Other Books by Robert Blumenfeld

Nonfiction
Accents: A Manual for Actors
Acting with the Voice: The Art of Recording Books
Blumenfeld's Dictionary of Acting and Show Business
Blumenfeld's Dictionary of Musical Theater: Opera, Operetta, Musical Comedy
Using the Stanislavsky System: A Practical Guide to Character Creation and Period Styles
Stagecraft: Stanislavsky and External Acting Techniques: A Companion to Using the Stanislavsky System
Teach Yourself Accents: The British Isles: A Handbook for Young Actors and Speakers
Teach Yourself Accents: Europe: A Handbook for Young Actors and Writers
Teach Yourself Accents: North America: A Handbook for Young Actors and Writers
Tools and Techniques for Character Interpretation: A Handbook of Psychology for Actors, Writers, and Directors
How to Rehearse When There Is No Rehearsal: Acting and the Media (by Alice Spivak, written in collaboration with Robert Blumenfeld)

Fiction
The Count of Sainte-Hélène, or The Lure of Infamy: A Novel of the Bourbon Restoration

Robert Blumenfeld

All the Tricks of the Trade: Everything You Need to Know about Comedy

A Practical Handbook and Complete Performance

Guide for Actors, Writers, and Directors

ISBN-13: 978-1502973832

ISBN-10: 1502973839

Library of Congress Control Number: 2014919616

CreateSpace Independent Publishing Platform

North Charleston, South Carolina

To my parents, Max David Blumenfeld (1911–1994) and Ruth Blumenfeld (b. 1915). I and my brothers share our parents' sense of humor. After all, we learned it from them! "Not from me," said my mother, when I told her about this dedication, "from Dad!" But she has a lovely wit and a brilliant, dry sense of repartee!

You can fool the town with Tragedy, but Comedy is a serious business.
-   David Garrick

Against the assault of laughter nothing can stand.
-   Mark Twain, *The Mysterious Stanger* (1916)

Table of Contents

Acknowledgements   xvii

Part One   1
Approaching Comedy: Tools and Techniques

Introduction   3
On Comedy: Why We Laugh

Chapter One   9
Comedy Tools and Techniques: Verbal and Physical
Comedy from the Joke to the Pratfall
   The Joke and Timing   10
      Be Serious! And Stand Still When You Deliver
      a Joke Line!   10
      Timing   12
      Find the Light!   13
      The Rule of Three   14
   More about Performing Stage Comedies of All Genres:
   Make It Real!   15
   Takes   17
   Playing Opposites   21
   Two Techniques: Behaving Like a Child and
   Having Your Mind Elsewhere   21
   Deadpan   24

Doubletalk   25

Imitation, Mimicry, and Mockery   27

Mugging, Gimmicks, Funny Voices, Gestures, and Walks   27

Cracking Up   29

Lazzi and Other Physical Comedy Techniques   29

Chapter Two   44

Creating Comic Characters: Stanislavsky's
Approach to Comedy

The Heart of the System: Don't "Act!" Instead, Be! And
"Behave" *As If* You Were the Character!   44

Be Truthful!   45

Every Action Has a Psychological Motivation   45

Be Specific!   47

Working with the System: Script Analysis
and Preparation   47

Using the System: Stanislavsky Plays Famusov in
Griboyedov's *Woe from Wit*   49

Chapter Three   53

Performing the Comedy of Manners: The Art
of Repartee, or Speaking Is Action

Chapter Four   58

Performing Farce and Commedia dell'Arte:
The Art of Pandemonium, or The Storm before the Calm

Chapter Five   70

Molière and the Italian Commedia

Molière [Jean-Baptiste Poquelin] (1622–1673)   70

Using the System: Stanislavsky Plays Argan in Molière's
The Imaginary Invalid   73

The Influence of the Italian Commedia on Molière's Comedies   78

Scene Analysis: Molière's *Les fourberies de Scapin*
(Scapin's Deceitful Tricks)   82

Chapter Six   89
Anton Chekhov and Stanislavsky
   Performing Chekhov's Realistic Psychological Comedies   89
   The Farces   92
      O vredye tabaka (On the Harmfulness of Tobacco)   94
   Scene Analysis: *Predlozheniye* (The Marriage Proposal)   96

Part Two   103
Mastering Period Styles: Each Play in Its Time

Introduction   105
What We Have Found Funny and Perceived as
Real Through the Millennia
   The Age-Old Plots and Stories   107

Chapter Seven   117
The Beginnings of Comedy: Ancient Greece and Rome
   Movement, Clothing, and Manners   117
   Ancient Greek Comedy: Farce and Satire   118
      Menander's *Dyskolos* (The Grouch; The Grump)   124
   Theater in Byzantium   127
   Ancient Roman Comedy and Farce   127

Chapter Eight   132
Medieval and Early Renaissance Comedy and Farce
   Movement, Clothing, and Manners   132
   Medieval Comedies   134
   La Farce du Cuvier (The Farce of the Tub)
   and *La Farce de maître Pierre Pathelin*
   (The Farce of Master Pierre Pathelin)   136

Chapter Nine   139
The Sixteenth Century: Italian Renaissance, Tudor,
Elizabethan, and Shakespearean Comedy
    Movement, Clothing, and Manners   139
    The Italian Renaissance Comedy of Machiavelli: *La mandragola*   141
    Tudor Farce: *Gammer Gurton's Needle, Ane Pleasant Satyre*
    of the Thrie Estaitis, Jack Juggler, and Udall's *Ralph Roister Doister*   143
    Performing Shakespeare's Comedies   147
        Playing Malvolio in *Twelfth Night*   150
    The Great Comedians of Shakespeare's Day   152
    The Parnassus Plays   155
    Scene Analysis: The Wooing Scene in *The Taming of the Shrew*   157

Chapter Ten   165
The Seventeenth-Century French Comedy of Manners;
English Restoration Comedy
    Movement, Clothing, and Manners   165
    Dancourt (1661–1725)   167
        Le chevalier à la mode (The Fashionable Cavalier)   168
    Regnard (1655–1709)   172
        Le joueur (The Gambler)   172
    English Restoration Comedy   174
    Colley Cibber (1671–1757)   178
    Cibber's *Love's Last Shift, or The Fool in Fashion* and
    Vanbrugh's *The Relapse, or Virtue in Danger*   180

Chapter Eleven   186
Eighteenth-Century Comedy of Manners and Farce
    Movement, Clothing, and Manners   186
    Libertinism: The Theme Underlying the
    Comedy of Manners   189
        A Libertine Character from Spanish Comedy: Don Juan   191
    French Comedy of Manners   193
    Marivaux (1688–1753)   196

Scene Analysis: Marivaux's *Le jeu de l'amour et du hasard*
(The Game of Love and Chance)   197
Theater in Denmark: The Comedies of Ludvig Holberg
(1684–1754)   205
    Jeppe paa Bjerget eller den forvandlede Bonde (Jeppe of the Hill;
    or The Transformed Peasant; 1722)   206
English Comedy   208
The Anglo-Irish Playwrights: Sheridan and Goldsmith   208
Scene Analysis: Sheridan's *The Rivals*   212
Eighteenth-Century Venetian Commedia Farce   222
    Goldoni's *Il servitore di due padroni* (The Servant of
    Two Masters)   225

Chapter Twelve   228
The Nineteenth Century: German, French, American, and
English Comedy
    Movement, Clothing, and Manners   228
    Early Nineteenth-Century German Romantic Farce   232
    French Boulevard Comedy   235
    Comedy in America   238
        Mrs. Mowatt's *Fashion; or, Life in New York*   240
        Tom Taylor's *Our American Cousin*   242
        Joseph Jefferson and *Rip Van Winkle*   246
    English and French Comic Opera   247
        A Summary of Techniques for
        Performing Comic Opera   248
        Performing Comic Opera with Authentic Style;
        Offenbach; Gilbert and Sullivan   249
        Stanislavsky in Gilbert and Sullivan's *The Mikado*   253
    English Comedy Genres: Extravaganzas, Pantomimes,
    Farce, Burlesque, Comedy of Ideas,
    Drawing-Room Comedy   256
        Scene Analysis: English Drawing-Room Comedy: Oscar
        Wilde's *The Importance of Being Earnest*   260

Chapter Thirteen   267
Farce and Comedy in the Twentieth and
Twenty-First Centuries: The Reality of
Absurdity, or The Absurdity of Reality
    Movement, Clothing, and Manners   267
    French Boulevard Farce Continues: Flers and Caillavet's
    L'Habit vert (The Academician's Green Coat)   269
    Tradition Expands: British Sex Farce Comes Alive!   273
    Theater of the Absurd   274
       An Absurdist Farce: Ionesco's *La cantatrice chauve*
       (The Bald Soprano)   277
    The Anglophone World of Comedy: Broadway and
    the West End   278
    Five Major English Comedy Writers: Noël Coward
    (1899–1973), Harold Pinter (1930–2008),
    Tom Stoppard (b. 1937), Joe Orton (1933–1967),
    Alan Ayckbourn (b. 1939)   280
    Two Americans: Edward Albee (b. 1928),
    Neil Simon (b. 1927)   287

Part Three   291
Comedy on Camera

Introduction   293
Performing Comedy on Screen
    A Summary of Techniques for Playing Comedy on the Film
    and Television Screen   297

Chapter Fourteen   305
Lessons and Tips from the Great Film and
Television Actors
    The Silent Film Comedians: Buster Keaton, Charlie Chaplin,
    and Harold Lloyd   307

The Early Talkies Comedians: The Marx Brothers,
Laurel and Hardy, W. C. Fields, and Mae West   309
The Mid-Twentieth Century: The Three Stooges, Danny Kaye,
Jerry Lewis, Walter Matthau, and Jack Lemmon   313
A Comic Innovator: Woody Allen   315
Another Comic Genius: Mel Brooks   317
Some More Contemporary Comedians: Billy Crystal,
Leslie Neilson, Will Ferrell, Albert Brooks, Jim Carrey,
Christopher Guest   318
English Film and Television Comedy   321
French, Italian, and Mexican Film Comedy   324
Some More American Films to Learn From   326

Chapter Fifteen   331
The Television Sitcom Then and Now: The Vaudeville
Skit Comes of Age

Appendix One: Major Comedy Writers from Ancient
Greece through the Twenty-First Century   343
Appendix Two: Major Comedy Screenwriters and Film Directors 373
Appendix Three: An Annotated Glossary of Comedy Terms   385
Selected Bibliography   419
About the Author   427

Acknowledgements

First of all, I want to single out for a very special acknowledgement those very dear friends who have contributed directly and indirectly to this book: Christopher Buck; Albert S. Bennett; Michael Mendiola and Scot Anderson; Peter Subers and Rob Bauer; Kieran Mulcare; Tom and Virginia Smith; Tristan Layton; Bruce Kitovich; David Bennett; William V. Madison; supreme comédienne and opera singer Agnès Bove; and composer Jean-Philippe Bec. They all have great senses of humor, and we always laugh a lot! My doctor and friend for forty years, the brilliant Ronald Grossman, tells very funny jokes. We laugh a lot together. I have known them all for many years, and they are valued and treasured members of my extended family.

And I express my gratitude and thanks for their love and support to the family into which I was born, especially my brother Donald Blumenfeld-Jones, and his wife, my sister-in-law, Corbeau; to my cousin, Jonathan Blumenfeld; to my mother's brother, my uncle, Seymour "Sy" Korn (1920–2010), who was unfailingly supportive and very knowledgeable about theater and literature; to my mother's sister, Bertha Friedman (1913–2001), and to her daughter, my brilliant cousin, Marjorie Loewer, who had a number of helpful suggestions as to what to include in the book.

Many thanks to the wonderful team at CreateSpace, whose editing and designing of the book have been superb. They are a joy to work with.

Lastly, I owe an incalculable debt to all the authors of the books in the bibliography, and to all the actors and directors I have worked with as an actor or dialect coach, and to the professors at Rutgers, who taught me elementary stage technique when I was in plays they directed—it was my one extracurricular activity all the time I was there, studying French language and literature; as well as to the teachers I studied with when I decided to become a professional actor, notably Uta Hagen and Alice Spivak, who became my friend and from whom I have learned a great deal over the many years we have known each other. I owe her special thanks for making some very good points in a conversation we had about this book.

All translations from French texts and plays and from Russian plays are mine. Inevitably, there will be notable omissions of famous comedies, sitcoms, playwrights, or actors dear to the reader, for which I apologize. Any errors, mistakes, or misconceptions are my own.

Part One

Approaching Comedy: Tools and Techniques

Introduction

On Comedy: Why We Laugh

Once upon a time in ancient Greece, *komoidia* (comedy), offspring of *komos* (revel) and *oide* (song), was a proud and happy noun. It meant a musical spectacle presented at the village religious festival in honor of the lubricious god of the fermented grape, Dionysus, whose cult was celebrated with wine and lewd satyr mimes and dances. Growing discontented with its parochial meaning, *komoidia* decided to expand its horizons, so it left the village to travel the world. It would hardly do to stay at home and miss out on all the adventures life had to offer!

As it went along on its voyage, *komoidia* broadened its meaning: it now referred to a comic play performed at urban theater festivals, such as the Athenian Dionysia. It could not help but go on from such a prestigious event to fame and fortune. And it was very happy in later times to be translated into many languages, including English. It was in this wise that Comedy became the Emperor of Laughter, and referred to the entire genre of theatrical works that are meant to provoke mirth, as well as to individual plays within the genre. Homage was paid, despite the grumblers, grouches, stuck-up snobs, and curmudgeons who said that Comedy was inferior to Tragedy, at which Comedy turned up its nose and laughed, asserting its power and basking in popular acclaim. It would never be obliged to relinquish its throne. And so it has lived happily ever after.

Comedy is a literary and theatrical genre with three distinctive features:

1. Comedy is written with the intention of being humorous and amusing, and of provoking laughter.
2. Comedies are about mundane life and our affections and desires, no matter what social milieu or environment they are set in, or what subgenre they belong to (comedy of manners, farce, romantic comedy, etc.).
3. Comedies end happily, even though we know that nobody lives in a blissful, happily-ever-after world.

The celebrated literary critic Northrop Frye (1912–1991), who had a lot to say about comedy, wrote in his masterpiece *Anatomy of Criticism* (Penguin, 1990), "Happy endings do not impress us as true, but as desirable, and they are brought about by manipulation."

Despite the fairy-tale endings, we learn more about life and human nature from comedy than we do from tragedy. So thought the English novelist and humorist George Meredith (1828–1909). In 1877, he gave a sober analytical lecture, later published under the title *An Essay on Comedy*, to the London Institution, a solemn organization devoted to developing scientific education. We are not all tragic heroes or heroines with fatal flaws, living on the heights of emotion and passion. (Thank goodness—who could stand it?) But we are all people living in specific circumstances as members of a particular social class. We are also wives, husbands, children, lovers, workers, or bosses pursuing our desires for happiness in the workaday world. This is the background of most comedies, even those that portray the gods, as does *Frogs* by Aristophanes, or deal with fantasies, as do Shakespeare's *A Midsummer Night's Dream* or Coward's *Blithe Spirit*. Meredith points out that the relations of parents and children in Shakespeare's history plays, *The History of Henry the Fourth*, *The Second Part of Henry IV*, and *Henry V*, which are all comedies of a sort, teach us more about such relationships than those in *King Lear*, as powerful and magnificent as that tragedy is. To put it in contemporary terms, the dysfunctional, sociopathic family in *King Lear* is farther from the experience of most of us than the mundane dysfunctionality depicted in the *Henry* plays.

Most people would rather go to a comedy than to an edifying drama or tragedy. Yet comedy has traditionally been looked down on and not taken seriously. The disapproving attitude toward it may have arisen precisely because comedy deals with ordinary people and everyday dilemmas, rather than with gods and heroes. When gods and heroes do appear in comedy, they are domesticated and tamed, mocked and parodied.

To put it another way, since comedy is not taken seriously, it has license to satirize, to tell home truths, and to pointedly mock and belittle not only individual foibles and idiosyncrasies, but also whole political regimes and politicians—as long as it is not so subversive as to call down upon itself the wrath of the regime. In Gilbert and Sullivan's *Iolanthe*, for example, the House of Lords and the upper classes are satirized, undermined, and held up to ridicule, but the rightness of the system is ultimately affirmed—protest, disruption, and revolution are not proposed: mocking laughter is a safe and permitted way of relieving political tension.

There are also cases where government wants to ban comedy precisely because it is offensive to the regime. The 2014 film *The Interview*, a comedy about the attempted assassination of the tinpot dictator of North Korea, caused a furor. The North Korean regime denounced the film and complained to the US about it. It was finally shown in the USA after fears of terrorist attacks had first caused cinema chains to cancel it. And even in North Korea people reportedly wanted to see it, much to the discomfiture of the government that banned it as subversive.

As Aristotle (384–322 BCE), the great ancient Greek philosopher of aesthetics and ethics, points out in his *Poetics*, composed around 325–323 BCE:

> Comedy…is the mimesis of baser but not wholly vicious characters; rather the laughable is one category of the shameful which involves no pain or destruction: most obviously, the comic mask is something ugly and twisted, but not painfully…

The concept of "mimesis" is central to Aristotle's thinking: all art is the imitation, or, more accurately, the reproduction, representation, or recreation of some aspect of real life.

"Wholly vicious characters" are the villains in tragedy—reprehensible characters whom we detest and execrate. We do not laugh at Iago or

Macbeth. But we do laugh at those characters who are not completely vicious, but who nevertheless have base, morally reprehensible qualities: misers, curmudgeons, connivers, crooks, hypocrites, certain politicians, snobs, and other sorts of narcissists people comedy through the ages, much to our delight.

When Aristotle says that comedy and the ridiculous involve situations that involve "no pain or destruction," he means that there is no real ultimate damage, as there is in tragedy. But there is no laughter without the suffering and pain on some level of the character at whom we laugh. As our preeminent American humorist Samuel Langhorne Clemens, better known as Mark Twain (1835–1910), wrote in *Following the Equator* (1897), "Everything human is pathetic. The secret source of Humor itself is not joy but sorrow. There is no humor in heaven."

Another great philosopher who wrote on the subject of why we laugh, the Frenchman Henri Bergson (1859–1941), published *Le rire. Essai sur la signification du comique* (Laughter: Essay on the Meaning of the Comic; the word *rire* also means "the laugh") in 1900. His book is essential reading for those who wish to understand the nature of comedy. For Bergson, laughter relieves tension, and thus makes life possible in society. Without it, the burdens life imposes would be too onerous. This idea agrees with some of Freud's.

In *Der Witz und seine Beziehung zum Unbewussten*, (Jokes and Their Relation [Wit and Its Relation] to the Unconscious; 1905), Sigmund Freud (1856–1939) discusses the psychology of humor, expatiates on the nature and meaning of wit and jokes—*Witz* means both a joke and wit in general—and explains what we find funny and why. One of the reasons we laugh is that we feel superior to the thing laughed at, and this causes a pleasurable sensation.

The English philosopher Thomas Hobbes (1588–1679) said something similar in *The Elements of Law Natural and Politic* (1640), chapter nine:

> ...the passion of laughter is nothing else but a sudden glory arising from sudden conception of some eminency in ourselves, by comparison with the infirmities of others, or with our own formerly.

In other words, laughter arises in us when we sense our superiority over something or someone. For Freud, the sense of superiority arises from our perception that a person has expended too little energy on mental functions such as reasoning or observation, and therefore reacts to situations in a way that strikes us as comic.

All of this implies keeping a certain distance between the person laughed at and ourselves. At the same time, we are involved with the situation, which we understand and with which we identify, because we perceive we might be implicated in the same kind of situation at any time. We go back and forth between distance and identification, so we are constantly laughing as the reversal of our expectations takes us by surprise.

One aspect of feelings of superiority arises from something common to all drama: the phenomenon of "double enunciation," or double meaning. The words mean one thing to the characters, and another to the audience, who know the truth of a situation, while the characters are unaware of it. The characters' confusion and mistaken notions, which are very common in comedies, cause them to talk at cross-purposes, and this is another source of our laughter. Also, whatever is incongruous and inappropriate causes laughter, and arouses our pleasurable feelings of superiority.

There is another reason we laugh, and this motivation adds a deeper layer, as Freud tells us: When we laugh at what is painful, uncomfortable, tragic, embarrassing, or horrific, we do so as an instantaneous reaction that serves to relieve out discomfort by repressing what we have found threatening and immediately pushing it out of our consciousness. Vermont poet, novelist, short story writer, and retired professor of English, Tom Smith, says, "We laugh at what makes us angry or afraid. It's not acceptable to run away or to attack, so we laugh. Laughter restores the chemical balance of the body, after the imbalance that comes with fear or anger."

And when you laugh, you also take your revenge on what has bothered you, on what has made you angry, and you ridicule the people who have hurt you. This is the opinion of the groundbreaking improvisational comic actor and Oscar and Tony award-winning director, Mike

Nichols (1931–2014). In *¡Satiristas!: Comedians, Contrarians, Raconteurs & Vulgarians*, a book of interviews by Paul Provenza and photographer Dan Dion (HarperCollins Publishers, 2010), Nichols had this to say: "Revenge drives most of the plots we love…And that revenge is sweet, because it's laughing at that prick that beat you up in high school." Or later on in life. A hilarious case in point: In the sardonic film comedy *Theatre of Blood* (1973), Vincent Price plays Edward Kendal Sheridan Lionheart, a disappointed Shakespearean actor, lambasted by the critics as a ham. Lionheart *is* a terrible ham, and when he does Shakespeare, we laugh. Denied the coveted London critics' circle award, he takes his revenge by pretending to commit suicide, then killing them off one by one, each in the manner of a different Shakespearean tragedy.

"Humor must not professedly teach, and it must not professedly preach, but it must do both if it is to live forever," wrote Mark Twain. The immortal humorists—writers in print, playwrights, screenwriters, and performers on stage and screen—expose what is ridiculous to humanity's scrutinizing gaze. And their joyous mirth has lightened the hearts of humankind through the ages. We laugh when we remember dilemmas and pandemonium now happily resolved, as Hobbes also points out. Another great American humorist, James Thurber (1894–1961) said, "Humor is emotional chaos recollected in tranquility."

What you have to offer to the world as a comic actor is your individuality, your own sense of humor, and your own style of delivery and characterization. In the process, you are going to have lots of fun and find vast enjoyment that helps you and everyone for whom you perform find a counter to the sadness of the world's ills, however fleetingly the antidote may endure. As the sadsack jester Jack Point says in Gilbert and Sullivan's *The Yeomen of the Guard* (1888), "For look you, there is humor in all things, and the truest philosophy is that which teaches us to find it and to make the most of it."

I

Comedy Tools and Techniques: Verbal and Physical Comedy from the Joke to the Pratfall

As some anonymous wit said, "Dying is easy; comedy is hard." It's especially hard if you have no sense of humor! But if you don't, chances are you wouldn't be interested in doing comedy in the first place. A sense of humor is comedy's prime prerequisite, after all. Once you have that—and it is individual, your own particular idea of what is funny, of what makes you laugh—you are more than halfway there.

When you do any kind of comedy, from stand-up to plays to films and TV sitcoms, you have to enjoy yourself. Have fun! Have lots of fun, but keep that fun behind your eyes, so to speak.

That may seem obvious, but since comedy is actually hard work, requiring immense concentration and energy, it needs to be pointed out that you also do need to be having fun. Observe any of the comedians discussed in this and later chapters, and you will see that they are all hell-bent on having fun with energy and gusto. When you enjoy yourself, the audience enjoys itself. But you can't let them know by any kind of signal that you are enjoying yourself, that you think you are being funny (unless that fact itself is the joke). You can't be obvious about it. You have to keep a straight face, to use a clichéd expression. The enjoyment has to be in the background of what you are doing. In other words, you know you're being funny, but you can't let the audience know you know, or, believe me, you won't be funny. The main, overall technique for performing comedy is very simple: Play comedy as seriously as a high-security secret, on a need-to-know basis. The audience doesn't need to know the joke, or even that there is a joke, until the right time.

Along with your individual sense of what is funny, and your enjoyment of it, you need to learn the techniques outlined in this chapter, many of which will come naturally to you. You need to absorb them, to make them as much a part of you as the grammar of the language you speak. The information in this chapter applies to all genres and to any kind of comedy, however disparate in style of writing and performance presentation, including romantic and absurdist comedy, comedy of manners, and farce.

The Joke and Timing

It is elementary that the basis of all comedy of whatever kind is the joke: a witty, funny, amusing, brief anecdote, witticism, droll one-liner, or wisecrack; or in a stage play, film, or television sitcom, a line (verbal joke) or action or comic bit (a physical, visual joke) that is meant to get a laugh.

Be Serious! And Stand Still When You Deliver a Joke Line!

The first rule for telling anecdotal jokes was nicely expressed by Mark Twain in his essay, "How to Tell a Story" (1897): "The humorous story is told gravely; the teller does his best to conceal the fact that he even dimly suspects that there is something funny about it." This is the first principle and the first technique for telling jokes, for doing entire comedies, and for playing funny or humorous characters whether in a comedy or a serious piece. We might paraphrase Twain thus: "The humorous character and comic piece are played gravely. The actor in a comedy does his best to conceal the fact that he even dimly suspects he is being funny."

Jokes depend for their effect on surprising the audience. There are two parts to telling any joke: First, you have to plant certain assumptions in the audience's mind. That is called setting up the joke. Then you reverse those assumptions with the final line, which surprises them, and gets the laugh; that line is called the punch line (also spelled punchline).

When punching a joke, point up the meaning of a line by vocally emphasizing or stressing the important words that convey it—without its being obvious that you want the audience to laugh. For a visual or physical joke, a bit of business or particular action will point the moment up. This finalizing business is called "putting a button on it," a term also used in musical comedy to refer to the finish of a number.

Some laugh lines are delivered as "throwaways." A throwaway is a line that is delivered in a casual, offhand way, as if it is incidental, and said in passing—so that it does not appear to be funny. Such a dry delivery can be hilarious. Sometimes, it takes a moment for the punch line to sink in, and for the audience to get the joke.

For the joke to work, that is, to get a laugh, both setup and punch line must be immediately clear and comprehensible.

In a play or sketch, you work with a partner—unless it is a monologue like Chekhov's one-acter O vredye tabaka (On the Harmfulness of Tobacco; several versions, written from 1886 to 1903). You or the partner is the "straight" person who sets the joke up, and whichever one of you isn't, is the "comedian" who delivers the punch line, without allowing the audience to guess when it is coming. In a monologue or solo stand-up routine, you have to do both jobs: you set up the joke, and deliver the surprise punch line.

Stand still when delivering a joke line in a comedy! If you have been moving around, stop when you get to that line. This will immediately concentrate the audience's attention even further on you. Don't fidget or make any extraneous movement or gesture. Any movement by you or anyone else on stage during the delivery of a punch line is distracting. Cultivate the habit of being still so that it becomes automatic and unconscious. It is essential to make the stillness feel natural to yourself, so that it will be real, and not a technical signal to the audience that you are about to say something funny. Remember that you still have to hide the fact that you are going to deliver a punch line; it still has to be a surprise. Even a throwaway line is more effective when the actor is still.

Timing

Getting the laugh depends on expert timing, and on a rhythm that you and your acting partner set up to carry along the sketch or the scene in a comic play. Timing is the technique of making something happen at the exact, carefully rehearsed moment when it is supposed to happen.

Once the audience laughs, you have to time out the laugh. To do that, you have to hold for it; that is, to remain silent and stationary, temporarily suspending the action of the play, while the audience laughs. You must stay in character while you do this, filling the pause for laughter with the character's inner life. When the laughter has subsided, but while some people are still laughing, the right moment for delivering the next line has arrived. You must seize that moment.

If you have two possible laughs in a line, get the first laugh as if it were the only one, by using a finalizing intonation pattern that says, in essence, "This is it. That's all I have to say." Then, when you have timed out the audience's laugh, proceed with the second half of the line, almost as if it is an afterthought, or a completely new idea—whichever is appropriate to the situation. This was a technique perfected by Bea Arthur (1922–2009) in her television series *Maude* (1972–1978) and *The Golden Girls* (1985–1992), both available on DVD. It worked every time, because she was absolutely real in her mental process and in her reactions. Discussing her acting methods and techniques, she said, "Sid Caesar taught me the outrageous, Lee Strasberg taught me what I call reality, and Lotte Lenya, whom I adored, taught me economy"—all lessons worth remembering whatever the genre, and which she embodied to the full. And she could hardly have chosen better models and teachers.

The audience response at every performance will be different, and as a result so will the timing. Also, you have to be in a concentrated, focused creative state all the time during performances, in order to be able to time the laughs.

An essential part of timing in any scene is picking up cues, that is, saying the next line without a pause, except when the audience laughs. You cannot step on the laugh, that is, you cannot cut off the laugh by speaking or moving; you must allow the laugh to happen. When you pick up your cues, the dialogue is seamless and this keeps the play moving. When there are pauses, they must be carefully rehearsed.

Pauses must be motivated, and they must not last so long that the audience thinks the actors have forgotten their lines. If the pause is motivated, this should not happen, and the audience's attention will not flag. What is the character doing during the pause? What are the thoughts that go through the character's mind? There are always thoughts, and they fill the pause. A pause may also be filled with physical actions: in the middle of trying to open a difficult container, while you are speaking, you might be constrained to pause and deal with the lid.

What makes something a joke is not only the punch line that punctures expectations, but also the way the joke is expressed, the manner in which it is told. To reiterate, although you know the joke is funny, the way you tell it has to be serious, or you will lose the effect of the surprise at the end and you won't get a laugh.

Remember this principle: joke lines in comedies are part of the *action*. In accord with this, an important technique is for whoever has the line following the laugh to say it with extra vocal energy that sets the comedy on its way again with renewed vigor. The audience reaction of laughter will also become part of the general rhythmic movement of the play, and, once again, it will vary at every performance.

Find the Light!

Another important rule regarding the delivery of jokes and laugh lines on stage: find the light, so you can be seen! A joke told in the dark will usually not get a laugh, depending on the circumstances. Finding the light involves checking where the light is brightest, followed immediately by moving into the "hot spot"; that is, the brightest spot.

The Rule of Three

Jokes often follow the "Rule of Three," which depends on context. The idea is that when a running gag, joke, or tagline is repeated, it is on the third repeat that the gag gets the laugh; a fourth repetition may elicit a groan instead of the desired laughter. A running gag is a joke or bit of comic business that recurs periodically in the course of a play or film; it is also called a running joke. The joke is designed to get the biggest laugh the last time it is played.

There is a wonderful example of the rule of three in Larry Coen and David Crane's *Epic Proportions*, a satirical farce that spoofed biblical epic films and the movie-making industry. (Crane later went on to create and write the hit TV sitcom, *Friends*; and Larry Coen is a distinguished member of the Boston theatrical community.) I had the good fortune to be in the original 1986 Off-Off-Broadway showcase production. There were generic scenes that might be in any of those old movies, and that had the audience howling. It was sometimes difficult to get through rehearsals, because we were cracking up and laughing so hard. We did everything absolutely for real. Under Paul Lazarus's brilliant direction, the cast of eight (most playing multiple roles) was wonderful, and Patricia Norcia was a memorable Cleopatra, among other roles. As part of our preparation, we all watched Cecil B. DeMille's (1881–1959) *The Ten Commandments* (1956). Under the circumstances, it became one of the funniest films I had ever seen.

Late in the play, three gladiators come in to fight Ramadidis, usurper to the throne, and each gladiator greets the queen in a similar fashion; Mark Kenneth Smaltz and Paul O'Brien were the first two gladiators, and I was the third one:

GLADIATOR # 1: (*Stepping forward.*) For you, my queen, with sword and shield, I shall defeat him! (*He brandishes his weapon.*)
GLADIATOR # 2: With spear and net, he will be mine!
GLADIATOR # 3: With a metal ball with spikes on it, I shall be victorious!

The first two declaimed in their noblest voices, standing upright and proud, and then I spoke in a rough voice, swearing in a Brooklyn accent to defend her with that "metal ball with the spikes on it." I hesitated slightly after the word "with," staring at the object because I couldn't think of what it was called (a mace). I got one of the biggest laughs of the night when I finally said "a metal ball with spikes on it," helped also by the fact that the other two were tall and stately and I, especially crouching over, was much shorter and looked ridiculous in my scant costume.

More about Performing Stage Comedies of All Genres: Make It Real!

To sum up, there are three basic rules to bear in mind when playing comedy on stage, and you have to make them automatic habits:

1. Joke lines in comedies are part of the action. Do not treat them as separate from the play. Keep the play moving forward at a good pace.
2. Don't wait for a laugh! You cannot anticipate as either an actor or the character that a laugh will be there, so you cannot wait for a laugh. Unless the character is deliberately joking or being witty, the character does not know he or she has said something funny until the audience reacts, and, technically speaking, not even then: the audience is not part of the character's world, even though the actor must take account of their reactions. Stanislavsky referred to the audience as the "third artist" involved in a performance (the author and the actor were the first two artists of the theater). What the audience receives and then gives back acts in tandem with the actors' performances and creates the comedy.
3. Don't step on a laugh! As I said above, when the audience laughs, you cannot step on the laugh; that is, you cannot inadvertently and ineptly come in too soon with the next line or bit of business. You have to allow them to laugh, and you must time out the laugh.

Act with lots of energy and concentration! Acting in comedy requires more physical energy and sometimes more vocal energy than drama. In other words, you play physical and verbal actions and pursue objectives with a heightened sense of desire, focus, concentration, and determination. Double that for farce. An exception: the psychological comedies of Chekhov, which demand the same energy you use for drama, as well as a deep exploration of the character's mental life. His farces, however, demand the same energy and pace as other examples of the genre.

The question of a character's sense of humor is often ignored, unless the part is written specifically with wit and jokes in mind. What does a character find funny, and why? Does the character use humor to get approval or disapproval, or to be the center of attention? These are questions to ask when you explore a character, particularly one who is supposed to be funny, or who wants to be, as in the case of so many witty characters in comedies of manners, who deliver their lines in order to make their interlocutors laugh.

"Never begin with results," cautioned Stanislavsky. It is tempting when performing in comedy to decide in advance exactly what you are going to do, where and how you are going to get the laughs, instead of allowing them to happen naturally because of what the character is living through: this is what we mean when we talk of a technical approach to character creation. The term "technical approach" may be confusing, but what we really mean is that such an approach leaves out internal psychological techniques, and begins with deciding in advance of rehearsal how lines are to be read, and how the character is to move. These are results, and they should not be predetermined, but rather found as you explore the character in rehearsal.

A comic moment and the timing of laughs can only be found in performance. You don't know if the audience is going to laugh, even if you want them to, and you have to act as if they weren't going to. If you act as if you expected a laugh, nine times out of ten you won't get it. In any case, to set anything so that you can repeat it exactly, *before* the process of exploration, is to inhibit the ability to act, which involves living and behaving as the character. True, the ability to repeat is a necessary part of the actor's art and craft, once you have rehearsed and set a performance. And setting a performance does not mean that the repetition of it should ever be mechanical. You must live in the moment. You must really listen and respond to the other actors. The way in which you play the comedy depends on real responses, whether you are playing broadly or using the technique of deadpan, or doing one of the many comedic takes.

Remember, too, that in comedy, the character fails continually to obtain objectives, and this is a source of humor. The character is always running up against a brick wall, falling down, and picking him- or herself up, and running into another brick wall. Every such encounter elicits laughter. For instance, when a character in a Feydeau farce is about to be caught in flagrante in a compromising situation, the person flees or hides, in a panic lest he or she be found out. The objective of consummating a relationship changes instantaneously to the goal of remaining safe and avoiding the consequences of one's actions. This instant change is a surprise to both character and audience, and is funny, as are the ploys and maneuvers to avoid the consequences. That objective usually fails, too, and the person caught out has to invent further excuses. And in the stubborn, head-on battles of people who want something from each other, we see then pursuing their conflicting objectives energetically, more than they probably would in real life, because for one thing they are contained within the short time it takes to perform a play.

Takes

A take is a reaction in the form of a pointed look, a stare, or a fixed look beginning in disbelief and ending in belief, at an object of fascination, when that object is recognized for what it is, and not for what it was originally taken to be. A take involves the recognition of someone, some thing, or some circumstance, and depends for its effect on the exact rhythm and tempo of the moves. Jack Benny was a master of all kinds of takes, and the DVDs of his films and television show can be studied with great benefit. The same thing is true of

Milton Berle and Phil Silvers. All three learned their comic techniques from performing in vaudeville. So did the iconic comic genius, Jackie Gleason, who cultivated the art of exaggeration and the overdone, but his takes—often way over the top—and slow burns, perfectly timed, were actually completely believable—because he believed them—and absolutely hilarious.

The technique of commenting on the action or on a remark was something they employed judiciously, although, as in the case of British comedian Frankie Howerd, it could be part of their act. To comment is to let the audience know how you as an actor feel about what is going on, perhaps by an attitude or a look of contempt or disapproval, even though the comment may be extraneous to the material you are performing. This is generally undesirable and to be avoided, unless going outside the material is part of a comic act. Commenting reminds the audience that you are performing and takes them away from their involvement in the story, substituting an immediate awareness of you as an actor. On the other hand, a character may comment by raising an eyebrow, for instance, and this is simply part of the action. The comment may even provoke a laugh. Or the actor may be directed to comment as the character by doing a take directly out front to the audience.

There are many different kinds of takes:

1. **The found object and the stare take:** You notice an object, such as a piece of paper money, a diamond ring, or another valuable thing, after you have walked past it, and you turn to stare at it before going over to it, and picking it up. You may use any of the following takes once you have noticed the object.

2. **The single take:** A turn to an object or person involving a fixed stare. A single take can be funny, as in George Burns' frequent reactions to Gracie Allen's inane remarks, because she takes everything literally and never understands anything in metaphorical or abstract terms. He simply looks at her, without turning away, when the realization dawns on him that she has understood something in a way that would never have occurred to him.

3. **The double take:** A comic bit, in which a look of blank incomprehension is instantly followed by a second look of immediate surprised comprehension. This take, done in three units or beats, involves looking at someone or something, looking away, and instantly looking back at the object of attention. On screen, the double take can be accomplished by simply using the eyes, focused first on one object, switched to another, and then back to the first, as a realization sets in. Part of the comedy comes from the fact that the audience already knows the reason for the disbelief and already knows what to believe. The late realization by the character, after the audience already knows what is going on, and their consequent anticipation of the character's reaction, is one of the causes of their laughter. But although the audience anticipates what is about to happen, you the actor can never do so.

4. **The rarer triple take:** This involves turning away from the object of attention, turning back, turning away again, and finally turning back and fixing the attention on the object—all done in a twinkling.

5. **The spit take:** Used especially in farce, this take involves a person drinking a liquid, and, being shocked or surprised while the liquid is still in the mouth, forcibly expelling it and spraying it all over the place, usually with a loud spluttering sound, e.g., when being clapped on the back by someone entering a room. If you use this take for the found object, you will be drinking before you notice it on the floor, and when you do, you can forcibly expel the liquid from your mouth in your astonishment.

6. **The swallow take:** This consists of audibly gulping while swallowing saliva, often accompanied by bulging eyes and a gesture of loosening a shirt collar, followed by dropped jaws, as a reaction of fright or surprise. It is very effective in film, e.g., when the camera can focus on the victim's prominent Adam's apple going up and down.

7. **The direct take:** This is a significant look in the audience's direction. But when performing in a play, don't look *at* them.

Select a point just above and behind them, on the back wall of the theater. Just after you have delivered the punch line, look fixedly in their direction. This is technical, and old-fashioned, very useful in Feydeau farces, for instance, but it must arise from the organic reaction of the character to whatever is going on. British music hall and television comedian Frankie Howerd (1917–1992) cultivated this sort of direct take, and it was part of his act both in stand-up and in comedies. In stand-up comedy, as opposed to plays, you may make direct eye contact with the audience, depending on the nature of your act: there are acts where audience members are singled out, perhaps challenged or made fun of in some way; and there are sometimes hecklers, who must be severely dealt with.

8. **The raised-eyebrow take:** This technique of commenting on what you have just said or on what someone else has said or done is performed as follows: If it is your joke, just before or after delivering the punch line, as an organic reaction, raise one of your eyebrows and turn your head slightly. This may be combined with the previous technique of looking in the audience's direction. If you cannot raise only one eyebrow, raising both will do just as well.

9. **The slow burn:** This variation on a take can be very funny. It was used to great effect by W. C. Fields, and by Charlie Chaplin's opponents in a number of his silent film classics. The slow burn is the long buildup of anger that is held back until it can be held no longer, and finally explodes. Jackie Gleason's reactions in his television series *The Honeymooners* were often slow burns.

10. **Taking out your anger:** This is a species of slow burn that involves the use of an object. For instance, perhaps you are slicing onions or hammering nails. You begin slowly and as you get more and more angry, your actions become more and more vehement.

11. **The instant switch:** A technique akin to the switch of attention in the double take is the "Instant Switch," also known as the "immediate, or instant reverse," of emotion from one

emotion to its opposite: frantic to suddenly calm, for instance, or its opposite: calm to suddenly frantic. "I love you! I love you! I HATE you!" Ted Knight as Ted Baxter in *Mary Tyler Moore Show* was a past master at this technique, which is a kind of instantaneous playing of opposites.

Playing Opposites

Among other essential techniques of which Stanislavsky was a great master is "playing opposites," which is of paramount importance in performing comedy. He always looked for the humorous side of every serious character. And he looked for the serious side of every humorous character. He searched for the good side of every villain. Playing opposites helps to round out the interpretation and give the character psychological depth and reality because it plays on the natural ambivalences and ambiguity of feeling that is part of everybody's characterological makeup.

Comedy itself uses opposites as one of its prime tools—see, for instance, the instant switch described above. An example is Neil Simon's *The Odd Couple*, in which two men, each divorced, are roommates, and total opposites: Oscar is a slob, and Felix is compulsively neat to the point of exasperation. The clever servant helping his sometimes not quite so clever master, who is in love, to achieve his goal, is ubiquitous in comedy throughout the ages, and takes any number of forms. In *The Play's the Thing* (see chapter thirteen, under "Five Major English Comedy Writers"), the servant has become an ingenious playwright, helping a young, naïve composer. In short, wherever you look, you find such opposites, even in tragedy, where there are scenes of comic relief.

Two Techniques: Behaving Like a Child and Having Your Mind Elsewhere

"The essential comic incongruity of the film clown is the contrast of a child in an adult body," wrote stage and film comedian Harry Langdon's

(1884–1944) nephew, Harold Langdon, in "Film Comedian—The Adult Child" (*Literature / Film Quarterly*, January, 1989). He says his uncle, who appeared in ninety-five films, was "the exemplar par excellence of my thesis."

The idea of this particular incongruity is not only valid analytically, but can also be turned into an actor's technique that applies equally well to comic acting on stage, and is especially useful in farce: you behave *as if* you were a child, using substitution as necessary (see chapter two). Conducting yourself like a mature, responsible adult, measured and thoughtful in your reactions, soft-spoken and rational in your expression of them, is not necessarily funny—although it can be in the right circumstances. But a "childlike" adult whose energetic behavior and reactions seem infantile and regressive, and whose naïve expression of desire is uncontrolled, is usually very funny.

Examples of such overt childishness in television sitcoms abound (Jacky Gleason, Lucille Ball, and so forth). In film, they include the behavior of many characters played by Jerry Lewis or Jim Carrey, the tearfulness of Stan Laurel and the peevish annoyance of Oliver Hardy; the exaggerated enthusiasm of Will Ferrell in *Elf* (2003), about an adult who behaves like a child (see chapter fourteen for more about all of them); and the wide-eyed reactions of Tom Hanks (b. 1956) in the "body swap" movie *Big* (1988), about a child trapped through magic in an adult's body.

In most plays, films, and sitcoms the character is not aware of behaving like a child: such unconsciously motivated behavior is not calculated in advance. It is spontaneous and instantaneously reactive. Think of the children you know. You may be able to use some of their behavior as a model.

As Mark Twain wrote, "The most interesting information comes from children, for they tell all they know and then stop." Children can be delightful, sweet, charming, funny, cute, brilliant, forthright, serious, earnest, and—most important—spontaneous in their reactions and in their way of expressing themselves. For comedic purposes, however, you will often have to adopt as well some of the more unpleasant aspects of childhood behavior, depending of course on the circumstances. You might be defiant, dogmatic, stubborn, insistent, demanding, or sulky—perhaps all at the same time—in the manner of some children when they are crossed. I want what I want when I want it and I want it now! And I won't back down! (Many adults behave exactly like this in real life, of course; it's only funny in a comedy.) You might throw a temper tantrum, or be cajoling and wheedling. Whatever you do, however extreme, however seriously and earnestly you take yourself and your desires, you have to do everything with full commitment. And you have to tell all you know, and then stop: your reactions have to be complete and final; yours is the last word.

If you are innocent, spontaneous, earnest, and naïve as the character in your reactions, if you are constantly surprised and enthusiastically excited or deeply shocked in the way a child can be, you will not anticipate what is coming up any more than a child would. You will be constantly either ecstatic or nonplussed. The desperate struggle to regain control after you are thrown off in some way can also be funny, depending on circumstances. In short, there are any number of comic possibilities for immature, unthinking, reactive behavior that make behaving *as if* you were a child a very useful comic tool.

In connection with the idea of such behavior, the idea of having your mind elsewhere, of anticipating what might come next, is also an excellent way of playing certain scenes. The clichéd question "Are we there yet?" is what children supposedly say when they are tired of traveling someplace. Instead of being in the moment, they are in the next moments. In their minds, they are not in the car or the plane: they are where they expect to be arriving. Many people are physically present, but elsewhere in their minds. As the character, you may want to concentrate on what is coming next: make that your action. You can't be bothered by the present. It's the future that preoccupies you. This will automatically put you above and beyond what is actually happening, and may even give you a vacant look that can be very funny, especially when the lines oblige you to continue talking with your partner.

Deadpan

Deadpan is the kind of comedy and of comic performing in which you use a neutral expression and react internally. The twinkle in the eye that communicates the comedian's pleasure and delight in being funny is almost hidden from the audience when uttering a joke or doing funny bits of business. But it is there. You just have to look extra hard to find it. Such underplayed comedy depends on an expressionless face and flat, but pointed delivery of lines, never telegraphing a joke.

Buster Keaton (1895–1966) is the prime example of such a deadpan comedian, with his hangdog look and poker face; you can see him in many films, and on YouTube. His timing was impeccable, and somehow, you knew he thought he was funny, but he never communicated that fact by the slightest sign. Yet he had to know, because he always got huge laughs. His sage advice about how to perform comedy was, "What you have to do is create a character. Then the character just does his best, and there's your comedy. No begging." By that last phrase, he meant no asking for laughs, or telegraphing that you think something is funny. He also said, "Think slow, act fast." This advice on tempo-rhythm is the essence of what happens in comedy and farce, when a character is trying to solve a dilemma, and can't seem to get it, then suddenly acts quickly. In Feydeau farces, for example, a problem presents itself, and stymies a character, who suddenly hides in a closet: this does not solve the problem, but puts off the solution. As the character stands there, panic written all over his or her face, we laugh.

The critic George Jean Nathan (1882–1958) said, "The test of a real comedian is whether you laugh at him before he opens his mouth." Keaton just had to stand there, and you would start laughing. The same thing is true of Jack Benny. In *To Be Or Not To Be* (1942) he plays Joseph Tura, a Polish classical actor in Warsaw. He enters as Hamlet for the famous soliloquy of the film's title, and just stands there, expressionless, apparently having forgotten his lines, and we see the prompter mouthing, "To be or not to be." This is truly hilarious, and only Benny could have gotten away with it. In reality, the character is nonplussed, because every time he starts that speech, a young man in uniform, played by Robert Stack, gets up in the middle of the row, and makes his way to the end, then leaves. He has a backstage assignation with Benny's wife, played by Carole Lombard in what would turn out to be her last film. In the 1983 remake, Mel Brooks takes a very different approach, as he must, being a very different person, and, taking himself very seriously indeed, gives us a kind of manic Hamlet, which is also very funny.

To summarize, the deadpan technique of comic delivery is to use dry wit and understatement, and deliver a joke or a punch line as if it were not funny. As always—I cannot stress this enough—you must appear not to be aware that what you are saying is droll. Take a further lesson from British actor and comedian Ricky Gervais (b. 1961), who relies on internal reactions, which we see reflected in his eyes. His delivery of lines—verbal actions—is a direct result of those internal reactions. When someone attacks him, Gervais uses a trademark smile to mask his anger—an example of playing opposites—and then replies, either as he smiles or just after. You can see this in DVDs of two television series, *The Office* (2005–2013) and *Extras* (2005–2007).

Doubletalk

The comedy of doubletalk plays variations on the theme of people who take themselves seriously, and pretend to more knowledge or erudition than is theirs. In one form of doubletalk, speech combines real words with nonsense syllables and words, forming a kind of gibberish.

The satiric mock-lectures of the brilliant "Professor" Irwin Corey (b. 1914)—"The World's Foremost Authority," as he billed himself—included a different kind of doubletalk, involving long, florid, convoluted clauses that went nowhere, but sounded profound and erudite. You can go to his website to read and hear some of his routines. He starts many of his "lectures" with the word, "However." Then he takes a slight pause while he appears to be thinking about what to say next. He launches immediately into an incomprehensible routine that appears to make sense, but goes nowhere—very original, and in fact, unique. He knows how funny he is being, but he appears to be deadly serious, and almost (but not quite) offended by the audience's laughter, which, gives him even more of an impetus to continue talking, as if he now insists on being taken seriously. When Irwin Corey went on and on with his rambling spiels, he was always playing the action of explaining his ideas and making his points. The fact that there were no ideas and no points to make was excruciatingly funny, and grew funnier as he continued: the effect was cumulative.

Al Kelly [Abraham Kalisch] (1899–1966), also an extremely funny master of double-talk, had a very different approach. It was as if one simply had difficulty in understanding him, and were sometimes listening to a foreign language. You knew the language well, but there were words you simply missed. He proceeds to mystify and baffle his interlocutors, who think they understand him at first. You can see samples of his work on YouTube.

Another form of doubletalk is to pretend to be speaking a foreign language. The multitalented actor, comedian, composer, jazz saxophonist, and writer Sid Caesar (b. 1922) was a master at this kind of doubletalk. If you didn't know German, French, Italian, or Russian, you could think he was really speaking any of those languages. He knew the way they sounded, and that is what he reproduced and imitated, throwing in a few real words and occasional phrases in English with the required accent. He captured perfectly the rhythms and intonation patterns that are such a necessary part of really speaking them. In fact, they are also part of doing a convincing accent in English, which Caesar could do perfectly. He amply demonstrated that talent in improvisational skits on his live television series, a precursor of *Saturday Night Live*, *Your Show of Shows*, which aired for ninety minutes every Saturday night on NBC from February 23, 1950 to June 5, 1954, closing after one hundred sixty episodes. Among its writers were Mel Brooks, Neil Simon, and Larry Gelbart. The variety show regularly included satirical sketches that required this kind of doubletalk, not only from him, but from the other regular actors on the show, Carl Reiner (b. 1922), Howard Morris (1919–2005), and Imogene Coca (1908–2001). One of his most famous skits was "The German

General," a satire of World War Two films, with Howard Morris; you can see it on YouTube. It originally aired on September 27, 1954 on the opening episode of *Caesar's Hour*, the show that followed *Your Show of Shows* several months later, and ran until 1957.

Imitation, Mimicry, and Mockery

Imitating or mimicking another person to his or her face is a device, rarely to be used, but useful sometimes in scenes where there is antagonism. One or two lines will usually suffice. In a passive-aggressive way, sometimes a character will shake his or her head and mug, mouthing words instead of saying them, behind another character's back. If that character turns, the character making the face may do an instant switch, and smile.

The imitation of well known actors can also be a useful comedic or character device, if the character is particularly given to such things. In the nighttime television crime drama series, *NCIS* (first season, 2003), Michael Weatherly (b. 1968) plays Special Agent Anthony DiNozzo. As the character developed, early on in the series he became a movie aficionado, often relating the crime under investigation to a particular film, and imitating the well known characters in such films as Alfred Hitchcock's *Psycho* (1960) or Jack Nicholson as Colonel Jessep in *A Few Good Men* (1992). Weatherly is brilliant and supremely funny, and his imitations are perfect, even uncanny. Sometimes, he throws a line away over his shoulder, and it lands squarely on the audience's funny bone. DiNozzo cares underneath his façade of amused insouciance. And the comic relief he provides helps to lighten what would otherwise be the overly grim atmosphere created by the grisly crimes.

Mugging, Gimmicks, Funny Voices, Gestures, and Walks

To mug is to make faces on stage or for the camera, especially using outlandish, exaggerated expressions meant to provoke laughter. This is rarely to be used and is usually the mark of a low comedian, but there have been masters, such as The Three Stooges, Jerry Lewis, or Milton

Berle, who made a specialty of it, at least during part of their careers. Sometimes a sound will accompany the mugging: a close-mouthed squeak of anger, or "homina-homina-homina" from Jackie Gleason in *The Honeymooners*. It is usually not a good idea to mug, unless it is really called for. Mugging is often a form of indicating, to be eschewed at all costs.

In scripts, a gimmick is a plot device that draws attention to a turn of events, for instance, in French farce, where people who know each other enter and exit through doors, just missing seeing each other. A gimmick is also a magician's secret device used in performing a magic trick—a gizmo or gismo. But when it comes to character, the word refers to a means of drawing attention to oneself by unusual actions, dress, and so forth. One of pianist and entertainer Liberace's [Władziu Valentino Liberace] (1919–1987) gimmicks, for instance, was his array of glittering costumes. One of the most common gimmicks is a funny voice, often accompanied by a funny gait.

A caveat: Avoid such gimmicks, unless they are really specifically called for, or unless you can make them your entire persona as a performer.

You have to be Ed Wynn to do what he did. Later known as a wonderful serious actor, Ed Wynn [Isaiah Edwin Leopold] (1886–1966) was one of the few comedians whose specialized voice—quavery, wavering, giggly, much imitated—and use of silly props and funny, ill-fitting costumes were not only memorable, but absolutely marvelous. He billed himself as "The Perfect Fool," and starred in 1921 in a Broadway revue with that title. From 1914 through the '30s, he was a Broadway comedian, and then went on to radio and television.

In general, a whiny, phony, nerdy voice, or a deliberately shambling or peculiar walk that draw attention to themselves are immediately unfunny. Unfortunate examples abound in some contemporary television sitcoms. Such egregiously tacky devices also violate the rule and first principle of the Stanislavsky system, which is to be truthful and honest. Applied as if with glue, like paper to a collage, and stuck onto a person, an eccentric voice and walk betray a superficiality and a technical approach that undermine the very basis of comedy, which is the reality that we can identify with, and that makes us laugh. A funny voice and walk come under the heading of indication, one of the cardinal sins in acting. Even the outrageous campy fop of Restoration comedy, waving his lace handkerchief about, and gesturing extravagantly, came from a real place, psychologically and sociologically. All characters in comedy must do that, or there is no point in watching them.

Cracking Up

A form of commenting on the material—"This is so funny!"—cracking up is a device used to attract attention, one often not controllable, and usually not terribly desirable. (Of course, cracking up can also be a spontaneous, uncontrolled reaction.) The actor breaks into laughter, attempting at first to hold back, in the middle of a comic routine, but the laughter sometimes becomes unrestrained. On the popular Carol Burnett (b. 1933) weekly television show, *The Carol Burnett Show*, (1967–1978), which consisted of unrelated, vaudeville-style skits, Harvey Korman (1927–2008) and Tim Conway (b. 1933) used to make a point of breaking up at least once a show, giving away to the audience how funny they thought the other one was. They were hilarious even doing that, because they meant it: they really did find each other funny.

Lazzi and Other Physical Comedy Techniques

If you do a commedia farce, such as Goldoni's *Il servitore di due padroni* (The Servant of Two Masters; see chapter eleven), you will also need to know and master lazzi, which include specialized movements, akin to acrobatics; standardized verbal quips, catchphrases, and dialogue exchanges; and various types of comic bits, routines, and tricks. Almost every character is involved in doing stunts and lazzi at some point. John Rudlin's *Commedia dell'Arte: An Actor's Handbook* (Routledge, 1994) is very informative. And Mel Gordon's *Lazzi: The Comic Routines of the Commedia dell'Arte* (PAJ Publications, 2001) lists two hundred and fifty lazzi in detail, both the verbal and physical varieties. Barry Grantham's *Playing Commedia: A Training Guide to Commedia Techniques* (Nick Hearn

Books, 2000) is chock-full of history, exercises, specific gestures, movements, mask work, and much more.

In the Piccolo Teatro di Milano's production of *Il servitore di due padroni* that I saw at the McCarter Theater in Princeton, NJ, there was a hilarious lazzo that I still remember vividly decades later. An elderly gentleman entered and looked around for a hiding place. Not finding one and hearing a noise in the distance, he knelt down on all fours with his back to the audience and covered himself with his cloak. Truffaldino entered, and, mistaking him for a chair, sat down on him, to reflect and debate with himself over some issue. In excruciating pain, the "hidden" man hit the stage floor with his hand three times. Truffaldino immediately said "Avanti!" (Come in!) and we howled. He looked around, shrugged his shoulders, and resumed his contemplation. Again, the hand banged the stage. Again, Truffaldino looked up and said "Avanti!" Even when it was repeated several times, we burst out laughing each time. The timing of "Avanti!" was perfect, and the absurd, comically sadistic lazzo was performed with complete reality.

A variation on this "lazzo of hiding" is described by Mel Gordon: Two characters, usually Harlequin and Columbine, are alone together in a room, when they hear someone knocking at the door. She tells him to hide quickly, since the person knocking must be Pantalone. But there is no place to hide, so Harlequin becomes a chair: He sits back on his haunches with his arms raised, and she throws a sheet over him, which covers him so that he looks like a low chair. Pantalone enters and sits on Harlequin's covered knees, resting his arms on Harlequin's. But he immediately jumps up, as if jabbed with a pin. Harlequin, unable to take the pain, had made a movement that caused Pantalone to rise. There is an obscene connotation to this lazzo, which I leave to the reader's imagination.

Here are some of the authentic kinds of lazzi listed in Gordon's book; the period sources he cites for them include both manuscripts and printed books:

1. Acrobatic lazzi: Many of the moves on the list of movements below belong to this category. Thomassin's standing

backward somersault (see chapter eleven under "Scene Analysis: Marivaux's *Le jeu de l'amour et du hasard*") is a famous one.

2. Lazzi involving comic violence and sadistic behavior, such as practical jokes.

3. Lazzi involving food, which would be much used, for instance, by the voraciously gluttonous Truffaldino in *Il servitore di due padroni*.

4. Logically absurd lazzi, which are often standardized verbal quips. Gordon cites the "Lazzo of the Six Fathers": Harlequin states that nothing can prevent his accomplishing his goals, because, after all, "I was begotten by six fathers."

5. Using stage props to perform tricks, such as juggling or tossing them back and forth between characters.

6. Verbal and physical lazzi that are scatological and/or sexual in nature.

7. Verbal and physical lazzi that show the rebellious side of servants dealing with their masters. These would be in evidence in such plays as Molière's commedia-like farce discussed in chapter five, *Les fourberies de Scapin* (Scapin's Deceitful Tricks), where Scapin tricks Géronte into hiding in a large sack, then beats him with a stick while pretending to be the would-be assassins who have been pursuing him.

8. Lazzi involving mime, such as the "Lazzo of the Chase," in which two characters chase each other as they run in place.

9. Lazzi of stupid behavior, as in the "Lazzo of the Chairs," in which two characters are seated next to each other on their own chairs, one guarding the other. The prisoner tries to escape by moving his chair slightly away, hoping eventually to move all the way out. The guard moves his chair closer, the prisoner moves away, and they are halfway across the stage when they stop. The prisoner smiles at the guard. After a slight pause, he recommences his move.

The takes described earlier are also pure physical comedy, requiring no words to provoke laughter. And they are used as well in conjunction with the kinds of movements described below. It is often the take preceding or following the movement that gets the laugh, as opposed to the actual movement itself. All farce requires fast-paced movement, so you must take movement classes to develop flexibility, and dance classes are wonderful for training in agility, grace, and ease as well. Yoga can also be very helpful, as can such books as Davis Rider Robinson's *The Physical Comedy Handbook* (Heinemann, 1999), which is full of useful information and techniques.

Physical comedy training is useful not only in farces, but also if you are playing a clumsy character, such as Yepikhodov in Chekhov's *The Cherry Orchard*, who drops things and bumps into everything, or a waiter in a television sitcom who spills soup on a customer. As always, such movements must combine external and internal techniques, and be psychologically motivated, or they will not be funny; that is, they must be done technically, by the book, but always for a reason.

More sound general advice for all these moves: Relaxation and concentration, as with all acting, are essential. You must be relaxed and at the same time in a state of readiness and full of the desire to perform—the creative state. Only then can you concentrate on the performance. So be as relaxed as possible, and avoid becoming physically rigid when you have to do one of the physical moves detailed below. You want to break a fall, for instance, only when you are relaxed and flexible, so that you can avoid injury. Practice all these moves so that they become second nature, and maintain flexibility while doing them. In performance, be careful not to show the audience by any look or physical preparation that you are anticipating the moves: these are not dives from a swimming board or the return of a serve in tennis, but supposedly spontaneous unrehearsed accidents.

1. **The trip:** When walking briskly or slowly, you suddenly trip over something, surprising yourself; this is a very quick move. Essentially, you trip over your own feet, even if you are pretending to trip over some obstacle in your path. The technique is actually to trip the back leg against the front leg: As you walk, when you lift the back leg, use the foot to push lightly

against the heel of the front leg, without using so much force that you hurt yourself. This will allow you to act as if you have been jolted forward. Immediately regain your balance. You can then stand and turn around in (simulated) surprise, or continue walking forward as if nothing has happened.

2. **Falling:** All falls require you to control your balance and to shift the balance of your weight. You must counterbalance one part of the body against another, and feel the heaviness of the body in the thigh, as you reach the floor, so that you can cushion the fall and avoid injury.

   a. **Forward:** You trip, and fall as if you are landing flat on your face. The technique: Begin with the same technique used for tripping, but instead of righting yourself, this will be the beginning of a fall. Step forward and, lowering yourself, stretch the other leg out as you do so, counterbalancing the forward leg. Keep the forward leg to the side, so that you avoid landing on your knee. In other words, once you have pushed the foot of the back leg against the front leg, as you are jolted forward, continue the movement, landing on the thigh of the same front leg that you pushed, while counterbalancing with the arms and the torso, so that you do not fall heavily and injure yourself. As you fall, break the fall with the upstage forearm, and cushion the fall on the forearms.

   b. **Backward:** You fall as if jolted backward. The following technique is done quickly, as each motion follows hard upon the next: Step back very slightly on either leg, lean forward slightly, and lower yourself to the floor so that the opposite buttock touches the floor first. Continue rolling along on the same side, and keep your head and neck up. As you are jolted backward, continue the movements, as for a pratfall, as detailed below, even though you will not be falling on your backside, but rather with your whole body stretched out.

c. **To the side:** This is easier, since you can cushion the fall with the length of your body, and with your arm and leg, on whichever side you fall. The idea is to crumple quickly to the floor, but with a series of unbroken movements: if you are falling to the left, first the left arm must begin to break the fall, helped by the left leg. The weight of the body must be evenly distributed.

d. **The pratfall:** This was sometimes a lazzo used by the Pantalone character in a commedia play, on receiving bad news. It is a scissors-kick fall onto your backside, or prat, as it used to be called. This can be dangerous, and you must be careful to control your balance. Your legs shoot out from under you, and you land on your rear. The technique: This fall, like all falls, is done in a series of movements that follow each other in quick succession, as in a real accidental fall. In this case, you will go up before you go down. Reacting instantly to whatever is causing you to fall, begin by throwing your arms out to either side. Kick up with your right leg and simultaneously jump or hop up with your left leg; or vice versa: left leg kick followed by a hop with the right leg. It will look to the audience as if the first leg caused you to lose your balance and carried your body upward. As you are rising upward, quickly move the left leg that you hopped on out in front of you; both legs will be in the air for a brief instant. Then instantly bring your right leg down onto the stage floor, and break the fall with your right leg, putting your weight on it and using it to lower your body to the ground. As you land, cushion the fall with your left buttock. If you wish, slap the stage floor with one or both hands, to create the sound of the impact; this is not always necessary. You will end in the position of sitting straight up, legs in front of you, looking slightly dazed or whatever reaction is required by the circumstances. Robinson's advice is to practice this slowly at first, and gradually bring the fall up to speed.

e. **Tumbling downstairs or down a mountain:** This acrobatic trick requires balance and dexterity, as you go head over heels down an incline or a staircase, and you have to touch the body to the ground or floor, being careful not to use the elbows or knees.

f. **Falling off furniture:** If you have to fall off a chair, kick the chair away with one foot, so that the chair appears to have become unbalanced all by itself, and cushion the fall as the chair shoots out from under you, trying to grab onto something to break the fall. In the farce film *Furry Vengeance* (2010), Brooke Shields as Tammy Sanders is awakened from a sound sleep by Brendan Fraser as her husband Dan when he has a nightmare. She screams and tumbles off the bed, in a one-two move that is perfectly done. She just falls, without a pause, and without thinking about it. There was probably a mattress or pad just below the bed, out of camera range, to break the fall, but in any case, she was well cushioned by the bedding, so she could not have been injured in the sudden move. Safety first, always!

g. **Practical jokes:** These vary from putting a bucket of water above a door so that when someone opens it, the water spills on that person to pulling a chair out from under someone who is about to sit, so that the person falls flat on the floor. Other practical jokes include putting a whoopee cushion on someone's chair, so that it sounds as if the person sitting down has farted; shaking someone's hand using a buzzer that shocks the other person; gluing something down so that when someone tries to pick it up, it won't budge; and giving someone a container to open, out of which springs a fake snake. A spit-take is a possible result to a practical joke. The advice on various kinds of falls is useful for many such jests, which are kinds of lazzi.

3. **Climbing down:** Whether you are climbing down from a ladder, a chair, or a boulder on a mountainside, you try and fail to climb down. This simple lazzo consists of reaching one leg down, preparatory to climbing to the floor or the ground, while holding onto something, such as the back of the chair. But the leg does not reach down far enough, so you have to try again, until at last you succeed in climbing down. You may put one leg down, bring it back up, put the other leg down, bring it back up, and repeat this as many times as you wish. You may also tumble off the furniture, as in the previous lazzo, or do a simple fall, when you think you are touching the ground, but are not. When climbing down a ladder, you may miss the next rung and have difficulty reaching the one below it.

4. **Slip and slide:** You step inadvertently onto an oil slick or, indoors, onto a puddle of grease, say in a kitchen, and you start to slip, then slide around. The slide may end in a fall. The technique, if you are indoors, is to grab on to something, a countertop say, and hold on for dear life, as you slide one foot after another, remaining in place; similar to running in place, but with a greater width between the feet so that you look uncontrolled. If you are outdoors, you may allow the slip and slide to lead to a fall; or you may regain your balance and walk away.

5. **The push:** With one outstretched hand, a person pushes another from behind, seemingly with force, and the pushed person reacts by moving forward and stopping, as if on a dime, and as if pushed with far more force than has actually been exerted. The pushed person may possibly continue walking as if nothing had happened, or may turn and confront the pusher.

6. **The head slam:** As you are opening a door or a French window, you accidentally slam your head against it. This may knock you out, or send you spinning, or simply cause you to stand there stunned. One reaction is simply to proceed with what

you were doing, and the lack of reaction can be funny in itself. The technique: As you open the door, simultaneously put your foot near it, so that it hits your shoe, making a sound, and snap your head back, as if the door had hit you. Immediately bring your had to the hurt spot, as you naturally would, and react, perhaps vocally, perhaps by gasping, or do not react at all: just stand there for a second. Your head must of course be near enough to the door to make any of this convincing. There is a nice variation on this in Shawn Levy's film *Just Married* (2003): Ashton Kutcher (b. 1978) lifts Brittany Murphy (1977–2009), his new bride, and carries her over the threshold of their hotel room, and just as he moves to go through the door, she slams her head against the frame. No doubt, the sound effects department supplied the noise, and she did the rest, jerking her head away, and pretending to be hurt. It looks very real!

7. **Faked injuries:** This may involve taking out your anger on something (see above). The technique: For instance, if you are hammering nails, hit the table near your hand and simultaneously scream in pain. You may also begin slowly and in a case where you get more and more angry, your actions become more and more vehement, the hit thumb being the climax of your anger. This may be funny in context, although it is difficult to laugh at such an awful occurrence.

8. **Partial concealment:** This is a ubiquitous comic device in farces. A person tries to hide, for instance behind the large double curtains of a window, and his or her feet stick out. This is one of many variations in farce films and stage plays, where the person in hiding is discovered by the person who is looking for him or her. What will the discoverer do? And how will the discovered person react? In *Just Married*, David Rasche (b. 1944) as Mr. McNerny discovers his future son-in-law, Tom Leezak, in just such a position in his daughter Sarah's bedroom, when he comes in to say good night to her. On his way out, he throws the name "Leezak" over his shoulder, as he is practically at the threshold.

9. **Inappropriate reactions: The unequal reaction, the minimal reaction, and the nonreaction:** The unequal reaction consists of a minimal reaction to something that would ordinarily be expected to cause a great amount of physical pain, such as a punch or being hit by a falling object. The nonreaction consists of a deadpan lack of reaction or of a very minimal reaction, compared to what one might expect, to some physical attack, whether a slap, a punch, being hit over the head, or the like. The nonreaction is usually followed by a slow turn, and a slow burn, as the victim prepares to retaliate with more massive force. In *The Bank Dick*, W. C. Fields, is hit on the head with a bottle of ketchup (probably made of some very light material, and painted to look like a real bottle of ketchup) thrown at him by his little daughter. He flinches, rubs his head slightly, and appears to mutter to himself. Then he leaves the house, and immediately returns with a huge potted plant that he is just beginning to throw at her, when his wife yells at him not to "touch that child!"

10. **The pie in the face:** Didn't your mother ever tell you not to play with food? The pies used in this stunt, once ubiquitous, especially in silent film farces, were filled with whipped cream, and virtually harmless. It was the reaction of those hit that made it funny. Reactions included the slow burn before the hit person threw the next pie. Buster Keaton tells us how they used to prepare the pies, which were not regular bakery pies. The prop people made two pie shells, which they glued together with a flour and water paste, because a regular pie plate might hurt and would also be distracting as it flew off the pie. The bottom of the pie shell was filled with another flour and water paste that stretched to hold the filling—lemon curd if the pie were to be thrown at a dark-haired or dark-suited person, blueberry puree if it was supposed to be thrown at a fair-haired person. This was then topped with whipped cream, and voilà—a throwable pie.

11. **The flying hat:** This rarely used trick involves trying to put on a hat that immediately flies off the wearer's head. W. C. Fields used a variation in a number of films that involved his using a cane, on which the hat was caught. Nonplussed, he then looked around to see what had become of it. Sometimes, he didn't even use a cane. Two techniques: 1. As you are about to put the hat down on your head, simultaneously press the middle finger against the thumb, giving a sharp flick with the finger against the thumb, "as if you were shooting a marble," says Robinson. Do this just as the hat brim reaches your head, simultaneously propelling the hat up and forward. The take you do afterward will get the laugh. 2. A Fields technique: reach behind yourself with the hat, so that it will have to miss your head, then look around to see what has become of it.

12. **Kicking the hat or other object:** On the ground or floor in front of you is a hat or other object that you stoop over to pick up. As you reach to pick it up, give it a slight kick with your toe, so that it flies away from you. When you go over to pick it up again, do the same thing. Use the upstage foot, so that the audience does not notice the kick. This strange lazzo is not only startling, but very effective, as the object appears to move by itself.

13. **The disappearing thumb:** This is the old trick that uncles have played on their young nephews and nieces: The thumb of one hand seems to be cut off, and to be able to move along the other hand, the thumb of which is folded down so as to be invisible. When I played Ko-Ko in Gilbert and Sullivan's *The Mikado* for Dorothy Raedler's American Savoyards, the production that she directed involved endless bits, and they required concentration. One bit, for instance, involved my slamming my samurai sword back into its sheath after I had drawn the sword partway out, and acting as if I had cut off my thumb. I slammed the sword and screamed, and then held up my hand with the thumb concealed, and moved my other thumb along. I then found my thumb again, and wiggled it.

One time, I slammed the sword so forcefully, and jerked my head at the same time, that my bald wig, with its pigtail on top, went flying off my head and landed on the very edge of the stage apron. The audience howled, and I simply picked the wig up, replaced it on my head, and shrugged. More laughter and applause.

14. **Slow motion:** In film, slow motion is used for actions and events that are meant to seem very slowed down in time. On stage, you simply slow down all your movements, exaggerating them at the same time.

15. **The corkscrew kick:** This movement is an old commedia trick, often used by the Harlequin character, and later used also in twentieth-century vaudeville and old comedy films, where you can see Groucho Marx or Buster Keaton doing it. It usually involves a change of direction, as the comedian going right abruptly turns on his heels and goes left. Géronte or, especially, Scapin might use it in *Les fourberies de Scapin*. The technique: Hop on one leg while you spin the other leg in a circle, then immediately reverse and hop on the other leg, spinning the opposite leg in a circle, before heading off in whatever direction you are going. Keep facing front while you do this move, cheat to the side with your hips, and you will create the optical illusion that your legs are actually spinning in a circle. Be very careful not to injure your knees.

16. **Difficulty in using objects:** The difficulties arise either from the awkwardness of the props/objects themselves, or from your own clumsiness as the character. The awkwardness in either case must be carefully rehearsed, and the problem to be solved must be dealt with in a real way, using the utmost concentration, as each step in dealing with the object is gone through in a prearranged, invariable order, so that it can be repeated in every performance. This is a purely technical matter, and must be incorporated into the actor's score so that it becomes organic, and seems spontaneous and unanticipated. Sometimes, the frustration is so great, that the actor will end up

kicking a piece of furniture, and faking an injury, compounding the comedy. Among the objects and their accompanying difficulties:

a. **Shoes:** Putting on shoes, as in Beckett's *Waiting for Godot*, where the characters, especially Estragon, have repeated difficulty in jamming feet into shoes that do not fit.

b. **Clothing:** Trying to put on a jacket, and being unable to find the sleeve openings; dealing with recalcitrant gloves or hats, as in the flying hat trick, above.

c. **Tricky objects:** These get away from whoever is handling them, and refuse to cooperate, as with a gooseneck microphone that will not stay in place, a microphone or music stand that refuses to stay screwed into position, but immediately slides down; a plate or bottle that insists on sliding along a slippery surface; or something that comes shooting out of a wrapper, such as a piece of candy or a sandwich, which you have had difficulty unwrapping. Lucy in the famous *I Love Lucy* episode at the chocolate factory had to deal with a conveyor belt.

d. **Setting up furniture or tents:** Unfolding folding chairs, chaise-longues, and/or folding tables at a campsite or for a picnic can be very difficult in these comic bits. Setting up a tent that keeps collapsing, for instance, or starting a campfire can be the occasions of very funny comedy.

e. **Dealing with large papers:** Unfolding and refolding charts and maps and trying to force them into place.

f. **Cooking:** Dealing with recalcitrant knives and vegetables or meats, trying to cut them up, or mixing a batter for cake or muffins can be the occasion of endless clumsy spills and splatters, and possible injuries that you must be very careful to avoid.

g. **Bottles or jars:** Opening a bottle on which the lid refuses to budge.

h. **Cigarettes and lighters:** Lighting a cigar, pipe, or cigarette when the lighter or match will not light.

i. **Liquids:** Pouring a drink, when the liquid may go all over the place, as attention is distracted.

17. **Playing Drunk:** There are degrees of drunkenness, from being slightly tipsy or high to falling down, and everything in between. They all require flexibility and fluidity of movement, and an extra careful attention to whatever the movement is, as Uta Hagen points out in *Respect for Acting* (Macmillan, 1973). Knowing that your senses have been impaired, you reach very carefully to put the glass down on a table, and sometimes just miss. In W. C. Fields's *The Bank Dick*, a falling-down drunk film director on location is marched along back and forth between two stalwarts who are trying to help him sober up. Every so often, he starts to fall, and they prevent him from doing so. The actor remains flexible throughout, and very loose-limbed, but, at the same time, had to be in complete physical control.

18. **Stage blows, slaps, and punches:** These depend for their effect upon the reactions of the actor being struck. They must be done by the numbers. The actor doing the striking must not really deliver a blow with force. Rather, the actor being struck must react as if it were real. As you are punched in the jaw, for example, throw your head back, and simultaneously make a loud vocal sound, as if the air were forced out of you. Similarly, if you are punched in the stomach, double up and make a vocal sound. Sometimes it is the actor being slapped who actually makes the sound of the slap by striking his leg with his hand and simultaneously throwing back his head, more or less forcefully depending on the strength of the blow. The result is a resounding hit that looks real. Another way is to have the actor being struck clap one hand against another, sometimes with the actor's back to the audience. In either case, the hitting arm completes its motion, but does not actually strike the other actor with any great force, despite appearances.

A light slap might, however, be done for real, as would a light stage punch.

19. **Three Stooges variations on physical abuse:** In the W. C. Fields film, *Never Give a Sucker an Even Break*, a move that the Three Stooges would use is done expertly by Fields: he grabs the nose of the other actor and gives the hand holding the nose a sharp rap with the other hand. The other actor's reaction is what makes this work. Any number of similar moves by the famous trio are also done without actually causing pain to the actor being attacked: moving the hand up and down so that the attacked actor has to follow the movement, then suddenly striking the actor or flicking his ear or rapping him on the top of the head. All such moves must be thoroughly rehearsed so as to avoid injury.

The one sacrosanct rule in physical comedy, as in fight scenes, is: Safety First!

II

Creating Comic Characters: Stanislavsky's Approach to Comedy

The Heart of the System: Don't "Act!" Instead, Be! And "Behave" *As If* You Were the Character!

Stanislavsky's logical system of creating characters is as necessary for comedy as it is for serious drama or tragedy. All plays demand reality and believability from actors, and the system allows you to develop an inner rationale and justification for your character in any kind of comedy, including those of Shakespeare and Molière, Chekhov's comedies of psychology, Wilde's drawing-room comedies, the light plays of Neil Simon, and even such absurdist pieces as Samuel Beckett's *Waiting for Godot*. The system is equally valid and necessary for comedy of manners, for farce, and for stylized performances that have elements of artificiality, including, for example, commedia dell'arte plays involving standardized gestures, lazzi, and the use of masks.

Stanislavsky tells us in *My Life in Art* that all acting depends on "the magical, creative *if*." Your goal in rehearsal is to become the character; that is, you have to behave *as if* you are the character. You have to behave *as if* every moment had never happened before, and were occurring spontaneously. And you must behave *as if* events have taken place when the character is not there, between the scenes of the play, and *as if* you have reacted to those events, and *as if* the character's own life had a continuity even when the character is not on stage.

How do you do this? You follow the principles and methods of the system. Begin by reading and analyzing the script, without setting anything; how to do this is explained below. You will find what you need as you rehearse, based on the ideas you have developed in your text analysis.

Be Truthful!

The first and most important principle of the system is to be truthful. Don't pretend you feel something when you don't. Be honest in your actions and reactions. Mean what you say. In other words, don't indicate; that is, don't try to show that you feel something by putting on what you think the emotion should look like.

Every Action Has a Psychological Motivation

The second principle underlies all the rest: Every action has a psychological motivation. Why do you do what you do? The mind makes demands that were stimulated by the body's demands, as Eugenio Barba and Nicola Savarese point out in *A Dictionary of Theatre Anthropology: The Secret Art of the Performer* (Routledge, 2006). When you act, "demands that are not real must become so." You are working with the life of a fictitious person. Just as in real life your reactions tend to be automatic, so when you play a character, you must make the character's reactions automatic, but never mechanical: you have to play everything for real, *as if* it were taking place in reality, and you have to learn to think like your character:

> This is the purpose of *perezhivanie*: to train the actor's mind to make demands, that is, [to respond to] stimuli, to which the body can do nothing other than react appropriately.

The Russian word used by Stanislavsky, *perezhivanie*, means "living through" a role. This is his prime concept of what the actor must learn to do in rehearsal, and must carry out in performance.

In fulfillment of this principle, you must find and carry out the correct psychophysical action(s), discovered primarily in the course of rehearsals, and impossible to discover experientially in any other way, so that you can behave *as if* you were the character.

In order to rehearse and to perform, you must experience. Remain open. Allow feelings to happen. Do not try to force them into existence. Use emotional recall of your past experiences that are analogous to those in the play as a substitution for the relationships and experiences in the play. Substitution, a rehearsal rather than a performance tool, is a conscious replacement of the fictitious objects, emotions, events, people, relationships, or places with objects, people, events, etc. from the actor's own life. This is very similar to the useful tool of endowment: the projection of physical or emotional qualities onto an object or person—for instance, endowing an empty suitcase as fully packed and heavy, so that you behave *as if* it is. As you remember, your body will react and feelings will awaken. In this way, you will understand viscerally what the character is living through. Substitution is particularly useful when you feel stuck and are not finding what you want in a moment or a scene. It is your "actor's secret," something only you know and that you do not want to communicate to others, lest it lose its power to help you as you want it to.

Although you may understand intellectually which emotions you think the character experiences, you do not need to worry about arousing feelings or emotions consciously: They will be there for you if you perform the correct series of psychophysical actions. As Stanislavsky thought, the trick is to awaken the unconscious through the conscious, and, once it is awakened, to let it alone. That is the meaning of the term "organic," a kind of performing that every actor aspires to achieve.

Moreover, your role and the development of your character will only be fully worked out as you work with your fellow cast members, from the first reading of the play on, in accordance with Stanislavsky's principle of "discovering through doing."

Be Specific!

The third principle and major key to the system, is: be specific. Know every detail of the given circumstances of the play (time, setting, and places, both those on stage and off), and of your character's life and relationships. Of prime importance is the character's relationship to everybody else. Specific interactions with the other characters must be explored in rehearsal.

In rehearsal and performance, you must listen and respond; this is essential. What you hear from the other characters, and, most importantly, how you receive what you hear, will automatically help you determine what to do and how you respond verbally. For the author's words to become yours, the thoughts that underlie them (the subtext) and that give them specific meaning in the context of the circumstances must become yours.

Working with the System: Script Analysis and Preparation

Working with the system begins with the analysis of the text: First, you read the play, to which you will respond without preconceptions. This response will arouse instincts and impulses that will prove productive: When you laugh at something, for instance, this is a good indication of where you may expect the audience to laugh. Next, you start to analyze the script, reading it for its story, and for your character's place in that story.

When you analyze a script, and when you rehearse, you have to look for what the words tell you about the character's mental life (psychology). This conditions what the character wants overall (the superobjective), and in each scene (the objective, goal, or task), and why. The throughline of the action, once all the scenes are put together, is the journey the character takes in fulfillment of the superobjective. You must also begin to explore the relationships with the other characters, which will be fleshed out in rehearsal.

Everything you do, everything you say comes from character, without which there is no comedy. And that comedy comes from the character's mental life, which determines the physical and verbal actions: these are what the character does and says to obtain the objectives. What are the intentions with which you say the lines? What lies beneath them (the subtext)? "The subtext," said Stanislavsky, "is what makes us say the words." The subtext is the intentional, emotional meaning of the words: What do you mean when you utter particular words in a particular way?

What is in the characters' way (the obstacles), what they have to overcome, is the reason for the story of the play: the course of true anything never did run smooth. You must confront what is in your way and overcome it. In comedy, you will fail to attain an objective, change tactics, and fail again and again, and this is one of the sources of humor. As my acting teacher Alice Spivak put it, "In comedy, all the objectives fail, and that is why we laugh."

The mental life of the character includes a knowledge of the period in which the play takes place. You have to understand, for instance, that the mindset, customs, deportment and manners of the era of Louis XIV that inform the comedies of Molière are different (despite similarities in sociocultural attitudes) from those of Victorian England—just as different as the clothing that you have to get used to. As the brilliant British stage and screen actor, Miriam Margolyes (b. 1941), who is superb at comedy, says in an interview in *On Acting: Interviews with Actors* (Faber and Faber, 2001):

> You can never do too much research. Take my show, *Dickens's Women*. I studied Charles Dickens's novels at Cambridge [...] I did extensive period research, not just the historical and political facts, but the social history of the time, the social mores and expectations. I also researched the language of the time, the words that were used and the ways in which sentiments were expressed.

Stanislavsky's *Building a Character* (Theatre Arts Books, 1949) expands on the system detailed in *An Actor Prepares* (Theatre Arts Books, 1936), and outlined above. Tortsov, the acting teacher in both books (representing Stanislavsky himself), advises his students not to be actors on stage, but human beings first and foremost. Do not hide behind your characters, he tells them. Instead, reveal yourself and your humanity through them. In other words, don't work up a set of gestures, movements, and expressions, but let them happen spontaneously as you rehearse. You will thus avoid clichés and be real in your playing.

As Stanislavsky tells us, even when you use models, and draw behavior from life to use for the character, you have to make the behavior individual and real. Don't perform the clichés associated with the swaggering soldier, the romantic young lovers, the boorish peasant, the haughty great lady, or the pretentious aristocrat, a type often found in comedies of manners:

> An aristocrat always carries a top hat, wears gloves and a monocle, his speech is affected, he likes to play with his watch chain or the ribbon of his monocle. These are all generalized clichés supposed to portray characters. They are taken from life, they actually exist. But they do not contain the essence of a character and they are not individualized.

As an actor, you need to develop "a heightened, detailed sense of observation." You will be able to include "certain elemental and typical features" in portraying character types, such as those mentioned here and the commedia dell-arte stock character types discussed in chapter five. At the same time, you must make such types individual, not simply "traditional, lifeless, hackneyed portrayals" that are "not live people but figures in a ritual." If you follow this advice, your characters will be that much funnier, because their specific behavior will be that much more unexpected and surprising, while remaining true to the character's milieu and circumstances.

Using the System: Stanislavsky Plays Famusov in Griboyedov's *Woe from Wit*

Stanislavsky gives detailed instructions and ideas for work on particular characters in three plays in *Creating a Role* (Theatre Arts Books, 1961), including Shakespeare's *Othello* and Nikolai Gogol's (1809–1852) biting political satire *The Inspector General,* which many will recall from a 1949 film adaptation starring Danny Kaye. He also analyzes several roles in Alexandr Sergeyevich Griboyedov's (1795–1829) great Russian classic satire of the middle class and its pretentions, the four-act verse play, *Gore ot uma* (Woe from Wit; the phrase means something like "too smart for your own good"), a farce about Moscow society after the Napoleonic Wars. The tag line that ends the play—"But what will Countess Maria Alexeyevna say about this?"—became a famous catchphrase in Russian, as did the title of the play and many of its other lines. Stanislavsky's portrayal of the fatuous, self-important, emotional bureaucrat Famusov was much appreciated. A wealthy landowner, but not an aristocrat, with many serfs in his possession, he is sycophantically attached to the nobility and aspires to gain their good opinion, and even to be accepted as one of them.

The play observes the classical unities of time, place, and action, and takes place during one day in the life of the Famusov household, beginning at dawn. Sofia, Famusov's sentimental daughter, is secretly in love with Molchalin, her father's secretary. The lecherous Molchalin, who has made advances to her maid, Lisa, has spent the night with Sofia in her room, but they have not made love. In true medieval chivalric and nineteenth-century romantic fashion, they have sighed, gazed into each other's eyes, held hands, and professed their undying love for each other. Chatski, a starry-eyed, independent romantic intellectual and poet madly in love with Sofia, who loved him until she discovered that Molchalin would be her very slave, returns that day from three years of travel abroad, during which he has searched for and failed to find the meaning of life. Almost his first act is to call on Sofia. He is an idealist who mocks the hypocrisy of society during an evening gathering of the crème de la crème in Famusov's home. Sofia is so put out by Chatski's sarcasm that she starts a rumor that Chatski is mad. Upset by her mean-spiritedness, Chatski flees the scene, and awaits his carriage. Sofia on her way to Molchalin's room, overhears Molchalin making further advances to Lisa. She denounces the venal secretary to her father, who thinks she is talking about Chatski, and excoriates the young man in turn. Chatski is thoroughly disgusted by now, and tells them all off. He will leave to resume his wanderings, and he hopes to find a place where a person of true feeling can be at home, much in the manner of Molière's misanthrope, Alceste. Famusov, taken aback by Chatski's outburst, and afraid that his reputation as an upright pillar of society may be at stake, panics over how the high and mighty will take the news of all these carryings-on: "But what will Countess Maria Alexeyevna say about this?"

In the chapters on Griboyedov's play, Stanislavsky divides work on the role into three periods, in a further refinement of his system: "the period of study," when you acquaint yourself with the part, analyze the text, study external given circumstances, such as the historical era, and create the internal circumstances, which includes internalizing the mindset of the epoch in a way specific to the character. The last thing you do during this period is to appraise the facts, and you have to know not only your own specific given circumstances as the character, but also the situation of everyone else. If you are playing Chatski, for instance, you have to know all about the Famusov household "and not just that part of it which directly concerns my role."

Second is "the period of emotional experience" of the part, during which you create the actions you will perform, based on the objectives and obstacles, as well as understanding the superobjective and throughline of action. Last comes "the period of physical embodiment," in which you put everything together so that it flows and you live through the part.

In discussing the preparation of Famusov for the 1906 MAT production, Stanislavsky talks about the list of facts he needed to study, including Famusov's flirtation with Lisa, for he is also attracted to the serving girl, who is herself attracted to Chatski. Famusov is a hypocrite, afraid of any misalliance, but not above a sexual liaison with a servant, provided it remain secret. Stanislavsky talks of all this in the first person, immediately identifying with the role, and at the same time, often refers to the character by his name. He imagines the other characters, as well as his own:

In this way, I acquire a feeling of sympathy for the people of my imagination. That is a good sign. Of course, sympathy is not feeling; nevertheless it is a step in that direction.

He tells us that he then proceeded to imagine himself in the costume, and to imagine what Famusov was like as a young man. He studied the relationships with all the other characters, and the specific moments in the play when we see him with each character. In short, he studied the role thoroughly from every point of view, and was thereby able to immerse himself in it, all the time referring to Famusov as "I." This is a brilliant lesson to all of us as to how to proceed, and, once again, to take the characters in a comedy as seriously as those in a drama or tragedy, and to give them a rounded psychological inner being. In his approach to this or, by extension, any comic masterpiece, Stanislavsky advises the actors to start from scratch, and not to predetermine anything. The situations, absurd and outlandish as they are, must be treated with absolute conviction and reality by everyone, or there is no comedy.

III

Performing the Comedy of Manners: The Art of Repartee, or Speaking Is Action

"On sweet urbanity, / Though mere inanity, / To touch their vanity / We will rely…" So sing the three young gentlemen who plan to disguise themselves in drag and invade the women's fortress-academy of Castle Adamant, where no men are allowed, in Gilbert and Sullivan's *Princess Ida*. These aristocratic swains are planning seduction, and their weapons include "verbal fences" to "charm their senses," and serenading the young ladies "With ballads amatory / And declamatory," as well as showering them with fragrant bouquets of flowers. Their cynical, and at the same time sweetly innocent refrain about the seductive ploys they plan to use is a perfect formula for the main form of action in the subgenre we call comedy of manners. Indeed, these comedies rely on language and on "sweet urbanity, / Though mere inanity" as tools for the characters to get what they want. They depend on wit, on what Stanislavsky called verbal action, for as he said, "Speaking *is* action." Unlike farce, comedies of manners contain little violence or physical comedy.

There are three things to bear in mind when playing comedies of manners:

1. You want to make the language and the wit so much your own that the thoughts you express appear to be really yours. And

you don't want to sound facile or glib, unless the character is that way.

2. You must know and assimilate the system of social manners, customs, and deportment that form the background to the plays in whatever era they are set. This demands research.

3. You must play the characters fully, flesh them out, and take their journey. Don't think you can simply say witty words and jokes: There is a real subtext (intentions that inform the way the lines are said) that you have to find, and real objectives, and real internal and external actions to play.

The ancient Greeks and Romans wrote comedies of manners, many now lost. And Shakespearean comedy offers us the witty exchanges of Beatrice and Benedict in *Much Ado About Nothing* and the court scenes in *All's Well That Ends Well*. A small sampling of the genre includes Molière's *The Misanthrope*, *The Bourgeois Gentleman*, and other plays; the comedies of Dancourt and Regnard; and English Restoration comedy. In the eighteenth century, Marivaux was famous for his frothy, delicious comedies of manners; Goldsmith and Sheridan wrote in that genre; and the nineteenth century saw the effervescent, witty drawing-room comedies of Oscar Wilde. The tradition continued in the twentieth with the brilliant and sometimes brittle plays of Noël Coward.

The wit in all these plays is always in the service of the loving or lubricious spider catching the fly that is the object of seduction in the honeyed web of humor, because, as we all know, you can't catch a fly with the vinegar of acerbity. And the acerbic characters in comedies of manners, whom the audience loves, usually catch the audience's laughter at their witty sallies, which is gratification enough for any actor.

The comedy of manners presumes the existence of a society with rules that must be observed in the domain of human and social relations, and it satirizes those prevailing codes of conduct, or sometimes the characters who break the rules. One of the principal ideas Bergson expressed in *Le rire* (Laughter) is that life as we live it has been "encrusted with the mechanical," that is, overlaid socioculturally with all kinds of strictures and conventions that often leave us hidebound both psychologically and behaviorally. We live according to what we have learned are certain social rules of conduct, in whatever era we happen to be born into. And we reproduce what we have learned unconsciously in an automatic, mechanical way. Our natural inclinations are thus repressed, perhaps necessarily, or life in any society would be impossible, as Freud would agree. But these rules, these mores, and the relationships that result from them, as well as the behavior involved, have replaced natural instincts, sometimes for the good, in repressing rapaciousness and greed; sometimes for the bad, in repressing the ability to love and be loved in a natural way, binding love about with conventions and fears that cripple our fulfillment. All comedy makes fun of or mocks these social rules and relationships.

Many comedies of manners are set in upper-class milieus, often in domestic settings that occasionally take one away from the drawing-room or bedroom, as to the hotel in Coward's *Private Lives*, or outdoors as in Sheridan's *The Rivals* or Wilde's *The Importance of Being Earnest*.

Wit, or what passes for wit, is the test of a person's worth. In the drawing room and the high society salon, urbanity reigns supreme—one must never forget civility and good manners. With the politest of intonations, characters who know they are funny and want their interlocutors to laugh, converse in witty exchanges replete with irony, and delivered with aplomb. The repartee stabs with a poignard, or thin-bladed jeweled letter opener, but seldom with the sword—one leaves that less subtle weapon to the Three Musketeers. The sophisticated, egotistical, and competitive characters are filled with desire, and often with snobbery and fatuity. Their passionate romantic feelings are hidden behind a façade of brilliant barbs. The sophisticated veneer of the rich and powerful hides the savagery of those who rule.

Comedy of manners is also called high comedy and drawing-room comedy, the first being a broader and more inclusive term, since comedies of manners need not be set in the rarefied aeries of the upper economic classes. But wherever the plays are set, breaking the rules of what is considered suitable conduct creates laughter. Look for where your character breaks the rules, or wants to, and is prevented from doing so: the frustration experienced can also be very funny.

Rules of etiquette and politesse have been set down in books at least since Athenaeus of Naucratis wrote his fascinating *The Deipnosophists* (The Learned Banqueters) in the second century. From medieval times to the present day, books of manners have continued to proliferate, and they are fascinating, because they show us real, as well as expected, unconsciously understood behavior. Politesse and good manners, which show a basic respect for other people, have had to be taught from ancient days, since people did not always naturally practice them. In the eras of aristocratic rule and privilege, there were all-important rules about how to treat those in a superior position in society, what conduct was expected, and how to show the proper respect by bowing and curtseying correctly, hand-kissing, and other forms of obsequiousness and sycophancy. The violation of these rules of etiquette could result in severe punishment in real life, depending on the period and the amount of tyranny exercised by the rulers. In addition to books of etiquette, the fiction, biographies, autobiographies, and memoirs of any period will give you great insight into the manners, deportment, mindset, and social expectations and behavior of the era.

If you play one of the characters in Wilde, Molière, or Restoration comedy who is quick with a witty rejoinder or an insulting quip, you are playing someone who compares him- or herself to another person, and who comes out on top. You can play such a character as someone who feels that he or she knows what other mortals don't, because on some level your character considers them beings of a lower order. Your basic, underlying attitude is, "I know, and you don't. I am sophisticated, and you are naïve. I am therefore superior." With this attitude, you may be kind or you may be mean, contemptuous, and nasty—that depends on the character. The latter attitude, however, may be too unpleasant for comedy, unless the contempt is kept in a very light vein, or unless such a character gets his or her deserved comeuppance, to the audience's delight.

Remember that the aim and desire of the witty character in the comedy of manners is to break out of the straitjacket of convention, and to flout public mores and standards of conduct. At the same time such a character is insecure, and wants to compete with the object at whom his or her remarks are directed, who is often a rival in love. To take one example, all of this is the basis for the character of Alceste in Molière's *The Misanthrope*, who may be right in his assessment of the frivolousness, banality, pretensions and hypocrisy of those around him, but who is wrong not to make allowances for human frailty, created by human need, longing, and insecurity: so thinks Molière.

To summarize, you must play all the characters in high comedy with the restrained passion, which sometimes breaks out of its restraints, and the amorous desires that underlie wit. At the same time, the sense of suitable decorum and good manners must be observed.

And you need vocal energy, and a sense of rhythm and pacing that will allow the performance to bounce along on intermittent waves of laughter.

As with all acting, you have to mean what you say. You have to be engaged with the actions, committed to the moment, and living in the moment. This demands concentration and immersing yourself in the given circumstances.

Quips, aphorisms, and insults must be delivered with a mordant sense of sarcasm and irony. Hurting other people verbally is actually funny—to the audience, not to the person being hurt. Even if you play the subtext kindly, you are still being insulting. In high comedy, the person who is stung usually knows how to come back, and has a rejoinder that is equally stinging, if not more so, provoking laugh after laugh.

Remember that you have to know how to move stylishly as well as to speak elegantly. So you have to understand how clothing conditions movement. Dame Edith Evans (1888–1976), whose career spanned fifty years, was superb and hilarious in high comedy, and brilliant in every other genre as well. You can see her as Lady Augusta Bracknell, a role for which she was famous, in the 1952 film adaptation of *The Importance of Being Earnest*. Her advice on the use of accessories: "Do everything with a fan except fan yourself with it."

IV

Performing Farce and Commedia dell'Arte: The Art of Pandemonium, or The Storm before the Calm

"Comedy is unusual people in real situations; farce is real people in unusual situations." Unusual, but not impossible. So wrote the legendary American animator, director, and writer, Chuck Jones (1912–2002), known for his Bugs Bunny and Daffy Duck cartoon features, which are themselves farces with unusual situations, and unreal characters in the form of anthropomorphized animals and birds.

The chaos, mayhem, and pandemonium, the confusion, hysteria, desperation and frustration with which farce abounds, and the attempts by the characters to evade the consequences of their actions and to avoid embarrassment, would be horrifying and sometimes even tragic in real life, but in a play or film, everything is resolved happily, as the characters go speeding through the events. As the English barrister and writer who created Rumpole of the Bailey, Sir John Mortimer (1923–2009), said, "Farce is tragedy played at a thousand revolutions per minute."

When playing farce, bear in mind the following three basic principles:

1. You must behave with complete conviction and reality in extravagant, absurd circumstances.

2. Farce, a fast-paced comedy, takes everything to extremes. This includes the desperate pursuit of objectives that fail, and the overwrought emotional reactions of the characters, who are prone to panic and to instantly switching emotions to their opposites: love to hate; calmness to frantic overwrought frenzy. The energy with which farce is played is also extreme: the fury of the storm before the calm.

3. As with comedies of manners, you must understand and assimilate the code of manners and the sociopolitical system of the period in which the farce is set.

The word "farce" comes from French, and means stuffing, in the culinary sense. In earlier centuries, a farce was a brief comic interlude stuffed, as 'twere, between the acts of a longer piece, often a verse tragedy, than which there was sometimes nothing verse. Bored audiences looked forward to a good laugh, and to a happy return to their naps once the farce was over and the tedious neoclassical ranting had begun again—a perfect soporific.

Although often condemned as vulgar and inferior, farce has always been wildly popular, partly because of its savage mockery of authority figures. In farce, they get their comeuppance, as they do not always do in real life. Poking fun at ancient Greek and Roman domestic tyrants began a tradition that continued with the portrayal of Satan as a comic figure in medieval religious pieces, went on with all the Pantalone types in the commedia dell'arte (see chapters five and eleven), and gave us the dictatorial, stubborn, hypochondriacal widower Argan in Molière's *Le malade imaginaire*. He has a contemporary descendant in the widow, Viola Fields, the character played by Jane Fonda in *Monster-in-Law* (2005). In this romantic farce, directed by Australian filmmaker Robert Luketic, and written by Anya Kochoff, the prospective mother-in-law is pitted against Charlotte (Jennifer Lopez), in a knock-down, drag-out fight for the affections of Viola's son, Dr. Kevin Fields (Michael Vartan). One of Viola's ploys is to pretend emotional and physical illness, but she has many others. She is not above faking a fainting fit in public when she isn't getting her way, and winding up in the hospital, where she continues her antics and plays on everybody's sympathy. And she pays her favorite restaurant waiter to come to the hospital and pose as her psychiatrist. Dressed in doctor's blues and a white lab coat, the "doctor" (Stephen Dunham) persuades Kevin and Charlotte that Viola needs to move in with them. When Charlotte discovers what Viola is up to, the mayhem begins in earnest!

Fonda and Lopez, and the supporting cast, including especially Wanda Sykes as Fonda's confidante and amanuensis—one of a line of sassy servants going back to ancient Greek and Roman comedy—are superb in the reality they bring to the extreme situations in which they find themselves. And that is the key to playing farce: behaving really. Fonda often overreacts—which is not the same as overacting—and this is a technique much employed in farce. As Sigmund Freud tells us, an overreaction indicates an inner unconscious conflict, inadvertently revived by some chance remark or incident. When the conflict is set off, like a firecracker, the person reacts in a way that sometimes may appear overdone to the spectator, but the person who experiences it from the inside is panicky and in need of resolution. This is, of course, a perfect lesson and precept for actors: once again, your acting must come from the reality of the internal and external situations. If you really believe in what you are doing, it will not seem overdone to you, and it will be organic and therefore appropriate to the circumstances. Think of the extreme overreactions of Jackie Gleason in *The Honeymooners*: we accept them because he truly means them.

Farce goes about as far as it can go—like the citizens of Kansas City in the famous lyric from Rodgers and Hammerstein's *Oklahoma*. When it reaches a limit of normal behavior, it surpasses it. You gotta go a little nuts! At every failure of an objective, the characters are prone to panic. They have to make an extreme effort to be self-controlled and not to allow violence to break out, which it sometimes does. Even if they appear to be, few characters in farce are relaxed or calm, at least for very long, and a tranquil mood can change to one of storm and stress in a twinkling. Characters take desperate measures and improvise desperate ploys to get what they want, to save themselves, or to conceal what they must; hence, the shoving of paramours into closets, the frantic escape of a terrified inamorato through a window, or the mad impromptu kiss of a husband and wife, during which a wide-eyed lover makes a hasty exit on tiptoe.

In the nineteenth century especially, histrionic or hysterical neurotics were a well known psychological category, often seen in farces. In Feydeau's *Mais n'te promène donc pas toute nue!* (Stop Walking Around Stark Naked!), discussed in chapter twelve, Madame Ventroux is a hysteric. Histrionics means hysterical behavior, theatrics, overly dramatic behavior, overreacting, and self-indulgent, extravagant acting; you will find just how far to go with this sort of thing when you are rehearsing.

Nineteenth-century British and French farce are full of hysterical types. Even earlier in theatrical history, Madame Patin in Dancourt's *Le chevalier à la mode* (The Fashionable Cavalier) and Mrs. Malaprop in Sheridan's *The Rivals* exemplify the hysterical character, who needs obedience, respect, and attention, and often fails to get them. Among later exemplars of the histrionic personality is Basil Fawlty in the television farce series *Fawlty Towers*. John Cleese plays a hotel owner, who is constantly beset by all kinds of problems that require instant solutions, thus driving him to a state of panic. Fawlty is particularly manic, as well as passive-aggressive. He compensates for his endless mistakes by making things up on the spot, in other words, by lying, and his attempts to hide his obvious embarrassment are terribly painful for him and hilarious to us.

Farce also abounds in obsessive-compulsive neurotics, and realistic comedy affords us examples as well. In general, obsessive-compulsive people are "anal-retentive": they just can't let go of their obsession, at least not without the greatest effort, and the obsession has become something they must compulsively attend to. Freud explains in his essay "Repression" that in obsessional neurosis withdrawal of the libido (sexual desire, and the awareness of it), which is the usual aim of repression, is accomplished, and an obsession substituted for it. But the repression is basically unsuccessful in providing a solution to the psychic conflict. It has only succeeded in substituting things that provoke anxiety for the anxiety aroused by the original libidinal impulses. People so afflicted go through life in an overwrought way. Obsessive-compulsive neurosis involves seemingly uncontrollable repetitions of actions or intrusive thoughts, and a concentration on a particular area of interest, to the exclusion of everything else. One of the first such characters in theatrical literature is Philocleon in Aristophanes' *Sphekes* (The Wasps), who is obsessed with doing jury duty, which he loves to excess. Truffaldino in Goldoni's *The Servant of Two Masters* is obsessed with food, and the super-macho male chauvinist Solyony compulsively douses his hands with perfume in Chekhov's tragicomedy *Three Sisters*. Among the many obsessive-compulsive comedic characters are the obsessively jealous Kitely in Ben Jonson's *Every Man In His Humor* and the compulsively neat Felix in Neil Simon's *The Odd Couple*. The compulsively snobby Hyacinth Bucket ("pronounced Bouquet"), who is a hysteric as well as obsessive, is hilariously played by Patricia Routledge (b. 1929) in the British sitcom, *Keeping Up Appearances* (1990–1995).

In *As Good As It Gets* (1997), Jack Nicholson plays Melvin Udall, an obsessive-compulsive who has a phobia about germs, is racist and anti-Semitic, and has to skip over particular cracks in the sidewalk on his way to his favorite restaurant, where he must always have the same table and the same waitress (Helen Hunt), or else he goes into panic mode. All of this in real life would be off-putting, to say the least, and perhaps even tragic, but with Nicholson's absolute personalized specificity combined with his near-panicky desperation, the character is hilarious, as he constantly fails to realize his objectives. Somebody is in his way on the sidewalk! He panics. Someone is sitting at his table! He panics. And he does everything with perfect innocence, with a perfect lack of knowledge that he is an idiot, and that most people who have the misfortune to deal with him can't stand him. Everything he does is justified in his own eyes. And that acute lack of self-awareness is also very funny. Ultimately, in this wonderful character study, it turns out that he has a heart after all, and can be generous and loving.

The same thing is true of another character with a very different full-blown obsessive-compulsive personality disorder in a farce that guys psychotherapy as a profession: Bob, played by the effervescent Bill Murray in *What About Bob?* (1991), with Richard Dreyfuss as his exasperated therapist, whom Bob will not leave alone. The manipulative patient follows the hapless Dr. Leo Marvin to his vacation home, and there the two opponents go at it hammer and tongues, while Dreyfuss, eventually maddened beyond endurance, tries to preserve a modicum of civility, particularly in front of his family, who just love Bob and think he is the most endearing person in the world. The complications and misunderstandings are typical of the best farces, and the entire cast has thrown itself into the given circumstances with perfect abandon. This film is a real lesson in playing farce.

The genre, or rather the way of constructing a play or screenplay and writing its characters, is remarkably flexible and broad, and can take place in any environment, from the university campus in Thomas's *Charley's Aunt* to the domestic setting of *The Odd Couple*. The most well known form of farce nowadays is the television sitcom. Aside from the plays and films just mentioned, the genre includes screwball movie comedies from the 1930s; Broadway comedies by Kauffman and Hart, who wrote madcap farces in which endless characters seem to appear and disappear, running in and out, as they do in some of Feydeau's pieces; and even drawing-room comedies like Wilde's *The Importance of Being Earnest* or *Lady Windermere's Fan*, which combine both genres. In the former, Lady Bracknell's constantly being nonplussed by everything that is said to her is a farcical reaction. She is imperious and appears to be in control, but inside she in a constant state of turmoil and prone to hysterical panic reactions. Everything takes her by surprise, and her reaction is extreme, as she tries to regain control of the situation and herself. Yet her outward behavior is extremely dignified—an example of playing opposites, discussed in chapter one.

Another element associated with farce is sexual innuendo. Remarks that were acceptable in mixed company in Restoration comedy were considered shockingly discourteous in the Victorian era, and this fact conditions how such moments are played.

Farce also includes rude and insulting behavior and verbal insults; chase scenes; and misinterpretations of people and events, leading to further confusion, mayhem, and pandemonium. All of this is typical of "French farce," also called "bedroom farce" or "sex comedy," such as those by the handsome nineteenth-century boulevardier Georges

Feydeau. There were so many bedroom comedies written by French playwrights that the name French farce stuck, although in the twentieth century the genre was taken over by the British. Absurd and silly as it is, the farce can nevertheless be realistic, as with Chekhov's *The Marriage Proposal* (see chapter six for a discussion). Or farce can be outlandish and weird, like some of Ionesco's absurdist plays.

One of the main elements of farce is the physical comedy known as "knockabout," which means literal rough and tumble physical action, and slapstick in which people knock each other around, in carefully rehearsed stage combat. Entertainment in which the humor consists of many such physical gags is called, in fact, a knockabout farce. Molière's *Les fourberies de Scapin* (Scapin's Deceitful Tricks), discussed in chapter five, has knockabout elements. So do many episodes of the *I Love Lucy* and *Honeymooners* television series.

The word "slapstick" comes from the stage implement used in commedia dell'arte, consisting of a handled flat board to which another flat board is attached at the top by a hinge, so that it makes a brief, loud, sharp bang when shaken by the handle. The slapstick was used to point up a comic line or droll bit of stage business, much like the drum roll in twentieth-century burlesque: buh-DOOM-boom. The bang of the slapstick might be followed by a whistle on a slide whistle.

In the eighteenth century, aside from the parodies of Italian opera, farce satires and spoofs of well known tragedies were also popular. In the early part of the eighteenth century, Dryden's heroic verse tragedies of the 1600s came in for increasing mockery. A farce parody with the deliberately unwieldy title *The Tragedy of Chrononhotonthologos: Being the Most Tragical Tragedy That Ever Was Tragediz'd by Any Company of Tragedians*, "Written by Benjamin Bounce, Esq.," reflects the names chosen by Dryden and others for their chief characters in the heroic verse dramas that were then considered the height of highbrow art and the apogee of theatrical loftiness. This hilariously bombastic spoof of Dryden, which expresses the simplest concepts, such as "The king is asleep," in circumlocutions, rodomontades and adumbrations that nobody would ever think to utter, was written in 1734 by Henry Carey

(1687–1743). Audiences at the time saw it as a political satire denouncing the unpopular Whig minister, Robert Walpole (1676–1745), considered the first de facto Prime Minister, and needling Queen Caroline (1683–1737), wife of King George II (1683–1760). Here is the beginning of the opening scene. I have preserved the original spelling and capitalization: The capitalized nouns are a great clue as to how to read this speech aloud, because they receive a natural stress, and make the point of these silly lines clear:

> SCENE I. *An Antichamber in the Palace.*
> (*Enter* RIGDUM-FUNNIDOS *and*
> ALDIBORONTIPHOSCOPHORNIO.)
> RIGDUM-FUNNIDOS.
> ALDIBORONTIPHOSCOPHORNIO!
> 　　Where left you *Chrononhotonthologos*?
> ALDIBORONTIPHOSCOPHORNIO. Fatigu'd with the tremendous Toil of War,
>
> 　　Within his Tent, on downy Couch succumbent,
> 　　Himself he unfatigues with gentle Slumbers;
> 　　Lull'd by the chearful Trumpet's gladsome Clangor,
> 　　The Noise of Drums, and Thunder of Artillery,
> 　　He sleeps supine amid the Din of War;
> 　　And yet 'tis not definitively Sleep;
> 　　Rather a kind of Dose, a waking Slumber,
> 　　That sheds a Stupifaction o'er his Senses;
> 　　For now he nods and snores; anon he starts;
> 　　Then nods and snores again; If this be Sleep,
> 　　Tell me, ye Gods! what mortal Man's awake!
> 　　What says my Friend to this?

The proliferate longwinded language of Aldiborontiphoscophornio is set in bas-relief against the more direct, real replies of Rigdum-Funnidos, couched in more ordinary terms, in this silliest of phantasmagorias, making the filigreed coruscations of elaborated verbosity even funnier.

Everyone who writes about farce says that the genre deals in cruelty and violence, but the violence, which may menace murder and turns into mayhem and confusion at the drop of a hat, does not actually result in lasting physical harm or murder. Any injury is of the mildest sort, as in the temporary incapacitation of the acerbic wit Sheridan Whiteside, based on the sometimes spiteful *New Yorker* magazine critic and Algonquin Round Table raconteur, Alexander Woollcott (1887–1943), in Kauffman and Hart's *The Man Who Came to Dinner* (1939); he played the part himself on tour in 1940, and on the west coast. The hit Broadway comedy/farce was made into a film in 1942 with Monty Woolley (1888–1963) reprising the title role he had created on Broadway. The film is a great lesson in farce acting, and in just how far one can go with extravagant behavior, although it may strike you as a bit old-fashioned nowadays. There have been Broadway revivals, and radio and television adaptations, and the play is often performed in summer stock.

Monty Woolley was an urbane actor, with wonderful, precise diction, and a great sense of humor, qualities useful in both comedy of manners and farce. He could bluster and tyrannize in the best tradition of the petty tyrants with which farce abounds. Whiteside could easily dispense with his wheelchair long before anyone knows it, but he keeps up the pretense of his incapacity because he has it too good: everyone shows him sympathy. They were overawed by him to begin with, and now they wait on him hand and foot, and cater to his every whim, as he drives everyone crazy. He is the most cheerful of curmudgeons, and glories in his newfound entourage of sycophants. Withal, he is genial, and kind, and can be moved by young love. He can also be very funny, and we all love insult humor, particularly when it is as clever as Kaufman and Hart's. It is this charming aspect that redeems the character and makes us able to enjoy him, rather than hating the rascally, sarcastic ironist who complains in a self-pitying tone, "Is there a man in the world who suffers as I do from the gross inadequacies of the human race?" And he means it! The line in context is very funny. Everyone is an idiot except for him, and his celebrity friends, who send him endless gifts. Presumably, they want to stay on his good side! His secretary, Maggie (played by Bette Davis in the film) is not afraid of him, and dares to be sarcastic to him in turn. At one point, she tells him, "Well, I must say you have certainly behaved with all of your accustomed grace and charm."

The play takes place in the small town of Mesalia, Ohio, where New York City radio personality Sheridan Whiteside has come just before Christmas to dine with the Stanleys, in order to garner good publicity: his image could use some redoing. The irascible Whiteside is known for his barbed wit and crusty personality, brooking no non-sense and puncturing pretention, while being more than a bit pre-tentious and snobby himself, and he is beginning to be uncordially disliked. But just as he is about to enter the house, he slips on a patch of ice, injuring his hip, and he is confined to a wheelchair. Whiteside informs Mr. Stanley that he is suing him "for a hundred and fifty thousand dollars" (he never actually does). Aghast, Mr. Stanley has allowed Whiteside to take over the house, where he treats the family like slightly dimwitted servants. Everyone caters to his every whim, including Dr. Bradley, the attending physician and his frantic nurse, Miss Preen, both of whom the intractable know-it-all drives crazy. He is what doctors call a bad patient. He tells Miss Preen, "Go in and read the life of Florence Nightingale and learn how unfitted you are for your chosen profession."

Supporting characters and principals in farce are often eccentric, with quirky character traits. A throng of reporters and celebrity visitors invades the Stanley home, including Banjo, a character based on Harpo Marx, and contributes to the mayhem, as Whiteside rules the roost, and runs up the phone bill. The endless parade of strangers exemplifies in the extreme what an anonymous somebody said about theater, and comedy in particular: "It's all entrances and exits, with punctuation in between."

The starry-eyed, naïve Mrs. Stanley is in awe of Whiteside, but Mr. Stanley, the easily riled but self-controlled factory owner, sees right through him. He is powerless to do anything, however, under the circumstances. Finally, Whiteside leaves, having recovered nicely, only to slip again on the ice as the curtain falls. There are, of course, romantic complications that are part of the plot, including Maggie's falling in love with Bert Jefferson, one of the reporters. All the romances are satisfactorily resolved, as is typical of farce.

George Bernard Shaw despised the genre utterly because of what he saw as the senseless, sadistic laughter at misfortune arousing the most bestial instincts in the audience. So he tried to reform it by writing farces with a social conscience, which farce notoriously lacks. Farce is nothing if not apolitical, even with such deus ex machina endings as the arrest of Tartuffe by the police of King Louis XIV at the end of the play, which is not strictly a farce, but is replete with farcical elements. The products of Shaw's supposed iconoclasm, which resulted in such plays as *The Philanderer* (1893), with its Feydeau-like complications; *You Never Can Tell* (1897), which is a kind of precursor of Kauffman and Hart's farcical comedies; and *Fanny's First Play* (1911), are seldom performed. He called them "farcical comedies" or "cerebral farces," but there was perhaps too much cerebration and too little farce for some tastes.

One of the problems with Shaw in all his plays, whether they are farces of comedies of ideas, is his language. He was prolix and verbose, and for actors, he provides a mouthful. Your diction has to be magnificent, and you cannot pause to make too many points or the audience will not only lose the thread, but will be there all evening, falling asleep. You have to deliver Shaw's lines with top vocal energy, which does not mean being manic—you have to fulfill the objectives in a rational way—but does mean being constantly on top of the verbiage. Your concentration and attention cannot flag for an instant, or all is lost.

Farce abounds in slapstick bits or lazzi, which must be done every time by the book. When performing farce, be single-minded and desperate! Most characters in farce have one-track minds, and are concentrated on one goal or objective, which they pursue doggedly and sometimes obsessively. They play to win, and frequently lose. What does your character want? You must, simply must have whatever it is!

Tempo-rhythm and pace are fast: Be fast! Only be slow if the character is deliberately slow in an exaggerated way. You may think slowly, but move quickly. Play the actions to their utmost and in deadly earnest, with energy and a sense of pace brought on by the urgency.

A final note on playing farce: Once you have worked everything out in rehearsal, you really have to let yourself go in performance. Don't think, just do it! In that way, farce practically plays itself, at breakneck pace, and with the constant clash and confrontation that constitute its essence. You may be exhausted at the end, but you will be exhilarated, too. You have earned that after-theater refreshment of your choice!

V

Molière and the Italian Commedia

Molière [Jean-Baptiste Poquelin] (1622–1673)

Actor, writer, and founder of France's national theater, the Comédie Française, Molière's influence on his contemporaries and on future generations of comedy writers can hardly be underestimated. He is the world's major writer of satirical comedies, including *Tartuffe ou L'imposteur* (Tartuffe or The Impostor), *Le bourgeois gentilhomme* (The Bourgeois Gentleman), *Le malade imaginaire* (The Imaginary Invalid), *Le Misanthrope*; and of farces such as *Les fourberies de Scapin* (Scapin's Deceitful Tricks), heavily influenced by the commedia dell'arte.

During his thirteen years as a strolling player, wandering the length and breadth of France, Molière learned his craft. But he would come into his own on the Paris stage, and his genius would flourish under royal patronage. George Meredith puts things beautifully in *An Essay on Comedy* when he tells us that the court of King Louis XIV, so corrupt and rigidly hierarchical:

…was a boon to the comic poet. He had that lively quicksilver world of the animalcule passions, the huge pretensions, the placid absurdities, under his eyes in full activity; vociferous quacks and snapping dupes [models for the doctors and Argan in *Le malade imaginaire*], hypocrites, posturers, extravagants, rose-pink ladies and mad grammarians, sonnetteering marquises, highflying mistresses, plain-minded maids, interthreading as at a loom, noisy as a fair.

Like every other writer, Molière drew heavily on the only things he could draw on: himself, his observations, his feelings, and his relationships. While all the time relying on accepted theatrical forms, which he transformed by the originality of his wit, he drew characters that had reality and depth. He was unhappily married to a member of his company, Armande Béjart (1642?–1700), and as Emile Gaboriau (1832–1873), once internationally famous for his brilliant detective novels (they influenced Conan Doyle in the creation of Sherlock Holmes), succinctly put it in 1863 in *Les comédiennes adorées* (Adored Actresses):

> ...[She was] a cold and implacable coquette, who was the despair of his life, and perhaps also, alas, the goad to his genius.
>
> Ever deceived as a husband, ever enamored as a lover, and in spite of his resolutions, Molière always comes back to this woman, whom he loved with an incurable love. She reappears in each page of his works. In *The Misanthrope* as well as in *The School for Wives*, it is she, always she. Molière's comedy, his irresistible comedy, is the painful drama of his private life.

Interestingly enough, we have a glimpse into the realism that Molière expected of his actors, no doubt even in extravagant farces, in an incident Gaboriau describes (quoting an uncredited period source) just before the premier of *Tartuffe*, in which La Molière (Armande Béjart) created the role of Elmire, whom Tartuffe attempts to seduce. Actors in those days provided their own costumes, and in her coquettishness, knowing that the controversial play about hypocrisy in religion would be received with displeasure, she decided to wear her most magnificent gown and extravagant jewels, so that at least she herself would be applauded. Molière went into her dressing room, and was horrified:

> "What do you mean by making this adjustment?" he cried. "Don't you know that in the play you are supposed to be in financial

distress? You are dressed and bejeweled as if you were going to a fancy society ball! Take that off immediately, and get dressed as befits the situation in the play!"

When the movements and gestures described in chapter ten on the seventeenth century become habit, they create an incomparable atmosphere and flavor of the era, but they must not be used too extravagantly, except for extravagant characters, and they must be natural and not pretentious; nor must they have attention drawn to them, except where they occur in elaborate ceremonies, as in Molière's *Le bourgeois gentilhomme* (1670), in which Lully's balletic interludes were part of the original conception. These interludes were partly satiric, and the king saw himself mocked in good-humored fashion, as the ballet, in which he took such personal interest and delight, was parodied. The plot concerns a middle-class nouveau riche merchant who wishes to become an aristocrat, and studies the manners and movement of the upper classes. His pretensions are mocked and he is shown that he must know his place in this hilarious, but rather reactionary, feudal-minded farcical piece, which continues to hold the stage because, although it is retrograde politically, it is more generally about the willingness of some people to exploit the weaknesses of others: the real, down-at-heels aristocrats want to take advantage of the wealthy middle class; the teachers of philosophy, fencing, music and dance, who know their pupil is incapable of learning what they have to teach and who despise him, want his money. And the play concerns as well the foibles and follies of obsessive-compulsive behavior—a twentieth-century term Molière could have known, of course, but he was familiar with the behavior—and the toll it can take on relationships that would otherwise be happy. This theme, with variations, will be found in many of Molière's satirical comedies of manners, including *L'école des femmes* (The School for Wives; 1662), *Tartuffe ou l'Imposteur* (Tartuffe, or The Impostor; 1664), and *Le Misanthrope* (The Misanthrope; 1666).

Using the System: Stanislavsky Plays Argan in Molière's *The Imaginary Invalid*

As the curtain rises on act 1, scene 1 of Molière's satirical farce *Le malade imaginaire* (The Imaginary Invalid; 1673), Argan, the hypochondriac of the title, is alone in his bedroom, seated before a table covered with trays of medications. He is piling up coins and counting out how much he owes the apothecaries and doctors. As Molière tells us, "he speaks aloud to himself":

> Three and two are five, and five are ten, and ten are twenty; three and two are five.
> "Plus, on the twenty-fourth, a small insinuative, preparative and emollient enema, meant to soften, humectify and refresh Monsieur's entrails?" What I like about Monsieur Fleurant, my apothecary, is that his descriptions are always very civil. "Monsieur's entrails, thirty sols." Yes, Monsieur Fleurant, but it's not enough to be civil, one must also be reasonable and not gouge sick people. Thirty sols for an enema! I am your servant, I've already told you so, you used to charge me only twenty sols, and twenty sols in apothecary's language is ten sols, so here they are: ten sols.
> "Then, on the same day, a detersive enema, compounded of a double catholicon, rhubarb, roseate honey, and other ingredients pursuant to the prescription, to sweep out, wash, and clean the lower belly of Monsieur, thirty sols." With your permission, ten sols.
> "Then, on the same day, a hepatic julep, soporific and somniferous, compounded to make Monsieur sleep…"

In today's currency, the sol would be worth approximately twelve dollars, and thirty sols ($360) is a lot of money for an enema even now! Argan enumerates many more treatments and medications, adjusts the payments, and counts them out. He has taken eight medications and had twelve purges this month, as compared to twelve medications and twenty purges the month before: "I'm not surprised that I don't feel as well this month as I did last month!"

"Take all this away," he says, having finished his business, and he looks around: "There's nobody here! No matter what I say, they always leave me alone—there's no way of making them stay here." And in self-pitying high dudgeon, he rings a bell furiously to summon the servants.

In 1913 at the Moscow Art Theatre, Constantin Stanislavsky was rehearsing Argan, and he was in trouble. In spite of all his knowledge, experience, and supreme artistry, in spite of his acclaimed comic performances, the inventor of the system of acting that is still used worldwide just wasn't funny. The character eluded him day after day. The much-anticipated production would be a disaster!

He had studied French culture and the period thoroughly, and he also appreciated the play's mordant parody of the medical profession—a surefire object of satire that is as old as theatrical history, and continues through such films as *House Calls* (1987), later a television series, and the hit sitcom, *Scrubs* (2001–2010). And he had divided the play into manageable units, and worked on each one separately, eventually putting them all together, building each scene and the play as a whole. But none of this was enough.

He finally discovered the problem: He hadn't found his character's core or "kernel," the correct superobjective—his overall desire and goal. Stanislavsky had thought it could be the unconscious desire, "I want to be sick." But he saw that this interpretation was leading to the disquieting, unfunny portrayal of a morbid delusional psychopath, who suffered from psychosomatic illnesses. The way the scenes were played was therefore all wrong. For instance, the clever, very funny, impertinent serving-maid, Toinette (one of an army of such characters in comedy through the ages), who sees right through him, became a heartless villain in her scenes with him instead of the voice of reason. And the doctors were cruel conmen instead of crafty, silly, conniving charlatans.

In searching further, Stanislavsky realized that Argan is actually mortally afraid of being sick, and that the sly, manipulative superobjective is really, "I want people to think I am sick." Aha! That is why this petty domestic tyrant surrounds himself with his trays of medications and calls in his doctors for endless consultations and purges. And that is why Argan tries to punish everybody in his family, manipulating them to get their sympathy and pity. "I am sick! Don't you care?" is the constant self-pitying message that cries out from his pitiable demeanor, as he peers up at everyone through half-closed eyelids. He gets sicker when he doesn't get what he wants, and brightens up when he does. He is fine when he is by himself, but as soon as someone comes into the room, he is ill, which doesn't prevent him from falling into a healthy rage with Toinette when she tells him that he is being an inconsiderate pest.

Stanislavsky's solution to the problem of Argan's superobjective put the comedy back in the comedy. It was also true to Molière's intentions. As the actor knew, Molière was not a cruel satirist, making fun of human misery and illness, but an insightful one who mocked human pretentions, foibles, and hypocrisy, whether conscious or unconscious.

When working on Argan, Stanislavsky was able to fuse the inner, psychological side of the character with the external physical side that he had discovered through hard work. That fusion is the essence of what the Stanislavsky system teaches actors to do. In the production photographs, he looks like a rueful sadsack, an outrageous clown bloated beyond recognition, and wrapped in voluminous gowns. His unruly hair spikes out from beneath his sloppy turban, and the corners of his half-open mouth seem perpetually turned down. All these externals were important so that the audience had an immediate sense of who he was, just by looking at him. As Vasili Toporkov informs us in *Stanislavski in Rehearsal* (Routledge, 2004), Stanislavsky believed that "[...] the search for physical characteristics should start with a deep understanding of the inner world of the character."

In addition to the satire of the medical profession, and the caricatural doctors in this play, there is a love story that forms the spine of the plot. Argan's daughter wants to marry the young man she is in love with, instead of the particularly unattractive son of a doctor whom her father has designated as her prospective fiancé. Argan is a tyrannical, misguided father who is forced by circumstances to see the light. Everything works out for the young lovers, and all's well that ends well.

The contrast of the two plots in one play, tied together to form one story, is typical of satirical comedy, which throws into relief different aspects of humanity and the human condition in order to hold them up for the audience's inspection. The double strand of the story allows us to compare the behavior of one group of characters, with whom we are meant to be in sympathy, with another, on whom we are to pass an adverse judgment.

Comedy is nothing if not judgmental. In *Le malade imaginaire*, we are meant to be on the side of the lovers and against Argan and the doctors. We nevertheless sympathize with him because Argan is a victim, first, of his own hypochondria; and second, of the unscrupulous quack physicians who take advantage of him. And they are so funny and so silly that we can't really hate them: we just laugh at their eccentricities and pretensions.

Argan is also sympathetic because he wants to be in control, and is not. There is an aspect of powerlessness in his seeking after power that we can all identify with. The theme of wanting to be in control of one's own life and failing in that goal is ubiquitous in comedy.

In *Le rire* (Laughter), Bergson wrote about Molière's treatment of physicians, who belong to a general social category of individuals at whom we laugh, because the categories themselves are elitist and exclusionary:

Every specialized profession gives those within its enclosed circle certain habits of mind and certain particularities of character, which cause them to resemble each other, and by which they are distinguished from the rest. Small societies are thus established in the bosom of the larger one. But if they isolate themselves too much from the mainstream, they risk harming social interaction. Now one of the functions of laughter is to repress these separatist tendencies. Its role is to turn rigidity into plasticity, to readapt the individual to the whole; in short, to round off the corners. We have here a type of the comic of which the varieties may be determined in advance. We will call this, if you like, the *comedy of the professions.*

We will not go into detail regarding these varieties. We would rather emphasize what they have in common. First of all, there is *professional vanity*. Each of M. Jourdain's teachers [in Molière's *Le bourgeois gentilhomme* (The Middle-Class Gentleman)] exalts his own art above all others. There is a character in Labiche who cannot understand how anyone could be anything other than a lumber merchant. Naturally he is a lumber merchant himself. Moreover, vanity will tend to become *solemnity*, in proportion to the chosen profession's more or less high dose of charlatanism. It is a remarkable fact that the more open to question a profession is, the more those who practice it feel invested with a sort of priesthood, and demand that everyone bow down before its mysteries. Useful professions are demonstrably meant for the public; but those of a more contested usefulness can only justify their existences by supposing that the public is meant for them; now, it is this illusion that is the basis of solemnity. The comic side of Molière's doctors arises in great part from this illusion. They treat the patient as if he had been created for the doctors, and nature itself as an appendage of medicine.

Another form of this comic inflexibility is *professional callousness*. The comic character is so narrow-mindedly involved in the rigid context of his function that he has no room to move around, or to be moved, like other people.

Professional vanity, undue solemnity, and callousness are great keys that open the door to playing the physicians in *Le malade imaginaire*. They expect, nay demand that all those in their presence bow down before the divinity of medicine, which they imply by their very attitude that only doctors, initiated as they are into the priestly mysteries, could possibly understand. Their dignity may not be invaded or challenged by the uninitiated laity. And if they are challenged or worse, defied, they react with callousness, disdain, and cruelty.

Argan bows down before what he takes to be his physicians' superior knowledge and attainments, and Molière gives them endless obscurantist mumbo-jumbo to recite, including a great deal of Latin.

Their remedies, with their jargon-vocabulary descriptions, as read out to us by Argan, are ineffective, especially given the state of the medical art in the seventeenth century, and the old saying that the cure is worse than the disease often applied to their prescriptions and treatments. They are hypocrites: they know better, but their only real interest is in themselves and what they can earn by their ministrations. They only want the patient to remain alive so they can bleed him dry. As Toinette tells Argan, "They have a good milk-cow in you!"

You can study "the habits of mind and certain peculiarities of character" of any profession and its individual members, being sure to individualize the character, and not simply to play clichés and stereotypes.

The Influence of the Italian Commedia on Molière's Comedies

Although dating from the late sixteenth century, what came to be called the *commedia dell'arte* came into its own in the seventeenth, and was particularly appreciated in Paris, as well as in Italy, where it flourished in the eighteenth century, especially in Venice, when it was given its name, for the scripted comedies of Goldoni based on the *commedia dell'improviso* (improvised comedy). Molière's comedies would be inconceivable without the Italian farce-comedies he saw. He was intimately acquainted with them, and with the Italian actors: for a time, his company and the Comédie-Italienne shared the stage.

Variations of stock character types from the Italian commedia farces are found not only in Molière, but also in Restoration and eighteenth-century English comedy, in nineteenth-century French farce, and even in Chekhov and the contemporary TV sitcom. Here is a list of the main classic stock character types found in the commedia dell'arte, as detailed by John Rudlin in his brilliant, indispensable book, *Commedia dell'Arte: An Actor's Handbook*; I have not listed certain minor character types. Each character had a distinctive kind of vocal delivery, particular kinds of movements and walks, and, depending on the historical period, wore specific masks or half masks representing their characteristic physical appearance. Physical tricks and comic bits and routines, called lazzi (discussed in chapter one), were always part of commedia, and all the types except the Young Lovers are basically kinds of clowns. Each type has many variations:

1. **The Zanni:** (Italian plural: the "Johns"; "the Venetian diminutive of Giovanni"; the word is probably derived from the ancient Roman *sannio*, meaning a buffoon in a Roman comedy; the English word "zany" is derived from this name.) A general category describing an unfortunate, dispossessed type, male or (as a later development) female, but withal clever and resourceful. He or she goes by many names, and gives rise to certain other types, male or female, as shown below. There were first (leading) and second (supporting) Zanni characters. The first included certain Brighella and Scapino characters. They are "the principal contributor to any confusion," says Rudlin, and that is their function in the story.

2. **Arlecchino:** (English: Harlequin; French: *Arlequin*) A category of Zanni, but distinguished from them by "having enough intelligence to hatch schemes, although they rarely work out as planned"; a servant, "usually to Pantalone." If he is a messenger, he is terrible at the job of carrying the message, because he is easily distracted by something of greater interest. He and Columbine are usually a couple. He is often a very acrobatic character, and knows all the comic bits and physical tricks called lazzi.

3. **Brighella:** (from Italian noun, *briga*: trouble; verb, *brigare*: to indulge in intrigue) A category of Zanni; a boss-like character, such as an innkeeper, a merchant, a recruiting sergeant; a character who had bettered his social status. His function in any story is to help it along, by arranging marriages, or foiling Pantalone and helping the Young Lovers. Figaro in Pierre Caron de Beaumarchais' trilogy and the operas based on it is such a character.

4. **Pantalone:** (Pantaloon) A rich old man, often one who wants to marry or is married to a much younger wife. He provides a

counter-throughline to the action, either by his desire to marry a young woman who is in love with a young man, Pantalone's son, for instance; or by trying to foil marriage plans by refusing to give a dowry. He is usually the target of machinations to deceive and foil him, although he is not really villainous, simply misguided. Two examples from Molière: Harpagon in *The Miser*; and M. Arnolphe in *The School for Wives*, who tries to hide his prospective young bride from the prying eyes of the world, only to lose her to her young, enterprising lover—a pure commedia plot, used over and over, with variations,

5. **Il Dottore:** (The Doctor) An old man, a scholar, often pedantic, or professional doctor, often a cuckold married to a young wife; frequently a bit of a dolt, or at least unperceptive, but could also be brilliant, and so self-involved and narcissistic as not to notice what is going on. He often functions as comic relief, rather than as a main character. He may be a verbose professor or a pedantic doctor, prolix in his use of Latin medical terms that nobody understands, as in *Le malade imaginaire*.

6. **The Male and Female Young Lovers:** They have various names, such as Silvio, Lelio, or Lindoro, for the men; Isabella, Angelica, or Flaminia for the women. They are usually at the center of the story, and we are supposed to root for them to win out over those who would spoil their love. They are usually the "straight" characters, and do not do lazzi or other comic routines, and they are seldom the butt of jokes.

7. **Il Cavaliere; il Capitano:** (The Gentleman; the Captain) A braggart; sometimes a boastful Spanish soldier, based on the fact that parts of Italy and other places in Europe were occupied at various times by Spain; a loud-voiced warrior who exaggerates his exploits and is actually a coward; sometimes a would-be, but inept seducer; based on ancient Roman comedies by Plautus, in the character of Miles Gloriosus, whom we see again in Sondheim's *A Funny Thing Happened on the Way to the Forum*. He has various names, such as Fanfarone or

Matamoros. He is often a would-be spoiler in the plot, and his boastful pretentions are unmasked, usually at the end.

8. **Colombina:** (Columbine) A category of Zanni; a clever maid-servant, always lucid and rational, but at the same time capricious and temperamental; also called a soubrette character; often the "personal maid to the prima donna," who is one of the young lovers. The plot sometimes hinges on her machinations, and she provides good, reasonable advice, while being an enabler. She is usually in love with Arlecchino, and sees through his wily plans.

9. **Pulcinella:** (French: *Polichinelle*; English: Punch, as in the *Punch and Judy* shows) A category of Zanni; he could be either a servant or a master, a magistrate, or even a poet or spy. He has a temper, and is a witty clown, quick with repartee. With an ironic attitude to life, he has little respect for others, and brooks no insults or contradiction. He is usually married. In commedia plots, he is also often a loner, and part of a secondary plot. He cannot hold his tongue, and "cannot help telling everyone everything."

10. **Scapino:** (French: *Scapin*, as in Molière's farce) A category of Zanni; a clever servant, usually to the leading male young lover. He is always concocting clever schemes to foil the old man character, who has often mistreated him, so that he want revenge, and sometimes money, which he cons from Pantalone. And he is well acquainted with the various comic bits and physical tricks called lazzi.

11. **Scaramuccio:** (French, English: Scaramouche) A category of Zanni; a clever servant, often to an impoverished gentleman; often a go-between for a pair of young lovers. He keeps the plot going. Scaramouche was the stage name of a famous Italian farceur, Tiberio Fiorilli (1608–1694), who went to Paris around 1644 and spent much of his career there. Not only was he a superb acrobat and mime, but he was also a skilled musician, whose trademark was the guitar that he always carried with him. He made a great impression on Molière. Others after Fiorilli continued to use the same stage name.

Types, as facile as they are, give you a basic framework on which to mold the character. The label by which a character is known is a good clue as to how to play that person.

Among the people Molière saw perform with the Comédie-Italienne in Paris was Domenico Giuseppe Biancolelli (1636–1688), known as Dominique, who refined and transformed his character Arlecchino (Harlequin) from a rather crude put-upon trickster to a more subtle, more intelligent joker. He was also the favorite Italian comedian of Louis XIV, who sometimes invited him to court, where he is said to have continued his antics and jokes. Once, when the actor was silently but obviously salivating over a dish of partridges, the smiling king ordered that he be given the dish. Dominique quickly thanked him, and asked, "May I have the partridges, too?" The dish itself was part of the king's gold plate.

Biancolelli was also a brilliant acrobat, renowned for his agility and for his lazzi, of which he was a supreme master. Molière was deeply impressed by his technical proficiency and the general disciplined professionalism of the Comédie-Italienne, and he would insist upon these aspects in his own company.

Scene Analysis: Molière's *Les fourberies de Scapin* (Scapin's Deceitful Tricks)

In 1922, Jacques Copeau (1879–1949) wrote in his essay, "Molière's Voice":

> The most beautiful eternity is that of a voice that after three hundred years still addresses humanity directly, touches us, living, articulate, with all the strength of its intonation, all the subtlety of its nuances…There are few immortal voices. The voice of Molière, for three hundred years now, has not ceased living and speaking.

Copeau was the founder and artistic director of the influential Théâtre du Vieux-Colombier, and he staged famous productions of Molière's plays, that rivaled those of the Comédie Française. In 1950, Copeau's mise-en-scène of *Les fourberies de Scapin* was posthumously published. The polysemous plural noun *fourberies* (singular, *fourberie*), describes Scapin's activities perfectly: it means deceptiveness, roguery, wiliness, knavery, schemes; or rascality in action, that is, some knavery carried out, such as deceiving someone in a con game. Scapin is a *fourbe* (clever rascal, wily schemer, etc.), a noun that is also an adjective meaning clever or wily.

Successfully mounted in New York, the production was redone in Paris to great acclaim. Besides directing, Copeau played the title role. The preface by that supreme actor and comedian, Louis Jouvet (1887–1951), to *Mise-en-scène des Fourberies de Scapin*, is as instructive as Copeau's account of how he staged the play. Jouvet played the pompous Géronte for the demanding director.

In *Les fourberies de Scapin* (1671), one of Molière's most popular farces, based on Terence's ancient Roman comedy *Phormio*, La Molière is the model for the coquettish Zerbinette, drawn from one of the commedia dell'arte's character types. Scapin is Scapino, one of the commedia's Zanni (servant) characters, a wily trickster and clown; his name is derived from the Italian word *scapare* (to escape), which refers to the character's constant outmaneuvering of his opponents and his escape from imminent disaster.

The play is set in Naples. Two youths from wealthy families, Léandre and Octave, manage to get themselves into hot water through falling in love. Neither has much money and both are awaiting the return of their fathers, absent from the city on business. Octave marries the penniless Hyacinthe, whose parentage is unknown, a great disgrace in that era. Léandre falls madly in love with Zerbinette, who has been kidnapped by gypsies and is being held for ransom. Scapin, the ingenious, clever servant of Léandre, helps his master to realize his dreams of marriage to Zerbinette by inveigling money out of Léandre's father, Géronte, who has returned in a fury to Naples, along with Argante, Octave's father, both eager to confront their scapegrace sons. Pretending that he needs money to pay the fees with which to annul Octave and Hyacinthe's marriage, Scapin gets Argante to give him a good amount, which he then gives to Octave. In addition, Scapin has his revenge on

Géronte, who had treated him badly: Having persuaded Géronte that Léandre has been kidnapped by Turkish pirates after going unawares into their galley, Scapin gets Géronte to give him ransom money. He then convinces Géronte that the brother of Hyacinthe is out to kill him (see the excerpt below for the reason). Scapin then gets Géronte to hide hastily in a large sack he provides, which he says is the only handy hiding place around. He then gives Géronte a sound drubbing. The beating is supposedly administered by the pursuing brother and his friends, whom Scapin pretends to imitate. The story is satisfactorily concluded when Géronte recognizes Hyacinthe as his daughter by a first marriage, and Argante, by a happy coincidence, recognizes Zerbinette as his daughter, long ago kidnapped by gypsies. His wiles, ploys, and rogueries discovered, Scapin is forgiven under the happy circumstances, and everyone rejoices.

The play has a famous line that is often quoted: Géronte, exasperated and nonplussed by Scapin's relating the story of how Léandre went into the Turkish galley all unaware of the intentions of his supposed hosts, says, "Que diable est-il allé dans ce galère?" (Why the hell [devil] did he go into that galley?) This sentence became a byword for questioning why someone has gotten involved in a precarious situation that could have been avoided.

Copeau's staging provides a model of interpretation, but, as Jouvet warns, the mise-en-scène both in its entirety and in its individual moments, is not a prescription, but a description. It is not a recipe, from which the dish can be cooked, but an indication of what Copeau did with the script. Every director must find his own way to bring the play alive, just as every actor must learn to think like the character, or else the play is lost before the process of rehearsal even begins: Nobody can reproduce somebody else's concepts. You have to get inside the play on your own. Still, Copeau's book provides an important promptbook of a successful historical production.

In "Moliere's Voice," Copeau tells us about a traditional exit that had crept into productions over the centuries. It occurs on the very last line of act 2, just after Scapin has given Léandre and Octave the money that he has managed to get out of their fathers. Léandre exclaims, "Let us promptly go and ransom her whom I adore!" They leave immediately, followed by Scapin. The "tradition" consists of Scapin calling back the two young heroes as they are on their way out, and saying, "Make way for knavery [fourberie]!" as he throws his cape over his shoulders with a grand gesture, and exits before them. Says Copeau:

> I don't know where this tradition comes from, nor how old it is, nor what actor, desirous of "making an exit," invented it. But what I am certain of is that it is false, absurd, contrary to all sound tradition, contrary to the spirit of the text, to the movement of the scene, to the rhythm of the act. To have created it, and especially to have maintained it, one had to have been deaf to Molière's voice.

Copeau tried to be faithful to what he saw as that voice. His book, *Mise-en-scène des Fourberies de Scapin*, contains the text on one page, and his detailed stage directions on the facing page, exactly as in a prompt copy; each is numbered, and corresponds with a number in the text opposite. In the excerpt below, from the opening of act 3, scene 2, Copeau's stage directions for the playing of each moment are here given in brackets. Scapin, the clever, rather sadistic trickster, is continuing to deceive Géronte with his wily maneuvers:

> [Géronte appears, proscenium left. He immediately summons Scapin, who turns round and speaks volubly from upstage.]
> GÉRONTE. So, Scapin, how is this business going with my son?
> SCAPIN. Your son, sir, is in a safe place. But you yourself now run the greatest danger in the world, and I earnestly wish you were at home!
> GÉRONTE. What?
> SCAPIN. At this very moment, as I am speaking to you, [1. Scapin has grabbed him a bit rudely by the arm, as if he had seized his prey, and he speaks almost directly into his ear, in a stage whisper, but accentuating each word] they are looking for you everywhere, to kill you. [2. Géronte pivots brusquely around, as if someone were behind him.]
> GÉRONTE. Me? [3. Strangled]

SCAPIN. Yes. [4. Low]

GÉRONTE. Who? [5. Loud. Scapin shushes him and continues to speak in a low voice.]

SCAPIN. The brother of this person whom Octave married. He thinks you have designs to replace his sister with your daughter, and that is why the marriage is being annulled; and with that in mind, he has determined to discharge his despair on you and to take your life in order to avenge his honor. All his friends, swordsmen like him, are looking for you on every side, and asking everyone for news of you. [6. Géronte groans and starts to move off upstage.] I even saw [7. Scapin catches up to him and brings him back.] soldiers from his company interrogating everyone they could find, and squads of them occupying all the streets leading to your house. [8. He lets go of him.] So you can't go home [9. Another groan from Géronte, who takes three steps right.] You can't go to the right [10. Géronte stops, takes two steps left.] or to the left [11. Géronte stops, raises his arms to heaven.] without falling into their hands. [12. Géronte leans on his umbrella.]

GÉRONTE. What shall I do, my poor Scapin?

SCAPIN. I don't know, Monsieur, and this is a strange business. I tremble for you from head to foot, and…Wait! (*He turns around, and pretends to go and see if there is anyone way upstage.*) [13: (Scapin) runs away, looks right and left. Géronte starts to tremble softly.]

GÉRONTE. (*Trembling*) Eh?

SCAPIN. (*Coming back*) No, no, no, it's nothing.

As the scene goes on, Scapin further controls and manipulates Géronte, to the point where Géronte can scarcely walk, as he stands there trembling. At times, Scapin actually moves him about physically. And Géronte is reduced by fear to taking small, hesitant steps. Scapin then has his revenge. At his suggestion, on the supposed approach of the would-be assassins, Géronte hides himself in plain view, in a huge sack that Scapin has provided, and he beats Géronte with a stick, as if he were the swordsmen who are pursuing him. This is all as much commedia as it is Molière, writing in the genre, rather than parodying it.

Here are some possible choices for each character:

1. **Superobjective:** *Scapin:* To serve my master, and so to be secure in my living conditions. *Géronte:* To make sure all is right with the family, and to ensure my son's happiness; I know what is best for him.

2. **Throughline of action:** *Scapin:* I invent various ploys and schemes to help my young master and his friend get out of hot water with their fathers, and I also scheme to get revenge on those who mistreat and disrespect me, namely Géronte. *Géronte:* I return to Naples to set matters right, and to induce my son not to continue his love affair with Zerbinette, who is not a suitable match, and I then fall for Scapin's stories, so that there, too, I seek to set things right. Eventually, all is revealed and made good, as I discover that Hyacinthe is my daughter, whom I thought lost to me, and Zerbinette is my friend Argante's daughter, so everything works out satisfactorily in the end.

3. **Counter-throughline:** *Scapin:* I contend with the unruliness and headstrong nature of my master, Léandre, and have to arrange things for him with his father, all of this being rather a pain in the neck. *Géronte:* I am furious at my son for his actions, and I suspect everything and everyone of trying to wrong me, because I am wealthy. This underlies all my actions, and I am nonplussed by what has happened to me, and to my son. "Why the hell did he go into that galley?"

4. **Adjectives describing the character:** *Scapin:* Wily, clever, intelligent, vindictive, manipulative. *Géronte:* Wary, authoritarian, insecure, strict, imperious.

5. **Point of view:** *Scapin:* I am a superior sort of fellow and very clever, and I have to be very careful to do what I want in order to maintain my security, and that means lying and playing tricks if necessary. *Géronte:* I am wary of everyone around me, and I don't know whom to trust, because I am a wealthy man, and many people are out to get me.

6. **What is the main event in the scene?** The revenge wreaked by Scapin on the unsuspecting, gullible Géronte.

7. **Where does the scene take place?** Outdoors, on the docks, in public.

8. **What are the other given circumstances—time of day; weather; your physical condition?** It is a warm day, which adds to the discomfort of the scene. Géronte is a bit wobbly on his feet, perhaps, because he trembles in fear. Scapin is in perfect physical shape, agile and flexible in his clown-like movements.

9. **What do you want—your objective?** *Scapin:* I want to manipulate Géronte so that he is terrified, and to take my revenge on him for his arrogant treatment of me. *Géronte:* I want to escape my would-be assassins and to be safe.

10. **What is in the way—the obstacle?** *Scapin:* He is, because I have to be very careful in what I do. *Géronte:* The assassins are after me, and they have blocked every avenue to my house, so there is nowhere I can go. I don't know what to do!

11. **What does your character do—your actions?** Copeau's staging gives us one idea of what each character does.

12. **Do you attain your objective by the end of the scene?** *Scapin:* Yes. *Géronte:* Yes—after all, there were no would-be murderers.

VI

Anton Chekhov and Stanislavsky

Performing Chekhov's Realistic Psychological Comedies

Known for both his brilliant, psychologically insightful short stories and his realistic theater pieces, Anton Pavlovich Chekhov
(1860–1904) is forever associated with the Moscow Art Theatre where
Stanislavsky produced, directed, and acted in his full-length plays. In
fact, Stanislavsky's way of working on those plays helped evolve his
system of creating characters.

Chekhov knew from the firsthand experience of his own and his
family's struggles all about the inhumanity and brutality of the socioeconomic order and rigid class structure of Czarist Russia. His attitude
to life and to people was full of compassion, and he translated his
feelings and his psychological perceptions into his fictional characters.
So real were they, that people used to say not "I am going to see *Three
Sisters*" but "I am going to the Prozorovs'."

The playwright might have agreed with the idea that Freud
expressed in *Jokes and Their Relation to the Unconscious*, about the origins
of the comic:

> The comic arises in the first instance as an unintended discov-
> ery derived from human social relations. It is found in people—in
> their movements, forms, actions, and traits of character, originally
> in all probability only in their physical characteristics but later in

their mental ones as well, or, as the case may be, in the expression of those characteristics.

Two other sources of comedy, as Chekhov saw it, are the cross-purposes of people in conflict with each other and hardly daring to be open about it; and the blindness and pretentiousness of egotism. He perceived the irony of solutions to our problems being right in front of us, and our simultaneous inability to perceive those solutions. We unconsciously prefer our known situation, and we indulge in egotistical self-pity, and torture ourselves and others in the process. This is certainly true of the principals in *Uncle Vanya* (1899) and in fact constitutes one of the themes of the play, as it does of *The Seagull* (1896; 1898), which for all its comic moments, ends tragically when Constantine commits suicide. So Chekhov's comedy is subtle, based in irony and empathy. In the full-length plays, it provokes a smile, rather than a laugh much of the time.

Chekhovian characters, like most people in real life, are incapable of living in an unexciting limbo. They need drama and they create it, like Masha, Vershinin, Kulygin and the other characters in *Three Sisters* (1901); or Madame Ranevskaya, Lopahin, and the rest in *The Cherry Orchard* (1904). And this self-created drama is another source of comedy for the observer, but of unhappiness for the protagonists.

Nevertheless, Chekhov was sure he had written full-length comedies that were as funny as his uproarious one-act farces, at which people almost literally rolled in the aisles. But, you may ask, how can one laugh at the death of the dear, sweet Baron Tusenbach? At the end of *Three Sisters*, he is killed in a duel by Solyony, a jealous, obsessive-compulsive psychopath, who is funny to us in a sinister way—before that horrible event? You can't, and you are not meant to.

The youngest of the sisters, Irina, did not love the baron, who was in love with her, but she was going to marry him anyway. It seemed her one chance for happiness. Now that it is gone, how unhappy will she really be, since she did not actually love him? This is scarcely the stuff of comedy, but rather of drama. We would be inclined to call this play a tragicomedy: The ending may be tragic for Tusenbach, but it is not necessarily so for Irina.

Nor is it tragic that Masha will not leave town to go with her beloved Vershinin when he departs with his regiment, but will remain with Kulygin (a part I had the pleasure of playing), the schoolteacher husband with whom she has fallen out of love. He is a prig, a pedant, a prude, and provincial in his attitudes, while pretending to be intellectually more than he is, but he is also a well-meaning, good-hearted man who loves his wife. He is a pantaloon, a descendant of the commedia dell'arte character, and a figure of fun, but one who provokes smiles rather than laughter. He fits the model of the hidebound, encrusted member of the establishment discussed by Henri Bergson in *Le rire*. Masha could do worse, and with Vershinin, the masochist married to a demanding, crazy wife, she might actually have ended up being even more unhappy, but she is incapable of seeing that. In any case, her passion for Vershinin may simply be born of the desire to get away from a life of boredom and provincial stagnation, rather than of true love for this rather ordinary, nice man.

All of these ideas enter into the playing of the parts, and are not mere literary speculation and analysis. They speak directly to the characters' psychology and their internal actions, and consequently to their behavior: the external actions that are the result of their thinking. And even these realistic psychological plays demand comedic techniques of timing and holding for laughs, as called for when there are funny lines.

In *Stanislavsky: A Biography* (Routledge, 1988), Jean Benedetti published a section of the prompt books of Stanislavsky's 1904 production plan for *The Cherry Orchard*, which he directed before he had even fully realized his system. He gives the characters a psychological background based in childhood experience. And he gives directions about the technical side of doing the play, about tone of voice and audibility.

When the nearly impoverished Madame Ranevskaya asks Lopahin if her beloved cherry orchard has been sold, Stanislavsky has Lopahin—the former serf on the estate whom she knew as a boy and who has now turned entrepreneur—examine his handkerchief, look down, and pause briefly before answering "guiltily" that "It has." When she then asks in a voice that is "barely audible" who bought it, and Lopahin tells her he did, shouting the line, she "sinks down and remains in that position for some time." Lopahin, even more embarrassed, "pulls at his handkerchief" as the situation grows even more awkward. Soon, "he tears his handkerchief in two and flings it away."

This particular rather melodramatic staging must have been very effective, but bear in mind that it is descriptive rather than prescriptive. Actors have to be allowed to find the moments, and usually are nowadays, without having such details imposed on them. Whether or not these plays are comedies provoking huge laughs depends on how the productions are staged, of course. At any rate, as Stanislavsky shows us, they have to be played realistically and seriously.

The Farces

Inspired by French boulevard farces, Chekhov called *The Boor*, *The Marriage Proposal*, and other one-act pieces "vaudevilles," one of the Russian terms for farce, and they are indeed based in the French manner of writing such plays. There are also farcical elements in the full-length comedies: the clumsy character Yepikhodov, who is always dropping things and falling all over himself, in *The Cherry Orchard*; Vanya trying to shoot the Professor twice, and missing in a scene of pandemonium at the end of act 3 in *Uncle Vanya*. As with the vaudevilles, these characters and incidents are psychologically motivated, and we might call the vaudevilles "psychological farces." Internal actions are of paramount importance, as the characters think, ruminate, and, most importantly, live inside themselves.

In *The Boor* (1888)—also called *The Bear*, a direct translation of its Russian title *Myedvyed*, which means both—Smirnov's boorishness and male chauvinism are contrasted with the widowed Madame Popova's romantic posing and fake mourning for a man who obviously treated her like dirt when she was alive, but whom she feels it is her duty to mourn. She only appears to be in a state of denial, however; underneath it all her sexual instincts, easily aroused, are as alive as ever. Chekhov has been seen as misogynistic for his portrait of Popova, with her pretensions and her masochism. But Chekhov is far from being misogynistic, and his genial satirical portrait of the "battle of the sexes" is tempered by his picture of male chauvinism, as Smirnov, posing as a macho sadist, is just as pretentious and exaggerated and silly as Popova. When Smirnov generalizes about women, he is ridiculous. Chekhov has him deliberately deal in clichés, and it is those Chekhov is making fun of and having fun with. The audience immediately sees what is really going on between these two histrionic, hysterical personalities. The subject of the play is how two people who are sexually attracted to each other avoid the subject of sex and lie to each other, and are pushed forward by their overwhelming, mutual desire.

Chekhov's characters exist for us in all the complexity and depth of actual living human beings even in his most outrageous farces, such as *Svadba* (The Wedding; 1889), with its gallery of inimitable eccentrics. The overreactions of the characters strike us real, because they are deeply felt, as they are, for instance, in another classic of the genre, *Yubiley* (The Anniversary; The Jubilee; 1891). Andrey Andreyevich Shipuchin, a nervous bank president, is trying to prepare for his jubilee while dealing with his narcissistic wife, Tatyana, whose name alludes to the romantic heroine of Pushkin's *Eugene Onegin*. She insists inopportunely on telling him everything that has happened to her. Tatyana, a satirical amalgam of Pushkin's heroine and the misogynistic conception of the stereotypical nagging self-centered wife, lives in her own world of romantic fantasies that are clearly sexual, but not about her husband, a satire of misogyny. Instead, they are centered around a stranger she flirted with outrageously on a train. At the same time, Shipuchin has to deal with an outraged, obsessed, tenacious woman customer, and with the misogynistic bank clerk who is trying to get rid of her so he can write a report. The committee sent to congratulate him enters in the midst of pandemonium, much to everyone's consternation. All these people are at the ends of their tethers in this awfully funny and silly farce, but, once again, everything seems so real. They are living examples of the dictum, "Comedy is other people's tragedy."

O vredye tabaka (On the Harmfulness of Tobacco)

The one-act monologue *On the Harmfulness of Tobacco* (which I have performed in two productions) was first published in 1886, and rewritten several times, the final version of 1902 being the best known. An inveterate smoker, Ivan Ivanovich Nyoukhin (the onomatopoetic name means "sniveler" in Russian), has been told by his wife to give a lecture on the harmful effects of tobacco at the local social club in the provincial town in which they live. Nyoukhin can't help instead launching into complaints about his life, as one thing leads him on to another. He is a complex character, sometimes ridiculous, sometimes pathetic, sometimes poignant, and full of nuances and subtleties, even though the line of his story and the situation in this one-act play are simple. Nyoukhin says the most ridiculous things, but he is not trying to be funny. One of his objectives is to maintain his dignity, and despite his sadness, he is not self-pitying.

Nyoukhin, who is just a little drunk (later on he surreptitiously takes a sip out of a flask), and who has no idea what to say, because he had probably not begun to prepare his lecture, hems and haws his way through the first part of his talk, and, except near the beginning, speaks about everything but tobacco. A teacher in his wife's boarding school, Nyoukhin prides himself on being an astute scientific observer, at the same time as he is a miserable, henpecked husband and an unhappy father, whose daughters laugh at him. When he says that they went into raptures over his article on the harmfulness of certain insects, or at least over the part about bedbugs, what really happened was probably that they went into gales of laughter. One gets the impression that his wife suggested the topic of the lecture after she, too, had seen his article. She probably screamed at him something like, "You idiot! What a stupid article! Why don't you give a lecture on the harmfulness of *tobacco*! On that you're an expert! And stop stinking up the house! Put out that cigarette!" Gradually, Nyoukhin reveals just how miserable and upset he is, and how much a failure he feels. His only desire, he tells us, is to run away and forget everything. The monologue ends on an ironic note when his wife shows up at the back of the lecture hall, and, terrified, he reverts to the subject he hasn't actually talked about all evening, and so ends the lecture.

What must his parents have been like? What was his childhood like? How did he end up marrying someone who treats him abusively and has him under her thumb? Why doesn't he have the courage to escape? Why doesn't he dare fight back? Was he ever in love with his wife? Did he ever really hope to make contributions to science? What must his dreams be like? These are some of the questions the actor playing Nyoukhin must ask when preparing the role, all of them based on the text itself.

And when it comes to performing the piece, the following questions are essential: What are Nyoukhin's immediate circumstances as he prepares to give his lecture? What is it like in the lecture hall? Is it too hot? Is it stuffy? What has he just been doing before he walks on stage? He has been taking a drink, probably, and having a smoke.

What is the first thing Nyoukhin wants (aside from running away to the ends of the earth the moment he sees the audience)? Perhaps he wants a glass of water. But there is none available, or in some productions, there may be. If there is, Nyoukhin wastes as much time as he can by drinking as long as possible, so as to avoid having to start the lecture. If there is not, he is simply stymied. Alcohol is dehydrating, and only alcohol allows him to confide in the group of strangers before him, as the lecture goes on. Of course, he would never confide in anyone he knew personally. But then, whom does he know? He has no friends. He feels completely alone and alienated. He has no one to talk to. No one understands or appreciates him, let alone loves him. He started life with dreams, but they have all been shattered, and his life has become a disappointment. As he comes out onto the lecture platform, his discomfort is compounded by his thirst.

If you are preparing this piece, you might try an imaginative exercise of the sort the writer's nephew, Michael Chekhov, might have suggested. Tell yourself: "I am standing here in front of the audience completely naked, and I want to hide, so I am looking around for a hiding place"; or "I desperately want to run away, but there is a ball and chain attached to my ankle and tied to a post right there on stage in front of me."

Scene Analysis: *Predlozheniye* (The Marriage Proposal)

Written in 1888–1889 and produced in 1890, *Predlozheniye* (The Marriage Proposal) was an immediate hit. I played Chubukov in one production, and directed another.

Dressed in his top hat and tails, Ivan Vasilievich Lomov (Chekhov took his name from the Russian word "lom," meaning a bit of waste matter; a scrap), has come to visit his neighbor, Stepan Stepanovich Chubukov, a landowner, seventy years of age. Chekhov derived his last name from the word "chubuk," which means a smelly, long-stemmed Turkish tobacco pipe; a great hint about the character, whom I had the pleasure of playing. Lomov has come to ask for the hand of Natalya Stepanovna, Chubukov's daughter, who is twenty-five, an age considered past marriageable back then: she should have been married already. Chubukov is overjoyed, gives his consent, and goes to find his daughter, whom he sends to see Lomov. As Lomov waits—according to Chekhov he is thirty-five, and "healthy, plump, but very hypochondriacal"—he talks to himself. His dilemma is a cruel one, his nervousness extreme, and he is a histrionic personality, which means that he self-dramatizes and overdramatizes, as well as constantly overreacting, not to be confused with overacting.

Here is the end of his monologue, and the first part of the first long scene between him and Natalya. The beats should arise naturally out of the rehearsal process, and happen, as always, as if for the first time.

LOMOV. [...] And right now, my lips are trembling and my right eyelid has started twitching...But the most terrible thing for me is sleeping. I lie down in bed and then I just start to doze off, when all of a sudden there's some kind of a spasm in my left side! And it jumps straight to my shoulder, and to my head...I kick off the sheets like a maniac and then I lie down again, but just as I start to doze off, there's another spasm in my side! And this happens twenty times…

NATALYA. (*Entering*) What the…? But Papa said, "Go on in. There's a buyer who came for his goods." It's only you. Hello, Ivan Vasilievich!

LOMOV. Hello, dear Natalya Stepanovna.

NATALYA. Excuse me for being in my apron and housecoat. We're shelling peas for drying. Why haven't you been over here for so long? Sit down…

(*They sit.*)

You want lunch?

LOMOV. No, thank you ever so much. I already had something.

NATALYA. Go ahead and smoke. There are the matches…The weather is marvelous, but yesterday it was so rainy the workers didn't do anything all day. How many haystacks did you finish? Would you believe it, I got ambitious and finished a whole field! And now I'm not happy about it. I'm afraid maybe my hay will rot. Maybe it would have been better to wait. But what's all this? It looks like you're in tails! This is news! Are you going to a ball, or what? By the way, you look handsome. But, seriously, why are you so dolled up?

LOMOV. (*Nervous*) You see, dear Natalya Stepanovna…The thing is that I've made up my mind to ask you to…listen to me. Frankly, you'll be surprised and you might even get angry, but I…(*Aside*) It's terribly cold!

NATALYA. What's this about?

(*Pause.*)

Well?

LOMOV. I shall attempt to be brief. You are aware, dear Natalya Stepanovna, that I have already, for a long time, from my childhood on, had the honor of knowing your family. My late auntie and her husband, from whom I, as you may perhaps know, got my land, as a legacy, always treated your papa and your late mama with deep respect. The Lomov family and the Chubukov family have always found themselves to be in a friendly, and one may even say, affectionate relationship to each other. In addition to which, as you may perhaps be aware, my land closely adjoins yours. As you may recall, my Bovine Meadows border on your birches.

NATALYA. Excuse me for interrupting you. You say "my Bovine Meadows." They're really yours?

LOMOV. Yes, mine.

NATALYA. Well, here we are again! The Bovine Meadows are ours, not yours.

They proceed to quarrel furiously over who owns the land, and Lomov feels more and more ill. Driven out by Natalya and Chubukov, who joins in the quarrel, Lomov is almost immediately brought back again, when Chubukov reveals to Natalya the reason for his visit. She calms him down, and Chubukov leaves the two of them alone. Now she knows what he wants! But he still beats around the bush, and then the subject of his hunting dogs comes up, as he digresses yet again. When he says his dog is the best, Natalya takes issue with him, and maintains that her dog is the best one. They start to quarrel again in earnest, when Chubukov enters, shuts them up, and orders the servant to bring champagne to celebrate their betrothal. All ends in merriment and rejoicing, as Lomov, although in a state of collapse, is now deliriously happy.

Here are some possible choices for each character:

1. **Superobjective:** *Lomov:* To be happy, and to feel calm and not ill, which can be accomplished by getting married, and joining the two estates. *Natalya:* To get married and be happy; to assert myself and have everything and everyone around me be aboveboard and honest.
2. **Throughline of action:** *Lomov:* I come to Chubukov's house to propose marriage to Natalya, and her father accepts me as a suitor. I then proceed to try to get my proposal across. *Natalya:* I have to deal with the terribly shy Lomov, and to understand what he is saying to me, which I make attempts to do.

3. **Counter-throughline:** *Lomov:* My own nervousness and hypochondriacal symptoms; Natalya's not realizing what I want, and interrupting me, so that we are continually side-tracked, even after Natalya knows what I want and her father brings me back to propose to her after I had left, furious over Natalya's arguing with me about the land. *Natalya:* I mistake the reason for Lomov's visit, and thinks he has come about the disputed land on their neighboring estates. Even when my father brings him back to propose to me after he had left in a huff, I have to assert myself and air my opinions.

4. **Adjectives describing the character:** *Lomov:* Nervous, high-strung, self-involved, neurotic, desperate. *Natalya:* Forthright, headstrong, willful, business-like, serious.

5. **Point of view:** *Lomov:* I am already thirty-five, and if I don't get married now, it will be too late. I can overcome my nervousness, because I have to, and I want people to sympathize with me. *Natalya:* I am a very busy, preoccupied person with no time or inclination for nonsense, and I would make somebody (like Lomov) a wonderful wife, because I am efficient and good-hearted and haven't a mean bone in my body, provided I am not contradicted by nonsensical people who do not know what they are talking about.

6. **What is the main event in the scene?** *Lomov:* I begin to propose marriage to Natalya. *Natalya:* I entertain Lomov, until…!

7. **Where does the scene take place?** *Lomov:* In Chubukov's salon. *Natalya:* In my living room.

8. **What are the other given circumstances—time of day; weather; your physical condition?** It is just after lunch on a late summer day at harvest time. The weather is sultry. *Lomov:* I am a wreck, physically and mentally, and I am too hot, because I am dressed up in a tailcoat for the occasion. *Natalya:* I am fine physically and mentally, and I am busy shelling peas, and doing other domestic chores that have been interrupted.

9. **What do you want—your objective?** *Lomov:* I want to propose to Natalya. *Natalya:* I want to find out what he wants.

I also want to do my work, and get him to leave as soon as possible.

10. **What is in the way—the obstacle?** *Lomov:* My nervousness and her lack of understanding. I thought her father had told her why I was here, but she seems indifferent. *Natalya:* He isn't really telling me what he wants. He beats around the bush and he won't shut up, and I don't know how to maneuver him into leaving.

11. **What does your character do—your actions?** *Lomov:* I pace; I sit; I talk; I try to overcome my nervousness; I talk. *Natalya:* I sit and talk with Lomov, while I shell peas.

12. **Do you attain your objective by the end of the scene?** *Lomov:* No. *Natalya:* No. (By the end of the play, they both will.)

As Stanislavsky pointed out, a two-character scene always has a leader and a follower. The leader is the person without whom the scene would not be taking place. So Lomov leads the scene when Natalya arrives. However, things change and at the end of the scene, Natalya becomes the leader of a new scene, and Lomov becomes the follower, as they discuss who owns the Bovine Meadows.

The painful shyness of Lomov, his passive-aggressive beating around the bush and his endless other neurotic symptoms (his dry throat and unquenchable thirst; his blinking eye; his aches and pains), which are a mask for his sexual desires and for his aggression, are so side-splittingly funny that when I first saw this play I nearly fell on the floor. (I was a high school student, and I had been ushering for The Princeton Players, a group that performed there every summer in the late 1950s; they did a superb production of *Marriage Proposal*.) Lomov's sexual desires are sublimated and assert themselves as soon as his land is discussed, when he immediately projects them onto the disputed part of his estate. He is confronted with the obstinacy of Natalia Stepanovna, who sublimates her sexual desire for him by being equally aggressively possessive about the estate. But there is nothing shy or passive about her aggressivity. When she realizes she has made a mess of things, she has hysterical fits that are hilarious to the audience. On the part of both protagonists, this is a way of avoiding the true topic of discussion, which is sex. The audience sees this clearly, and that is why the play is so painfully funny. But it is only funny if the actors play their parts with absolute reality.

Part Two

Mastering Period Styles: Each Play in Its Time

Introduction

What We Have Found Funny and Perceived as Real Through the Millennia

I talk a great deal in this book about being real in your playing of comedy. But like our perception of what is funny, our perception of what is real in acting changes with time. And this means that the way we perform changes as well. Audiences laugh not only at content, but also at the manner in which we play that content, and styles of acting have varied over the centuries.

The ancient Athenians thought the acting they saw was real. Solon (638–558 BCE), the great lawgiver, believed that Thespis's playing was so lifelike that it was dangerous! Actors were respectfully called *technitai* (artist-technician; performing artist), but the usual common name for them was *hypocrit* (one who pretends to be something other than he is, literally an "answerer"; for instance, an actor who responds to a line delivered by the chorus), with no disapproving moral stricture attached to the word, despite the meaning it took on later. In any case, the Athenians accepted the reality of what they saw despite what we would now consider the extreme stylization of the performance practice: the actors all used masks; actors played multiple roles; both male and female roles were played by men. But if the actors believed in the given circumstances and played with truthfulness, even if they declaimed the lines rhetorically, the audience would have been absorbed in the world of the play and believed in its reality.

The public would have been startled and thrilled by gods and goddesses appearing as if by magic on the *theologion* [literally, the god place]. This was the roof of the *skene*, a building at the back of the raised stage, where dressing rooms were located; not only does our word "scene" for a portion of a play derive from this Greek word, but also the word for "stage" in some contemporary Romance languages, e.g., *scène* in French, *scena* in Italian, *escenario* in Spanish. It backed onto the *proskeniun*, which, so it is conjectured, was decorated with painted scenery representing a palace entrance, temple, or other appropriate place. We are used to painted scenery in the contemporary theater as well, of course, and we suspend our disbelief in its unreality. And the Athenian spectators would have been horrified by the dead bodies wheeled out onto the forestage on the *ekkylema*, a flat wheeled cart stored in the *skene* and used to show the result of violent offstage action—Agamemnon and Cassandra lying inert, with Clytemnestra gloating over them, for instance, in Aeschylus's tragedy *Agamemnon*.

We have something else in common with the ancient Athenians besides accepting what we see as real within the limits of the conventions that we have learned: we can still laugh at the plays they laughed at, just as we can still be moved by the tragedies that elicited their tears, so little have human desires and follies changed over the eons.

We can see differences in acting style in the films of different decades. And we often perceive the acting from the 1930s and 1940s as being less real than it is in contemporary films. However, as Alice Spivak says, "Styles change. That doesn't mean it's not real." Certainly the actors in the old films felt that they were playing moments truthfully and inhabiting their characters, whose needs and wants they had made their own.

How often have you heard someone say, "Why, it seems like only yesterday that I..." And yet, the events had happened decades before. New York City actor and community activist Albert S. Bennett said of the sergeant in the film *The Hurt Locker* (2008), which takes place in Iraq, "He was exactly like my sergeant in basic training!" And Albert served during World War Two, some seventy years ago. Everything that happened before you were born seems like ancient history to you.

But for those who lived within a certain time frame, the events of the period have an immediacy and a presence that is exactly the same as yours as you live in your own time.

The Age-Old Plots and Stories

Mrs. Levy loved the theater. Mr. Levy hated it. But she dragged him along anyway, until finally he rebelled and refused to go to even one more play. "But why do you hate the theater?" she asked. "Why?" he answered, "I'll tell you. In the theater it's always the same. When he wants, she doesn't want. When she wants, he doesn't want. And when they both want, down comes the curtain!"

He had a point. There are some plots that have been used so often, it almost seems as if you couldn't do a play without them. Take, for example, boy finds girl, boy loses girl, boy and girl find each other again, and are united.

The satire of eternal human foibles gives certain pieces of all eras their durability: Molière still speaks to us, and Aristophanes has his appeal. Occasional revivals of Restoration comedies and eighteenth-century pieces are always well received, and Oscar Wilde's humor, like Noël Coward's, can still send us into gales of laughter. Anton Chekhov's comedy was so psychologically astute that his plays have not dated, and his farces are still extremely funny.

Since theater began, certain stories have been told and retold, with variations that make them interesting. It is the era in which they are set that dictates how we perform them, using the period's particular carriage, deportment and manners: the periods in which Molière and Chekhov plays are set are major conditioning factors in how they are played. But the basic stories have remained the same since Greek and Roman authors dreamed those plots up, and since the Italian commedia troupes adopted them and incorporated the standardized Roman comic characters. The knowledge of these conventional stock types did not die with the Roman Empire, but has survived to the present day. The same stories are still told in modern dress on television sitcoms. Generally speaking, they concern romance and love, the course of which never did and never will run smooth. If it did, there would be no conflict, and if there is no conflict, there is no story, no drama, and no comedy.

The number of basic dramatic plots has been set at seven or at twenty, depending on the author. Georges Polti (b. 1868–?) in his classic *Les trente-six situations dramatiques* (The Thirty-Six Dramatic Situations; 1895), published in 1924 in a translation by Lucille Ray, outlines what he conceives of as the thirty-six possible basic situations used in plots as a whole or, often, in part and in combination. He based his book on a list by Johann Wolfgang von Goethe (1749–1832), who said he got the idea from the Italian writer of theatrical fairy tales, Carlo Gozzi (see chapter ten). Polti applies his idea to serious drama, and here is my own list of the principal comedy plots through the ages. They are standard stories, used again and again.

You will notice that some plays appear more than once on the list, in accordance with the idea that plots are often only partial, and elements may be combined to make a more complicated story. Those listed below could equally well be plots for tragedies, except that the comedies have happy endings.

What makes these simple plots interesting are the endless adornments, complications, and variations to which they are subject. In most cases after the medieval era—when simple plots are the norm in the surviving comedies (there are seldom any subplots)—the main plot thread is surrounded by principal themes and characters that take us well beyond the simple story, which, from repeated use, would otherwise make for monotonous theater. Molière's plays are cases in point: On the direct thread of one of the variants of plot number one, for instance, he hangs his trenchant, penetrating portraits of human foibles and pretensions and his mordant satires of various professions, and these are more important than the romance—although not to the young couple, to whom the eccentric characters opposing their love are obstacles to be surmounted. From the very nature of the plot, the superobjectives, throughlines, main objectives and obstacles begin to emerge. The individual scripts will of course give you the specific verbal and physical actions that constitute the play.

The first two plots on the list, with their variations, are the most common throughout theatrical history, and are often used in combination. The third is a usual element in any comedy plot, as well as being a frequent main thread. Nearly every plot listed is combined with some variation on plot 1. In social satire, this is very usual, and the object of the satire, which is what the audience focuses on, is often secondary to the love story, in terms of plot. You will see that some plots are interrelated, such as "2. The Biter Bit" and "7. The Social Climber," but the latter variation on number 2 is so often used that it deserves its own category. And now, without further ado, here are those plots that have stood the test of time, and that still arouse our laughter:

1. **The Course of True Love Never Did Run Smooth**. Two lovers find that they are not allowed to be together, and must hide their love and bide their time, possessing their ardent souls in patience, meanwhile deceiving those who would keep them apart. There are five common variations—they have variations themselves—of this plot, consisting of obstacles that the lovers must surmount. They are the skeletons that are fleshed out and clothed with everything from social satire to a farce with romantic complications:

    a. The father of the young lady or young man wants to marry her or him to someone else, with whom she or he is not in love.

    b. The guardian of the young lady wants to marry her himself.

    c. Someone in authority opposes the marriage, or the consummation of the love. This person, whether man or woman, is sometimes a rival, as in cases of adultery, where the husband is often the opponent of the young man.

    d. There are two (or more) rivals for the young lady's or young man's hand, one of whom she or he is usually in love with. Mistaken jealousy, which constitutes an obstacle in itself, often complicates this plot.

e. Cuckoldry: A man is in love with another man's wife, and she with him. He cuckolds the husband, who may or may not find out.

In the end, all difficulties are resolved and the lovers are united, through both their own efforts, and often with the help and connivance of a third party, as in *The Barber of Seville*, where Figaro aids and abets the young couple. A commonly used plot device is for the suitor to insinuate himself in disguise into the house where his beloved lives, often more or less imprisoned, as in *The Barber of Seville*, where Almaviva disguises himself as a music teacher, highly recommended by Don Basilio, a friend of Rosina's guardian, Bartolo. Shakespeare had Hortensio disguise himself as a music teacher so he could woo Bianca in *The Taming of the Shrew*, just as Lucentio, having fallen in love with her, and she with him, disguises himself as a Latin tutor.

A. Greek, Roman: Terence's *Phormio* (combination of partial plot a and 2 and 3, below); Plautus' *Aulularia* (The Pot of Gold; plot a; discussion, chapter seven) and *Amphytrion* (plot e; discussion, chapter nine under "Tudor Farce").

B. Medieval: Anonymous elegiac comedy adaptations of Plautus's *Aulularia* and *Geta*, adapted from *Amphytrion*; see chapter eight.

C. Renaissance / Elizabethan: Udall's *Ralph Roister Doister* (the woman Ralph is in love with is married; discussion, chapter nine); Machiavelli's *La Mandragola* (The Mandrake [Root]; discussion, chapter nine; combination of plots e and 6, below); Shakespeare's *The Taming of the Shrew* (discussion and scene analysis, chapter nine; combination of plots a, d, and 4, below).

D. Seventeenth Century: Molière's *L'école des Femmes* (The School for Wives; plot b), *Le malade imaginaire* (The Imaginary Invalid; see discussion, chapter five; partial plot a), *L'avare* (The Miser; combination of partial plots b and d), and *Les fourberies de Scapin* (Scapin's Deceitful Tricks; discussion, and scene analysis, chapter five;

combination of partial plots a and 2 and 3, below); Congreve's *The Way of the World* (plot d); Cibber's *Love's Last Shift* (combination of plots c and 6; discussion, chapter ten).

E. Eighteenth Century: Beaumarchais' *Le Barbier de Séville* (The Barber of Seville; plot b; discussion, above and in chapter eleven); Sheridan's *The Rivals* (combination of plots c and d; discussion and scene analysis, chapter eleven).

F. Nineteenth Century: August von Kotzebue's *How to Die for Love: A Farce in Two Acts* (discussion, chapter twelve; plot d); Mrs. Mowatt's *Fashion, or Life in New York* (discussion, chapter twelve ; combination of plots d, 3, 5, 6, and 7); Oscar Wilde's *The Importance of Being Earnest* (see discussions and scene analysis, chapter twelve; plot c).

G. Twentieth Century: Coward's *Private Lives* (plot e, but the couple was previously married, and they run off together; discussion, chapter thirteen); Coward's *Blithe Spirit* (plot d; discussion, chapter thirteen); Sondheim's *A Funny Thing Happened on the Way to the Forum* (combination of plots a, c, and d).

2. **The Biter Bit**. In French, the phrases are "le trompeur trompé" (the deceiver deceived) or "à trompeur, trompeur et demi" (to the deceiver, a deceiver and a half), since turn-about is fair play. This could also be a plot element in number one on this list: two lovers who experience an obstacle to their love, as in *The Barber of Seville*, where the guardian who tries to foil the lovers is foiled himself. There are a lot of variations, among them:

    a. Someone contrives mischief in order to gain something, or to avoid the consequences of his actions, and is in turn the victim of mischief.

    b. Someone masquerades as someone else for his own gain, and is eventually exposed.

c. Someone, usually a man, carries on an illicit and perhaps adulterous love affair, and is chastened and brought to see the error of his or her ways. The mischief-maker, two-timing lover, or hypocrite gets his comeuppance. Political satire often uses this plot, and the corrupt politician is exposed to public ridicule.

A. Greek, Roman: Menander's *Dyskolos* (The Grouch; discussion, chapter seven); Plautus's *Amphitryon* (partial plot, combined with 5 and 6); Terence's *Phormio*.

B. Medieval: *La Farce de maître Pierre Pathelin* (The Farce of Master Pierre Pathelin; discussion, chapter eight).

C. Renaissance / Elizabethan: Shakespeare's *The Merry Wives of Windsor*; Ben Jonson's *Volpone*.

D. Seventeenth Century: Dancourt's *Le chevalier à la mode* (The Fashionable Cavalier; discussion, chapter ten); Molière's *Tartuffe*, *L'Avare*, and *Les Fourberies de Scapin*.

E. Eighteenth Century: Beaumarchais' *Le mariage de Figaro* (The Marriage of Figaro; discussion, chapter eleven).

F. Nineteenth Century: Taylor's *Our American Cousin* (discussion, chapter twelve).

G. Twentieth Century: Kaufman and Hart's *The Man Who Came to Dinner* (discussion, chapter four); *Kind Hearts and Coronets* (1949 film); Sondheim's *A Little Night Music*, book by Hugh Wheeler (1916–1987), based on Ingmar Bergman's (1918–2007) film comedy, *Smiles of a Summer Night* (1955).

3. **Mistaken Identity and Erroneous Judgment**. A case of mistaken identity or of erroneous judgment is resolved, but not until after numerous risible complications have resulted in misunderstandings making for amusing plot twists and turns. This is a common plot element or device in farce, as well as a plot thread.

A. Greek, Roman: Plautus's *The Two Menaechme* and *Aulularia*; Terence's *Phormio*.

B. Medieval: Elegiac comedy adaptation of Plautus's *Aulularia*.

C. Renaissance / Elizabethan: *Jack Juggler* (discussion, chapter nine); Shakespeare's *All's Well That Ends Well; As You Like It; The Comedy of Errors; Twelfth Night.*

D. Seventeenth Century: Molière's *Les Fourberies de Scapin* and *L'Avare;* Cibber's *Love's Last Shift;* Vanbrugh's *The Relapse* (discussion, chapter ten).

E. Eighteenth Century: Marivaux's *Le jeu de l'amour et du hasard* (The Game of Love and Chance; partial plot; discussion and scene analysis, chapter eleven); Sheridan's *The Rivals.*

F. Nineteenth Century: Mrs. Mowatt's *Fashion, or Life in New York* (partial plot); Taylor's Our American Cousin; Wilde's *The Importance of Being Earnest, An Ideal Husband,* and *Lady Windermere's Fan;* Chekhov's one-act farces, *The Boor and The Marriage Proposal* (discussion and scene analysis, chapter six); Henry Becque's farce *La Parisienne* (The Parisian Lady); Brandon Thomas's *Charley's Aunt.*

G. Twentieth Century: John Guare's *Six Degrees of Separation* (partial plot, combined with 7).

4. **The Shrew or the Domestic Tyrant Tamed**. A hen-pecked or, alternatively, an authoritative husband, or male chauvinist, gets his shrewish wife or inamorata to obey him through various contrivances and clever ploys. Sometimes the tables are turned, and it is the woman who tames the unruly man, a domestic tyrant; this plot is often combined with number 5, below.

A. Greek, Roman: Aristophanes' *Lysistrata.*

B. Medieval: *La Farce du Cuvier* (The Farce of the Tub; discussion, chapter eight).

C. Renaissance / Elizabethan: Shakespeare's *The Taming of the Shrew.*

D. Seventeenth Century: Vanbrugh's *The Relapse.*

E. Eighteenth Century: Holberg's *Jeppe paa Bjerget eller den forvandlede Bonde* (Jeppe of the Hill; or The

Transformed Peasant; partial plot; discussion, chapter eleven).

F. Nineteenth Century: Chekhov's *Myedvyed* (The Bear), in which both the male tyrant / boor and the female romantic hypocrite are tamed.

G. Twentieth Century: Cole Porter's musical, *Kiss Me, Kate*, based on *The Taming of the Shrew*; Sondheim's *A Funny Thing Happened on the Way to the Forum*.

5. **Teaching a Lesson: The Naïve Deceived Then Disabused**. Someone is tricked into believing he or she is someone else. Many amusing complications and misunderstandings result. When aroused from his or her condition, the person realizes the truth of the situation, and learns a moral lesson.

A. Greek, Roman: Plautus's *Amphytrion* (partial plot).

B. Medieval: Geta, elegiac comedy adapted from *Amphytrion*; *De vetulla* (On the Old Woman; discussion, chapter eight).

C. Renaissance / Elizabethan: Udall's *Ralph Roister Doister*; Shakespeare's *The Taming of the Shrew* (opening and closing scenes with Christopher Sly); *The Tempest; A Midsummer Night's Dream*.

D. Seventeenth Century: Vanbrugh's *The Relapse*.

E. Eighteenth Century: Holberg's *Jeppe paa Bjerget eller den forvandlede Bonde* (Jeppe of the Hill; or The Transformed Peasant) and *Den politiske Kandestøber* (The Political Tinker).

F. Nineteenth Century: Mrs. Mowatt's *Fashion, or Life in New York* (partial plot).

G. Twentieth Century: Coward's *Blithe Spirit*.

6. **Love's Labor Won**. A young lady in love contrives by various clever ploys to win the love of a man who at first is not in love with her; or vice versa: a young man wins the love of a young lady who was at first indifferent, or dared not admit her love.

A. Greek, Roman: Plautus's *Amphitryon* (partial plot).

B. Medieval: *De tribus puellis* (The Three Girls; discussion, chapter eight)

C. Renaissance / Elizabethan: Machiavelli's *La Mandragola* (The Mandrake Root); *Ralph Roister Doister*; Shakespeare's *All's Well That Ends Well; As You Like It; Much Ado About Nothing; Love's Labor Lost; Twelfth Night; A Midsummer Night's Dream*.

D. Seventeenth Century: Cibber's *Love's Last Shift* (combination with plot 1 c).

E. Eighteenth Century: Goldsmith's *She Stoops to Conquer*.

F. Nineteenth Century: Mrs. Mowatt's *Fashion, or Life in New York* (partial plot).

G. Twentieth Century: Philip Barry's *The Philadelphia Story*.

7. **The Social Climber.** Someone full of hubris and snobbery desires to rise in social status, and usually does not succeed, but learns a lesson about life. Often, there are people who connive to bilk the social climber of his or her wealth, and these villains come in for their share of disapproval, as the unfortunate wealthy but snobbish climber is taken advantage of by those of the impecunious, unscrupulous higher class. Nevertheless, the social climber is the object of satire and opprobrium: the moral of this plot is that people should know and keep to their places. In some plays, this is a variation of "The Biter Bit" or the "Teaching a Lesson" plots. There are often combinations with other plots, as in Molière's *Le bourgeois gentilhomme*, which also has number 1 c as a plot element. Although no longer very common, this sort of story was often used in the sixteenth, seventeenth, eighteenth, and nineteenth centuries, when the social class one was born into counted a great deal more than it did beginning in the latter half of the twentieth century, after World War Two.

A. Greek, Roman: Plautus *Stichus; Curculio*.

B. Medieval: *Le vilain ânier* (The Peasant Muleteer; discussion, chapter eight).

C. Renaissance / Elizabethan: Lyndsay's *Ane Pleasant Satyre of the Thrie Estaitis* (An Amusing Satire of the Three Estates; discussion, chapter nine); Shakespeare's *Twelfth Night*.

D. Seventeenth Century: Molière's *Le bourgeois gentilhomme*; Dancourt's *Le chevalier à la mode*.

E. Eighteenth Century: Sheridan's *The Rivals*.

F. Nineteenth Century: Mrs. Mowatt's *Fashion, or Life in New York* (partial plot); Taylor's *Our American Cousin*; Griboyedov's *Woe from Wit* (discussion, chapter two); Shaw's *Candida*.

G. Twentieth Century: Shaw's *Pygmalion*, which is this plot in reverse, since Eliza is the victim of someone who desires to pass this Cockney flower girl off as an aristocrat; Guare's *Six Degrees of Separation*.

VII

The Beginnings of Comedy: Ancient Greece and Rome

Movement, Clothing, and Manners

The principle garment of ancient Greece was the long or short, light-fitting chiton, a kind of tunic, of which there were several kinds. In Rome, the tunic or gown was also the main article of clothing, with the toga draped over it. Cloaks were also worn in both Greece and Rome. The toga, too, came in a variety of styles and could have a bordering stripe indicating a person's rank. The idea of distinguishing people by colors they were allowed to display carried over into the theater, as shown later in this chapter. Footwear was also quite light, except for the heavy laced boots worn by soldiers. Movement in both eras is comparatively free, and certainly allows for the physical comedy that was ubiquitous in all these plays.

Manners could be quite formal at court receptions and banquets, but otherwise dining was relaxed and casual. Consult *The Deipnosophists* (The Learned Banqueters) by Athenaeus of Naucratis (second century CE) and the *Noctes Atticae* (Attic Nights) by Aulus Gellius (ca. 125–ca. 180 CE) for as complete a look at ancient manners and etiquette, conditioning the behavior in the ancient plays discussed below, and in general in the plays over these centuries. We learn in *The Deipnosophists*, for instance, that people ate with spoons and knives and sometimes with their right hands while reclining on couches, and not usually sitting upright, before low tables, which had been brought in already laden with food. After the main course, they were taken out, cleaned, and reset with sweets and other delicacies. Although forks existed, they were used for cooking and for religious ceremonies, but not for individuals to eat with. Table manners were decorous, and people even washed their hands before a meal, and changed their shoes before entering the dining room.

The Roman author Valerius Maximus (first century CE), an author about whom nothing is known beyond his work, *Memorable Doings and Sayings*, has given us invaluable information about Roman social customs, which would apply to the staging of comedies by Plautus and Terence. He tells us, for instance, that when walking in the street, the man of highest rank was followed by someone of lower rank, except for the small son of the person of rank, who could precede him. So even back then, the stuff of comedy is there in the mockery of class distinctions that we see in Roman comic plays.

Ancient Greek Comedy: Farce and Satire

There are two major comedy writers of ancient Greece whose work has survived in any extensive way. The first is Aristophanes (445–385 BCE), who wrote eleven plays that we know of, exemplifying the Old Comedy. His most famous plays are *Lysistrata* (411 BCE) and *Batrachoi* (Frogs; 411 BCE). The latter involves a contest in Hades umpired by Sophocles and sponsored by Dionysus, disguised as Hercules. Will Aeschylus or Euripides be selected to return to earth and revive the dying art of tragedy? Dionysus had thought Euripides would win, but in the end, he prefers Aeschylus and returns with him to the world of the living. The Chorus of Frogs leaps about and croaks, as it comments on the proceedings.

In 1974, Stephen Sondheim and Burt Shevelove "freely adapted" *Frogs*, turning it into a musical that was performed at the Yale University gymnasium swimming pool. In a revised version, it had a limited Broadway run in 2004 at the Vivian Beaumont Theatre. The rivals were William Shakespeare, and the man who didn't think much of him, George Bernard Shaw. Shakespeare won.

In *Lysistrata*, the Athenian women, led by Lysistrata, refuse to have sexual relations with the men until they stop making war with Sparta. The play has been used as the subject of several musical theater pieces, including a 1902 Berlin operetta by Paul Lincke; the Broadway musical *The Happiest Girl in the World* (1961), an Offenbach pastiche with lyrics by E. Y. Harburg and a book by Fred Saidy; and the opera *Lysistrata or The Nude Goddess* (2005) by Mark Adamo, with a libretto by the composer.

Menander (343/342?–291/290 BCE), the second great comic playwright, wrote an unknown number of plays, probably more than one hundred, most lost, exemplifying the New Comedy. Five extensive fragments and two major scripts survive: *Dyskolos* (The Grouch; 317 BCE)—nearly complete; and *Samia* (The Maiden from Samos; ca. 321/316? BCE)—about one-third complete.

We know the names of many more comic playwrights of the ancient world than those two, but we have only occasional fragments, such as those by the major Old Comedy writers Cratinus (519–422 BCE) and Eupolis (446–411 BCE), and those by Epigenes of Athens (fourth century BCE), a writer of the Middle Comedy period, along with its most important playwright Alexis (ca. 370–ca. 270 BCE), who apparently was known for his mythological parodies. Manuscripts mention many others, such as the Roman freedman Gaius Maecenas Melisssus (first century CE), who wrote comedies of manners. But we have nothing concrete that would permit us to reconstruct a whole play. We do not even have one complete manuscript by Menander, but we have more material than we have for others, and he was adapted by Roman playwrights, so we have a good idea of what the originals must have been like. And we do know something about conditions in the theater, theatrical presentation, and the conventions that prevailed at the Dionysia and at the Lenaea, the January theater festival.

Surviving Greek and Roman comedy is nothing if not bawdy, and even raunchy. Vase renderings of scenes show this, and are some of the few records we have of scenes from the popular farce called the *phlyax.* Among the many ancient dances are the *kordax,* a rude comic dance, and the *sikkinis,* an equally lewd dance done by the Satyr characters. When performing these plays, you have to let yourself go: Leers, innuendo, and a ribald attitude to obscenity and to lustful enjoyment are all called for, depending, of course, on how the play is directed.

Buttressing the point of view that comedy, laughter, and sex are all related, comedy began, according to Aristotle, with the short pieces called "satyr plays," lewd ancient Greek pieces full of sexual allusion and ribaldry, featuring the phallus, and glorying in pan-sexuality. The characters were satyrs, and later authors of tragedies wrote many. Now lost, they were performed following a trilogy of tragedies, to provide comic relief. They evolved from and were sometimes part of the religious rites involved in the worship of the omnisexual, passionate god Dionysus, who was also the god of drunkenness, wine, and abandon. Comedies were preformed after the tragedies at the god's festival, the urban Dionysia in Athens, a festival that revolved around phallic worship.

Only men acted in the Greek theater, so they played all the women's parts, from Clytemnestra and Electra to Jocasta, and all the lewd comic women's parts as well. The actors may have worn pieces of cloth, scarves, or even gowns that were symbolic of the gender they were portraying. A saffron tunic was probably worn in comedy by male actors playing female parts. The male characters certainly wore a cloth penis, called a *phallos,* sometimes quite a huge one that protruded below their short tunics, as we can see in vase paintings of dramatic presentations. Many actors also displayed their own organs, with the foreskin drawn over the glans, because it was considered obscene to display that part of the penis. Why? Who knows? People have always had their hang-ups about sex.

The urban Dionysia evolved from the annual rural festivals celebrating the grape harvest and new wine. Aside from being the god of wine, Dionysus, like his Roman counterpart, Bacchus, was the god of the dark side of humanity, the deep, hidden desire for destruction, or what Freud would later describe as the death instinct. The phallic symbol was the god's sign, considered a great ornament to be worshipped for its power and procreative qualities.

It was part of the institutionalized rituals of the urban Dionysia to display phalloi in the parade, called the *phallophoria*, to the amphitheater where the dramatic contests and performances took place, on the hillside below the Acropolis. Carts carrying huge phalloi were accompanied by the revelers, the priests, the patrons of the festival, and the citizens of Athens, along with representatives of the colonies of the empire, and the metics, as the resident aliens were called. The hugest phallus was ritually adored, and bulls were sacrificed. The proceedings were accompanied by a feast, transported as part of the parade by food carriers, and by drinking wine. Obscene songs were sung, and lewd dances performed. It must have been lots of fun!

The Old Comedy, the most ancient form of the genre, exemplified by Aristophanes, included a number of standard or stock characters, which he used in his plays. The three most important were the contrasting *alazon* (braggart) and *eiron* (dissembler); and the *bomolochos* (lurker; particularly someone who hung around a religious altar so that he could grab food scraps from the sacrifices), a sly, shrewd, self-seeking, low-class person who connived at hoodwinking people for personal gain. The *alazon* is a figure of authority, and full of boastful overweening pride. In the commedia, he would become the Pantalone or the Capitano; and in Shakespeare, such characters as Malvolio in *Twelfth Night*. The *eiron*, the ancestor of Harlequin in the commedia and the host of clever, enabling servants since, was shrewd and smart, but hid his cleverness, and opposed the *alazon*, who took delight in displaying his. The *eiron* could be a friend or clever servant of a lover or hero. Lord Goring in Wilde's *An Ideal Husband* also belongs to the *eiron* type. The *bomolochos* also reappears in later comedies, as a literal-minded servant and as a social climber or parasite, more sophisticated than in the ancient comedies. Molière's Tartuffe is an example. The descendants of these types are legion, and they are still with us even in television sitcoms.

The Middle Comedy that replaced the Old Comedy is known only by hearsay, since we have no examples beyond fragments. And we know the New Comedy that superseded it from fragments and the two plays by Menander mentioned above, but more from Roman adaptations than Greek originals. New Comedy apparently used the stock characters and generalized plots that would evolve into the commedia dell'arte by the sixteenth century, whereas the Old Comedy was specific and topical, dealing with individuals and current issues and events, and did not employ standardized conventions and devices, even though it had a standard dramatic structural form. One of the innovations in New Comedy was in costumes: the old symbolic costumes, phalloi, padded bellies on men that made them look funny, and padding to represent women were discarded in favor of a more natural look and a more realistic way of dressing.

Because it was not taken seriously, nor was meant to be, comedy was for a long time excluded from the Dionysia. But, as Aristophanes averred, it was actually a most difficult form to master. When this was recognized, comedy was included in the festival, once the lewd songs had evolved into longer plays.

The rules of the festival had changed thanks to Aeschylus (ca. 525–456 BCE), the writer of tragedies: Aristotle informs us in the *Poetics* that "Aeschylus innovated by raising the number of actors from one to two, reducing the choral component, and made speech play the leading role," which had hitherto been played by singing, whether accompanied or a capella. Eventually, three actors were allowed, perhaps an innovation of Sophocles. This change made it easier to write comedies.

The Old Comedy included music and obscene songs, as well as filthy jokes, slapstick, grotesque characters, absurd situations, and stories of the gods and their interactions with humankind. As Aristotle informs us, it also developed "formal features," and was eventually highly structured, like tragedy; but within the structure, there was still plenty of room for ingenious actors to be very funny. From a director's point of view, the following structure is a help in shaping the development of the play, and showing where the climaxes are.

The essential device and heart of Old Comedy was the epirrematic *agon*. The *agon* is the conflict in any drama, and in a comedy it is the central debate on some issue:

1. **Prologue**: The opening of the play, with a soliloquy or a dialogue for two characters that introduced the play's subject.

2. *Parados*: The entry of the chorus, right after the prologue.

3. **Symmetrical scenes:** These were written in particular verse forms and meters. The scenes were in two sections, resembling each other in form, hence the term symmetrical.

4. *Parabasis*: In this kind of symmetrical scene, the chorus or a single actor talked directly to the audience, and represented the author's point of view.

5. *Agon* (**conflict**) **scene:** This usually followed the parabasis, and the audience now saw a debate about the subject of the play; this debate was at the heart of the play's issues, such as who would win the contest for best dramatist, Aeschylus or Euripides, in *The Frogs*; or what to do about the war, in *Lysistrata*. The *agon* begins with an ode sung by half the chorus. This is followed by a command—the *katakeleusmos*—by the coryphaeus (head of the chorus) to the first debater to speak (he will lose the debate), and the actor begins the presentation of his ideas—the *epirrheme*—amid interruptions, concluding with an appeal—the *pnigos* (choking)—delivered breathlessly. The second debater now repeats the whole process, with the other half of the chorus singing an *antiode*, the speaker giving the *antipirrheme* (opposite point of view), and then the whole chorus gives its decision, which will be followed by more dialogue.

6. **Episodes:** These were the following dialogue scenes, sometimes continuing a discussion of the issues, but often simply presenting comic interludes and scenes, in which songs were included. There could be a wedding scene, called a *gamos*, betokening a happy ending.

7. **Exodus:** The conclusion of the story, and the exit song of the actors and the chorus.

Aristophanes seems not to have stuck completely to the formal structure outlined here, but to have inserted, especially in the episodes, irrelevant skits, and songs. In fact, he seems very close to vaudeville, and in some modern productions, you could get out your tap shoes, straw hat, and cane, and in the comic sketches, assume your broadest vaudeville manner of caricatural portrayals.

Menander's *Dyskolos* (The Grouch; The Grump)

Menander chose not to follow the established format at all, and by doing away with the formal structure of the Old Comedy, paved the way for even greater freedom of comedic expression within plotted plays that told a story. He also incorporated dance interludes between each of the usual five acts. Menander was considered by many ancient scholars to be a very great writer, a brilliant poet, and profoundly insightful. And we see in his surviving plays that he went in a different, more realistic direction from Aristophanes, as he did in the very funny *Dyskolos* (The Grouch; The Grump). We see the descendants of this character in Molière's *The Misanthrope* and Neil Simon's *The Odd Couple*.

The title character of this five-act farce, which revolves around the plot thread "the course of true love never did run smooth," is a reclusive curmudgeon, a cantankerous misanthropic farmer. Why does anyone become this way? Because he is deeply disappointed in what life has given him, and most especially in other people, who have lost his trust. But rather than being the subject of a tragedy, such feelings are the subject of mockery, scorn, and derision: these attitudes are deemed ridiculous, and can be overcome by a little real love, according to our comic poet. The lesson for the actor, as always, is to play this character with all due seriousness, to take his suffering seriously, and to feel his pain. The comedy is in the character's overreactions: To the most trivial offenses, real or imagined, he reacts with rage.

The story of *Dyskolos* is complicated: Knemon, the grouch of the title, lives on his rocky farm in hilly Phyle, not far from Athens, with his daughter (known only as the Girl) and his elderly female servant, Simikhe. Knemon's life is constant drudgery, as he toils endlessly on his unproductive farm, and he hates everyone and will not speak to his neighbors. The countryside round about and a nearby grove are sacred to Pan, god of nature, and when he passes by the grove he grudgingly acknowledges the god. Nearby, Knemon's wife, Myrrhine (a silent role), and his disowned son by a previous marriage, Gorgias, have set up a household with one servant, Daos, away from the unbearably bad-tempered man. Pan himself delivers the customary prologue, in which he tells us that he has decided to help Knemon's daughter better herself because she has been worshipful to him and the nymphs who inhabit his sacred grove. To that end, he has made a rich city boy, Sostratos, fall madly in love with the Girl while he is out hunting with a friend, Chaireas, a social climber and a parasitic sycophant, with descendants in seventeenth-century French and English Restoration comedies. Sostratos has sent a servant, Phyrrias, to make inquiries about the Girl's family, but he has been driven away by Knemon, who threw stones at him. Petrified, Chaireas leaves hastily, as Knemon enters. He is as nasty as can be to Sostratos, who is taken aback, but when Knemon leaves, and just as Sostratos is about to leave as well, in order to find and seek advice from his father Kallipides' clever servant, Getas, the Girl enters to fetch water, since the infirm Simikhe has dropped the bucket down the well. Sostratos offers to help, by getting fresh water from Pan's grove. Meanwhile, Gorgias's servant Daos sees Sostratos and the Girl in conversation, and goes to tell Gorgias about it. As all the characters depart, we have the first dance interlude, performed by the worshippers of Pan. In the second act, Gorgias accuses Sostratos of being like all idle rich young men, treating the lower classes with contempt, and of having bad intentions toward his sister, and Sostratos explains that he loves her and wants to marry her. He and Gorgias, mollified and now happy, become fast friends. Sostratos puts on work clothes, and Gorgias accompanies him into the fields to find Knemon. Now Sikon enters, dragging a sheep. He is a cook, and a stock character type in the New Comedy. Sikon is taking the sheep to Pan's grove to sacrifice it, because Sostratos' mother has had a nightmare in which she saw her son toiling in the fields. In the third act, Getas tries to borrow a jug from Knemon, who threatens him, and is about to follow him with his whip, when Sikon comes in, wanting to borrow a kettle in which to cook the remains of the sheep. He flees in terror before the wrath of Knemon. Meanwhile, poor Simikhe has dropped the hoe down the well, as she was trying to retrieve the lost bucket, and now Knemon cannot work, and he cannot implore Pan's or anyone else's help, because everyone round about hates him. Pan's worshippers now enter and perform another dance. In the next act, Knemon climbs down into the well to find the hoe, and falls in. He is now helpless. The terrified Sikon hears his cries for help, but is too afraid to do anything. Sostratos, having returned with Gorgias, not knowing what has happened to Knemon, enter his house to find him, so that Sostratos can at last ask for the Girl's hand in marriage. Hearing his father call out, Gorgias climbs down the well, and rescues his father, who is convinced that he is now a dying man. He entreats Gorgias, whom he now acknowledges as his son, to find a husband for the Girl, and Gorgias proposes that Sostratos should marry her. He agrees, and upon the arrival of Kallipides, everyone except Knemon goes to worship in Pan's grove. Kallipides, not sure at first that he wants a pauper girl to marry into his family, is shamed into admitting that his attitude is at the very least unkind, and when it is suggested that his daughter, Sostratos' sister, is a suitable match for Gorgias, he readily agrees, and the marriage is arranged. A feast is held in celebration of the double wedding, but Knemon, as misanthropic as ever, refuses to attend. Sikon and Getas decide to teach him a lesson. As Knemon is sound asleep, they take him from the house, dumping him outside. They then go inside, and make a terrible din, and when the ever cantankerous Knemon awakens, and has difficulty standing up, they ask him if this is his house. "Of course," he says. They tell him they want to borrow his pots and pans and a large punchbowl to prepare the feast. He is forced to listen to them as they babble on about how wonderful the feast is going to be, until finally, they pull him up and make him dance, pointing out how clumsy he is. Unable to bear them, he opines that it might be better to go to that feast than remain dancing with these two after all. He does so, and is welcomed and treated with honor, and crowned with a garland of flowers, so that the play ends in revelry and dancing and with the hope that he will finally overcome his misanthropy.

Here we have the sentimental ending that brings a tear of joy to the spectator's eye, the sort of ending that would become characteristic of comedy through the ages. This somewhat diffuse, complicated play has its many delights, not the least of which is the scene in which Sikon and Getas have their rather gentle revenge on Knemon. The graceful dance interludes, too, add some magic to the proceedings. Underlying the play is the worship of Pan, and of nature as providing for the needs of all, if only we would appreciate what it has to offer. The typical moral of this play is that love rules the day, and such attitudes as Knemon's are to be eschewed.

Theater in Byzantium

In Greek Byzantium, capital of the Empire and home of the Greek Orthodox Church, and especially in the city of Constantinople, the people loved theater, and comedy flourished, among them those by the beloved Menander. Alongside them, lewd shows involving sexual display were also as popular as strip joints and pole dancing are today. Procopius's (500–565) rather biased early medieval *Secret History*, written around 550 or 558, gives us several possibly apocryphal anecdotes about the wife of Emperor Justinian I (483–565), the Empress Theodora (500–548), and her obscene performances before she became a member of the royal family. One of her acts consisted of standing nude on the stage, save for a ribbon tied around her waist, because the law forbade anyone to appear entirely naked on stage. Bending backward so that the audience could see between her legs, she had slaves sprinkle barley seeds "into the calyx of this passion flower," from which geese, brought on stage at that point, "would next pick the grains with their bills and eat." I refer you to Procopius's scathing book for some other most amusing details and stories.

Ancient Roman Comedy and Farce

In ancient Rome, the major comedy writers were, first, Plautus (251?–184? BCE), who wrote perhaps twenty-one comedies, of which twenty survive intact. Many were based on Greek models, now lost. The dates of most of his plays are unknown. The comedies include *Asinaria* (Asses); *Miles Gloriosus* (The Braggart Warrior; ca. 205 BCE); *Stichus* (200 BCE); *Aulularia* (The Pot of Gold; 195 BCE); *Pseudolus* (191 BCE); *Rudens* (The Rope); *Amphytruo* (Amphytrion); *Menechmi* (The Two Menaechme); *Curculio*, one of the sources of composer-lyricist Stephen Sondheim's *A Funny Thing Happened on the Way to the Forum* (1962); and *Casina*, adapted from a Greek New Comedy, *The Men Who Drew Lots*, now lost, by Diphilus (342–391 BCE), supposedly the author of more than one hundred comedies, all lost, of which we have fifty titles.

Second came Terence (195?–159 BCE; Roman), six of whose plays survive, some perhaps adapted from Greek plays, now lost; *Andria* (The Women of Andros; 166 BCE); *Hecyra* (The Mother-in-Law; 165 BCE); *Heautontimorumenos* (The Self-Tormentor; The Masochist; 163 BCE); *Eunuchus* (The Eunuch; 161 BCE); *Phormio* (161 BCE); and *Adelphi* (The Brothers; 160 BCE).

The word "actor" is exactly the same Latin word used in ancient Rome, and it had exactly the same meaning that we give it: first, one who does something; and second, a performer who plays parts in a public presentation, that is, one who interprets roles and pretends to be a character. Another word was *histrio*, which also meant actor, and survives in English as the rare noun "histrion" and the common adjective "histrionic."

There were stock characters in Roman comedy. In plays of the *atellana* (Atellan farce), a genre of farce from the town of Atella in the Campania region, where Plautus acted in his youth, there were supposedly four such types: the *Maccus* (a boaster and drunken tippler); *Bucco* (a glutton and braggart); *Pappus* (a gullible, prissy, pedantic old man); and *Dossenus* (a clever, self-serving, and covetous trickster). The audience knew something immediately about who the characters were, because the actors wore representative masks and color-coded costumes, as they had in the Greek theater. The Latin word for mask is *persona*. The *pantomimus*, or mime actor, usually did not wear a mask. As in Greece, actors were men, although some dancers and mime artists were women, classified as prostitutes. In the days of the later empire, women began to perform, apparently in comedy only.

In ancient Rome, the color code delineating character was as follows:

1. **Purple:** A wealthy man.
2. **Green:** A senator, judge, or someone else in a position of authority.
3. **Yellow:** A female character; a yellow tassel indicated that the character was a god or a demi-god.
4. **White:** An old person; white clothing and, often, white wigs were worn.
5. **Red:** A red wig indicated that the character was a servant or slave.

Mimes often wore a parti-colored robe called a *centunculus*, prefiguring the diagonal multicolored or black and white costumes of Harlequin in the commedia dell'arte. All actors wore the sock or the buskin. The sock, from ancient Roman for a low shoe (Latin: *soccus*) was worn by comic actors; and the buckskin half boot, the cothurnus, was worn by tragedians. Presumably, this convention is of ancient Greek origin. The archaic term "sock and buskin" thus became a metonymy for the drama: the sock for comedy; the buskin for tragedy.

In addition, actors wore such accouterments as swords to show that the character was a soldier, carried a carving knife and wore an apron if the character was a cook, or carried a cane or staff when playing old people. The stock characters in Roman comedy, taken over from those in Greek New Comedy, included the *adulescens* (youth) and the *virgo* (the young lady with whom the *adulescens* was in love, or who is in love with him); the *senex* (old man) and *pater* (father); the *matriona* (mother) and the *uxor* (wife); the *leno* (brothel-keeper; pimp) and the *meretrix* (prostitute); the *miles gloriosus* (braggart warrior); the *servus* (servant), plural, *servi* (servants)—he was always disreputable and dislikable—and the *ancilla* (serving maid). If these types seem familiar, they should: not only have they been used over and over again in western theater through the ages, but they are represented in their Roman manifestations in Sondheim's *A Funny Thing Happened on the Way to the Forum*. The book by Larry Gelbart and Burt Shevelove is based on a number of plays by Plautus, whose *The Two Menaechme* was the basis of Shakespeare's *The Comedy of Errors*, musicalized in 1938 by Richard Rodgers (composer) and Lorenz Hart (lyricist) as *The Boys from Syracuse*. The book by George Abbot for this first musical adapted from Shakespeare does not use a word of Shakespeare's text!

Aside from the atellana, there were several other genres of ancient Roman comedy, including those adapted from Greek sources, combining some of them into one play, called a *fabula* or *comoedia palliata*. The process of doing this was called *contaminatio*. The *fabula praetexta* was a serious or comic play, drawn from Roman history, and the *fabula togata*, from the Roman garment called the toga, was a comedy with contemporary Roman themes. It was also called a *tabernaria*, or a comedy that took place in a private or domestic setting. There was also a popular genre called the hilarotragedy, tragicomedies that were parodies of well known tragedies, similar no doubt to the Greek paratragedy, which also burlesqued or satirized tragedy. And there were Dorian farces performed in the Greek cities of southern Italy by *phylakes* (talkers of nonsense; prattlers), many of whom were amateur actors. Presumably they inspired the atellana.

The comedies of Plautus and Terence are in the genre of the fabula palliata or the tabernaria, and mostly all revolve around love stories, and the wiles and machinations of the lovers to be together, and to overcome the obstacles of those who would oppose their union. In other words, we have the oldest of elemental romantic comedy plots, and one that is still exploited to this day in such films as *The Monster-In-Law*, discussed in chapter four—the mother-in-law was a figure of comedy even in ancient Rome, where Terence wrote *Hecyra* (The Mother-In-Law). The same plot informs the delightful *Just Married* (2003), starring Ashton Kutcher and Brittany Murphy, both tremendously personable and charming, as a honeymooning couple in Europe, who have to overcome numerous obstacles, and are pursued by Christian Kane, the ex-boyfriend who is in love with her and has been sent by her disapproving parents to break the couple up—without success, of course.

It is notoriously difficult to translate jokes from one language to another, particularly when the jokes depend on wordplay. There are unique expressions in every language that have connotations that don't exist in the translator's language. This is famously the case with the Latin of Plautus, for instance, whose endless comic wordplay and double meanings require explanatory footnotes. And to explain a joke is almost to ensure that it won't be funny. But at least we can understand the humor by dint of the explanation.

Plautus' plays and their universal themes have been adopted by other writers who have given us their variations. In *Aulularia* (The Pot of Gold), the miser Euclio is a total paranoid, more attached to his gold than even Harpagon, his descendent in *The Miser* by Molière, who based his play on Plautus's comedy, which he had read in the translation by Michel de Marolles (1600–1681). Obsessive and compulsive, he goes nearly mad at the very thought that his hidden store of gold could be stolen.

In a conversation typical of comedy, that of two people who are at cross-purposes because they misinterpret what each is saying, Euclio and his daughter's suitor Lyconides, who is completely ignorant of the hidden treasure, asks for her hand in marriage. He also admits that he has already slept with her, and wants to confess this fault in order for Euclio to see that he is an honorable man and worthy of his daughter's hand. But he says all this indirectly, in an ambiguous, euphemistic way that Euclio misinterprets: "…the wicked deed that causes you all this distress was my doing; I confess it." Euclio thinks Lyconides means that he has stolen the gold and, in despair, says that he is a ruined man. Lyconides understands him to be talking about his daughter, and apologizes all over again, leading to Euclio's enraged response that apologies are unacceptable. Lyconides says that, "having touched, my only plea is that I may possess entirely." At this, Euclio practically has an apoplectic fit. Of course, all misunderstandings are cleared up satisfactorily.

VIII

Medieval and Early Renaissance
Comedy and Farce

Movement, Clothing, and Manners

Women wore long gowns over undergarments, and men wore tights or tight-fitting breeches. They wore gowns over tunics (earlier in the period), or short jackets (doublets) over their hose, later in the era. The loose or tight gowns (sometimes pleated), with no collar, and with either great wide hanging sleeves or narrow ones, were fastened at the neck, and belted around the waist. The long gown with a hood sewn onto it was common, and younger courtiers replaced it with colorful, and even flashy jackets and hose that showed off their legs.

In Chaucer's England, the typical basic garment for both men and women was the "coathardie," a tight-fitting sleeved tunic or gown, closely fitted at the waist, that was of varying lengths for men—to the tops of the thighs, or to the bottom of the knees—and usually close to floor-length for women. The coathardie had a front slit, buttoned or laced from the neck to the waist. The sleeves, often embroidered or with strips of cloth sewn on for ornamentation, could also be slit and buttoned or laced part or all of the way up. Movement is clearly restricted by the clothing, although still loose and free enough to allow for the physical comedy called for in some of the farces of the period, such as *The Farce of the Tub*, discussed below.

Period books of manners include the useful *The Book of Keruynge* (The Book of Carving), printed in 1508 by Wynken de Worde (d. 1535) and devoted largely to the arts of the table, but the book also describes in detail how the chamberlain, who is enjoined to be "dyligent & clenly in his offyce," is to dress his lord and perform other duties. The book is based on earlier medieval sources, especially John Russell's (fifteenth century) *The Boke of Nurture*, written ("by me," says Russell) around 1430, and published in 1460. Russell served Humphrey, Duke of Gloucester (1391–1447), "a Prynce fulle royalle, with whom Vschere [Usher] in Chamber was Y, and Mershalle also in Halle [the dining hall]." The idea of being cleanly is very important in an era when high, strong odors, both of the kitchen and of the street, were the norm, and people seldom bathed. Very instructive on this point is Sarah Gordon's *Culinary Comedy in Medieval French Literature* (Purdue University Press, 2006).

All but forgotten today, the sixteenth-century Russian classic, the *Domostroi*, laid out rules of etiquette for the nobility that are instructive not only for life under the tsars, but for etiquette in western medieval Europe; the book's attitudes are medieval rather than Renaissance. Translated, edited, and introduced by the independent scholar of Russian history, Carolyn Johnston Pouncy, *The Domostroi: Rules for Russian Households in the Time of Ivan the Terrible* (Cornell University Press, 1994) is essential reading for any play set in these periods, when feudal attitudes and the separation of the sexes in separate household quarters prevailed, and with many similar rules and relationships all across the broad European landscape. There are, of course, specific Russian cultural attitudes and ways of conducting household affairs. The constant attention to religion counseled by the book's anonymous author(s) is also pervasive in Western Europe during the medieval / early Renaissance era. For instance, section 23, entitled *How Christians Should Heal Themselves of Illness and Every Affliction (This applies to Tsars, Princes, Chancery Personnel, Bishops, Priests, Monks and All Other Christians)*, instructs everyone to "seek a cure in God's mercy, in tears and prayer, by giving alms to the poor" as a means of interceding with God for a cure. And everyone is expected to lead a Christian life. Other religions are not mentioned, but we know that they were considered heathen and unworthy of God's approval, let alone divine blessing. Rules of etiquette and deference to those of higher rank are laid out clearly, along with detailed instructions on managing a household.

A person living in fifteenth-century France would undoubtedly have known what Boucher tells us in *20,000 Years of Fashion* about how hierarchy was displayed in clothing, Specific colors for the ubiquitous long gowns worn by the upper economic classes were reserved for specific professions or occupations: "black, red, and violet were often reserved for magistrates, judges, and officials. These colors might change according to the province: the magistrates of Charles of Burgundy wore black gowns…" Even if such things are never stated in a piece, they are essential background, part of the character's inner road map of the period.

Manners at court were formal. Anyone doing comedies from this era should know how to bow, curtsey, and show deference to people of higher rank. Men made a full or half bow, sometimes low, sometimes with less of an inclination, from the waist, bending both knees slightly. Women curtsied low, sometimes all the way to the ground, with one leg held behind the other. In less formal situations, women would keep the knees and feet touching, and bow slightly from the waist, bending the legs at the same time. These salutations were used both when entering and leaving the presence of a noble.

When paying homage to a lord or sovereign, men made a full genuflection, bringing the left leg behind the right and kneeling on the left leg; and women curtsied, kneeling on both legs before rising as gracefully as possible. The body remained straight up while performing the man's bow, with no inclination, but with the right hand held over the heart. It was customary to kiss the sometimes gloved hand of a monarch, and the ring of a high clergyman, and for men to kiss women's hands. But note that the lips would not actually touch the hand, but were merely held above it.

Medieval Comedies

In a fascinating book, *Répertoire du Théâtre Comique en France au Moyen-Age* (Repertoire of Comic Theater in Medieval France), published in 1886, the scholar and professor of medieval French literature at the University of Paris, Louis Petit de Julleville (1841–1900), informs us that we have the texts and performance data for more than two hundred and fifty medieval French comedies. The authors of most of them are unknown. They were done in every major city in France. We also have fifty more titles, of which the texts have not come down to us. This rich trove does not even take into account the many serious morality plays and tragedies that have survived the ravages of time.

Among the medieval era's genres is elegiac comedy, written in Latin in medieval France, in elegant rhymed couplets; most of them are dramatic poems rather than plays. The subject is often sexual conquest and/or love, as it is in *De tribus puellis* (The Three Girls), in which three young maidens vying for the title of best singer encounter the narrator of the story, and ask him to judge them. The plot is clearly based on the encounter of Paris and the three goddesses on Mount Ida in the ancient Greek myth, about which one of the girls even sings. The narrator has fallen in love with the third girl, and sleeps with her as the poem ends. *De vetulla* (On the Old Woman), is about an aging, amorous Ovid (43 BCE–17/18 CE), the Roman poet who wrote *Amores* (Love Affairs) and *Ars amatoria* (The Art of Love). Deceived by a go-between, he is so disappointed that he renounces love altogether. The ca. twenty texts that we have are from the thirteenth and fourteenth centuries, many of them adapted from Greek and Roman plays.

However, most of the surviving comic plays are from the fifteenth century. Before that, for several centuries of the long medieval era, there is a paucity of material, aside from the elegiac comedies, with only two from the fourteenth century and merely four from the thirteenth, when we may conjecture that theater began again to be a widespread form of entertainment, after a probable lapse of several centuries, beginning with the decline of the Roman empire. Professor Julleville gives summary information on all the plays.

The domestic or societal stories, such as the *fabliau* (comic tale) *Le vilain ânier* (The Peasant Muleteer)—more a dramatic poem than a play—appear to be as real as Neil Simon comedies are today. The theme of *Le vilain ânier* is upward social mobility, beginning to be talked about and experienced in the late medieval era. The play / poem is about a donkey driver who transports manure, enters a spice merchants' street, and faints at the unaccustomed odors; he is revived by the odor of dung, and is aware that he cannot, despite his wishes, rise in life to become a spice merchant.

Even in serious pieces dealing with the lives of saints, comic interludes called farces were stuck into the middle of the plays in order to retain the audience's no doubt flagging attention. Religion may have been pervasive, but it still had the fine power to bore, even in theatrical presentations. Like their early counterparts in the ancient world, medieval farces dealt in obscenity and lewdness, supposedly in order to disapprove of these manifestations of human nature. This is the opposite of the ancient attitudes about sex as a natural, and naturally amusing, aspect of human life; the medieval world is already more repressive than the Greek and Roman worlds. So if you do these plays, you have to awaken the side of yourself that is, or at least pretends to be, shocked at open displays of sexual feeling. This does not preclude a yearning, a longing for the love of a distant, unattainable love object, such as we see in medieval romances as the model of chivalry.

La Farce du Cuvier (The Farce of the Tub) and *La Farce de maître Pierre Pathelin* (The Farce of Master Pierre Pathelin)

Written anonymously around the mid-fifteenth century, *The Farce of the Tub* is a three-character play with a similarity to Shakespeare's *The Taming of the Shrew*, discussed in chapter nine.

A woman of spirit and independence, the Wife (Femme) of the put-upon Jacquinot, connives with her Mother (Mère) to force Jacquinot to sign a long list of domestic duties that he will perform, thus relieving Wife of the necessity of doing the work by herself, although she will still be in charge of it. Wife and Mother have thought of everything, or so they believe. Jacquinot will have to take care of the baby, make the bread and do the cooking, wash the dishes, clean the house, and help her do the laundry. If he is in any way derelict in his duty, Wife will punish him with a sound drubbing. This is a theme we will see again through the ages: the wife who threatens to beat her husband reappears, for instance, in Holberg's eighteenth-century comedy *Jeppe paa Bjerget eller den forvandlede Bonde* (Jeppe of the Hill; or The Transformed Peasant), discussed in chapter eleven.

The happy couple has a huge tub for washing the dirty laundry, and into the tub they pour boiling water in which they soak the linens. Because wringing out the huge sheets requires two people, Jacquinot and Wife are twisting a huge sheet when he accidentally, or perhaps by design, lets go of his end, and, kerplop! Wife falls into the deep tub, in which she thrashes about, unable to climb out. She begs him to help her, but he takes out the paper he had signed, and proceeds to go through his allotted tasks one by one, as slowly as he can, while she continues to scream for mercy. He cannot find anything on the list that would oblige him to help her get out of the tub. "That's not on my list," he says, in one of the world's first repeating catchphrases. Ten times she pleads, and ten times he says, "That's not on my list!" So there she stays until she agrees to abrogate the agreement. Like Katherine in *The Taming of the Shrew*, she promises to be humble and submissive and obedient to her husband's will. He pulls her out of the tub. But the curtain comes down on an uncertainty: Will she keep her promise? Jacquinot has the final line: "I'll be happy if she sticks to this bargain!"

Along with *The Farce of the Bathtub*, the most well known medieval French comedy is *La Farce de maître Pierre Pathelin* (The Farce of Master Pierre Pathelin), written around 1465. It was so popular that it spawned sequels, much like sitcom spinoffs. It is a political satire with five characters, and its performing time is about one hour, which is about what the actors could expect audiences of that era to stand for—literally: they stood or walked about as the actors performed on a raised platform.

The plot concerns the sly, conniving village lawyer, Pierre Pathelin; his wife, Guillemette; and a clothier, Guillaume Joceaulme, from whom Pathelin obtains six yards of cloth on credit. When Joceaulme shows up to collect his money, Pathelin, aided and abetted by Guillemette, pretends to be delirious. He raves on and on in several French dialects.

The hapless clothier gives up, and leaves. But he now takes Thubault Aignelet, a shepherd, to court. The shepherd has been stealing Joceaulme's sheep for years, but the clothier lacked proof, which he is now able to supply. As it turns out, the shepherd's lawyer is none other than Pathelin, who tells him to answer "Baa" to every question put to him by the Judge, the only honest character in the play. That way, the shepherd will seem insane, and the Judge will rule in his favor. Of course, the clothier recognizes Pathelin, now miraculously recovered, and tries to sue him at the same time. This confuses and befuddles the well-meaning Judge, who, in his discombobulated state, rules against Joceaulme. When Pathelin tries to collect his legal fee from Aignelet, the shepherd only answers, "Baa." Thus is the biter bit, in a plot typical of such farces: "le trompeur trompé" (the deceiver deceived).

A line from *The Farce of Master Pierre Pathelin*, which the Judge uses as Pathelin tries to distract him, became a famous catchphrase: "Mais revenons à nos moutons!" (But let's get back to our sheep); in other words, let's return to the subject under discussion, let's get back on track.

The urbane citizens of medieval France found the physical and verbal comedy in farce funny, and the situations were supposed to reflect conditions in their own lives. The stories date from at least the Greek and Roman days. Half-remembered, or perhaps unearthed by some monk who gave the old Latin plays to an interested friend, the plays were then adapted to contemporary circumstances. The simplicity of medieval plays, without subplots, makes the actions easy to figure out, and the objectives and obstacles are self-evident.

IX

The Sixteenth Century: Italian Renaissance, Tudor, Elizabethan, and Shakespearean Comedy

Movement, Clothing, and Manners

Men and women wore a long-sleeved shirt that fitted over the head as an undergarment—silk for the rich, linen for the poor. Men's shirts were often thigh-length. Some came with ruffs attached. Tights, often seen in Shakespearean productions, were ubiquitous.

Over their shirts, or smocks, women wore either a "kirtle," a kind of floor-length, fitted gown; or else an upper garment called a "bodice" and a "petticoat" (skirt). The bodice, which was like a combination of a bra and a vest, came together in a point at the front bottom, and was either laced or fastened with hooks and eyes; it could be sleeveless or sleeved, and had a flattening effect on the bosom. And they wore ruffs around their necks. To achieve a fashionable, bell-like shape below the waist, women wore "farthingales," which could be beautifully embroidered and ornately decorated. The farthingale was a skirt that was ribbed with hoops to make it flare out.

Men sported long cloaks or short capes, sometimes with sleeves, and doublet and hose (tights); and they, too, often wore ruffs, or elaborate collars. The doublet, a close-fitting jacket with buttons down the front, was actually worn by both men and women, who wore theirs over a sleeveless bodice. The doublet was fastened to the hose with lace ties, called points.

Clergymen and older men often wore long gowns, sometimes with long sleeves with openings near the top through which their sleeved arms fitted; when standing, hands were clasped in front, as in portraits of Elizabeth's venerable ministers of state.

An important book of manners and etiquette essential to understanding and reproducing the behavior of the period is Baldassare Castiglione's (1478–1529) *The Book of the Courtier*, first translated into English in 1561. Its principal point is that broad knowledge and attainments, as well as the art of elegance, refined manners, and good deportment require *sprezzatura*, which means concealing artifice so that everything one does appears natural and unforced.

Equally important is the *Galateo, ovvero dei Costumi* by Giovanni della Casa, Archbishop of Benevento (1503–1556). In 1576, Robert Peterson of Lincoln's Inn, about whom very little is known, published his translation into English as *Galateo, Of Manners and Behavior in Familiar Conversation*. The book was meant for people of all social classes. The word *galateo* comes from the name of a courteous Neapolitan doctor who wrote a book on education, and whose tone della Casa adopted, as he himself tells us, when writing his own book. It became so famous that the word passed into the Italian language with the meaning of "a book of etiquette, good manners, and breeding."

For the Elizabethan man's bow used for curtain calls, at court, or in any formal situation, put the left foot forward and the right foot back, while gracefully bending the right knee (breaking the leg, or "making a leg"), and simultaneously bowing from the waist and placing the right hand over the heart, all in a single elegantly executed movement.

Women curtsied in a similar fashion by placing the right leg almost directly behind the left, lifting the skirts delicately at the sides with both hands, and taking the body down without bowing forward, while nodding the head very slightly.

Elizabethan clothing can be difficult to move in, because it can be so elaborate, with collars and cuffs, sometimes made of lace, and ruffs being all the fashion. But when designed for the stage, it should allow the physical comedy and nimbleness called for in such plays as *The Taming of the Shrew*, Thomas Dekker's (1572–1632) *The Shoemaker's Holiday, or the Gentle Craft* (1599) and *The Honest Whore* (1604) or Ben Jonson's (1532–1637) *Volpone* (1605–1606), and *Bartholomew Fair* (1614).

The Italian Renaissance Comedy of Machiavelli: *La mandragola*

Along with their rediscovery of ancient Greek and Roman philosophy and literature, the late Medieval / early Renaissance Italians rejoiced again in the ancient Roman comedies of Plautus and Terence, whom playwrights such as Pietro Aretino adapted for the Italian theater. As Italian comedies both in their original language and in translation spread throughout Europe and England, they virtually shaped theater for the next centuries. In particular, Niccolò Machiavelli's comedy *La mandragola* (The Mandrake [Root]), produced around 1518, was a seminal work, much admired and often imitated, for the intricacy of its plotting and the realism of its characters. The intricate plotting of this wry, ironic, almost cynical comedy inspired the structure and stories of Shakespeare's *All's Well That Ends Well*, *Twelfth Night*, and *Measure for Measure*, and the comedies of later writers.

In 1513, Machiavelli wrote *Il principe* (The Prince), the book that gave rise to the adjective Machiavellian, a byword for sinister, cynical, and underhanded backstairs political plotting and maneuvering, for using people mercilessly and deceptively, and for employing any means necessary to achieve one's own ends, including immoral, unethical, and even criminal proceedings. Although the book is descriptive rather than prescriptive, it was almost immediately misinterpreted as being the latter, and Machiavelli was seen as advocating immoral ideas and precepts. Shakespeare's wicked, manipulative Richard III, and Iago, evil incarnate, are embodiments of what came to be called Machiavellianism. Whether or not Shakespeare actually read Machiavelli is an open question: Shakespeare had access to the private libraries of his noble patrons, and read voraciously when he could, but there was no Elizabethan translation. It is possible that he read Machiavelli in Italian, but in any case the Florentine's name and ideas were well known, often in distorted, clichéd, misunderstood form.

Over the centuries, *La mandragola* has been denounced as immoral. As it ends, everyone is happy, but evil triumphs over accepted morality and the sacred bond of marriage. And the happiness is based on the lies the characters tell each other. The piece almost begs the question, can true happiness be the result of such falsehood?

The main theme of the play is one common throughout the history of comedy, that of cuckoldry. Shorn of some of its complications, the story of the play is as follows: The beautiful Lucrezia is the virtuous wife of Messer Nicia, a naïve and credulous lawyer. Callimacho is almost beside himself with desire for her. Messer Nicia is passionate about wanting a child, and, as a last resort, has determined to consult a doctor. When the conniving Callimacho hears of this, he poses as a medico, assisted by his unpleasant, parasitical servant Ligurio. Callimacho gives the befuddled Nicia a drug distilled from the mandrake root that he says will make the barren Lucrezia fertile, but he warns Nicia that it will kill the first man to make love to her. Nicia must therefore administer the medication, then find a man to make love to his wife before he does. Callimacho, a master of disguise, makes himself up as a callow youth, and allows himself to be "entrapped" by Nicia into entering Lucrezia's bedroom. Once the schemer is there, her mother and a venal friar, Fra Timoteo, who has been bribed and suborned by Callimacho, and has informed the mother about the nefarious results of the mandrake-root potion, persuade Lucrezia that making love to this anonymous unknown swain is the best course of action. To Nicia's delight, Lucrezia becomes pregnant. Callimacho, posing as Nicia's friend, now becomes a frequent guest in the house. He proves a delightful companion to Nicia, and also manages to become Lucrezia's secret lover, since she is as madly in lust with him as he with her. And as the play ends, everyone is going to church!

Tudor Farce: *Gammer Gurton's Needle, Ane Pleasant Satyre of the Thrie Estaitis, Jack Juggler,* and Udall's *Ralph Roister Doister*

Among the most well known and occasionally revived late medieval, Tudor-era plays is *Gammer Gurton's Needle*, presumably produced in 1533, depicting the life of the lower economic classes, the peasants and serfs. And in a rare example of a satirical morality play, we have the only extant Scottish morality play and the only theatrical work by the Scottish nobleman, Sir David Lyndsay (1490?–1555?), *Ane Pleasant Satyre of the Thrie Estaitis* (An Amusing Satire of the Three Estates; 1540). The play is a clarion call for the elimination of corruption in the body politic and the ecclesiastical establishment. The three estates are the Barons, the Bishops, and the Merchants. Allegorical scenes alternate with farcical interludes, as Diligence summons the three estates before Divine Correction, recently come home to Scotland after a very long absence. Among other characters vying for the favors of the Three Estates are three of the Vices: Deceit, Flattery, and Falsehood, all disguised as clergymen. The Bishops have arrested two of the Virtues, Charity and Verity, as heretics, but they are freed by Divine Correction. Finally, King Humanity, aroused from his slumbers, convenes a parliament of the Three Estates, and the Barons and Merchants agree to reform, and to drive away the vices Sensuality and Covetice, who had led them to the parliament in the greedy hope of gain. But the Bishops are accused of various vices, and of being jesters in disguise, and they must repent the error of their ways. Eventually, Deceit and Falsehood are hanged for their crimes, along with Theft, but Flattery, being a mere fool, is allowed to escape their fate. Folly closes the play with an epilogue, in which he asserts that "the number of fools is infinite." When James V (1512–1542), King of Scotland, saw the play, he loved it, and immediately exhorted the clergy "to reform their fashions and manner of living."

Around the time Nicholas Udall was writing his famous farce *Ralph Roister Doister*, many similar plays, now lost to us, were popular. Some anonymous works survive, usually in partial form, such as *Jack Juggler*, an interlude, meant to be done between the acts of some longer play, now lost. Written around 1553, it was not published until probably 1562; both dates are conjectural. Apparently based on Plautus's *Amphytrion*, a retelling of an ancient Greek myth, the farce shows that ancient Roman culture was by now in the process of being revived in England, and that Italian Renaissance ideas were beginning to travel abroad during the late medieval period. In fact, the prologue to this interlude talks of Cicero and classical learning.

In *Amphytrion*, a myth used any number of times and in many versions since Plautus wrote his comedy, Jupiter is in love with the mortal, Alcmena, wife of the general Amphitryon of Thebes. Amphytrion is away fighting a war, and Jupiter transforms himself into the imposing, handsome warrior, coming down to earth to seduce Alcmena. The god Mercury, his sly son, accompanies him disguised as Amphitryon's slave Sosia, who had gone off with Amphitryon to the war. Jupiter succeeds in seducing Alcmena, and when Sosia and Amphitryon return home, Mercury helps Jupiter by a delaying tactic, duping Sosia into believing that he, Mercury, is actually Sosia. Jupiter and Amphitryon accuse each other of being the false Amphitryon, but the truth is at last revealed. Amphitryon forgives his wife, and Alcmena gives birth to twin sons: one is Jupiter's, the other Amphitryon's.

The title character of the anonymous early Tudor farce, Jack Juggler, is a kind of Satan personage from the morality plays, based in this case on Plautus's whimsical trickster god Mercury. When the stupid, incredibly gullible pageboy Jenkin Careaway is sent by his master, a "gallant" named Boungrace, to accompany his mistress, the "Gentlewoman" Dame Coye, home to dinner, he is accosted by the roguish scamp Jack Juggler, who loves practical jokes, and at the same time, prays to "Christ and Saint Stephen." Jack persuades Jenkin that he, Jack, is really Jenkin, and that Jenkin's errand has already been accomplished, and his mistress has arrived safely home. The befuddled page therefore goes home again, only to be met by his master with a sound drubbing for neglecting his duty. Such is early Renaissance—and ancient Roman—humor!

In 1869, the English scholar, writer, and professor of English literature, Edward Arber (1836–1912), who had a particular interest in old manuscripts, published an edition of *Ralph Roister Doister* "carefully edited from the unique copy now at Eton College." He also wrote a biographical essay about the polymath Nicholas Udall: "A Brief Note of the Life, Works, and Times of Nicholas Udall, M.A., Teacher, Dramatist, Translator, Preacher. In succession Master of Eton College, Rector of Braintree, Prebend of Windsor, Rector of Calborne, and Master of Westminster School." It includes the following information about wages and living conditions, useful for any play set in this period:

> The Rev. Dr. Goodford, the present Provost of Eton, has most kindly afforded me interesting information obtained by him from the MS. records of the College; viz., the Audit Rolls and the Bursar's Books, respecting Udall's connection with Eton:
> The salary of the Master at Eton was then £10 a year, or fifty shillings for each of the four terms. In addition, he received 20s. for his 'livery,' and other small sums, as for obits (*i.e.* attending masses for the dead) [*e.g.* Udall received for obits, 14s. 8d. in 1535, and the same in 1536]; and for candles and ink for the boys [*e.g.* Udall received for these purposes, 23s. 4d. in 1537, and the same in 1538.] If the assumed multiple of 13 truly express the relatively greater purchasing power of gold and silver more then than now: the salary and emoluments cannot be considered excessive.

In other words, multiply the sums by thirteen, and you arrive at the base salary of £10 as being worth £130 in the Victorian era, which in contemporary terms would be approximately £12,000 or $20,000 per annum, not very much, as Professor Arber says.

As tutor to Princess Mary (1515–1558), one day to be Queen Mary I, Udall observed women's education at first hand, and the information that follows is also useful for anyone doing projects set in this period. As Professor Arber tells us:

In his *Pref. to John*, partly translated by Princess Mary, partly by Rev. F. Malet, D.D.; Udall gives us the following account of female education in his day: which can only, however, apply to a few women, like Elizabeth [the future queen, 1533–1603], Mary, and Lady Jane Grey [1536/1537?–1554].

"But nowe in this gracious and blisseful tyme of knowledge, in whiche it hath pleased almightye God to reuele and shewe abrode the lyght of his moste holye ghospell: what a noumbre is there of noble women (especially here in this realme of Englande,) yea and howe many in the yeares of tender vyrginitiee, not only aswel seen and as familiarly trade in the Latine and Greke tounges, as in theyr owne mother language: but also both in all kindes of prophane litterature, and liberall artes, exactly studied and exercised, and in the holy Scriptures and Theologie so ripe, that they are able aptely cunnyngly, and with much grace eyther to indicte or translate into the vulgare tongue, for the publique instruccion and edifying of the vnlearned multitude [...] It is nowe no newes in Englande to see young damisels in nobles houses and in the Courtes of Princes, in stede of cardes and other instrumentes of idle trifleyng, to haue continually in her handes, eyther Psalmes, Omelies, and other deuoute meditacions, or elles Paules Epistles, or some booke of holye Scripture matiers: and as familiarlye both to reade or reason thereof in Greke, Latine, Frenche, or Italian, as in Englishe."

Written in rhymed couplets, *Ralph Roister Doister* was an immediate success when it was produced, probably at Eton, where the boys presumably performed it in ca. 1553. This farce has a lot in common with ancient Roman farces, and may have been adapted from a lost play by Plautus or Terence. The prologue informs us that we are about to see a moral tale. In act 1, scene 1, Matthew Merygreke, Ralph's conniving friend, comes in singing lazily, thinking that the world owes him a living, and that all he has to do is persuade his friends to help him out with whatever he needs. In act 1, scene 2, the almost willfully naïve Ralph Roister Doister—easy prey because he is upset, in need of help, and gullible—and his somewhat unsavory, manipulative friend meet.

Christian Custance is a wealthy widow affianced to Gawyn Goodluck, a rich merchant. Matthew Merygreke, a friend, or rather a hanger-on of Ralph Roister Doister, who gives him money, persuades Ralph to woo her. When he presents himself in the most pompous manner possible, his suit is unsuccessful, so Ralph and his friends try to abduct her. But their plot is foiled by her servants. The timely arrival of Goodluck just afterward ensures that the play will end happily ever after.

Performing Shakespeare's Comedies

William Shakespeare's (1564–1616) comedies include the six plays that we now call problem plays, which are tragicomic, ironic, and moralistic: *The Merchant of Venice* (1596–1597); *Twelfth Night, or What You Will* (1601); *Measure for Measure* (1603); *All's Well That Ends Well* (1606–1607); *The Winter's Tale* (1609–1610); and *The Tempest* (1610–1611).

The outright comedies, with happy endings, and elements of farce and sometimes of fantasy, are *The Two Gentlemen of Verona* (1589–1591); *The Taming of the Shrew* (1590–1591); *The Comedy of Errors* (1594); *Love's Labor's Lost* (1594–1595); *A Midsummer Night's Dream* (1595); *The Merry Wives of Windsor* (1597–1598), the only comedy set in Shakespeare's own era and country; *Much Ado About Nothing* (1598–1599); and *As You Like It* (1599–1600).

The Shakespearean actor is immediately confronted with two tasks: to bring a character to life in all its reality and profundity; and to deal with Shakespeare's gorgeous, but archaic language, Early Modern English, whether prose or verse. In fact, the language is very accessible, as Patrick Tucker points out in his very interesting book *Secrets of Acting Shakespeare: The Original Approach* (Routledge, 2002). Other books that will help you deal with the language include Cicely Berry's *The Actor and the Text* (Applause, 1992); Peter Hall's *Shakespeare's Advice to the Players* (Theatre Communications Group, 2003); David and Ben Crystal's *Shakespeare's Words: A Glossary and Language Companion* (Penguin, 2002); and my own volume, *Stagecraft* (Limelight, 2011).

Shakespeare most often uses iambic pentameter for his verse. An *iamb* (pronounced "I am"; but "iambic" is pronounced "eye AM bik") is a *foot* (unit of verse) containing one weakly stressed syllable followed by one more strongly stressed syllable; there are five iambs (or iambic feet) in a line of iambic pentameter, in the following rhythm: te TUM / te TUM / te TUM / te TUM / te TUM. In general, you must ignore that rhythm, which will be there anyway—the audience will hear it—and just speak the lines so they make sense.

Shakespeare frequently writes *blank verse*; that is, unrhymed verse. When he does use rhymes, as with the rhyming couplets that frequently punctuate the endings of scenes, you should not usually stress them. As with the rhythm, the audience will hear them. However, there are moments when you must be aware that the rhymes are there for deliberate effect. And rhymes, like Shakespeare's puns and other wordplay, can be a source of humor, as Kristin Linklater points out in *Freeing Shakespeare's Voice: The Actor's Guide to Talking the Text* (Theatre Communications Group, 2002).

In act 3, scene 1 of *The Comedy of Errors*, for instance, the "rhymes are sprayed about like bird-shot," as she says. Based on Plautus's *The Two Menaechme*, the plot of *The Comedy of Errors* hinges on the fact that Antipholus and his slave Dromio have traveled from Ephesus to Syracuse, and that, unknown to each, they have twins who live there. The Syracusan Antipholus and Dromio are married to Adriana and Luce, causing further complications, which are only resolved when the father of the twin Antipholus brothers, Aegon, sees them together, and sets matters to right. The twins were separated in a shipwreck, and he is thrilled to be able to see them again. In this scene, with its naughty jokes about farting, Antipholus of Ephesus and his Dromio want to get into Antipholus of Syracuse's house:

ANTIPHOLUS OF EPHESUS. Go fetch me something, I'll break ope the gate.
DROMIO OF SYRACUSE. (*Within*) Break any breaking here and I'll break your knave's pate.
DROMIO OF EPHESUS. A man may break a word with you, sir, and words are but wind. / Ay, and break it in your face so he break it not behind.

DROMIO OF SYRACUSE. (*Within*) It seems thou want'st breaking: out upon thee, hind.

The fast pace of this exchange and of the rest of this rhymed scene should delight the audience, and make the scene easy to play, as each Dromio, not having seen his twin, vies for verbal position and plays the conflicting actions. As with every comedy, tempo-rhythm is one of the most important aspects of keeping the play moving forward. The jokes are played as part of the action.

Shakespeare's incisively drawn characters are wonderful to work on, psychologically complicated and multifaceted. And you use the same system for creating characters, rehearsing, and performing as you do with any other play.

The comedies are full of slapstick farcical exchanges and physical bits, as well as of hints of the comedy of manners that was to develop in the following centuries into a full-blown subgenre. We have the witty exchanges of Benedict and Beatrice in *Much Ado About Nothing*, for example, and the farcical verbal and physical sparring of Katherine and Petruccio in *The Taming of the Shrew*, discussed below, as well as the outrageously farcical wedding scene when Petruccio arrives to claim his astounded bride.

If your character speaks with an accent, like the French and Welsh characters in *Henry V* or *The Merry Wives of Windsor*, for example, you must do the accents with especially good diction, because the language is sometimes hard for the audience to grasp.

In general, good diction and strong vocal energy are essential. This requires diaphragmatic support, and the energetic use of the tongue and lips, without overdoing articulation, since you don't want to sound artificial. Still, the articulation of the consonants (when one part of the vocal apparatus touches another) has to be clean and crisp, as in the sounds of "d," "t," "b," and "p," for instance. An excellent book on clear stage speech is Edith Skinner's *Speak with Distinction* (Applause Theatre Books, 1990). And for more on these accents, see my own *Teach Yourself Accents: The British Isles* (2013) and *Teach Yourself Accents: Europe* (2014).

And do see the wonderful DVD of *Acting in Shakespearean Comedy* made by the English actress Janet Suzman for the BBC, along with her book, *Acting with Shakespeare: Three Comedies* (both from Applause, 1996). Her principal point is that the basic actor's approach to both tragedy and comedy is the same: you plunge yourself into the given circumstances, explore relationships, and decide how to play the character's actions. "You search for the truth of the matter," she says.

It is important to understand the deportment and manners of the Elizabethan period, especially if a production is set in that time. But even when it is not, a certain mindset regarding the rightness of monarchy as a political system is implied in the text, and underlies the sociocultural attitudes and the behavior of the characters.

Playing Malvolio in *Twelfth Night*

Created by Richard Burbage in 1602, Malvolio in *Twelfth Night* has been interpreted by many famous actors, and in 1971, I had the pleasure of playing the arrogant, pedantic, priggish, puritanical steward of Olivia's household in the journeyman production at the American Shakespeare Festival in Stratford, CT.

I sought the advice of the magnificent Morris Carnovsky (1897–1992), who was playing Prospero in *The Tempest* that season. He had been a member of the seminal Group Theatre in the 1930s, which practiced the Stanislavsky system, and he was also an acting teacher. As Prospero, he was uncannily real in his performance. (I understudied Sebastian and Antonio, and watched him from the back of the house every time.) His deep, rolling baritone encompassed every note and tone, from the plaintive to the thundering raging volcano, to the soothing tender loving voice of a father with his daughter. He used personal substitutions so well that when he talked of "my brother, called Antonio," you could almost see his brother, so clear were his feelings about the man who had betrayed him.

Carnovsky had played Feste at the American Shakespeare Festival, and Malvolio at the Globe in San Diego. When I asked him how he approached the part, he wrinkled up his face so that he looked like a prune, and I burst out laughing. He then proceeded to be very prissy, straightening out an imaginary bow tie with total concentration, and looking around him the whole time, to see who might be looking at him. In short, he became Malvolio, every inch a narcissist, and showed me by example how to behave. Then he said, "Remember, to Malvolio, everyone smells slightly." This very imaginative, Stanislavskian advice struck a responsive chord immediately, and I did indeed adopt it. Even Olivia, with whom Malvolio is infatuated, has a slight unpleasant odor about her, as far as he is concerned, so that I kept my distance from her, and was wary even when approaching her. This advice was also very sound for a play set in an era when people did not bathe or wash much, if at all.

Malvolio has more than once put people of higher rank in their place, and they will have their revenge. In act 2, scene 5, Olivia's uncle, Sir Toby Belch, a Falstafffian toper; Sir Andrew Aguecheek, his not overly bright friend; Fabian, a servant and a friend to Sir Toby; and Olivia's servant Maria, one of those clever maids descended from ancient comedy, leave a letter they have forged in Olivia's handwriting lying where Malvolio can find it. The four hide in the garden to see the results of their joke.

The theatrical convention common to comedies of all eras is that the protagonist is unaware of the pandemonium going on behind his or her back. The convention is quite funny in this play, as Sir Toby rages and has to be restrained by Fabian. The trick for the protagonist in playing such a scene is to be so involved in the immediate circumstances and so self-involved that the conventional unawareness becomes plausible and acceptable to the audience. I found this easy to do as Malvolio, because he is such a narcissistic egotist. At every interruption from the others, continuing my stream-of-consciousness inner monologue, I became mesmerized and lost in my thoughts and dreams of love and power, although some of the interruptions are so brief that it was not necessary to do even that much. We all had to be very aware of picking up cues, and dovetailing the responses, of not stepping on laughs, nor waiting for them, and of keeping the scene moving forward. The effect of this scene depends on its tempo-rhythm, and on everyone working together, a true example of the importance of ensemble playing.

The Great Comedians of Shakespeare's Day

One of the great comic actors, much celebrated in his day and long thereafter, much loved and much mourned at his death, was Richard Tarlton or Tarleton (1530–1588), popularly known as Dick Tarleton. As a member of the theater group, the Queen's Men, he amused Queen Elizabeth, and he was given the post of Court Jester until he overstepped the bounds and made jokes about Raleigh and Leicester. He was known for both the naturalness of his characterizations and for his witty responses to hecklers, to whom he would ad lib rhymes. After his death, a famous book of jokes, *Tarlton's Jokes*, was published in several small volumes, but whether they were actually his is conjectural: his name was probably used to sell the books. Ben Jonson said of him, "The self-same words spoken by another would hardly move a man to smile, which uttered by him would force a sad soul to laughter."

The virtuosic Will Kemp, also spelled Kempe (1585–1602), considered his successor, was often compared to him, but was apparently a more accomplished, less crude actor. Known for his skills in clowning and physical comedy, as well as for his extemporal wit and ad libs, Will Kemp wrote a delightful, lightly humorous book that is a mine of hilarity, *Kemps Nine Daies Wonder: Performed in a Daunce from London to Norwich*, published in 1600. To win a bet, he had actually danced his way from the capital to the great provincial town, taking pauses for rest and refreshment, and doing his "morrice" dances, for which he received money from eager and appreciative spectators who thronged the countryside for the event. The occasion for this was his retirement from the stage, and it was a last sort of tour by someone who was fairly well traveled, having performed at stately Elsinore Castle for Christian IV, King of Denmark (1588–1648).

An adept and nimble dancer, Kemp was a master of the jig, which was a short musical afterpiece, or sometimes a curtain raiser in the

Elizabethan theater, consisting often of obscene or ribald songs and dances. It included the dance that was itself also called a jig, a lively one in 3/4 or 3/8 time, expressive of excitement and joy, as in the traditional Irish jig. The lively song performed while doing such a dance was called a jig as well. This song and dance number, of which contemporary Irish step dancing is reminiscent, was used in a number of Shakespearean comedies.

Kemp's little book is interesting not only for the amusement it affords, and as an autobiographical picture of the great comic actor, with his sly sense of humor, but also for a glimpse at aspects of the era's culture. We have this interesting revelation, about how pickpockets apprehended during a performance in a London theater could expect to be treated:

> In this towne [Burntwood] two Cut-purses were taken, that with other two of their companions followed mee from Lōdon (as many better disposed persons did): but these two dy-doppers [Elizabethan slang: a "dopper," originally "dobber" in the Norfolk dialect, is a penis, and also a fool and a knave; the word "dy" means double, so these are double fools] gaue out when they were apprehended, that they had laid wagers and betted about my iourney; wherupon the Officers bringing them to my Inne, I iustly denyed their acquaintance, sauing that I remembred one of them to be a noted Cut-purse, such a one as we tye to a poast on our stage, for all people to wonder at, when at a play they are taken pilfring. This fellow, and his half-brother, being found with the deed, were sent to Iayle [jail].

For Shakespeare, Kemp most probably created the roles of the Grave-digger in *Hamlet*, Launce in *Two Gentlemen of Verona*, Launcelot Gobbo in *The Merchant of Venice*, Dogberry in *Much Ado About Nothing*, Peter in *Romeo and Juliet*, Touchstone in *As You Like It*, and possibly Falstaff in *Henry V*—although the part may have been played by John Lowin [1576–1659], who had apparently created Falstaff in the two *Henry IV* plays and would again in *The Merry Wives of Windsor*. Kemp played

Justice Shallow in *The Second Part of Henry the Fourth*. And he appears as a character in the third of the anonymous *Parnassus Plays*, discussed below.

Shakespeare and Kemp did not always see eye to eye. Hamlet's famous advice to the players in act 3, scene 2 includes the following admonition on how *not* to play comedy. It may refer to Kemp's unruly adlibbing ways—anything for a laugh, especially if it was obscene. That's not much different from what some comedians and comic actors do nowadays:

> And let those that play the clowns speak no more than is set down for them, for there be of them that will themselves laugh, to set on some quantity of barren spectators to laugh too, though in the mean time some necessary question of the play be then to be considered; that's villainous, and shows a most pitiful ambition in the fool that uses it.

One of the reasons for ad libs is that the actors had little time to rehearse or memorize sometimes complicated material, and worked from cue sheets or sides, as we now call them, in which their lines and the cues preceding them were written out by the prompter, the equivalent of a modern stage manager. They had heard the play read in its entirety by the playwright, and a list of the scenes in order was presumably posted backstage, to be consulted during performances. So actors had to play what they were given, much as a contemporary film or television actor has to audition with sides without ever seeing a complete script. For more on the subject of working in the Elizabethan English theater, see the magisterial *Actors and Acting in Shakespeare's Time: The Art of Stage Playing* (Cambridge University Press, 2010) by John H. Astington.

The third great Elizabethan comedian, successor to Kemp, was Robert Armin (1563–1615). He created such roles as the Drunken Porter in *Macbeth*, Touchstone in *As You Like It*, Thersites in *Troilus and Cressida*, and Feste in *Twelfth Night*. He was known for his intelligent, if cynical wit and his melancholy, and was considered perfect for these roles. He also wrote comedies, and performed in plays by Ben Jonson.

The Parnassus Plays

The trilogy known as *The Parnassus Plays* (1597–1601/2) is of uncertain authorship. The lost manuscripts of the first two of these satirical comedies, *The Pilgrimage to Parnassus* and *The Return from Parnassus*, were unearthed in a collection of papers at the Bodleian Library at Oxford University only in the late nineteenth century, as the scholar, librarian, and historian William Dunn Macray (1826–1916) informs us in the preface to the 1886 edition, which he edited. The third play, *The Return from Parnassus (Part II), or The Scourge of Simony*, was popular enough to have been printed twice in 1606. The plays were called "Christmas toys," and were written and performed at the university as part of the season's festivities, much in the manner of lampoons mounted by Harvard's Hasty Pudding Club, a descendant of these Elizabethan university theater organizations.

The trilogy concerns the wanderings of two scholars, Studioso and his cousin Philomusus (he who loves the Muses), whose father, Consiliodorus, sends on their way with advice reminiscent of that given to Laertes by Polonius in *Hamlet*. The two wayfarers set off for Mt. Parnassus to pursue learning and the scholarly life. But they find they cannot make a living as scholars, so they get involved in all kinds of other schemes in order to make money. In the course of their wanderings, they meet Luxurioso, and Stupido, who adores Shakespeare. And they run into the famous actors, Will Kemp and Richard Burbage (1568–1619), creator of such roles as Hamlet, Othello, and Malvolio for Shakespeare, his friend and fellow sharer in the Lord Chamberlain's, later the King's Men (the company's name was changed in 1603, when James I mounted the throne). We have one of the few glimpses of these actors as their contemporaries saw them, in a way similar to what one might see on a *Saturday Night Live* skit. Eventually, the two students make their way home from Parnassus, having learned much about life and less about academic knowledge than they expected; they find that the latter is less than useless.

Act 4, scene 3 in *The Return from Parnassus (Part II)* with Burbage and Kemp is very interesting, because they make an attempt at training Studioso and Philomusus in the art of acting. This is a satire of the well known scene in which Hamlet instructs the players and gives them the famous advice on how to "speak the speech." And we learn something about how master actors worked with their apprentices: not so much on character, although there is some of that, as on the delivery of lines, with proper intonation patterns, pauses, and so on. Their method is also the one autocratic pre-Stanislavskian nineteenth-century directors used when staging plays: They gave not only movements but also actual line readings to the actors, who were expected to reproduce them exactly. In the short rehearsal periods allowed during the Elizabethan age, this was no doubt an expedient and even necessary way of working:

> BURBAGE. M[aster]. Stud[ioso]., I pray you take some part in this booke, and act it, that I may see what will fit you best. I thinke your voice would serue for Hieronimo: obserue how I act it, and then imitate mee.
>
> STUDIOSO. 'Who call[s] Hieronomo from his naked bed, And,' &c. [Hieronymo is a leading character in Thomas Kyd's (1558–1594) popular revenge melodrama, *The Spanish Tragedy*, written sometime between 1582 and 1592; it had numerous revivals and was often parodied.]
>
> BURBAGE. You will do well after a while.
>
> KEMPE. Now for you, me thinkes you should belong to my tuition, and your face me thinkes would be good for a foolish Mayre or a foolish iustice of peace. Marke me. 'Forasmuch as there be two states of a common wealth, the one of peace, the other of tranquility; two states of warre, the one of discord, the other of dissention; two states of an incorporation, the one of the Aldermen, the other of the Brethren; two states of magistrates, the one of gouerning, the other of bearing rule; now, as I said euen now, for a good thing cannot be said too often, Vertue is the shooing-horne of iustice, that is, vertue is the shooing-horne of doing well, that

is, vertue is the shooing-horne of doing iustly, it behooueth mee and is my part to commend this shooing-horne vnto you. I hope this word shooing-horne doth not offend any of you, my worshipfull brethren, for you, beeing the worshipfull headsmen of the towne, know well what the horne meaneth. Now therefore I am determined not onely to teach but also to instruct, not onely the ignorant but also the simple, not onely what is their duty towards their betters, but also what is their dutye towards their superiours.' Come, let me see how you can doe; sit downe in the chaire.

> [The phrase *a foolish justice of peace* is an allusion to Justice Shallow, the part created by Kemp in *The Second Part of Henry the Fourth*. The word *shoeing-horn* means something that facilitates an action, like the implement that helps someone put on a shoe. In Elizabethan slang, it also means a go-between or a decoy. The word *horne* (horn) itself means an erect penis; it also refers to the horns of cuckoldry.]

PHILOMUSUS. 'Forasmuch as there be,' &c.

> [Philomusus begins to recite from the Bible, Jeremiah 10: 6: "Forasmuch as there is none like thee, O Lord; thou art great and thy name is great in might."]

KEMPE. Thou wilt do well in time, if thou wilt be ruled by thy betters, that is by my selfe, and such graue Aldermen of the playhouse as I am.

BURBAGE. I like your face and the proportion of your body for Richard the 3; I pray, M[aster]. Phil[omusus]., let me see you act a little of it.

PHILOMUSUS. 'Now is the winter of our discontent Made glorious summer by the sonne of Yorke.'

BURBAGE. Very well, I assure you. Well, M. Phil. and M. Stud., wee see what ability you are of: I pray walke with vs to our fellows, and weele agree presently.

Scene Analysis: The Wooing Scene in *The Taming of the Shrew*

Shakespeare's Bawdy: A Literary and Psychological Essay and a Comprehensive Glossary (E. P. Dutton & Co., 1947) by the prolific New Zealand-British lexicographer Eric Partridge (1894–1979) is a brilliantly informed book about the vocabulary of sex and obscenity in Elizabethan English. It's fun to read all by itself, as well as being a useful reference tool. All the wordplay in the excerpt from act 2, scene 1, from one of Shakespeare's earliest plays, *The Taming of the Shrew* (1590–1591), presented below, is amply explained by Partridge, but some of it is quite obvious without explanation, because we have retained some of the same sexual slang to this day ("cock" meaning "penis," for example). There are however many examples throughout Shakespeare that require the kind of elucidation Partridge provides. The Bard of Avon had a very sexy sense of humor and wasn't afraid to be vulgar or to make lewd jests.

The sociocultural attitudes seemingly displayed in this farcical romantic comedy strike most of us nowadays as abysmal and contemptible: misogyny, with its assumptions about the inferiority of women, and their evil nature, based on the story of Eve in Genesis succumbing to the wiles of Satan; woman viewed as chattel belonging to man, whom in their Christian marriage vows they swear to love, honor, and obey. But Harold Bloom thinks it a misinterpretation to see the play as misogynistic, because this evil and socially regressive attitude is offset by the mockery Katherine makes of it in her speech near the end of the play about being submissive and obedient, in which the heavy irony of her pronouncements should be made clear by the actress, seeming obedience being a form of manipulation and control, in the service of getting what one wants. " "True obedience" here is considerably less sincere than it purports to be, or even if sexual politics are to be invoked, it is as immemorial as the Garden of Eden," says Harold Bloom in *Shakespeare: The Invention of the Human* (Riverhead Books, 1998), and he concludes his discussion of this play by telling us that Shakespeare is suggesting that, compared to men, "women have the truer sense of reality." Modern audiences tend to be on Katherine's side. Her spiritedness is admirable, and why should she give in to Petruccio, to sacrifice her freedom in order to become his servant and chattel?

The opening of the play, the Induction, tells the story of Christopher Sly, a drunken tinker whom a lord has taken to his house, where he dupes Sly into believing he is a nobleman. Sly is induced to watch a play, which is about the taming of Katherine, elder daughter of the wealthy merchant, Baptista (a part I played twice), by Petruccio. The rivals who seek Bianca, her younger sister's hand, pay Petruccio to get Katherine to agree to marry him, which he does. The impatient, wealthy rivals have to do something to fulfill their desire to possess Bianca, because Baptista refuses to give her in marriage before he has married off Katherine. Bianca, who has the reputation of being an angel, is really more of a shrew than her sister, who is strong-minded and independent, but by the end of the play has realized the error of her ways and grown obedient to her husband, so we are led to believe. In any case, Bianca is in love with Lucentio, and the two connive eventually to outwit the rivals and to marry. The play concludes with the characters with which it began, and Christopher Sly is persuaded that he has been dreaming a wonderful dream. Because of the play he has seen, he finds the courage to go home to his wife.

And now, here is part of the wooing scene, notable for its puns and wordplay. Petruccio doesn't even know Katherine, but he is not timid about being sexual with her, and even she does not appear to perceive this as particularly disrespectful, however much she professes to despise him. Indeed, the scene can be played as if she is actually attracted to him sexually, and he to her. This dialogue is partway into the scene, after a somewhat more formal introduction of himself by Petruccio, who pretends not to notice how antagonistic Katherine is being, and is deliberately sarcastic about her supposed mildness and virtues, which is of course the exact opposite of everything he has been told about her. Despite the lack of stage directions, there are indications in the lines themselves of the physical actions to be played, as you will see:

PETRUCCIO. [...] Hearing thy mildness praised in every town,
Thy virtues spoke of, and thy beauty sounded,
Yet not so deeply as to thee belongs,
Myself am moved to woo thee for my wife.

KATHERINE. Moved! in good time: let him that moved you hither

Remove you hence: I knew you at the first

> [At the first: immediately; right away. Perhaps Katherine starts to move away from him at this point.]

You were a moveable.

PETRUCCIO. Why, what's a moveable?

KATHERINE. A joint-stool.

> [A movable: a piece of furniture, i.e., something you can move (cf. French "meuble": furniture). A joint-stool: a folding stool or chair, which can be moved around, folded and unfolded. We still sometimes hear "joint" used to mean the male sexual organ. Katherine means that Petruccio has only one interest, and she knows what that is! The implication is also that he is fickle, i.e., movable. Perhaps she is moving around the room at this point, hence Petruccio's pun, as he catches up with her.]

PETRUCCIO. Thou hast hit it: come, sit on me.

> [Essentially, Petruccio is telling her that she is right. Perhaps he pulls her down onto his lap, an example of a stage direction implied in the lines.]

KATHERINE. Asses are made to bear, and so are you.

PETRUCCIO. Women are made to bear, and so are you.

> [Partridge reminds us that "bear" has two meanings here: to bear children; to support the weight of a man on top of her.]

KATHERINE. No such jade as you, if me you mean.

> [A jade is a worn-out stallion. Partridge says, "Kate's imputation here is that Petruchio is insufficiently virile to be able to **ride** her." He defines "ride" as "to mount sexually." Perhaps at this point, Katherine pushes him off her.]

PETRUCCIO. Alas! good Kate, I will not burden thee;

For, knowing thee to be but young and light...

> [Perhaps Petruccio is sarcastic because she has just pushed him away, and he has felt how strong she is.]

KATHERINE. Too light for such a swain as you to catch;

And yet as heavy as my weight should be.

[I am of a proper, correct weight. Is she running away from him again at this point?]

PETRUCCIO. Should be! Should...buzz!

[Petruccio here takes the word "be" as "bee," the insect; hence Katherine's following riposte. Partridge writes, "This is the Elizabethan convention—Shakespeare's, anyway—for that 'rude noise' (an anal emission of wind)...known as a *raspberry*"; perhaps in England, but a raspberry in American slang is a similar loud noise emitted from the mouth. Either way, the word buzz is suggestive of rude disapproval. Perhaps he begins here to chase her around the room, as the word "takes," below, indicates he might be doing.]

KATHERINE. Well ta'en, and like a buzzard.

[The buzzard is not known for its cleanliness. In the next line, "turtle" means the bird, turtledove.]

PETRUCCIO. O slow-wing'd turtle! shall a buzzard take thee?

KATHERINE. Ay, for a turtle, as he takes a buzzard.

PETRUCCIO. Come, come, you wasp; i' faith, you are too angry.

KATHERINE. If I be waspish, best beware my sting.

PETRUCCIO. My remedy is then, to pluck it out.

KATHERINE. Ay, if the fool could find it where it lies.

PETRUCCIO. Who knows not where a wasp does
wear his sting? In his tail.

KATHERINE. In his tongue.

PETRUCCIO. Whose tongue?

KATHERINE. Yours, if you talk of tails: and so farewell.

PETRUCCIO. What, with my tongue in your tail? nay, come again,
Good Kate; I am a gentleman.

[The sexual wordplay here is obvious. The words "come again" have a double meaning: reply once more; and the obvious sexual connotation of a second orgasm.]

KATHERINE. That I'll try.

(*She strikes him.*)

PETRUCCIO. I swear I'll cuff you, if you strike again.

KATHERINE. So may you lose your arms:

If you strike me, you are no gentleman;
And if no gentleman, why then no arms.

> [The reference is to a heraldic coat of arms.]

PETRUCCIO. A herald, Kate? O, put me in thy books!

KATHERINE. What is your crest? a coxcomb?

PETRUCCIO. A combless cock, so Kate will be my hen.

KATHERINE. No cock of mine; you crow too like a craven

> [She means "like a coward," with an obvious pun on "raven."
> Again, the sexual meaning of the preceding lines is obvious.]

Here are some possible choices for each character:

1. **Superobjective:** *Petruccio*: To get married and be happy and wealthy. *Katherine*: To assert myself and have everything and everyone around me be aboveboard and honest; to do as I wish; to be happy in the long run.

2. **Throughline of action:** *Petruccio*: I arrive and look for something to make my fortune. When I find out about the marriage, I proceed to woo and win Katherine, and then to tame her. *Katherine*: I wish to remain free, but I am attracted to him. I am forced by my father to marry him, and even though I do so against my will, he teaches me a lesson in what it means to be obedient and loving at the same time. That way, I get what I want.

3. **Counter-throughline:** *Petruccio*: I have to fight Katherine's intransigence. I do so every step of the way. *Katherine*: I resist every step of the way, until I realize where my true happiness lies.

4. **Adjectives describing the character:** *Petruccio*: Brash, forward, determined, self-interested, humorous. *Katherine*: Forthright, willful, self-protective, intelligent, wary.

5. **Point of view:** *Petruccio*: She is attractive, and I can win this game of wooing her, because I can tell she finds me attractive, too, but she is a shrew and withal quite intelligent, so I shall have to gauge how to get round her. *Katherine*: Men are

impossible, and want to destroy my independence and make me into their chattel, but I do find him attractive; nevertheless, I won't give in to this conceited popinjay.

6. **What is the main event in the scene?** The wooing of Katherine by Petruccio.

7. **Where does the scene take place?** *Petruccio*: In Baptista's reception room, where I have never been before. *Katherine*: In my reception room.

8. **What are the other given circumstances—time of day; weather; your physical condition?** It is a hot summer day in the Florentine mansion of Baptista. Both characters are in peak physical condition and very strong, but Petruccio is physically stronger.

9. **What do you want—your objective?** *Petruccio*: I want to get her to bend to my will; to marry and bed her. I find her attractive. *Katherine*: I want to find out what he really wants, aside from marrying me. I also want to get him to leave as soon as possible. But he is attractive, so I am content to banter for a while, until it becomes unbearable.

10. **What is in the way—the obstacle?** *Petruccio*: Katherine, who is headstrong and impossible to deal with, high-spirited and has a comeback for everything. *Katherine*: Petruccio and the very fact that he is here. He isn't really telling me directly what he wants. He beats around the bush and he won't shut up, and I don't know quite how to maneuver him into leaving.

11. **What does your character do—your actions?** Everything in a farcical scene like this depends on the staging. Only with the blocking in place can you determine exactly what the actions are. *Petruccio*: I size things up when I enter. I banter with her. I get physical with her, and maybe even take her over my knee. *Katherine*: I size him up when he enters. I avoid physical contact by moving away from him every time he approaches me. I resist when he catches me.

12. **Do you attain your objective by the end of the scene?** No, for both characters.

In order to perform this farcical scene, the actors have to be aware of tempo-rhythm and pacing. The exchange is in the form of sticho-mythia—rapid-fire exchanges of sharp, pointed dialogue, found also in some modern comedies, such as Noël Coward's *Private Lives*. This literary device is a perfect clue as to pacing and timing, and the laughs in this scene clearly depend on both.

X

The Seventeenth-Century French Comedy of Manners; English Restoration Comedy

Movement, Clothing, and Manners

The style of seventeenth-century plays depends on simplicity and elegance of movement. And movement for actors can be rendered very cumbersome by the costumes, the more authentic they are, whether French or those of the English Restoration. Slow and stately are the watchwords. Elegance, refinement of manners, and graceful deportment are the hallmarks. The bows, flourishes, and curtseys must be practiced so that they become second nature. How to remove the man's plumed hat and to put it on after bowing, all in one elegant, refined gesture; and how and where to hold the lady's gown so as to allow her to curtsey gracefully are essential skills.

Antoine de Courtin's (1622–1685) celebrated *Nouveau Traité de la Civilité qui se pratique en France parmi les honnêtes gens*—translated into English in1671 as *The Rules of Civility; or Certain Ways of Deportment Observed in France, amongst All Persons of Quality, upon Several Occasions*—lays out clearly the laws of correct deportment and polite manners in seventeenth-century France, and it was adopted as a model of courtesy and politesse in England as well. For Courtin the deference due to men of rank was the first and most important rule of etiquette, and inferiors must always be aware of their status and behave accordingly. This attitude informs the high comedy of

Molière, and we see that when such rules are transgressed—when, for instance, people try to rise above their station, as M. Jourdain does in *Le bourgeois gentilhomme*—the consequences are ridicule heaped on the transgressor, or worse. M. Jourdain is of the opinion that his wealth counts as much as aristocratic birth in gaining entrée into the world of the nobility, but for the aristocracy, his money counts for nothing. It is a useful tool to the often impoverished noblesse, but is of no more worth than the merit of achievement in providing what only blood can offer: the privilege of status. Everyone not "to the manor born" is contemptible in their eyes, and automatically vulgar and déclassé. Only the nouveau riche and the parvenu made an ostentatious point of parading around town in a new gilt carriage with plush red velvet seats and a team of well-groomed horses. Nobody need wonder that there was a revolution a little over a century after this play was first produced.

The following information is elementary, and there are many nuances of the period's manners to be studied and learned:

1. When encountering someone of equal rank, men incline the head slightly. Aristocrats usually touch the brim of their hats to persons of equal rank, or doff them with a flourish to show off the plumes that adorned them. They usually return a nod from someone of lesser rank, but if they have been displeased and still wish to he polite, they simply look at the other person as a sign that they had seen him or her.

2. Men must bow to someone of superior rank, and women must curtsey, sometimes only slightly. Women may use their fans to hide the lower part of their faces, as a further sign of deference. As several sources inform us, three bows when entering and leaving the royal presence were de rigueur, in England as well as in France.

3. Courtin tells us that when kissing the hand of a person of higher rank or a woman of any rank, in public, men must the right hand to take the proffered one, glove removed. And they do not actually touch their lips to the hand, but make a show of doing so.

4. The man's bow in Restoration England and in France: Stand with the right foot slightly forward and turned out slightly to the right; nod forward from the head, right hand on heart. Bow from the waist higher or lower, depending on the status of the character being saluted, and without bending the leg. Courtin tells us that the higher a person's rank, the lower the bow.

5. Women curtsey in the following manner: Grasp both sides of the gown elegantly, then rise up slightly before moving down toward the floor as low as possible. Keep one foot behind the other for balance. When women enter a room, they must make a slow and stately reverence to the assemblage, curtseying low to the floor.

6. Men and women must always allow persons of higher rank to pass out of a room before they do. They make way with a nod and sometimes with an elegant gesture, bowing to the person who is leaving.

If you are performing Molière, read the vivid, sometimes mordantly satiric *Memoirs* of Louis de Rouvroy, duc de Saint-Simon (1675–1755), which begin in the year 1691, when the almost unvarying daily routines of French court life were already well established. One had to be very careful and scrupulous in one's conduct, as in one's appearance and dress. Life at the court of Versailles, depending as it did on manners and politesse and precedence, seems sometimes like that very high comedy to which it forms the background in the plays of Molière and Dancourt. So extraordinary was Saint-Simon's talent, that the story he tells is endlessly engrossing, despite the occasional longueur or lapse of taste when he chooses to tell us of the scandalous, grossly ribald behavior of some august personage.

Dancourt (1661–1725)

Dancourt was the stage and penname of a gentleman of rank, Florent Carton, sieur [lord] d'Ancourt, a lawyer, actor, and prolific dramatist. In 1685, having eloped with Thérèse de la Thorillère (1663–1725), the daughter of an actor who had been one of Molière's colleagues, he and his wife joined the Comédie Française. Much acclaimed for his playing of the title role in Molière's *The Misanthrope* and other leading parts, Dancourt was even better known for more than sixty sparkling, cynical comedies of manners. The targets of his realistic satire were the pretentiousness and snobbery then prevalent in all social classes. He had quite a vogue in Paris, but, bored with the theater, he retired to his country estate in Berry to live out the rest of his life as a gentleman-farmer.

Le chevalier à la mode (The Fashionable Cavalier)

One of his most popular plays was the five-act comedy, *Le chevalier à la mode* (1687), often considered his best work. It shows the growing ascendance of the rich, middle-class merchants during Louis XIV's reign. The storming of the Bastille took place one hundred and twenty-two years after the premier of this play, in which we can see the seeds that would lead to the overthrow of the monarchical system. The increasingly wealthy bourgeoisie, whom the aristocracy despised, began by demanding more respect from the class of sybaritic, sycophantic courtiers, and ended by securing more political power. Molière's *Le bourgeois gentilhomme* preceded Dancourt's comedy by seventeen years, and is on a similar theme, as are several of Dancourt's other plays. To enter the social class above theirs, they either had to be ennobled for services to the crown (relatively infrequent) or, much more often, to marry into the nobility. Since the aristocracy was frequently impoverished, despite the rents from their estate tenants, there were many such matches, which the nobles considered misalliances, but which they had no choice but to make, if they did not wish to go bankrupt.

Madame Patin is a naïve, wealthy, middle-class Parisian widow, enamored of the villainous Chevalier de Ville-Fontaine. She is desperate to marry into the aristocracy, and wants to sever relations with the members of her husband's middle-class family, whose manners she finds vulgar, bourgeois, and unaristocratic. Constantly feeling put upon, she despises her own class, and wishes she had been born into a noble family, but not just any kind of noble family: the Chevalier belongs to the prestigious *noblesse de l'épée* (nobility of the sword), who owe their position to military prowess, and can trace their ancestry back to the crusades in many cases. She wants to reject her ardent suitor, the prim M. Migaud, who belongs to the *noblesse de la robe* (nobility of the gown), ennobled, some of them quite recently, for their legal, financial, and administrative services to the crown. In addition to his lower status, M. Migaud's name is against him: "Can you imagine me as Madame Migaud?" asks Madame Patin, disdainfully. The name rhymes with the French word *nigaud* (nee GO), meaning an idiot or a fool. Her own married name, *patin*, means skate, and also a broad-soled cloth slipper worn to clean floors with; for francophones, this is close to the word *pantin*, meaning a jumping jack toy or a clownish puppet. Her clever, loyal maidservant, Lysette, who provides sensible, good advice, says she can imagine her employer as Madame Migaud! But Madame Patin behaves haughtily in his presence nonetheless. As it turns out, the Chevalier tries to seduce Madame Patin's virtuous niece, Lucille, and in the end, rebuffed and upset, Madame Patin, her eyes opened, goes on with her life a wiser and a sadder woman, and with no marriage prospects in view.

At the opening of act 1, scene 1, Madame Patin is almost hysterical, as she enters her house in high dudgeon, "with much precipitation and in disarray," and is met by Lysette:

LYSETTE. What is it, Madame? What's the matter? What's happened to you? What have they done to you?
MME. PATIN. A snub! Ah, I'm suffocating. A snub...I can't speak. A chair!

What had happened? As Mme. Patin tells us, "The Marquise of I don't know what...had the audacity to take up the middle of the road in her carriage, and to force me to back up twenty paces." She also called Mme. Patin a "bourgeoise," the supreme insult. And the poor lady had instantly returned home, nearly fainting and in high dudgeon.

The first scene should be played at top speed. That way, it will have its full, hilarious effect. Madame Patin's first words, "A snub," provide the first laugh of the evening: the word itself is funny, and the overreactive, hysterical suffering of the snub's victim even funnier, although we don't yet know her; the word in French, *avanie* (ah vah NEE), is also funny. For the wounded Madame Patin, living in that era, this "snub" is a major incident. No doubt, however, the audience of the time was expected to find her exaggerated reactions ridiculous. Dancourt's idea appears to be that people ought to know their place and stick to it, but that idea will be subverted as the play proceeds, and we find out that class does not mean everything. Hypocrisy and bad manners belong to people of every class.

This play speaks volumes about the period. What do we learn? First, that materialism is coming to the fore: What is considered prestigious by the bourgeoisie is a show of wealth, an expensive equipage, and lots of servants. This is part of ostentatiously displaying how rich one is. Secondly, we learn from dialogue in the very first scene that the aristocracy doesn't have the money to keep up a display of wealth, and that riding around in the equivalent of an old jalopy or an antique car is even more prestigious than a new, fabulously equipped SUV. The marquise was driving in an old carriage, and Mme. Patin in her spanking new equipage. We learn what the trappings of wealth are, as Lysette describes them: crimson velvet, gold trim, beautifully groomed horses, and so forth. We also learn in scene 1 that rank has its privileges and prerogatives, and that you had better back up and give the aristocrat the right of way. And we learn that the newly rich merchant class, which thinks that its money counts for everything, wants respect, and is furious at being singled out as bourgeois. But they are indeed the bourgeoisie, and their ideas, values, and manners are bourgeois, that is, materialistic, uneducated, and somewhat rude and boorish. Of course, they do not wish to be told this, and they are unconscious of being boors and vulgarians. Underneath the façade of wealth, they feel inferior to the natural-born aristocrats, for whom materialistic values are contemptible: it is the spiritual, god-given values of the divine rights of kings, and the merits conferred by high birth that count for them. Thus the aristocracy masked its venal nature and its acquisitiveness: their birth bestowed almost mystical privileges unavailable to the low-born. This the bourgeoisie cannot allow. They have their pride.

We know very early on whom we are dealing with in the Chevalier, and, through him, the aristocracy is portrayed in a very bad light. In act 1, scene 7, Ville-Fontaine and his valet, Crispin, have the following exchange, in which the objectives and verbal actions are clear:

CRISPIN. Oh! Oh! What? The mistress of the house talks of marriage, and you are thinking of marrying her? Do you love her?
CHEVALIER. *I*, love *her*? You poor fool!
CRISPIN. Then what are you talking about?
CHEVALIER. I shall marry her if I like, but I hate her like the plague, and it won't be her I marry!
CRISPIN. No, the devil take me if I understand you.
CHEVALIER. I am in love with the forty million livres of income that she possesses.

If the Chevalier had a mustache, he would twirl it! The livre was the basic unit of French currency, worth at this period between two and three dollars in today's money, so Ville-Fontaine is looking forward to enjoying between eighty and one hundred twenty million dollars annually, after he pulls the wool over Madame Patin's eyes.

In other words, the principal lesson in these scenes, as one reads between the lines, is about the mindset and worldview of the characters, the assumptions about the social order, and the overwhelming desire for prestige, respect, and consideration. This is the sort of thing you as an actor have to learn about and understand, because it is part of the inner roadmap, and the internal life, of any character you play in a seventeenth- or eighteenth-century play, or in one set in that period. The logical, Stanislavskian principle is that the outer behavior and deportment, the manners and the way of wearing the costumes, are conditioned by the inner life of the character.

Regnard (1655–1709)

On the same high level with the comedies of Molière and Dancourt, although less well known, the plays of Jean-François Regnard also partook of the penchant for satire and the mockery of those who would climb above their station, but in a more gentle manner than either of his contemporaries. His writing is not as incisive as Molière's but his plays are very amusing and were highly successful in his day.

Regnard was a wealthy man, having inherited a fortune from his father, a fish merchant, who died when he was three. He was highly educated, well traveled and a sportsman. During a trip to Italy, where he lived for two years, he was captured by Algerian pirates, and was ransomed after seven months, which must have seemed an eternity. He later fictionalized the episode in a novel, *La Provençale* (The Lady from Provence; 1731), published posthumously.

In 1683, after two years of traveling around Europe, Regnard returned to his native land and purchased the office of Trésorier de France au Bureau des Finances de Paris. Despite its pompous title, this job was almost a sinecure involving the minor keeping of accounts, and it gave him the leisure time to write for the theater, his passion. All government offices were for sale, and a fee was paid annually for every position from that of a court usher in a provincial town to that of a minister of state in Paris. This was one major source of income for the crown. The system led, of course, to corruption, graft, and bribery as well. The purchase of certain offices exempted the buyer from paying taxes. The whole idea of buying government offices and positions would be abolished by the French Revolution in the next century.

Le joueur (The Gambler)

Regnard's most successful play was *Le joueur*, produced in 1696. And the highly regarded *Le légataire universel* is still sometimes revived by the Comédie Française. Nowadays we would call *Le joueur* a wry, black comedy that ends on a rather sour, although not tragic note. Its subject is something we know well: addiction, and the addictive personality. It might make a good film.

The charming young Valère is an agreeable, good-looking, personable chap with much to recommend him, but he is unfortunately addicted to gambling. The love of his life, Angélique, who requites his love, can't bear his obsession, and agrees to get engaged to Dorante, Valère's uncle, but this is a tentative arrangement, and they have not yet signed a contract. The gambler is now in despair, and furious with both of them. But he repents, and agrees to give up his gambling, while his father Géronte agrees to pay his debts if he will indeed be as good as his word. Valère thus wins back the heart of Angélique. As a token of their newly committed love, she gives him a jewel-encrusted miniature portrait of herself. He cannot resist the temptation to pawn it, so that he can return to the gaming tables, and, having won, he puts off going to the pawnshop to redeem the portrait, so that he can continue gambling. Meanwhile, Angélique has been informed of all this, and Dorante has gone himself to redeem the portrait. Valère, having fallen, continues in his devil-may-care, gambling ways, thinking that Angélique is ignorant of his activities, and he loses all his money. Nonetheless, the dispirited Angélique gives him one last chance, and confronts him, asking him to produce the portrait. He lies to her, and his servant lies as well, and pleads with her to take him back, but she knows what kind of life she will lead if she marries him, and she rejects him. Instead, she will marry Dorante. Géronte, enraged at his son's refusal to give up his gambling even after he has paid all his debts, and hoping to teach him a lesson, takes the drastic step of disinheriting his son. Valère still hopes at the end of the play to make a fortune at the tables. As he says to his valet in the very last line, "Come, come, let us console ourselves, Hector. And some day, at the gaming table, we'll make good our losses in love."

In act 5, scene 7, Valère lies to Angélique about the portrait, with the connivance of the clever Hector. The play is written in the usual classical alexandrine verse, twelve syllable to a line. Angélique has asked Valère to produce the portrait in the presence of Dorante. Mme. La

Ressource (the lady with whom Valère pawned the miniature portrait); and Nérine, Angélique's maidservant, are also there:

> VALÈRE. Yes, you rascal! Speak! What have you done with it?
> HECTOR. (*Holding his hands behind his back; speaks low to Mme. La Ressource*) Madame La Ressource, one moment, without letting on, lend me back what we pawned.
> VALÈRE. Ah! You dog! You two-faced traitor! You've lost it…
> HECTOR. Sir…
> VALÈRE. (*Drawing his sword*) Your death will…
> HECTOR. (*On his knees*) Ah, sir, stop! And don't kill me! When I saw in this portrait how beautiful Madame was, I brought it to an artist, who is making me a copy.

But Angélique is not duped, of course, and she says to Valère, "Do not think to continue abusing me with such useless tricks, you ungrateful man!" He protests that he does not deserve such an epithet, but in vain. "Perfidious as you are," says she, "This portrait that I gave you as proof of my most passionate love…In spite of your oaths, perjurer, you pawned it the very same hour!" She is unhappy momentarily since, as we saw, the play ends on an ironic note that in this case takes us close to tragedy, but remains in the realm of comedy.

English Restoration Comedy

Sir William Davenant (1606–1668), Shakespeare's putative godson, returned from exile in France with his king, Charles II (1630–1685), now restored to the throne of his ancestors. Davenant was pleased on July 19, 1660 to pen the following royal decree at the behest of his master:

> Our will and pleasure is that you prepare a Bill for our signature to passe our Great Seale of England, containing a Grant unto our trusty and well-beloved Thomas Killigrew Esquire, one of the Groomes of our Bed-chamber and Sir William Davenant Knight,

to give them full power and authoritie to erect Two Companys of Players consisting respectively of such persons as they shall chuse and apoint; and to purchase or build and erect at their charge as they shall thinke fitt Two Houses or Theaters.

Thus was born the Restoration theater, ending the long period during the Puritan Interregnum under Oliver Cromwell when theater was not permitted and the playhouses were closed. Two rival theatrical companies were formed: Sir Thomas Killigrew's (1612–1683) King's Company, and Sir William Davenant's Duke of York's Servants, known as the Duke's Company, under the patronage of the future King James II (1633–1701). In theory, no other theaters were permitted, and the decree also authorized the two producers to determine salaries, and to put on fully mounted productions of plays with or without music. They flourished throughout the era, along with others that were eventually allowed, and were reopened to great rejoicing after the Great Fire of London forced their temporary closure in 1666—events vividly described by that inveterate theatergoer Samuel Pepys (1633–1703), and his brilliant polymath friend John Evelyn (1620–1706) in their invaluable, eminently readable diaries. To Pepys we owe many descriptions of plays and players, on all of which he had definite and usually enthusiastic opinions.

The era of Restoration theater is usually said to end around 1715, although some put it earlier. The period is known especially for the comedies written by such authors as Colley Cibber, William Wycherly, William Congreve, John Vanbrugh, and Sir George Etherege, among others. But heroic verse tragedies were also produced in abundance, and some writers gained reputations for profundity for having written what we now consider unplayable, prolix pieces where posturing and posing are at a premium, and real human emotion is seldom to be found.

The comedies of the period, on the other hand, are rife with human situations and types that were well known at the time, and that we still enjoy today. Extravagance in dress, symbolic of social pretentions, is a common Restoration theme, as are libertinage and amorous intrigues. As the monarch and his court resumed the sort of life not seen by anyone in Britain during the thirty years Puritan interregnum, people of social standing and those who aspired to it demanded more and more deference. The quest for respectability and for being kow-towed to forms the nub of a number of plays of the period, as with Molière and Dancourt.

First, study the period's mindset, deportment, manners, and cloth-ing, which you will find discussed at the beginning of this chapter. The information applies to England, much influenced by French manners and deportment, as well as to France, where Charles II had spent his youth at the court of his cousin Louis XIV.

Part of the fun in English Restoration comedies comes from making fun of the dress that grew more and more elaborate and extravagant as time went on. In some circles, it was de rigueur to compete to see who could sport the most unwieldy outfit, and move in the most graceful fashion, showing the high aristocratic back-ground of the wearer who never in his or her life had to earn a liv-ing, and who scorned the lower classes, like those Chinese mandarins who grew their fingernails inordinately long to show that they were always being served and were above having to do anything for them-selves. Colley Cibber was a master at satirizing these attitudes, both in writing and in acting, as you will see below in the discussion of his highly successful comedy, *Love's Last Shift, or The Fool in Fashion* and its sequel, George Vanbrugh's *The Relapse, or Virtue in Danger*, in which Cibber performed to great acclaim. His characterization of Lord Foppington must have been one of the supreme comic perfor-mances of the age.

The next thing to understand in playing these comedies is the nature of the character types that reflected the new and nouveau riche mores of the period, which, again, were very much the same as those in France: the fop, extravagantly overdressed and underintelligent, more emotionally involved with his huge peruke, and his ever more ornate coats and breeches, which were adorned if not festooned with endless lace and ribbons, than with other people; the aging aristocratic lady who is losing her charms, but behaves as seductively as if she were decades younger; the wily self-serving servants and servile tradesmen and professionals out to bilk their employers and customers.

In an age when women were finally allowed on the English stage, as they had been long before in the continental theater, a typical character was the *précieuse* (the French word means "pretentious woman"), portrayed, for instance, in Molière's one-act satire *Les précieuses ridicules* (The Ridiculous Pretentious Ladies); or the blue-stocking feminist intellectual and would-be poets, as in Molière's five-act comedy of manners *Les femmes savantes* (The Learned Ladies). These misogynistic plays, like others from the period, decry and lampoon women's education, and, by extension, women's intellectual capacities, rather than simply satirizing pretention, which is their ostensible target.

You must deal with the ornate Restoration English, making its syntax clear to the audience, and you must be constantly thinking, because these plays are intellectual, and the conversations in them are often intellectual debates. As Simon Callow says in his excellent book, *Acting in Restoration Comedy* (Applause, 1991), "Restoration comedies demand the most exhausting kind of acting: sustained thinking…These plays live in the play of ideas, which can only be achieved by thinking through each line…You have to be ahead of each thought, in perfect command of the sequence of ideas."

The period's grammar must become your own natural habit and way of speaking, which is not too difficult, as it is fairly close to ours in many ways. Think of the language as part of the "given circumstances," and you can then incorporate it into your characterization, just as you can the theatrical conventions of the aside and the soliloquy, common not only in Shakespeare, but also in these plays, and indeed through the eighteenth and nineteenth centuries. The aside is a theatrical convention consisting of a brief address to the audience or to the character's self in the middle of a scene. The action is suspended while the aside is delivered. And a soliloquy is a monologue revealing inner feelings or ideas, spoken by a character in a play who is alone on stage; hence, *to soliloquize*: to deliver or indulge in such a monologue.

Colley Cibber (1671–1757)

Colley Cibber, actor, theater manager, playwright, and memoirist, has much to teach contemporary actors. Much decried and derided in his own day, he was what playwright Paul Rudnick, in an article called "Random Rules for Comedy" in *The Dramatist* (November / December, 2005), called a "laugh whore." Such "shameless" actors should be worshipped, Rudnick tells us, because they ensure the success of comedy. They crave laughs, and they know how to get them. Cibber certainly did. Do read his florid autobiography, *An Apology for the Life of Colley Cibber* (1740); his writing style is a hilarious coruscation of prolixity.

He spanned the ages: His career began during the heyday of Restoration comedy, and continued on into the eighteenth century. Cibber's critics and detractors thought him crass, vulgar, tasteless, and much given to effect, and to form and fluff over substance. Among his most well-known and scathing castigators was the brilliant, viper-tongued satirical poet, Alexander Pope (1688–1744), who made his contempt for Cibber even clearer in his voluminous notes to the epic poem, *The Dunciad* (1728). Pope also wrote that Cibber, who made what he thought of as improvements in classic plays, was responsible for the "miserable mutilation" of "hapless *Shakespeare*, and crucify'd *Molière*" and that his execrable productions were done with "less human genius than God gives an ape"—and those were the mildest barbs he aimed at his despised target. But Cibber's versions of Shakespeare proved popular, and even in modern times Cibber's interpolated lines had such conviction that Lord Olivier (1907–1989), used one of them from the last act in his film of *Richard the Third* (1955), after Richard has recovered from his nightmares: "Conscience, avaunt! Richard's himself again!" Well, it does sound like Shakespeare, doesn't it?

Colley Cibber admired good acting when he saw it, as in the case of the most illustrious actor of the Restoration period, Thomas Betterton (1635–1710), equally at home in tragedy and comedy. Among Cibber's associates, there are several whose acting he described, and his descriptions provide excellent lessons in comic acting, in how to play parts really and consistently. Here is some of what he has to say about the comedienne, Mrs. Susannah Mountfort (1667?–1703), later Mrs. Verbruggen, married to the gifted, temperamental actor, John Verbruggen (16?–1708), known for being somewhat undisciplined and working from inspiration, rather than systematic preparation:

> In a play of D'Urfey's [prolific playwright Tom Durfey (1653–1723)], now forgotten, called "The Western Lass," which part she acted, she transformed her whole being, body, shape, voice, language, look and features, into almost another animal; with a strong Devonshire dialect, a broad, laughing voice, a poking head, round shoulders, an unconceiving eye, and the most bediz'ning dowdy dress [actors in those days supplied their own costumes] that ever covered the untrained limbs of a Joan Trot.

She was also popular playing men's parts in drag:

> People were so fond of seeing her a man, that when the part of Bayes, in "The Rehearsal" had for some time lain dormant, she was desired to take it up, which I have seen her act with all the true, coxcombly spirit and humor that the sufficiency of the part required.

Two other notable comedians, who, with Cibber, formed a triumvirate as managers of London's Drury Lane Theatre, and whose acting he described, also provide valuable lessons in how to perform comedy: the Irish actor Thomas Dogget (1670–1721), who excelled in low-comedy roles, and Robert Wilks (1665–1732) from Worcestershire. Of the former, Cibber said, "He was the most original and the strictest observer of nature of all his contemporaries… He could be extremely ridiculous without stepping into the least impropriety to make him so." Apparently, Wilks had an unpleasant voice, but he devoted minute study to his parts, and interpreted them peerlessly, creating many characters in Cibber's plays and in those of his intimate friend George Farquhar. His most famous role was that of Sir Harry Wildair in Farquhar's *The Constant Couple*. Cibber thought his playing sometimes too forceful. And he added:

> But whatever he did upon the stage, let it be ever so trifling, whether it consisted of putting on his gloves, or taking out his watch, lolling on his cane, or taking snuff, every movement was marked by such an ease of breeding and manner, everything told so strongly the involuntary motion of a gentleman, that it was impossible to consider the character he represented in any other light than that of reality.

It is worth noting that this versatile actor was also acclaimed for his Hamlet.

The principal lesson Cibber himself has for us today can be summed up in one word: exuberance. Cibber was constantly excited by himself and his own ability to make people roar with laughter. He was extravagant and ebullient, and above all, exuberant. He loved what he did. He gloried in it, and was satisfied. He undoubtedly loved the adverse criticism leveled at him, and he deflected all the arrows, which he thought had missed their target. He laughed even at himself. All of this is wonderful grist for the actor's comedic mill. Love what you do. Enjoy yourself. And, even more, do it with gusto and high spirits, which you may have to restrain, but which the audience will sense could bubble to the surface at any moment.

Cibber's *Love's Last Shift, or The Fool in Fashion* and Vanbrugh's *The Relapse, or Virtue in Danger*

Both written in 1696 and both huge successes, Cibber's and Sir John Vanbrugh's (1664–1726) sentimental comedies of manners present to us the minor character Sir Novelty Fashion, who becomes Lord Foppington in Vanbrugh's sequel; the part was played in both pieces by Cibber, who had written it for himself. It made the plays the phenomenal hits they were, and the character's overweening vanity, outrageous remarks, and rampant flirtations caused audiences to collapse with laughter. In Vanbrugh's sequel, the part was expanded, capitalizing on Cibber's acclaimed performance. Even his wig could be funny! As Lord Foppington (the character's name says it all), Cibber had his huge periwig carried on stage in a sedan chair by two hefty servants. The wig was almost as large as the diminutive actor himself. Its heralded arrival provoked uncontrolled laughter, especially when he made a great point of putting it on with the most elaborate ceremony, and with over-done, pompous dignity. In his notoriously squeaky voice, he treated his servants with the utmost contempt and ordered them about with a defensive attitude, because somewhere inside himself, Foppington knows he is ridiculous and that people, including those same servants, are laughing at him behind his back, while showing him exaggerated deference to his face.

Love's Last Shift is a romantic, sentimental comedy with a typically complicated Restoration plot: Having been deserted by the rake Loveless ten years before the play begins, after only six months of marriage, Amanda has no idea what has happened to him. But Young Worthy, a friend to the couple, encounters him by chance in a park and informs her that the dissipated, impoverished Loveless, a man well acquainted with bottle and brothel, has, in fact, returned to London after his travels abroad, whither he went to escape his creditors, and believes her to be dead. Young Worthy is a bit of a jackanapes and rascal who enjoys intrigues and complications, and he agrees to help her regain the love of her husband, in his spare time, as it were. Worthy has been wooing Hillaria on behalf of Elder Worthy, his older brother. At the same time, he courts Hillaria's cousin, Narcissa, for himself. Young Worthy manages to trick Loveless into having an affair with Amanda, whom he does not recognize, and who poses as a high-class courtesan. Loveless has the most passionate night of lovemaking that he has ever experienced, and he is entranced. When Amanda reveals her identity, Loveless is full of remorse, and swears to reform and return to her. Meanwhile, Young Worthy inveigles Sir William Wisewoud, father of Narcissa, into signing a marriage contract with him, under the pretense that the contract is for the Elder Worthy, who is Sir William's choice of a husband for his daughter. Thus Young Worthy wins the hand of his beloved, and leaves the Elder Worthy free to marry Hillaria, which he does.

Vanbrugh's sprightly writing in the sequel captures perfectly the tone of Cibber's previous comedy, and adds original touches of character, expanding on Sir Novelty's even greater vanity now that he has been created a lord by favor of the king.

The Relapse begins where *Love's Last Shift* left off, and shows us a discontented Loveless, chafing under his marriage vows, and deciding to have an affair with Berinthia, his wife Amanda's cousin, an attractive widow with whom he falls in love, even though Amanda has warned him against her. Meanwhile, Worthy, "a gentleman of the town," tries to seduce Amanda, but she resists his advances and remains faithful to her husband. In a subplot, the penniless Tom, known as Young Fashion, brother of Lord Foppington, contrives to marry the wealthy heiress Miss Hoyden (the word "hoyden" means a rambunctious, unruly young lady), daughter of the country gentleman Sir Tunbelly Clumsey. Fashion pretends to be Lord Foppington, who had been trying to seduce Miss Hoyden into marriage, and, thus disguised, arranges a marriage contract for himself behind his brother's back.

On his first appearance, in act 1, scene 3, Lord Foppington has entered in his dressing gown—slap my Vitals! This is Lord Foppington's favorite oath; it literally means hit me in the genitals. He promptly rebukes his page, who has just greeted him with the word "Sir":

LORD FOPPINGTON. Sir, Pray, Sir, do me the Favour to teach your Tongue the Title the King has thought fit to honour me with.
PAGE. I ask your Lordship's pardon, my Lord.
LORD FOPPINGTON. O, you can pronounce the Word then, I thought it would have choak'd you—D'ye hear?
PAGE. My Lord.
LORD FOPPINGTON. Call *La Verole*, I wou'd dress [...]

La Verole is the name of his haughty French servant, hired because French people are considered above the English in matters of taste and dress. The word "vérole" means pox or syphilis; this would have been known to the audience, who would have roared at it, no doubt.

Lord Foppington's page summons his tailor, shoemaker, seamstress, and barber to do the honors of attiring him in his ornate apparel. Before they enter, led in by La Verole, he says, in a direct address to the audience:

> Well, 'tis an unspeakable pleasure to be a Man of Quality— Strike me dumb—My Lord—Your Lordship—My Lord *Foppington—Ah! C'est quelque Chose de beau, que le Diable m'emporte* [Ah, this is something handsome, may the Devil take me].
> Why the ladies were ready to pewke at me, whilst I had nothing but Sir *Novelty* to recommend me to 'em—Sure whilst I was but a Knight, I was a very nauseous [nauseating] Fellow—Well, 'tis ten thousand Pawnds well given—slap my Vitals—

Sir Novelty has paid for his title, as he makes clear, and paid a great deal of money at that. In 1696, King William III (1650–1702) instituted a new coinage, and at this period the pound was worth perhaps as much as three hundred pounds in today's currency, if we go by purchasing power, perhaps more; a year's income for the wealthy. So Lord Foppington has purchased his title for approximately three million pounds! You will notice the spelling "pawnds," which all by itself indicates his odd vowels and drawling way of speaking. He pronounces all the words with the "ow" diphthong in the same way, as "aw": town becomes "tawn"; house becomes "hawse," rhyming with the usual British pronunciation of "horse," and so forth. Simon Callow points this sort of thing out in *Acting in Restoration Comedy*, where he talks of Lord Foppington's "curious vowels." Foppington also substitutes "a" for "o," so "shot" is pronounced "shat," for obvious comic effect. Vanbrugh took his orthographic cue for Foppington's extravagant, affected, simpering pronunciation from Colley Cibber's performance as Sir Novelty Fashion in *Love's Last Shift*.

In contemporary terms, the Restoration foppish accent is like the affected, ultra-posh Sloane Rangers accent of the upper-class denizens of the Sloane Square and South Kensington area of London about thirty years ago, in the 1980s, which Callow thinks should not be used, however, for Lord Foppington himself, specifically because he thinks the actor should pay attention to and obey Vanbrugh's vowels. They should be pronounced as written, as when Foppington says, "Oh, Lard—madam, your ladyship's welcome to tawn" or, speaking of his father's having committed suicide, says, "...he shat himself," instead of "he shot himself."

Though it fell into desuetude, the Sloane Rangers accent. also called Sloaney-speak or Sloaney-speech, that might be useful in most Restoration comedies for the characters of fops and pretentious characters generally is now being heard again. Some of its hallmarks are:

1. The lips are tight, with the corners tensed, and the mouth slightly closed during speech.
2. The usual upper-class British RP (Received Pronunciation) dropping of post-vocalic (after a vowel) "r," even though the letter is used in spelling.
3. The occasional drawing out and lengthening of vowels and diphthongs, giving the accent a languid, drawling quality.
4. The heavy use of the schwa (the weak vowel "e" in *the*, when it is before a consonant: *the story*) in unaccented syllables, so that often only consonants are heard.
5. The pronunciation of the "o" diphthong in *home* like the "ay" in "say": *haym, Slayn Squayuh 'nd Sith Kenzngtn* (Sloane Square and South Kensington); <u>I</u> *raylly daynt knay* (I really don't know).
6. The pronunciation of the "ow" diphthong in *town* like the "i" diphthong in *dine*: *dinetine* (downtown); *hise* (house); *mith* (mouth); *hi you?* (how are you?); *ay saw a mise* (I saw a mouse.)
7. Frequent glottal stopping at the ends of words ending in "t" (the glottal stop replaces a "t" by closing the glottis over the vocal cords for an instant)—here represented by the question mark—such as *it, what, not, hot,* and *got*: *i?s ra(r)ely ho? i?* (It's really hot out) would be an extreme amount of glottal stopping, but *It's ho? it* (It's hot out) would be usual, with a glottal

stop on only the middle word and the other final "t" sounds lightly pronounced.

In act 2, scene 1, when Amanda and Foppington are talking of books, she opines that they are "the best Entertainment in the world." He fatuously replies:

> I am so much of your Ladyship's mind, Madam; that I have a private Gallery (where I walk sometimes) is furnish'd with nothing but Books and Looking-glasses. Madam, I have guilded 'em, and rang'd 'em, so prettily, before Gad, it is the most entertaining thing in the World to walk and look upon 'em.

Amanda tells him she prefers the inside to the outside of a book, and Foppington says, "That, I must confess, I am not altogether so fond of."

With these few deft strokes, Vanbrugh, capitalizing on Cibber's original character, has shown us who Foppington is: a "peacock popinjay" who "turns up his noble nose with scorn" at whoever may be lowly born, to use W. S. Gilbert's felicitous phrases in *The Yeomen of the Guard*. His overriding concern with his appearance and dress, his desire to be the best-dressed person around, with the most lace and ribbons and the widest breeches, brand Foppington as an extreme narcissist, who prefers fashion to people, and judges everyone by what they are wearing and how they wear it. This is a very particular mindset, and an excellent example of specificity, since he knows exactly which fashions are to be preferred. Every character should be as specific as this one.

XI

Eighteenth-Century Comedy of Manners and Farce

Movement, Clothing, and Manners

Men wore powdered wigs, embroidered greatcoats with lace at the sleeves, and lace jabots, as well as tricorn hats, with or without plumes. They used snuff, gracefully taken as a pinch between thumb and forefinger.

Over their elaborate, laced corsets and other undergarments, women wore bustles and long, often extravagant gowns. Married women wore caps at home, and wigs and fancy hats when out in society.

Grave and dour, Philip Dormer Stanhope, Fourth Earl of Chesterfield (1694–1773) was a man disappointed in life, and with very little reason, since he was rich beyond imagining. He wrote on March 9, 1748 in one of his edifying letters (of which there were hundreds, all most revealing of the period and of the writer), to his son, Philip (1732–1768):

> True wit, or sense, never yet made anybody laugh; they are above it: they please the mind and give a cheerfulness to the countenance [...] how low and unbecoming a thing laughter is: not to mention the disagreeable noise that it makes, and the shocking distortion of the face that it occasions...

The dyspeptic Lord Chesterfield's bilious, sneeringly derisive approach to laughter is risible. But I doubt if Philip found it so. He stayed as far away from his august sire as he could, or dared. The straitjacket was not for him, nor the rigid inflexibility of his sire's approach to life. Occasionally, the august lord did give good advice: Brush your teeth, and wash. (But no bathing: that could be dangerous to one's health! And indeed it could be, in an age when water was unsafe and filled with disease-carrying germs.)

Dozens of books of etiquette were published, and Chesterfield's famous letters alone are a mine of information about period manners, and social attitudes. As he wrote to his son on September 27, 1749, concerning "a vulgar man," as opposed to a true gentleman, "His clothes fit him so ill, and constrain him so much, that he seems rather their prisoner than their proprietor." The movement of the arms was freer than it had been in seventeenth-century coats, because the cuffs and lace ruffles, when worn, were not as huge. "Take particular care that the motions of your hands and arms be particularly graceful; for the genteelness of a man consists more in them than in anything else," Lord Chesterfield counsels his son on May 2, 1751.

Men touched the front corner of their tricorn hats when passing each other in the streets and when greeting women, or raised them a short way. To persons of greater rank, men bowed by removing the tricorn hat with their left hand holding the front of the hat, lowering it elegantly and gracefully, and turning the hat so that it faced outward, while bringing the right hand over the heart and bending slightly from the waist. After entering a house, if the hat were not taken by a servant, a man would hold it under his left arm, pressed to his side. Gloves would be removed and held as well. Men bowed twice: once on entering a room; and, after taking one or two steps, again, to salute the assemblage. At a ball or reception, when moving through the room, men bowed or inclined the head from side to side, or nodded, as a greeting. When leaving a room, two bows while moving backward were customary; three, if departing from the royal presence: Step to the right, and bring the left foot forward, then bow from the waist, without bending the legs. Move the arm with the hat in it very slightly outward from the body; the other hand touched the heart, or not, as the person wished. Then take several steps backward, and bow again. These movements should all be graceful, elegant and small; nothing extravagant. Early in the nineteenth century, during the Regency, it was customary for men to bow slightly from the waist, while holding both hands over the heart.

Women curtsied by grasping both sides of their gowns, putting one foot behind the other, and, on very formal occasions lowering themselves to the floor, while keeping the torso upright. They then also inclined their heads slightly before rising, again, keeping the torso in an upright position. But the usual gentle, graceful curtsey was a very slight one, using the same position of the legs just described, and bending the knees ever so slightly. As they passed through a room at a ball or reception, women might incline their heads slightly to either side as a greeting to those they wished to acknowledge.

Servants curtsied partway down or bowed, inclining the head, on entering a room and on addressing their masters.

In public especially, women used fans ubiquitously. There was a coded way of using fans, which is detailed in several books of the period. There are appropriate reactions to the signals in the form of responses that might include a slight nod of the head in acquiescence or an indignant or unhappy look, or a look of surprise or pleasure.

The many possibilities include:

1. To say "I love you," a woman would place her fan over her heart, or draw the fan across her cheek, looking softly and coyly at the object of her affections.
2. If she touched the tip of the fan to her lips, it meant "Be quiet"; and if she touched the handle of the fan to her lips, it meant "Kiss me."
3. But if she pointedly drew the fan through her hand, this signaled that she hated the person she was looking at.
4. If a lady hid her eyes behind her fan, it meant that she found the person she was looking at attractive, and was feeling shy.

5. If she switched her fan from her right to her left hand, that meant she wanted to get to know her interlocutor better.

6. But if she switched it from her left to her right hand, that meant that the other person was being too forward.

7. When a woman fanned herself slowly, this was a signal that she was married.

8. But if she wanted someone to follow her, all she had to do was to stop fanning, and move away, carrying the open fan discreetly in front of her face.

9. Pointedly opening and shutting the fan was an angry gesture that meant "You are being cruel."

François Boucher's detailed breakdown in his magisterial *20,000 Years of Fashion: The History of Costume and Personal Adornment* of the ways in which the French Revolution altered costume and habits of dress in the directions of greater lightness and less elaborateness and luxury is essential knowledge. The attitude to dress in this particular era, and the tendency to despise those who dressed expensively as traitors to the people, who could not afford luxuries, is of vast importance when doing a comedy set in this period; the social relationships are inevitably reflected in individual, personal relationships. The changes in styles of dressing betoken a growing sense of entitlement on the part of the dispossessed masses, and allow greater freedom of movement. There was a consequent change in the hierarchy of social structure, however short-lived it proved to be. With the rise of Napoleon, the old attitudes and personal relationships would reassert themselves.

Libertinism: The Theme Underlying the Comedy of Manners

The eighteenth century is known as the Age of Enlightenment, during which the European and American worlds saw a greater understanding of the human condition, of government, of science, and of the arts and their power to help bring about change. It was also the century of libertinism. If you read certain kinds of eighteenth-century literature, it appears that people could hardly wait to get that gorgeous, cumbersome clothing off. In the privacy of the boudoir, amid the powdered wigs, lace jabots, gold-filigree greatcoats and long, ornately decorated gowns, all was perpetually in disarray as libertines and their lubricious conquests indulged their versatile, voracious, and multifarious sexual passions. Tear off that bodice! Undo that corset! Pull down those breeches! Everyone seemed to be rampant and panting and lustful!

For full and titillating descriptions of sexual behavior and acts, you have only to read the works of the libidinous Donatien Alphonse François, Marquis de Sade (1740–1814), a freethinker and atheist whose orgasmic ecstasy and lewd priapic fantasies are omnisexual, and whose propensity for the kind of activities for which we now use his name was unrivalled. He survived the French Revolution only because he was one of the prisoners in the Bastille when it was stormed on July 14, 1789, but despite that, the salacious and unruly Sade was imprisoned again by Robespierre. Although he had renounced his titles, Citizen Sade would have been guillotined had Robespierre himself not preceded him on the scaffold, putting an end to the Terror. And once that unhappy episode was over, Sade became a marquis again, and demanded the respect due to his rank and station. For more information on this fascinating personality, read the absorbing book by the French historian and editor of Sade's correspondence Maurice Lever, *Sade: A Biography* (Mariner Books, 1994).

The epistolary novel *Les liaisons dangereuses* (Dangerous Liaisons), written in 1782 by Pierre Choderlos de Laclos (1741–1803), was much adapted in the twentieth century: There are two plays, several films, and a number of radio and television series based on the novel, and even a ballet and two operas. The book gives us yet another picture of this libertine age, and revolves around the unscrupulous attempts at seduction by conscienceless aristocrats. In the hands of the rapacious, mordant Vicomte de Valmont and the lascivious, psychopathically jealous Marquise de Merteuil, former lovers and present rivals, sex is a sadistic weapon they use to humiliate, degrade, and destroy each other, and those whom they would seduce. As they play endless games, they pretend to be innocent, and concerned about their prey, their beautiful prey, whom they find irresistibly attractive. Their only objects are the pleasure of the orgasm and the destruction of reputations. We can see here in germination and by implication the nineteenth-century reaction to this sort of thing, particularly when anything approaching sexual desire was displayed in public. Chaperoned visits of young unmarried couples were de rigueur in French, Spanish, Italian, and English culture, and had been for two centuries.

Libertine attitudes existed alongside a flourishing, frowning disapproval of such carryings-on and a repressive attitude toward sexuality that came to prevail, especially in the growing bourgeois classes, which found their power increasing with their incomes.

A Libertine Character from Spanish Comedy: Don Juan

The graphic arts of the period are replete with numerous drawings and etchings (come up and see my etchings sometime!) of a pornographic nature. The ubiquitous theme of the vile irreligious seducer, who beds women and abandons them, and suffers the torments of hell for his sins was seen as a warning to dissolute profligates to beware of divine retribution. The libertine most famously portrayed in fiction is the invented Spanish character of Don Juan, a nobleman of Seville. The character dates from the more pietistic age when the Inquisition was in full force. The eighteenth-century spin on the story was perhaps less disapproving and puritanical, although it was ultimately just as moralistic, and was no doubt laughed at by many who thought the very idea of heaven and hell ridiculous.

One of the earliest to tell the tale of sin and divine retribution was the baroque playwright and Roman Catholic priest Tirso de Molina, whose *El burlador de Sevilla y el convidado de piedra* (The Joker of Seville and the Stone Guest) was produced in 1630. His play is set in the fourteenth century, and the Don is a Catholic, who knows he is committing sins and defies God.

In Molière's play *Dom Juan, ou Le festin de pierre* (Don Juan or the Feast of Stone; 1665), the same point is made as in Molina's comic drama: sin leads to disaster and the sinner is punished by the hand of God, in this case in the form of the hand of the stone statue who seizes the Dom's hand in his. We may see that hand as symbolic of pleasuring the self, and such an activity is condemned.

The self-serving venality of the petty bourgeois is also satirized in the character of the Dom's valet, Saganarelle, played by Molière himself. The play ends in terror and the horror of the Dom's fate, but Sganarelle's principal concern is with his wages, and whether or not he can now expect to be paid.

Dom Juan is an atheist, which plunges him further into darkness; his beliefs alone ensure him a place in hell. But, as usual with Molière, one doesn't know how much the playwright is serious, and how much he is actually satirizing religious belief, in his best tongue-in-cheek manner, so that he could proclaim his innocence of any evil intent if necessary. *Dom Juan* is susceptible of bringing religion itself into contempt, or at least of making people think about it more than the political establishment thought good for them, and for itself. To bring the long-established institution of religion into disrepute was a heinous revolutionary act in their eyes. Where would it end? Eventually, as we know, it would end in the French Revolution, with its anti-religious attitudes and appalling slaughter of members of the clergy, bloody acts no less intolerant, bigoted, and horrible than those of the Inquisition.

Carlo Goldoni's (1707–1793) first play was *Don Giovanni ossia Il Dissoluto*, of uncertain date, but the Don's most famous incarnation is no doubt in Mozart's (1756–1791) opera *Don Giovanni* (1787), the full original title of which is *Il dissoluto punito, ossia il Don Giovanni* (The Dissolute One Punished, or Don Giovanni). At the end of the opera, the stone statue of the Commendatore drags him down to hell. Don Giovanni had killed him when the Commendatore had caught the vile seducer trying to rape Donna Anna, the old soldier's daughter. Donna Anna, her fiancé and protector Don Ottavio, and Donna Elvira, whom Giovanni had seduced and abandoned, arrive at the Don's palace to denounce him for the murder of the Commendatore, and Leporello, the Don's reluctant but conniving servant, tells them everything that has transpired. The opera ends with a tacked-on, unconvincing moralistic chorus sung by all the principals: this is the proper end that awaits those who do evil, they sing.

The libretto is by another exemplar of the freethinking libertine type, though on a lesser scale than that of his protagonist: Lorenzo Da Ponte (1749–1838), who based his story partly on incidents in the life of Casanova. Da Ponte, né Emmanuele Conegliano, was an Italian poet and the librettist of thirty-six operas, immortalized especially as the author of the texts for three of Mozart's greatest operas: *Le nozze di Figaro*, *Don Giovanni*, and *Cosí fan tutte*. Born into a converted Jewish family in the Republic of Venice, he studied for the Catholic priesthood, but was expelled from the seminary for committing adultery. He left Italy for Vienna, where he became a leading light in the city's operatic world, providing libretti for all of the major composers of the period. Eventually, after a colorful life, which he relates in fascinating detail in the four volumes of his amusing autobiographical memoirs, Da Ponte left Europe for New York, where he became Columbia University's first professor of Italian literature.

His acquaintance and contemporary fellow Venetian Giacomo Girolamo Casanova di Sengalt (1725–1798), usually known simply as Casanova, was also a real life Don Juan, as his extensive memoirs indicate, although they are probably full of lies. Nevertheless, as a source for the manners, mores, and deportment of the eighteenth century they are supremely authoritative, and very useful for actors.

French Comedy of Manners

There were a number of genres of comedy popular in France in the eighteenth century, to all of which the libertine, freethinking atmosphere form a background. The light-hearted comedy of manners, devoid of social criticism, but set in upper-class milieus, and exemplified in the works of Marivaux, is the most well known. His pieces are still performed by the Comédie Française. Commedia dell'arte plays, usually performed in French by the Comédie-Italienne, for which he wrote, were very much loved, and the genre of opéra comique, much in the style of the English ballad opera, were greatly appreciated.

Alongside them are satirical comedies that are more critical in tone, such as the five-act verse comedy *La métromanie, ou Le poète* (Metermania, or The Poet; alternatively, *Mad for Meter*, *A Mania for Meter*, or *Meter Mad*; usually known as *The Poetry Craze, or The Poet*), produced to great acclaim in 1738. Its author was the epigrammatist and author of five plays, Alexis Piron (1689–1773), a poet himself, and he had his tongue firmly in his cheek when he penned this tale of two poets who write under pseudonyms and fall in love with each other, a kind of early version of the film *The Shop Around the Corner* (1940), based on the 1937 Hungarian play *Parfumerie* by Miklós László. One of the two is M. Francaleu, writing as a Breton poet named Mlle. de Mériadec de Kersac. The other is his prospective son-in-law, Damis, writing as M. de l'Empirée. When the nature of their correspondence in the *Mercure de France* and their true identities are finally revealed, because they have come together to rehearse a play by M. Francaleu, still writing pseudonymously, Damis remains in love with his fictitious inamorata, much to "her" astonishment, and that of Damis' commonsensical uncle Baliveau, who tries to make his obsessive-compulsive nephew see reason. The prospective real fiancée, Lucille, characterized by her servant Lisette as self-absorbed, hedonistic, frivolous, and egotistical, and who was in love with Damis' poetry, is won over by Dorante, who adores her and will marry her. For them, we see unhappiness ahead. But Damis is ecstatic: The eternal poet with his head in the clouds is obsessed with finding the right word, and his craze for rhyme and meter will take over his life.

It is interesting that in casting his play, M. Francaleu tells Dorante, who is introduced to him by Damis as a possible replacement for actors no longer available (one of them has died—"He was dead wrong to do that," says Damis), that an actor must "experience in order to feel, and feel in order to pretend well." With these words, he approaches the ideas of Stanislavsky. And this line shows us as well that realism was expected in the theater of Piron's day.

Another of the unavailable actors is unwell because he has been inoculated against the smallpox, and this, too, tells us something about the period, when medical science was advancing slowly and imperfectly, and people came down with that dread scourge, now largely gone from the earth.

Far better known today, perhaps largely thanks to Rossini's and Paisiello's operas based on the first play, and Mozart and Da Ponte's based on the second, are the first two plays of the satirical *Figaro* trilogy by Pierre Caron de Beaumarchais. The second play *The Marriage of Figaro* includes overtly subversive social satire, and was considered particularly shocking, with the portrayal of aristocrats as venal, libertine, and uncaring. By order of King Louis XVI (1754–1793), the play was banned in 1779 on grounds of indecency. The ban was lifted in 1784, and the play was finally performed. Even then, Beaumarchais was briefly imprisoned.

In the play, the famous "droit du seigneur" (the lord's right) is called into question: this is the feudal right of the aristocrat to sleep on the first night of a marriage with the bride of any of his servants or peasants. Figaro does all he can to ensure that this insidious privilege will not be exercised, as Count Almaviva pursues Figaro's bride to be. The Countess Rosina whom the Count had wooed and won aided by Figaro in *The Barber of Seville*, finds her husband unfaithful and philandering. Figaro, who is now their servant, is engaged to Susanna, whom the lecherous Count pursues relentlessly. Suzanna, the Countess, Figaro, and the post-pubescent pageboy Cherubino, enamored of the Countess and just feeling the hormones racing through his blood, make every effort to prevent the Count from attaining his objective. When the suspicious Count, a domestic tyrant with a double standard, finds Cherubino in the Countess's bedroom, he banishes him by sending him into the army, but Cherubino manages to avoid leaving. The Count will be brought to heel and taught the error of his ways, and the Countess will regain the lost affections or at least the promised fidelity of her husband.

The other major genre of comedy, invented by Pierre-Claude Nivelle de La Chaussée (1692–1754), is a kind of antidote to frivolous, freewheeling attitudes about love: the comédie larmoyante (tearful, lachrymose, or sentimental comedy) is romantic comedy with a dramatic twist and tragic overtones, written to cater to bourgeois, middle-class tastes and ideas about sexual morality. These plays always have a moral, a characteristic they share with the trilogy of *Figaro* plays, and with satires generally, but their tone and intentions are not satirical but moralistic.

In La Chaussée's five-act verse comédie larmoyante, *Le préjugé à la mode*, the fashionable prejudice of the title is that it is unseemly to be in love with one's wife. Nevertheless, the philandering libertine, D'Urval, is in love with his spouse, Constance, although he has long led the life of a hedonistic seeker after sexual pleasures. She is also in love with him, even as two noblemen, Damis and Clitandre, vie for her affections. But D'Urval is afraid to be mocked with the kind of ridicule prevalent at the time, and portrayed in the French film *Ridicule* (1996), an excellent recreation of the period, as well as an engrossing movie. D'Urval's friend Damon, to whom he confesses his feelings, urges him nevertheless to declare his reawakened affection for Constance, and D'Urval sends her a diamond and a note expressing his tender love for her. But she thinks they are from one of the two noblemen, and returns them. One of her admirers tells D'Urval that he has a portrait of her, and, wildly jealous, D'Urval leaves her, but he returns disguised as Damon, to test whether his friend is actually another rival. D'Urval, discovering that Constance adores him, reveals his identity, and all is forgiven.

Marivaux (1688–1753)

With his penchant for fun and his witty dialogue, Pierre Carlet de Chamblain de Marivaux added to the theater a sense of airy lightness. The decorous persiflage in which his characters indulge became known in French as *marivaudage*, meaning playful banter and badinage, expressed in elegant language, whether the character was a servant or a person of "breeding." Marivaux' style of dialogue was different from that of Molière, whose *L'école des femmes* (The School for Wives) tells a story similar to any number of Marivaux' comedies of manners: These plays, filled with seeming insouciance, are about the quest for love and power, and inordinate, even pressing desires masked by the politesse and civility of the characters, some of whom would stop at nothing to get what they want.

Scene Analysis: Marivaux's *Le jeu de l'amour et du hasard* (The Game of Love and Chance)

The word "jeu" (literally, play or game), is usually translated in this title as "game." The word also means gaming or gambling, and in medieval days it meant "play," in its theatrical sense: *The Play of Love and Chance*. The translation "interplay" is also accurate, so the title could be *The Interplay of Love and Chance*. All three connotations exist simultaneously in French, and Francophones would have a sense of the title's ingeniousness. The word also means "acting," and people talk of an actor's "jeu," meaning his or her acting or playing.

This comedy in three acts, produced in Paris at the Comédie-Italienne in 1730 with great success, is considered Marivaux' masterpiece. Its themes and story were already familiar to those who had attended the Comédie-Italienne and seen such plays as *Les Effets du jeu et de l'amour* (The Effects of Play [i.e., gambling] and Love), written and produced in 1729 by Lélio, the pseudonym of the actor and writer, Luigi Riccoboni (1676–1753), a member of one of the principal families of the famous company. He also wrote, among other books, the first history of theater in Europe, *Réflexions historiques et critiques sur les différens Théâtres de l'Europe Avec les Pensées sur la Déclamation* (Historical and Critical Reflections on the Different Theaters of Europe, with Thoughts on Declamation), an excellent book, published in 1740. And in 1655, Philippe Quinault (1635–1688) had written a comedy called *Les Coups de l'amour et de la fortune* (The Blows of Love and Fortune). This prolific French playwright and librettist had collaborated with a number of famous composers, most notably Lully, for whom he wrote the scenarios for many ballets and for his opera *Alceste*. Despite the similarity of titles, Marivaux had no need to steal this old plot of deception and masquerade, which harks back to the ancient Greek comedies, and he used the well known commedia characters of the Young Lovers and of Harlequin (Arlecchino) as he did in fifteen other plays.

A number of actors played the Harlequin roles at the Comédie-Italienne, among them the exceptionally popular star, Carlin, the French stage name of the Italian actor Carlo "Carlino"

Antonio Bertinazzi (1710–1783), who often wore a black mask when performing the role. In her *Souvenirs* (Memoirs), the famous Rococo painter Madame Louise Elizabeth Vigée-Lebrun (1755–1842), who saw him in Marivaux comedies when she was a little girl, describes him thus:

> His inexhaustible sallies of wit, the naturalness and gaiety of his playing, made him altogether an exceptional actor. Although rather fat, he had a surprising agility and lightness in his movements. I was told that he studied his gestures, which were so flowing and graceful, from watching kittens at play, and it is true that he had their suppleness.

Actually, portraits show him as fairly thin, which he probably was thirty years before this description was penned, when he played Arlequin in a number of pieces for Marivaux. And he has the drollest of expressions on his face, as if he is about to burst out laughing.

In *Le jeu de l'amour et du hasard*, the valet Arlequin (Harlequin) was created by Carlin's predecessor, Thomassin, the stage name of Tomaso Antonio Vicentini (1682–1739), known for his athleticism and dexterity. In an Italian commedia version of the Don Juan story performed in Paris, in which he played Harlequin, the Don's valet (Leporello in Mozart and Da Ponte's opera *Don Giovanni*), Vicentini executed a lazzo for which he was famous. In the last scene, Arlequin, having ushered in the statue of the Commendatore, hid under a table, but was forced to come out when Don Juan invited the statue to stay to dinner, which Arlequin had to serve. He had poured a glass of wine for himself and toasted Donna Anna. The statue nodded its head in acknowledgement, and Vicentini, appearing to be shocked out of his mind, did a standing backward somersault, still holding the glass. He landed on his feet without having spilled a drop.

Marivaux' writing in this play without villains is witty, light-hearted and elegant, as befits the manners and rococo atmosphere of the times. His characters are insouciant and pleasant people, who overcome their courtship problems and indulge in their amorous intrigues cheerfully and with good will, like figures in a painting by François Boucher (1703–1770) or Jean-Honoré Fragonard (1732–1806), both of whose hedonistic, titillating works fill idyllic, pastoral settings with voluptuous swains and paramours. In fact, there are no sociopolitical or economic problems on the play's horizon, certainly not for these wealthy characters and their well cared for servants. The roseate skies betoken not the sunset of the regime and the system of monarchy that would begin to topple sixty-nine years later, but the dawn of a happy time, midway into the reign of Louis XV (1710–1774), who so famously said later on, when he was jaded and tired, and had lived through financial disasters and family intrigues, famines and wars, "Ça durera mon temps, après moi le déluge!" (This will last out my time, after me the deluge!)

The play is as much about the game and interplay of illusion and theatricality as it is about love and chance: The play's setting is Orgon's town house in Paris. Silvia is surprised to learn that her father Orgon has asked Dorante, a young man neither of them has ever met, to court her. A young woman of spirit, she decides to see what he is really like by changing places with her maidservant, Lisette. Orgon agrees to the deception, and Silvia's brother, Mario, finds the idea intriguing, and, for his own amusement, will tease the disguised couple. The entire household is informed, so that no mistakes will be made that might reveal the truth before it should be known. Orgon, enjoining his son to be discreet, tells Mario privately that he has had a letter from his friend, Dorante's father, informing him that Dorante himself has also decided to test his possible future wife, and to disguise himself as his own valet, Arlequin. (It is worth noting that Marivaux used the Harlequin character in fifteen of his plays.) So Orgon, whom Dorante had not wanted informed, and Mario are the only people aware of the double deception that is about to take place. Dorante arrives, using the name Bourguigon (Burgundy) and presents Arlequin to them, disguised as Dorante himself. (Arlequin's entrance scene—act 1, scene 9—is the first truly hilarious scene in the play, which has nevertheless been delightful up until then.) Silvia and Dorante thus meet each other for the first time disguised as their servants, and the servants meet, disguised as the masters. Silvia is soon attracted to "Arlequin" (Dorante), and finds "Dorante" (Arlequin) impossible and intolerable. Dorante can't abide "Silvia" (Lisette), but finds himself falling in love with "Lisette" (the real Silvia). Both Silvia and Dorante are chagrinned to think that they have fallen for servants, whom it would be impossible for them to marry. Dorante, who can't stand the masquerade any longer, reveals his identity to Silvia, still disguised as her maid, Lisette. She is overjoyed, but decides to continue her own masquerade a bit longer, in order to test him further. She will get him to propose to her, even though he still thinks her a servant. Meanwhile, Mario, whom Dorante has never met, appears by arrangement with Silvia, and passes himself off as "Lisette's" lover. Dorante is jealous and enraged, and departs, disconsolate and upset. But he decides that he truly loves "Lisette," so he returns to claim her in marriage, and, despite the difference in their social stations, he proposes to her. She is delighted to find him the most honorable and noble of men, and enchanted that he is truly in love with her, and she reveals her true identity. Dorante is thrilled, and thanks Mario for forcing the issue. Meanwhile, the real Arlequin has fallen in love with the real Lisette, and the play closes with the happy prospect of a double marriage of masters and servants.

Typical of dialogue in this period is the extensive use of asides, as in the following example from act 1, scene 2. Orgon has just heard his daughter's proposal to disguise herself as Lisette, and have Lisette temporarily take her place to greet Dorante:

MONSIEUR ORGON. (*Aside*) Her idea is amusing. (*Aloud*) Let me think a bit about what you said. (*Aside*) If I allow her to do this, something unusual may happen, that she isn't even expecting herself...(*Aloud*) So be it, my daughter, I will allow you to disguise yourself. Are you quite sure, Lisette, that you can bring off your part in this?

The aside is thus a convenient vehicle for informing the audience of a character's real thoughts, and, in this case, for the character, who may be blocked to move off for a second, to pretend to be thinking, as he says he wants to do. Or he may simply turn his head toward the audience, then turn back to speak to his daughter. In any case, he has already made up his mind, and is simply musing about what may ensue. When he speaks again, Orgon does not reveal what he has been thinking. Although it is not very difficult to master, the aside still demands some versatility, and the ability to change technically and seamlessly from one form of dialogue (musing, in this case) to another (speaking to an interlocutor). This is a variation of the comedy technique called the "instant switch," discussed under takes in chapter one.

From Arlequin's hilarious entrance on, the tempo-rhythm of the play will get faster, until it reaches its happy climax. The pace has been more leisurely, although still lively, up until his entrance. Disguised as Dorante, Arlequin puts on outlandish airs and carries on like trash, acting as if he almost owns the place and is already married. He is even seductive with the false Lisette, before whom he preens as he ogles her. When "Lisette" leaves to fetch Orgon, Dorante reproaches Arlequin: "You promised me you would leave your stupid, trivial way of talking at home. I gave you such good instructions! I told you to be serious! Well, I see that I was a fool to trust you."

Naturally, Arlequin promises to improve: "I'll do better from now on. And if serious isn't enough, I'll give you melancholy. I'll even weep, if I have to."

"I don't know what I've gotten myself into," says Dorante, "this little adventure is getting me down! What should I do?"

To which the insouciant Arlequin, obviously enjoying himself, replies, "Isn't that wench attractive?"

"Shut up!" says Dorante, "here's Monsieur Orgon!"

It is in act 2, scene 12 that Dorante reveals his true identity to Silvia, still disguised as her impertinent maid, Lisette. Class distinctions, considered suitable at the time, are preserved: People of the same class actually fall in love with each other. The idea is that breeding will tell; Marivaux is nothing if not socio-politically conservative. Here is an excerpt from the first half of the scene, which will show you, even in translation, the stylishness of Marivaux' elegant writing and his felicitous manner of portraying the delightful and pleasing ardor of love:

DORANTE. Ah, I was looking for you, Lisette.

SILVIA. Well, it wasn't worth the trouble to find me, because I am running from you!

DORANTE. Stay, Lisette! I must speak to you for the last time, on a matter of importance to your masters.

SILVIA. Go tell them! Every time I see you, you torture me! Leave me!

DORANTE. The same is true for you! But listen to me, I tell you, and you will see everything change its aspect once I've said what I have to say.

SILVIA. Very well, speak! I will listen, since it seems my indulgence towards you is bound to be eternal.

DORANTE. Will you promise to keep a secret?

SILVIA. I have never betrayed anyone.

DORANTE. You owe the confidence I have in you to the esteem in which I hold you.

SILVIA. I believe you. But try to esteem me without telling me, because this smells of a pretext.

DORANTE. You are deceived, Lisette. You promised to keep a secret. Let's end this! You have seen my passion. I could not prevent myself from loving you.

SILVIA. Well, there we are! I will prevent myself from listening to you! Goodbye!

DORANTE. Stay! It is not Bourguigon who speaks to you!

SILVIA. Oh? Then who is it?

DORANTE. Ah, Lisette! It is now that you shall judge of the pain my heart has felt!

SILVIA. It is not to your heart that I am speaking, but to you!

DORANTE. Nobody is coming?

SILVIA. No.

DORANTE. The present state of things forces me to tell you this. I am too honest a man to stop them in their course.

SILVIA. So be it!

DORANTE. Know that he who is with your mistress is not the person you think him to be.

SILVIA. Who is he then?

DORANTE. A valet.

SILVIA. And?

DORANTE. It is I who am Dorante.

SILVIA. (*Aside*) Ah! Now I see clearly into my heart.

DORANTE. In this disguise I wanted to penetrate a little into what your mistress was like, before marrying her. Before I left, my father allowed this, and what followed seems like a dream: I hate the mistress whom I was to marry, and love the servant, who could only find in me another master. What should I do now? I blush for her to tell you this, but your mistress has so little taste that she is enamored of my valet, to the point where she would marry him if she were allowed to do so. What side should I take?

SILVIA. (*Aside*) Let us conceal from him who I am!...

And she continues to do so, in order to test him further. Here are some possible choices for each character:

1. **Superobjective:** *Dorante*: To find love, and happiness in marriage. *Silvia*: To find love, and to be happy in marriage.

2. **Throughline of action:** *Dorante*: I disguise myself as my valet in order to have a good look at what my designated bride is like. I fall in love with her maid. I reveal to her who I am, and feel I have no choice but to leave. I love her so much that I return. And it turns out that she is actually my prospective bride, so I am happy to end things by marrying her. *Silvia*: I am frightened by the prospect of marrying just anybody, after having seen my friends' unhappy experiences of marriage. So I disguise myself as my maid in order to be able to observe my prospective husband. He is a horror, but, to my chagrin, considering social circumstances, I fall in love with his valet. But his valet is actually Dorante in disguise. Still, when he reveals himself

to me, I decide to continue my own masquerade to see further what he is like. I discover how true and loyal and faithful and goodhearted a person he is, willing to sacrifice all for love, and I finally reveal myself to him, and know that I will be happily married to the man I love, and who requites my affections.

3. **Counter-throughline:** *Dorante:* I must maintain my disguise, and make sure Arlequin maintains his, for as long as possible. *Silvia:* I must maintain my disguise and make sure Lisette maintains hers, for as long as possible.

4. **Adjectives describing the character:** *Dorante:* Intelligent, amorous, self-protective, incautious, forthright. *Silvia:* Intelligent, sweet-tempered, understanding, self-assured, self-protective.

5. **Point of view:** *Dorante:* I have enough proper self-respect to have to be sure she is the right one, and I love this servant more than the mistress I was supposed to marry, and ultimately that counts more than social class and the opinion of society. *Silvia:* I cannot allow myself to be roped into a marriage that I don't want, and I must be sure that I do want it, and that he is the right person, which I will find out before giving my consent.

6. **What is the main event in the scene?** The revelation of Dorante's true identity.

7. **Where does the scene take place?** In the reception hall of Orgon's house in Paris.

8. **What are the other given circumstances—time of day; weather; your physical condition?** It is a pleasant summer day, and warm in the house. Both characters are in fine physical shape, but Silvia is feeling upset and depressed, both because she is in love with a man she takes to be a valet, and at the prospect of marrying a man she has grown to detest, if not despise.

9. **What do you want—your objective?** *Dorante:* My love is stronger all the time, and I can no longer stand to hide it. I want to reveal my love for Silvia to her, and perhaps she can help me decide what to do in these impossible circumstances. I want to decide what to do about all this. *Silvia:* I want to

decide what to do, once I learn the truth. I continue the masquerade partly in order to gain time. The aside, "Ah! Now I see clearly into my heart!" shows that I have loved him all along, and sensed that he was not the valet I took him for: His manner was too refined and he was to polite to be of that low class.

10. **What is in the way—the obstacle?** *Dorante*: I am in love with a servant, Lisette, as I think, and I would never be allowed to make a marriage below my station. Also, in immediate terms, someone may come in at any moment, as I am revealing my love. Perhaps I think I hear a sound, and turn to see, when I say, "Nobody is coming?" *Silvia*: I am in love with a valet, and that makes marriage impossible. When he reveals himself, this is no longer an obstacle, but I am afraid still, because I need to know more about what he is like.

11. **What does your character do—your actions?** *Dorante*: I enter and find her. I make her stay and listen to me. I tell her what is on my mind, and who I really am. *Silvia*: I have gone in here to get away and think, but I stay when he asks me to. I don't want to encourage him, so I am snippy with him. And I stay because I really want to, because I actually love him. When I have heard him out, after my initial snippy remarks, I decide to continue in my masquerade for a while longer.

12. **Do you attain your objective by the end of the scene?** *Dorante*: Yes, in that I have revealed who I am and declared my love; but ultimately no, because I still don't know what to do about it. *Silvia*: Yes.

Theater in Denmark: The Comedies of Ludvig Holberg (1684–1754)

In Denmark, the cynicism of libertinage and the corruption of mores was not a usual theme in comedies of manner, but political satire proved very popular since the class system was very much in evidence.

Ludvig Holberg was an astounding polymath. He taught Latin and History at the University of Copenhagen, wrote major histories of

Denmark, books on international law, and on many other subjects. He wandered through various European lands, absorbing everything he could about the local customs and people, and he was able to use everything in his writing.

Holberg is known as the father of comedy in Denmark. Using as his models the commedia dell'arte plays, published by Evaristo Gherardi in Paris in French in 1707, and the comedies of Molière, as well as Shakespeare and English Restoration comedy, he created a uniquely Danish comedy, with characters drawn from the life he saw around him. His plays may have been modeled on those others, but Holberg transformed them, and he painted deeper psychological portraits than is true of even Goldsmith and Sheridan, where plot is more important than character.

Professor Oscar James Campbell, Jr. (1879–1970), the American expert on Holberg, and the translator of his plays, wrote *The Comedies of Holberg* (1914), in which he classifies Holberg's stage works, which are often revived in Denmark, into four categories:

1. Domestic comedies of character
2. Simple comedies of character
3. Comedies of intrigue
4. Comedies of manners

Holberg's great interest in portraying people with psychological depth gives actors characters with a rich emotional and cognitive life. He wrote comparatively few comedies of manners, and most of his plays fall into the first two categories. In his domestic comedies of character, he takes one principal male personage and writes him in depth, showing his foibles and follies, ridiculing them, and holding them up for the world to see clearly.

Jeppe paa Bjerget eller den forvandlede Bonde (Jeppe of the Hill; or The Transformed Peasant; 1722)

Based on the situation with which Shakespeare opens *The Taming of the Shrew*, *Jeppe of the Hill*, one of Holberg's domestic comedies of character, takes the plot of Shakespeare's prologue and expands it into the main story. In *Shrew*, the tinker Christopher Sly, drunk beyond imagining, is fooled into believing he is a rich man, and in *Jeppe*, the title character, an ex-soldier turned peasant, is made to think he is the local baron and landowner who runs the peasants' lives. The story is actually much older than Shakespeare, and is also to be found as long ago as *The Thousand and One Nights* of Arabian literature, where drunkards are traduced and betrayed into believing that something patently false is true.

Jeppe is married to a shrew, who has generally tamed him, although he goes off to get drunk all the time, in spite of his misgivings about the consequences when he returns home to Nille, who keeps a switch that she has named Eric handy so she can beat him with it when he misbehaves. And Jeppe, as Professor Campbell puts it, "is an extraordinarily complete and vivid human being." Indeed, Jeppe is cringing and brave, cowardly and curmudgeonly, shrewd, clever, bombastic, satiric, pompous, sarcastic and insightful by turns, as well as put upon and the victim of fate. And he sees everything through drink-sodden eyes, for he loves his beer and brandy.

Nille sends Jeppe to town to buy her some soap, but instead of proceeding on his errand, Jeppe stops in for a drink in a tavern across the way from the house. It is run by his convivial, if untrusting old comrade in arms, Jacob Shoemaker. Jeppe gets so drunk that he falls asleep on a dung heap. The local baron and his servants find Jeppe and haul him off to the castle, change his clothes, and put him to bed. When he wakes they convince him he is the baron, and he proceeds to lord it over them. Drunk and asleep again, Jeppe is dressed in his filthy peasant garb and taken back to his dung heap, on which he wakes. He is promptly arrested by the judge and put on trial, all as a joke, then condemned to be executed by hanging. To give himself courage, and although he faces death bravely, Jeppe asks for a glass of brandy, which he is granted, and he falls asleep again, since it contains a sleeping potion. When he wakes, he is on a gallows, the rope safely under his armpits. His wife comes along and he convinces her that he is dead, but the truth is revealed when she beats him with Eric and he feels pain. The judge stops the beating and sends Nille packing. The practical joke in which the baron and the others take such delight is now over, but Jeppe, convinced that he was a baron and was dead, and is now alive, proceeds to lord it over Shoemaker, and to drink away the money he was given as a compensation. The epilogue, spoken by the baron, tells us the moral of the tale: People should know their station. Elevating a peasant to a position of governance is a mistake, because only those to the manor born are worthy to rule. In short, a cobbler should stick to his last. But Holberg is being ironic! As Professor Campbell neatly sums it up, "Here a character [Jeppe], apparently the creature of a time-worn farcical story, is made to represent in vital human terms the results of a debasing social and economic system."

English Comedy

Colley Cibber still flourished, and the century also saw the plays and collaborations of George Colman "the Older," and the extravaganzas of George Colman "the Younger," both of whom were also theater managers. And the famous actor-manager David Garrick (1712–1779), the most noted actor of his era, famous for his reforms in acting and theatrical presentation, and the father of modern realistic acting, also wrote and produced comedies and farces. But the most enduring plays of the era were written by Goldsmith and Sheridan.

The Anglo-Irish Playwrights: Sheridan and Goldsmith

The theatrical output of Oliver Goldsmith (1728 / 1730?–1774) and Richard Brinsley Sheridan (1751–1816) was not prolific, but they wrote masterpieces, and their humor is still much appreciated. Goldsmith's ironical five-act comedy of manners, *She Stoops to Conquer, or The Mistakes of a Night*, receives constant revivals, as do Sheridan's plays.

Goldsmith, whose parents were English, was born and raised in Ireland. After completing his education and not knowing what to do with himself, he traveled around Europe, winding up in London and taking all kinds of jobs, until he finally settled on writing as a career.

His novel, *The Vicar of Wakefield*, brought him fame immediately when it was published in 1766, and earned him the friendship of Garrick and other influential literary and artistic figures who wanted to know him. But in 1768 his first play, *The Good-Natured Man*, was an unfortunate failure, and has rarely been revived. Aside from *She Stoops to Conquer*, he wrote one other play, *The Grumbler*, which remained unfinished at his death.

She Stoops to Conquer sends up social and class attitudes, and is at the same time precursive of the romantic era's sensitivity and sentimentality in matters of love. The country Squire Hardcastle and his wife, Lady Hardcastle, await the arrival from London of Mr. Marlowe, a prospective fiancée for their daughter Kate. Although an aristocrat, Marlowe is uncomfortable and shy around upper-class women, but forward and at ease around lower-class women. Kate realizes immediately that in order to win him, she will have to pose as lower class, so she pretends to be a barmaid, and thus stoops to conquer. There are droll misunderstandings, and plot complications involving subplots as well as the main thread, but in the end Kate succeeds in her plan.

Sheridan was born in Dublin, and both his parents were in the theater. His father, Thomas Sheridan (1719–1788), son of an Anglican clergyman and godson of Jonathan Swift, was a well known actor; and his mother, née Frances Chamberlaine (1724–1766), the daughter of an Anglican clergyman, was a novelist and playwright. They decided that it would be more advantageous to live in England, and the family moved to London in 1758, where Thomas Sheridan, giving up his acting career, established a school of elocution, and Frances Sheridan had two plays produced at the Drury Lane by Garrick. Richard Brinsley Sheridan taught at the school until it went bankrupt, driving him to write plays in a desperate attempt to recoup some of the family fortunes. In 1780, Thomas Sheridan, who wrote four books, published *A General Dictionary of the English Language*, "one main Object of which, is, to establish a plain and permanent Standard of Pronunciation"; it also included a long section on grammar. The "List of Subscribers" (purchasers) included David Garrick and the Trinity College Library in Dublin.

Sheridan fell in love with Elizabeth Linley (1754–1792), a singer, and this fiery, temperamental man, quick to take offense, fought two duels to defend her honor. He married her in 1773, and insisted that she give up her career, which she did some years later. Her father was the English composer Thomas Linley (1733–1795), who wrote a dozen operas, and is best known for the score to *The Duenna*, produced in 1775, with a libretto by Sheridan. Elizabeth performed in the piece, and Linley's son, Thomas (1756–1778), a violinist and composer, collaborated with his father on the score.

After the success of Sheridan's plays, particularly *The Rivals*, which made him famous, Sheridan and his father-in-law, in partnership with a certain Dr. Ford, became theater managers of the Drury Lane, having purchased Garrick's shares.

Sheridan had been befriended by some notable political figures of the day, especially the Whig, Charles James Fox (1749–1806), and decided to go into politics himself, and in 1780, he was elected to the House of Commons. Popular for his wit and famous for his oratory, he was highly successful as a parliamentarian, serving until 1812, nor was he above indulging in the ubiquitous custom of the day, taking small bribes. He was also extravagant, and racked up a mountain of gambling and other debts, many of which he incurred in rebuilding the Drury Lane twice over. Once he was no longer an MP, and had no immunity from creditors, they descended upon him like wolves, and his last years were spent in penury. The only other play he ever wrote after he became an MP was an adaptation of Kotzebue's tragedy *Pizarro*, produced in 1794.

Reminiscences of Michael Kelly, of the King's Theatre, and the Theatre Royal Drury Lane (1826) by Michael Kelly (1762–1826), the Irish tenor, theater manager, and composer, and a close friend of Sheridan, is full of droll anecdotes about everyone he knew in the world of music and the theater, including Dr. Arne, Charles Dibdin, Samuel Arnold, Giovanni Paisiello, and Mozart, whom he describes at rehearsals of *Le nozze di Figaro*, in which Kelly originated the roles of Don Curzio, the magistrate, and Don Basilio. Mozart was enthusiastic, encouraging, and altogether charming.

Kelly tells us this anecdote about his acquaintance, the bel canto singing teacher, violinist, and composer, the castrato Ferdinando Mazzanti (171?–179?), "who had been formerly a celebrated soprano singer in Italy and Germany," and was visiting London at the age of seventy:

> ...and he told me, that the first time he ever went to an opera in England, the performance was "The Beggar's Opera Travestied," at the Little Theatre in the Haymarket, which he mistook for the Opera House in the same street. The part of Polly on this occasion was represented by the elder Bannister [the distinguished actor, Charles Bannister (1738–1804)], who gave her tender airs with all the power of his deep and sonorous bass voice; and he told me that his astonishment and horror were unspeakable, when he saw the part of a young woman acted by an old man; for he had not been informed, nor did he even guess at the time, that the part of Polly was burlesqued; on the contrary, he thought it had been so intended by the author, and always so acted.

That his friend was so horrified is amusing, in light of the fact that Mazzanti himself had been a soprano singer before his retirement from the stage, but no doubt he only sang male roles.

The Beggar's Opera was the first and is still the best known of the ballad operas, which were comedies with music. The music for its more than sixty-nine songs was adapted from various sources, including folk tunes and Handel operas, and arranged by the German-born English composer and pedagogue, Dr. Johann Christoph Pepusch (1667–1752), who also composed some original music for it, including the overture. The text and lyrics are by John Gay (1685–1732), and it was first produced in London at Lincoln's Inn Fields in 1728. The idea for the story about the gallant two-timing highwayman Macheath, pardoned for his crimes just as he is about to be hanged, was suggested to Gay by his brilliant friend Jonathan Swift (1667–1745), author of one of the great satires about humanity, *Travels into Several Remote Nations of the World, In Four Parts. By Lemuel Gulliver, First a Surgeon, and then a Captain of Several Ships*, known simply as *Gulliver's Travels* (1726; revised, 1735).

Sheridan had his eccentricities and often neglected his affairs, hence his problems in later life. Michael Kelly describes a number of instances in his *Reminiscences* of Sheridan's sometimes odd behavior. Kelly was preparing to sing Ferdinand in a revival of *The Duenna*, and, having gone over his part, left the house, leaving the printed copy of the play "on the table." He returned home to find Sheridan correcting it, and Kelly preserved this unique copy. "What could prove his negligence more," asks Kelly, "than correcting an opera which he had written in 1775, in the year 1807; and then, for the first time, examining it, and abusing the manner in which it was printed?"

On another occasion, after the Duke of Bedford had "put a distress [lien] on the Drury Lane Theatre for nonpayment of ground rent," Sheridan petitioned for the lien to be taken off, and the duke had apparently agreed to an arrangement whereby Sheridan promised to pay him £10 a night out of ticket sales until the back rent was paid. More than a year passed, and "Sheridan was astonished at receiving no reply to his letter," so he went "in an angry mood" to the duke's attorney—"I was with him at the time"—and complained to the lawyer, who assured him that the duke had indeed replied, "Above a year before."

On hearing this, Sheridan went home, examined the table on which all his letters were thrown, and among them found the Duke's letter, unopened, dated more than twelve months back. To me, this did not appear very surprising; for, when numbers of letters have been brought to him, at my house, I have seen him consign the greatest part of them to the fire, unopened.

Scene Analysis: Sheridan's *The Rivals*

The Rivals, produced at London's Covent Garden Theatre in 1775, the year the American Revolution began, was Sheridan's first play, written when he was only twenty-three, but it shows a mature understanding of life far beyond his years. The play was a flop at its premier, partly because of its bawdy humor, in an age heading toward puritanical attitudes in matters sexual and reacting against ubiquitous libertinism. The play also lasted an hour longer than had been intended. In addition, the part of Sir Lucius O'Trigger was played by John Lee (?–?), who did not seem to know his business that evening, and was roundly booed by the audience. He had been primarily a tragedian, famous for being one of the actors to play Iago opposite Garrick's rival, Spranger Barry (1719–1777), who performed the role of Othello after Garrick had decided not to do the play.

Lee was known also for being temperamental and for taking excessively long pauses. This is a good lesson for modern actors: Pauses must be meaningful, full of thought and internal action, and not self-indulgent. And they must advance, rather than impede the action.

He was known as well for his vanity, and the pains he took over his appearance. After being hit with an apple that evening, Lee stepped to the footlights and asked, "By the pow'rs, is it personal? Is it me or the matter?" The part was perceived as offensive to the Irish, and the audience reacted to the insults, as well as to the bad acting. Sheridan immediately withdrew the play, and rewrote it, shortening the scenes, tightening up the dialogue, and rewriting the role of Sir Lucius. He recast the part as well, with the fine Irish actor Laurence (also spelled Lawrence) Clinch (?–?), a Dubliner then resident in England. Clinch's acting is said to be partly responsible for the play's success. Sheridan also apologized for the unintended insult. When the play was remounted, it proved a great and lasting hit. The original cast of this comedy of manners included some the greatest comic actors of the age:

Edward "Ned" Shuter (1728?–1776), whom David Garrick said was the greatest comic actor he had ever met, and who created the role of Squire Hardcastle in Goldsmith's *She Stoops to Conquer*, played Sir Anthony Absolute. He was also quite a character himself: A great drinker and raconteur, he would hold court, and regale his hearers with anecdotes and jokes. He was also extremely religious, and would preach when drunk. He was a noteworthy Falstaff, whom he understood perfectly.

The versatile leading man and comedian Harry Woodward (1717–1777), who created the part of Sir Anthony's son, Captain Absolute, began his career when but a boy, and went on to play Mercutio in *Romeo and Juliet*, Touchstone in *As You Like It*, and, notably, Petruccio in *The Taming of the Shrew*, in which he was extravagant and grotesque in the wedding scene. Woodward was also known for his graceful movement, and he played Harlequin in a number of plays. In 1773, he spoke the prologue written by Garrick for *She Stoops to Conquer*.

The part of Mrs. Malaprop was created by the distinguished Jane Green (?–1791), who used the stage name Mrs. Green, as she had formerly used her maiden name when she acted as Miss Hippisley, until 1747. She had played Ophelia to Garrick's Hamlet, and would later create the role of Lady Hardcastle in *She Stoops to Conquer*, in which she also made her farewell performance in 1780.

In Henry Fielding's (1707–1754) "comic romance," *The History of the Adventures of Joseph Andrews and of His Friend, Mr. Abraham Adams*, the novel he published in 1742, Mrs. Slipslop tries to seduce young Joseph, who has not understood a single word she has said, and, tongue-tied, can only reply, "Yes, Madam."

> "Yes, Madam!" replied Mrs. Slipslop with some warmth, "Do you intend to result my passion? Is it not enough, ungrateful as you are, to make no return for all the favors I have done you: but you must treat me with ironing? Barbarous monster! how have I deserved that my passion should be resulted and treated with ironing?"

Mrs. Slipslop may have been Sheridan's inspiration for one of his most famous and beloved characters, Mrs. Malaprop, who is slipshod in her speech. Her name has passed into the language: A malapropism is the unconscious, unintentional use of a wrong word in place of the right one that was intended. Mrs. Malaprop is always using a word that is close in sound to the one she really means to use, as in what is probably the best known of her malapropisms, "She's as headstrong as an allegory on the banks of the Nile." Her name comes from the French phrase, *mal à propos*, one meaning of which is "inappropriate." Here is another example: "Ah, and the properest way, o' my conscience!—nothing is so conciliating to young people as severity…prepare Lydia to receive your son's invocations;—and I hope you will represent her to the captain as an object not altogether illegible."

Bob Acres, the part later played to such acclaim by Joseph Jefferson (see chapter twelve), was created by the quaint and whimsical John Quick (1748–1831), who also created Tony Lumpkin in *She Stoops to Conquer.* This very versatile actor was small of frame and had a naturally funny voice with a squeak to it, which no doubt served him well as Rigdum-Funnidos in a revival of *Chrononhotonthologos.* He played scores of roles in his long and distinguished career, among them the First Gravedigger in *Hamlet.* And he was the favorite actor of King George III (1738–1820), who enjoyed conversing with him so much that he often invited him to Buckingham Palace. The English biographer and playwright, James Boaden (1762–1839), who wrote the lives of several famous actors and actresses, said of him:

> In all Shakespeare's clowns, he freely executed the conceptions of his great author, and said no more than was set down for him. His Dogberry [in *Much Ado About Nothing*] may be said to have been as perfect a personation as any representation even by Garrick himself.

As Garrick, the greatest actor of his age, said, "You can fool the town with Tragedy, but Comedy is a serious business." The actors mentioned here took that business very seriously, and everyone in comedy today should follow their lead: They studied their parts assiduously, and played their characters in a real way, without trying to be funny. Garrick himself performed equally well in both tragedy and comedy, and the facetiousness of his remark belied the powerful felt nature of his characterizations: In tragedy, he moved the audience by his real playing, and in comedy, he provoked laughter by his drollery.

There are psychological dramas in which there is a conflict between two conscious impulses, as there is in *The Rivals,* with its comedic

portrayal of conflict between generations; and there are psychopatho-
logical dramas, in which there is a conflict between a conscious impulse
and a repressed one—think of Hamlet and his internal conflict over
avenging his father's murder. No matter which type of drama or comedy we talk about, underlying them all is the idea that they are the "ter-
rain," as Freud calls it, on which "the action that leads to the suffering
is fought out."

This witty, farcical comedy of manners takes place in Bath, where
the gentry go to take the waters. Not accidentally, it is a play about
the beginnings of a social revolution. Mrs. Malaprop wants her
niece, Lydia Languish to marry the dull, provincial country squire,
Bob Acres. But when Sir Anthony Absolute arrives in Bath and proposes to Mrs. Malaprop that Lydia should marry his son, Captain
Jack Absolute, Mrs. Malaprop, seeing this as a more advantageous
match, drops Acres, and consents to the new arrangement. But
Lydia is in love with "Ensign Beverly," who is really Jack Absolute
in disguise. He masquerades as a poor person in order to win Lydia's
love, because he believes that if she loves him as a pauper, she will
really love him, even when she discovers who he is and that he has
money—a great deal of money, in fact. In addition, Lydia Languish
is extremely sentimental and unrealistic and has her heart set on marrying a poor man, so that Jack must pretend to be poor in any case.
Mrs. Malaprop and Sir Anthony have learned of Lydia's romantic
attachment to "Beverley," and strongly disapprove of the impoverished ensign, without ever having met him, of course. Sir Anthony
tells Jack that he has found him a wife, and the enraged young man,
not knowing that it is Lydia, quarrels with his father. To complicate
matters further, if Lydia marries without her aunt's consent, she will
lose her fortune to Mrs. Malaprop. Bob Acres, furious at what he
takes to be the insult to his honor is egged on by his friend, the
Irishman, Sir Lucius O'Trigger, to challenge Ensign Beverley to a
duel, and he sends his friend Jack Absolute to issue the challenge to
Beverley! Meanwhile, Sir Lucius, wounded in his love for "Delia," his
secret correspondent, whom he thinks is Lydia, but who is in reality
the infatuated Mrs. Malaprop, challenges Jack Absolute to a duel! He

accepts the challenge, and they all meet as prearranged. Everything is then explained, and Lydia, in love with Jack, agrees to marry him, while Sir Lucius rejects Mrs. Malaprop. Bob Acres, who had not really wanted to fight in the first place, but had felt obliged to do so, withdraws his challenge. There is also a subplot: Jack's friend, young Faulkland, jealously in love with Lydia's cousin and confidante, Julia, resolves his difficulties over what he has taken to be her provocative conduct toward other men, and the two are united. In short, everything ends satisfactorily and everyone lives happily ever after.

Here is an excerpt from act 1, scene 2, which is set in "A Dressing-Room in Mrs. Malaprop's Lodgings." Mrs. Malaprop has discovered Lydia's liaison with Beverley, and she points the finger of scorn at her niece, and addresses Sir Anthony, as they enter the room: "There, sir, there sits the deliberate Simpleton, who wants to disgrace her family, and lavish herself on a fellow not worth a shilling!" She wants Lydia to "illiterate him, I say, quite from your memory." And she admonishes Lydia, "Now don't attempt to extirpate yourself from the matter; you know I have proof controvertible of it." She also tells Lydia that she has no right to have a preference for anyone, and that she, Mrs. Malaprop, has someone in view for her to marry. She does not tell Lydia that the person in question is Captain Jack Absolute, whom she has just been discussing with his father. And she orders her niece away: "Take yourself to your room.—You are fit company for nothing but your own ill-humors!" Upon this remark, Lydia storms out, angry and upset. Sir Anthony, who is taken aback by the young lady's attitude, is now alone with the fuming Mrs. Malaprop:

MRS. MALAPROP. There's a little intricate hussy for you.
SIR ANTHONY ABSOLUTE. It is not to be wondered at, ma'am,—all this is the natural consequence of teaching girls to read. Had I a thousand daughters, by Heaven! I'd as soon have them taught the black art as their alphabet!

[Lydia has been reading the latest novels, but has hastily concealed them upon her aunt's approach, since Mrs. Malaprop might disapprove, and prominently displayed instead a book of Fordyce's sermons and Lord Chesterfield's *Letters* of advice to his son (see above). Lucy, Lydia's maid, has informed her in distress that "the Hairdresser has torn away as far as Proper Pride." In other words, the hairdresser, who makes house calls, as was common in that period, has used the pages for curling papers. "Never mind," says Lydia, "open at Sobriety." Fordyce was the Scottish clergyman, James Fordyce (1720–1796), who died in Bath, appropriately considering the setting of this play. In 1766, he published his edifying *Sermons for Young Women.*]

MRS. MALAPROP. Nay, nay, Sir Anthony, you are an absolute misanthropy.

SIR ANTHONY ABSOLUTE. In my way hither, Mrs. Malaprop, I observed your niece's maid coming forth from a circulating library!—She had a book in each hand—they were half-bound volumes, with marble covers!—From that moment I guessed how full of duty I should see her mistress!

MRS. MALAPROP. Those are vile places, indeed!

SIR ANTHONY ABSOLUTE. Madam, a circulating library in a town is as an evergreen tree of diabolical knowledge! It blossoms through the year!—And depend on it, Mrs. Malaprop, that they who are so fond of handling the leaves, will long for the fruit at last.

MRS. MALAPROP. Fy, fy, Sir Anthony! you surely speak laconically.

SIR ANTHONY ABSOLUTE. Why, Mrs. Malaprop, in moderation now, what would you have a woman know?

MRS. MALAPROP. Observe me, Sir Anthony. I would by no means wish a daughter of mine to be a progeny of learning; I don't think so much learning becomes a young woman; for instance, I would never let her meddle with Greek, or Hebrew, or algebra, or simony, or fluxions, or paradoxes, or such inflammatory branches of learning—neither would it be necessary for her to handle any of your mathematical, astronomical, diabolical instruments.—But, Sir

Anthony, I would send her, at nine years old, to a boarding-school, in order to learn a little ingenuity and artifice. Then, sir, she should have a supercilious knowledge in accounts;—and as she grew up, I would have her instructed in geometry, that she might know something of the contagious countries;—but above all, Sir Anthony, she should be mistress of orthodoxy, that she might not mis-spell, and mis-pronounce words so shamefully as girls usually do; and likewise that she might reprehend the true meaning of what she is saying. This, Sir Anthony, is what I would have a woman know;—and I don't think there is a superstitious article in it.

The whole idea of arranged marriages is called into question in this play, although it would be a common custom through at least the first two decades of the twentieth century in western culture, and still is in some cultures. Women are always in a subordinate position in such a sociocultural situation, treated like chattels, to be bought and sold. Women are not to be treated as the equal of men, not even to be broadly educated, and feminism is unthinkable. Children must obey their parents in all things, including marrying the person chosen by the father. This is the mindset common to all the characters, even those who rebel against it.

Mrs. Malaprop and Sir Anthony Absolute are both narcissistic, manipulative egotists, but they are not malignant, so we can laugh at their foibles, eccentricities, and obsessions. And they mean well in their authoritarian approach to running their children's lives for what they think is the children's own good.

Mrs. Malaprop is pompous and stuck-up and unconscious of her misuse of language. Julia speaks in act 1, scene 2 of "…her select words so ingeniously *misapplied*, without being *mispronounced*." The humor comes partly from the air of authority she gives to even her most trivial utterances, while making the most egregious mistakes. And everything she says is absolutely serious. When preparing Mrs. Malaprop you have first of all to analyze the language, that is, to figure out what she actually means, then to give the words the meaning she actually intends.

What sort of inner conflict is it in Mrs. Malaprop that leads her to be so imprecise, thus unconsciously undermining her own authority? Deep insecurity and a feeling of not being loved are at the core of this histrionic, hysterical character. And the underlying feeling that she does not deserve to be loved leads to the unconscious, masochistic desire to be punished, which would take the form of being mocked, if anyone dared to point out to her how absurdly stupid her warping of the English language makes her appear. But nobody would dare indulge in mockery to her face, because she preserves her air of authority as a defense.

Sir Anthony Absolute's name, like many names in seventeenth- and eighteenth-century plays, represents the basis of the character: Everything he says is absolute, as if it were a divine, oracular utterance. He is inflexible and utterly convinced that he is right about everything. There is little give and take between him and his interlocutor, to whom he often barely listens. But underneath it all, he loves his son and wants what is best for him, so that his severity is tempered by his affection, and is, indeed, a result of it.

Here are some possible choices for each character:

1. **Superobjective:** *Mrs. Malaprop*: I want to be respected, and obeyed. *Sir Anthony Absolute*: I want to see my son happily married, in the way I think best for him, and I want his respect and obedience.

2. **Throughline of action:** *Mrs. Malaprop*: I keep a firm eye on Lydia, and try to thwart her, until all is revealed, and turns out well for everyone. *Sir Anthony Absolute*: I keep a firm eye on my son and try to make sure he does what I want, until all is revealed, and turns out well for everyone.

3. **Counter-throughline:** *Mrs. Malaprop*: I don't trust Lydia, and she seems to be evading me, and I have to find out what is really happening. *Sir Anthony Absolute*: My son keeps avoiding me and I am not in the best mood, so I don't always see clearly what is going on. I tend to lose my temper, instead of analyzing the situation calmly.

4. **Adjectives describing the character**: *Mrs. Malaprop*: Insecure, dictatorial, imperious, untrusting, suspicious. *Sir Anthony Absolute*: Authoritarian, strict, opinionated, inflexible, well-meaning.

5. **Point of view**: *Mrs. Malaprop*: The younger generation doesn't know what is good for it, and I, in my superiority of knowledge and behavior, must teach them, and make my niece in particular learn to be obedient and chaste, and to stop reading those disgusting novels. *Sir Anthony Absolute*: Everyone ought to know his or her place, to keep it, and to keep it well. Women, for instance, should not be overeducated: it doesn't suit them. And young people, like my son, should obey their parents, who know what is best for them, as I absolutely do for him.

6. **What is the main event in the scene?** The argument about what women should and should not learn.

7. **Where does the scene take place?** In Mrs. Malaprop's dressing room in her house in Bath.

8. **What are the other given circumstances—time of day; weather; your physical condition?** It is late morning, and the weather is fine. Both characters are in good condition.

9. **What do you want—your objective?** *Mrs. Malaprop*: I want to speak up to him, and oppose some of his ideas. *Sir Anthony Absolute*: I want to convince her that I am right, and women should know their place.

10. **What is in the way—the obstacle?** *Mrs. Malaprop*: My insecurity. My desire to be respected and loved. I don't dare be too forceful: I lack the courage to do more than protest weakly. *Sir Anthony Absolute*: My obstinacy. My insistence on always having the upper hand. She doesn't appear to agree with me, and I have to control my temper.

11. **What does your character do—your actions?** For both characters, the actions are verbal. There may be activities, such as drinking chocolate or other stage business, depending on the staging. *Mrs. Malaprop*: I listen and react, mostly in silence,

responding somewhat hesitantly to everything he says, until I get a chance to expound my own ideas. *Sir Anthony Absolute*: I expound my ideas on women and learning, pressing home my points as forcefully as I can without being impolite.

12. **Do you attain your objective by the end of the scene?** *Mrs. Malaprop*: Yes, in part. At least I say something. *Sir Anthony Absolute*: Mostly, yes. At least she agrees with me on some things.

Eighteenth-Century Venetian Commedia Farce

The French illustrator and author Jean-François-Maurice Arnauld, Baron Dudevant, known by his penname, Maurice Sand (1823–1889), son of Baron François Casimir Dudevant (1795–1871) and the famous romantic novelist and political activist, George Sand (1804–1876)—the couple separated in 1835—wrote a magisterial study of the commedia dell'arte, *Masques et bouffons (comédie italienne): Textes et Desseins* (1860), to which his mother wrote the preface. It was translated under the English title, *The History of the Harlequinade*. Regarding the decline and fall of the commedia, he wrote:

> At the end of the eighteenth century, when the Italian comedy was dying in France, having been fused into comic opera and French comedy, it was also expiring in a literary sense in Italy, but not without one last flicker, perhaps the most brilliant since the days of Ruzzante.

Ruzzante was Angelo Beolco (1502–1542), known as Il Ruzzante, from a running character he played, the peasant Ruzzante. This was possibly his real name, the word "beolco" being tacked on afterward; it derives from a rural dialect word, "befolco," meaning ploughman or country bumpkin. One of the founders of the commedia, he was a Venetian actor and writer famous for his twelve comedies of rustic life, which were early commedia pieces.

By "one last flicker," Sand means the plays presented by Count Carlo Gozzi (1720–1806), the Venetian writer known for his fairy-tale, commedia dell'arte tragicomedies. The most famous were *L'augellino belverde* (The Pretty Little Green Bird), a version of which was mounted on Broadway in 2000 by Julie Taymor; *L'amore delle tre melarance* (The Love of Three Oranges); and *Turandot*. The latter two were later made into operas by Prokofiev and Puccini, respectively; and all three were an attempt to use commedia themes and characters in a way different from Gozzi's great rival, Goldoni. They were meant as a challenge to the more genial, extroverted Goldoni's idea of realism in the theater. Gozzi attempted to keep the commedia form alive as the manager of a Venetian commedia company starring the highly popular Antonio Sacco (1708–1788), a brilliant Truffaldino, as the Harlequin character was often known.

Somewhat puritanical and withdrawn, Gozzi summed up his era in *Memorie inutile* (Useless Memoirs), written in 1777, but first published in 1797, and translated in 1890 by the English poet, literary critic, scholar, and writer on aesthetics, John Addington Symonds (1840–1893), whose translation I use here:

> The spectacle of women turned into men, men turned into women, and both men and women turned into monkeys; all of them immersed in discoveries and inventions and the kaleidoscopic whirligigs of fashion; corrupting and seducing one another with the eagerness of hounds upon the scent; vying in their lusts and ruinous extravagances; destroying the fortunes of their families by turns; laughing at Plato and Petrarch; leaving real sensibility to languish in disuse, and giving its respectable name to the thinly veiled brutality of the senses; turning indecency into decency; calling all who differ from them hypocrites, and burning incense with philosophical solemnity to Priapus [the Roman phallic god]:— these things ought perhaps to have presented themselves to my eyes in the form of a lamentable tragedy; yet I could never see in them more than a farce, which delighted while it stupefied me.

Gozzi's two rivals for supremacy on the Venetian stage were Carlo Goldoni and the ex-Abbé, Pietro Chiari (1712–1785), whom he despised. Chiari wrote more than sixty comedies, and in 1762 he left Venice and went to Paris to be manager-director of the Comédie-Italienne. As for his rivalry with Goldoni, Gozzi had this to say, in his acerbic, jealous, and bitter moralistic manner:

> I recognized in him [Goldoni] an abundance of comic motives, truth, and naturalness. Yet I detected a poverty and meanness of intrigue; nature copied from the fact, not imitated; virtues and vices ill-adjusted, vice too frequently triumphant; plebeian phrases of low double meaning, particularly in his Venetian plays; surcharged characters; scraps and tags of erudition, stolen Heaven knows where, and clumsily brought in to impose upon the crowd of igno-ramuses. Finally, as a writer of Italian—except in the Venetian dia-lect, of which he showed himself a master—he seemed to me not unworthy to be placed among the dullest, basest, and least correct authors who have used our idiom.

Posterity has not agreed with this harsh verdict, and reveres the pro-lific Goldoni for his comic genius. Famous worldwide as the fore-most practitioner of commedia dell'arte, Carlo Goldoni was even in his own day the most loved Venetian playwright and librettist of the century. In fact, it was Goldoni who coined the term commedia dell'arte, to distinguish his hilarious comedies, with their sparkling dialogue and fast-paced action, from the entirely improvisational pieces based on scenarios that commedia troupes performed. He also wrote many comic opera libretti, notably seventeen with the delight-ful composer Baldassare Galuppi (1786–1785), from whom his name is inseparable. As opera came into its own, comic opera flourished. It would be inconceivable without the commedia of the previous century, or those who practiced it in the eighteenth, particularly in Italy. Galuppi—called affectionately *il Buranello*, from his native town, Burano, near Venice—was a hard-working composer of all kinds of instrumental music, sacred music, and more than one hundred serious and comic operas.

Goldoni's *Il servitore di due padroni* (The Servant of Two Masters)

In 1745, this play was produced to immediate acclaim in Venice, and then in other European cities, where it was done in translation. It was written at the request of Antonio Sacco, who created the role of Truffaldino. This is a scripted play with elements of the commedia dell'improviso, so that improvised lazzi are woven into the scenes, and there are standard commedia characters as well. This is what Goldoni meant by coining the term commedia dell'arte, in which the scripted scenario does not rely on improvised dialogue.

The plot is typically complicated, and the play can be difficult to follow when you read it, but it comes to life in the theater, as it did in the production I saw when the famed Piccolo Teatro di Milano performed it many years ago at the McCarter Theatre in Princeton, NJ. At that point I did not know more than a few words of Italian, but the physical comedy and situations were so clear that this was not a handicap, although I did of course miss the wordplay, puns, and other verbal jokes.

This is a simplified version of the story: Together with her servant Truffaldino, Beatrice arrives in Venice disguised as her brother Federigo, who has been killed in a duel by her lover Florindo (the Capitano commedia character), whom Federigo had forbidden her to marry. She takes rooms in Brighella's inn, where much of the action will unfold. Then she goes with Truffaldino to the house of the wealthy and suspicious, conniving merchant Pantalone. Truffaldino is to announce that "Federigo" is there to collect a debt owed to her brother by Pantalone. Astounded, he asks Truffaldino what on earth he means by saying Federigo has arrived, when Federigo is dead! Of course, Truffaldino convinces him that he is mistaken. After all, "Federigo" is waiting downstairs! Meanwhile, since it is to Venice that Florindo has fled for safety, Beatrice has been looking for him, and when she finds him, she will use the money for their flight and subsequent marriage. But Pantalone sees in her, disguised as she is, a suitable match for his daughter Clarice, who had been betrothed to Federigo, but is now in love with and betrothed to Silvio, the son of Pantalone's friend, Dr. Lombardi (the Dottore commedia character). Enraged, Silvio challenges "Federigo" to a duel. Meanwhile, Florindo has hired Truffaldino as a servant, not knowing that he is already Beatrice's servant. Truffaldino, a glutton if ever there was one, has seen an opportunity for more free food! At one point, Beatrice mistakenly accuses him of having eaten her cat! He sees no reason why Beatrice should know that he has two jobs, and manages to sew confusion on all sides, as he runs around Venice on errands for his two masters, receiving letters and the instruction, "This is for your master"—who is of course unspecified. Mixed up as he is, Truffaldino, in his terrible confusion, develops an awful stutter, confusing his interlocutors further. He even accidentally puts things belonging to each of his masters in the trunk of the other. Beatrice and Florindo each recognize the misplaced items as belonging to the other, and each confronts Truffaldino, who, thinking quickly, tells each one that the other is dead. The separated lovers are now in despair, and emerge from their rooms in the same inn—where by a typical coincidence they have never seen each other—prepared to commit suicide by stabbing themselves with daggers. Of course, they immediately recognize each other, and fall into each other's arms. Beatrice now casts off her disguise, and her betrothal to Clarice is canceled. The duel is called off, and Silvio weds Clarice, while Beatrice, having collected the debt from Pantalone, marries Florindo, who will presumably be pardoned for the duel he fought with Federigo. Truffaldino will marry Pantalone's maid, Smeraldina (the Columbine commedia character), and remain in service to the wary Pantalone.

The most famous scene in this hilarious farce is the one in which Truffaldino serves two banquets in two separate rooms at the inn to the guests of his masters, trying to keep everything straight while simultaneously eating as much food as he can, stuffing his mouth and running around in a mad tizzy.

Performing in this play, or in any of the dozens of commedia farces like it, requires the most incredible agility and movement skills, especially of course for the Harlequin character. But nearly all the characters have to be able to do the kind of lazzi described in chapter one. And everyone must have all the other comedic techniques down pat as well. A superb sense of timing is essential. And you must play every moment with the utmost seriousness of purpose and the almost insane, single-minded desire to reach your objectives, large and small.

XII

The Nineteenth Century: German, French, American, and English Comedy

Movement, Clothing, and Manners

Men wore long frock coats with buttons in the nineteenth and early twentieth centuries, and they are therefore ubiquitous costume pieces in farces and comedies of manners. The great Russian director Vsevelod Meyerhold (1874–1940) said, "In a tail coat one must keep to half movements. Elbows have to be held closer to the body. Gestural thrusts must be short, movements light." The stiff collars and cravats that men wore meant that men had to hold their heads up. And the elaborate heavy women's gowns make movement rather formal and slow, but not as difficult as that in eighteenth-century wear.

Accessories included gloves, lorgnettes, fans and reticules or small purses for upper-class women; pocket watches (no wristwatches), gloves, and the occasional monocle for men. Hats for women could be large and elaborate, and were sometimes veiled. Men wore top hats and, later, derbies or fedoras, and carried canes. By midcentury, visiting cards were de rigueur, and there were many rules concerning their use and presentation, detailed in numerous books of etiquette.

There were refined, elaborate rules of conduct that governed "good" society, and good behavior; and there was no "hail fellow, well met" attitude even among close friends meeting in public. Decorum and propriety were the watchwords of the day. In private, of course, greater intimacy and familiarity could be permitted, as it is, for instance, between Jack and Algernon in Oscar Wilde's *The Importance of Being Earnest*, discussed later in this chapter.

If you are doing nineteenth- and early twentieth-century comedies, read *In Search of Lost Time* by Marcel Proust (1871–1922), among other things a brilliant chronicler of the manners, fashions, and mores of his era. There are also many books of etiquette for the period. For more information on expected social behavior of the mid- to late nineteenth century, read Baronne Staffe's *Usages du monde: Règles du savoir-vivre dans la société moderne* (Social Customs: Rules for Correct Manners in Modern Society), widely read in France. Although the term *savoir-vivre* figuratively means "correct manners," more literally the term means "to-know [how] to-live," and that is what the book is about: how to conduct yourself and how to behave properly in social circumstances. Published in 1889, it had reached its one hundred-thirty-first printing ten years later. Although well to do, Baronne Staffe (1843–1911) was not a baroness, and not even an aristocrat by birth. She was born Blanche Soyer in Savigny-sur-Orge, one of Paris's sothern suburbs, and lived reclusively in her villa, receiving the royalties that made her wealthy from the sale of this and similar books she had authored. Her principles were revered and followed by several generations of French people.

She covers every event in human life, from birth through death, and tells us what the proper procedures are in dealing with each one of them. As so many nineteenth-century English and American writers on etiquette do, Baronne Staffe discusses the obligatory topics of visiting cards, and of social visits and how they are to be carried out. Unlike the English-speaking authors, however, the Baronne adds that with regard to "intimate visits," they "…are measured by the amount of empathy, of friendship; they are free of all rules." This would not be approved of by the more puritanical Anglophone writers, but this attitude tells us a great deal that is relevant to French high comedies, and indeed to the farces of such authors as Georges Feydeau. The relations between the sexes appear easier and more natural than in English plays of the same period.

Baronne Staffe tells us in her avant-propos, entitled "True Elegance":

Everything changes with time, but much more in appearance than in reality, in form rather than in content. Those things based on principle are the same, in all centuries and in all places: there are only surface differences.

Therefore, correct manners have varied in their *expression*. But if you really think about it, you will realize that today as when it began, the goal of politesse is to "make those with whom we live happy with themselves and with us." That is why—to speak only of modern times—one will find in the traits of the chic man of our fin-de-siècle the characteristics of those who have been called in the course of the centuries a chevalier, a man of honor, a courtier, and a great lord; that is why, under the name of woman of the world, there lives the chatelaine, the woman of quality, the great lady.

Contemporaries of steam and electricity, we cannot have the slow and majestic manners of the century of the peruke; nor are the filigreed gallantry or the languorous compliments of the century of powdered wigs at our command.

Her initial point is well taken: manners remain inwardly the same, in that politeness and respect must always rule, no matter what the outward forms. And this guiding principle is the foundation of the comedy of manners: you have to play the social game, which means abiding by social customs and being unfailingly polite, even when you don't want to be. When this principle is violated, and characters are rude to each other, we laugh. But politeness can also be a mask for aggression and conflict, as it is in the scene where Gwendolyn and Cecily make each other's acquaintance in *The Importance of Being Earnest*. Here, too, the audience knows what is expected when two people meet each other, and awaits refined manners and cool politeness on the part of these upper-class characters. But the audience is not deceived by the show of politeness in this scene, where the immediate hostility and animosity, and the passive-aggressive behavior of both characters, are therefore very funny, because of the incongruity between real and false politesse.

Although she did not mean to be funny, Baronne Staffe no doubt had quite a sense of humor, and could envision specific situations where insults and insult humor were prevalent. She has this to say, for instance, with regard to visits and social calls, and it is a clue as to how to play scenes where certain incidents at high society events occur:

It is very impolite to affect a glacial air toward the other visitors whom you find already there or who arrive after you...

Another way of torturing the masters of the house is to take a haughty or malicious tone towards someone received at the same time. The hosts have no other way of covering the impoliteness and rudeness of the offender than by showing their sympathy to the one attacked, while at the same time being careful not to irritate the personage who has permitted himself such a prank. Sometimes the disdain and animosity are reciprocal, and I ask you to imagine the figure the hosts make between two such roosters with their hackles up...

But this is often how characters in comedies of manners behave! Baronne Staffe might be describing the dramatic action of a high comedy, rather than prescribing manners. The opening society party scene of Oscar Wilde's *An Ideal Husband* provides an example of just this sort of behavior, as barbs are exchanged, and opinions expressed.

And here is Baronne Staffe's advice to young mothers paying visits:

Some young mothers commit the egregious mistake of taking their babies with them on a visit. There is no worse torture to inflict on the mistress of a house careful of her furniture and bibelots. As good, as well behaved as young children may be, after five minutes of immobility and tranquility, their little legs will begin to move, sending kicks into the chairs; their adorable little fingers will begin to scratch at the satin upholstery of the armchairs, and then, little by little, the baby will slip away, and wind up next to a table covered with artistic porcelain statuettes, with ivories, etc. [...] and [...] will thus put them into great danger.

The lady of the house sees this, dares say nothing, her blood boils, she would like to shove the child a hundred feet under the earth, or at least she thinks so. Mama carries on talking, and notices nothing, or perhaps she calls her babies over to her, scolds them… and allows them to begin again; in either case, what an unbearable annoyance for the hosts and even for the other visitors!

Baronne Staffe's advice is to leave children at home in the care of a trusted servant, or to take them to their grandparents' house while mama is out calling, or to take them to a house where there are other children to play with. There are some childish characters in farces or high comedy that could be played like the unruly children she describes, and in party scenes, the hosts' reactions—blood boiling, but not daring to say anything—could be a great way of playing certain scenes.

Early Nineteenth-Century German Romantic Farce

Despite its reputation for melodrama, seriousness, and emotionalism, the romantic movement in the theater also saw comedies that were in a direct line of descent from the urbane, sophisticated eighteenth-century comedies of manners. Along with the Austrian actor and writer, Johann Nestroy (1801–1862), August von Kotzebue (1761–1819) is one of the originators of the fine tradition of German romantic comedy. Although he started writing for the theater in the eighteenth century, Kotzebue's plays, including his many melodramas, belong more properly to the nineteenth, and to the dawn of the romantic movement in the arts.

Of aristocratic background, he was a dramatist of a conservative cast of mind, and supported the regime in Prussia, where he was born in the city of Weimar, later so famous as the seat of the short-lived republic established after Germany's defeat in World War One. Germany in von Kotzebue's day was not yet a united country, but a series of small kingdoms, principalities, and dukedoms. Prussia and Bavaria were the two largest and most powerful kingdoms, but it was Prussia that would eventually assert its hegemony and assume the leadership of the new country of Deutschland in 1871.

In 1819, Kotzebue was murdered for his beliefs by the firebrand activist and university student, Karl Ludwig Sand (1795–1820), a member of one of the ultraliberal Burschenschaften (student associations) that stood for nationalism—then considered a liberal idea—and for social and political reform in the repressive atmosphere of the day. Using the murder as an excuse, the government of Prussia dissolved the associations shortly after the assassination, and Sand, who became a martyr in the eyes of the nationalists seeking a united Germany, was executed.

August von Kotzebue's *How to Die for Love: A Farce in Two Acts* was adapted for the English stage anonymously from his 1811 one-act farce *Blind geladen* [literally, Loaded Blind; Loaded with Blanks], and produced in 1812. It is clearly based in commedia traditions. One of two typical braggart warriors in this very funny and charming, if very slight piece is named Captain Blumenfeld. You can imagine how I laughed when I read such lines as "Blumenfeld is a pleasant fellow."

Baron Altorf insists that his daughter Charlotte choose for a husband one of the two rivals for her hand, Captain Thalwick or Captain Blumenfeld, who are close friends. Both are madly in love with her. But she cannot decide, because, although she likes them both, she is in love with neither. So she hits upon a stratagem whereby they will choose among themselves, but without violence: no duels allowed. As the baron explains, "…whichever can induce the other to o'erstep the boundaries of my estate (you know the landmarks about the village) has won her." The two soldiers bribe each other's servants to obtain information, and indulge in various tricks and ploys. There are funny and cynical lines about the wiles of servants and the nature of politics and journalism. In one trick, Captain Blumenfeld sends Captain Thalwick a letter that is purportedly from his dying mother, begging him to return home to see her on her deathbed. But Thalwick is not deceived for one second. He tells his servant Trap, who has brought the letter to him and begs him to go home: "You rend my heart with your pathetic appeal. There is only one little doubt that strikes me."

"And what doubt, Sir, can a son have in such a situation?" asks Trap.

"My mother has been dead these ten years," answers Thalwick. Finally, Thalwick wins the day by a ruse: Despite their agreement not to fight, he challenges Blumenfeld to a duel, knowing that Blumenfeld's pistols are at the gunsmith's, and offering the use of his own, which he has loaded only with powder. Blumenfeld, incensed by the insults Thalwick hurls at him, accepts, and they fire in turn at each other. Thalwick then pretends he is shot, and exhorts Blumenfeld to fly for his life, which he does, going over the boundary. Once all is revealed, the Baron gallops after him, and all ends happily as Blumenfeld not only forgives his rival and friend, but is glad to be invited to the wedding feast. Thalwick concludes the merry jest, written in prose, with a rhymed couplet: "And now with Charlotte let me *living* prove / Joys earned by showing "How to Die for Love."

Fast-paced and energetic, and sometimes even frantic, this little gem has to be performed without thinking too much. Just carry out the actions as they are laid out in the script, and pursue the clear objectives, and you cannot go wrong. This farce is a classic example of the genre, and is as genial as a gentle noonday sun shining brightly on a flowing stream that leaps and bubbles along without a pause. Indeed, it would be a mistake to have any pauses, which would simply slow down the progress of the proceedings. The piece only lasts about half an hour. If it were ever revived, *How to Die for Love* would make part of a nice evening of pleasant short pieces about events leading up to marriage, such as Chekhov's one-act "vaudevilles," *Predlozheniye* (The Marriage Proposal; 1889) and *Myedvyed* (The Boor; 1890).

The gentlemen-soldiers should not be played as stock braggart warriors. Each has his own personality, and you should play each of them with real, individual traits and characteristics, drawing on yourselves and your own charm to create a personality without clichés. Play opposites: Take the braggart warrior and play him as a diffident, well-meaning person, rather than as a swaggering, loudmouthed boaster. If some of the lines are blustering, you can bring that side of the character out.

The same idea of playing opposites holds true with the Baron and Charlotte. Play the old gentleman not as a haughty, domineering aristocrat, but as a genial, kindly gentleman who wants what is best for his daughter. And play Charlotte as a young woman of spirit, not as a spinster dominated by her father and afraid for her future. That side of the character will be apparent in any case in some of the lines, but if you play against them the character will be that much more real.

French Boulevard Comedy

What has come to be called "le théâtre du boulevard" (boulevard theater) began in the time of Napoleon I, came into its own as the nineteenth century wore on, and continued into the twentieth and beyond. It originally referred to the great and small theaters (now mostly gone) located near a number of streets and along the Boulevard du Temple and the Boulevard Saint-Martin in what is now the fourth arrondissement of Paris. In 1862, when Baron Georges-Eugène Haussmann (1809–1891) was supervising his great reworking of the city, he demolished the neighborhood, replacing it with the present Place de la République. The kind of light and sophisticated comedy and drama presented there still flourishes, hence the continued use of the term.

At these hugely popular venues, which were gathering places for all social classes, comedy, melodrama, drama, tragedy and farce, both spoken and musical, were performed. Elsewhere in Paris, the satirical and romantic operettas, the "opéras bouffes," of Jacques Offenbach (1819–1880) and of Hervé [Louis Auguste Florimond Ronger] (1825–1892), who also acted and sang in his own pieces, were especially popular in the era of Napoleon III (1808–1873). But the fourth arrondissement was a theater district much like Broadway; there is currently no theater district in Paris as there is in New York or London: theaters are scattered throughout the city; nevertheless, the term "boulevard theater" remains in use, and now refers uniquely to popular entertainment such as that presented at those long gone playhouses. The boulevard theaters, like many elsewhere in Paris, were not usually state-subsidized like the Comédie Française, but were mostly private ventures.

For a glimpse at what the ambience and the theaters themselves were like, see Marcel Carné's film *Les enfants du paradis* (The Children of Paradise; 1945), which recreates the early nineteenth century perfectly and is a superb film from every point of view. The title refers to the uppermost balcony, where the cheapest seats were found; it was nicknamed "paradise" because it was so high, and just below the ceiling; cf. the British term, "the gods."

Feydeau's *Mais n'te promène donc pas toute nue!* (Stop Walking Around Stark Naked!)

The numerous farces and comedies written by the French authors listed in appendix one come mostly under the heading of boulevard theater. Georges Feydeau is considered the greatest nineteenth-century author of farces. Despite his comic genius, Feydeau could be quite tasteless. He could be misogynistic, and thought nothing of getting laughs by making fun of speech defects, foreigners and their accents, and people with various physical conditions and deformities. But he also mocked social institutions, politicians, quacks, shams, charlatans, pretentious bores, and other more legitimate targets of satire, such as people who refused to wash or whose vanity was overweening. His hilarious *Mais n'te promène donc pas toute nue*, although first produced in 1911, shares the mentality, moral outlook, class attitudes, and mores that belong to the Belle Époque of fin-de-siècle France and Edwardian England.

In France, the Third Republic had been the form of government ever since the end of the empire of Napoleon III in 1871, and the capitalist, bourgeois, money-getting ethos was the norm, despite the survival of the old, still wealthy aristocracy, portrayed in the works of Marcel Proust. Puritanical attitudes and strict Church morality were widely considered codes to live by. All of this informs Feydeau's rollicking farce. The violation of these implicit codes of conduct causes the characters who uphold them to go slightly mad. The milieu of this piece is the upper middle-class environment of political leaders, members of the ruling bourgeoisie.

The Comédie Française production made for television in 1971 is available on DVD, and it is absolutely hilarious. The bare plot outline that follows does not give you an idea of the sparkling dialogue, or of the intensity with which the situations are lived out by the unsurpassed actors in the old production. The story of this long one-act play is less complicated than in some farces, but still contains the elements of mistaken identity, inappropriate behavior, incongruous juxtapositions, and very high stakes for the major players.

The entire play takes place in the salon of Deputy Ventroux (played on the DVD by the hilariously exasperated, desperate Jacques Charon [1920–1975]), a member of the National Assembly. He and his young wife, Clarisse (perfectly realized by the insouciant Micheline Boudet [b. 1926]), have a thirteen-year-old son, Auguste (an off-stage character: we hear his voice, but he never appears). The deputy reproaches his wife with walking around nearly naked in front of Auguste and their servant, Victor (interpreted impertinently by the supercilious Jean-Luc Moreau [b. 1944]). "What's the difference?" she says. When he enters the room, Ventroux is furious to discover that Victor has been paying careful attention to their offstage quarrel while cleaning the windows, and promptly sends him out of the room, outraged that he has been listening at the door. "But, Monsieur," says he, "I was at the window!" And he goes off in a huff, leaving the window wide open. Enter Monsieur Hochepaix, the Mayor of Mousillon-les-Indrets (played with perfect buffo bravura by Louis Seignier [1903–1991] on the DVD), who wants some political favors for his constituents. Clarisse appears in her light, nearly transparent housedress, as usual, and Ventroux is furious with her all over again, particularly since the mayor is his political opponent, and this conduct is scandalous. But all of a sudden, Clarisse is stung on her rear end by a wasp. Convinced that the sting is serious, and that she is in dire danger, she begs her husband to suck the venom out of the wound, but he refuses. She then turns to the mayor, who also refuses. Instead, they will call in a doctor, and she goes to her room to lie down. M. Romain de Jaival, a journalist (based on several real-life models, and expertly played by Alain Feydeau [1934–2008], grandson of Georges Feydeau) is now announced. He has come to interview Deputy Ventroux for the

Figaro. Ventroux asks him to wait, and takes Hochepaix with him into the next room, so they can finish their conversation. Clarisse comes back in, and mistakes de Jaival for the doctor. She has him examine the painful wound, and remove the wasp's sting. Ventroux enters, and nearly goes mad, explaining to his wife that this is a journalist! Suddenly, he notices his neighbor Clemenceau staring in through the window and laughing: He has been watching everything. Ventroux exclaims, "Oh! I'm screwed! My political career is over!" Meanwhile, Clarisse, with disarming insouciance, blows kisses at Clemenceau, whom Feydeau means to be the real Georges Clemenceau (1841–1929), twice prime minister of France, and a prime mover in the negotiations over the Treaty of Versailles that ended World War One.

The central incident of sucking the venom out of the wound is based on a real event: The Feydeau family and some friends went on a picnic in the forest of Rambouillet, and Feydeau himself tried to help his friend, a certain Madame Picaud, in just that way after she had been stung by a wasp. Feydeau's jealous wife was furious, and accused him of "acting less out of therapeutic devotion than from maniac lubricity," according to Henry Gidel in his biography *Feydeau* (Flammarion, 1991).

Comedy in America

By midcentury, American theater was expanding with the frontier, and every town and city had its theater. In the west, these were often makeshift platforms under crude tents, but in the cities they were beautiful plants with comfortable seating. Amidst the plethora of verse tragedies, musical extravaganzas such as *The Black Crook*, musical comedies like those of Harrigan and Hart, and the import of British plays, there were numerous new American plays, many in the genre of social comedy—American comedy of manners—which proved popular from the middle of the century on. Mrs. Sydney Bateman (1823–1881), James K. Paulding (1778–1860), Henry Oake Pardey (1808–1865), and Cornelius Matthews (1817–1889) all wrote successfully in that genre, although their plays are now forgotten.

By the end of the century comedies portraying new immigrant groups, usually in stereotypical fashion, were also popular. These plays too have long ago disappeared from the stage. For instance, a comic Swedish immigrant trilogy—*Ole Olson* (1889), *Yon Yonson* (1890) and *Yenuine Yentleman* (1895)—by playwright and actor Augustus "Gus" J. Heege (1862–1898) was very popular in its day, but nobody remembers them now. He performed in the plays himself, and prepared for his roles by living among and observing the inhabitants of "Little Scandinavia" in northern Wisconsin. Although he claimed to be authentic in his speech and was vouched for by Scandinavian-Americans, a skeptical *New York Times* review of December 29, 1891 stated "the Swedes and Norwegians we have in the East do not speak English in the Yon Yonson way."

A number of comedic characters from American fiction were popular with audiences, most notably Washington Irving's Rip Van Winkle, performed to great acclaim by Joseph Jefferson. A spoof of the well known narrative poem by Henry Wadsworth Longfellow (1807–1882), on which it is as loosely based as possible, *Evangeline; or, The Belle of Arcadia* (1874) was a musical by Edward E. Rice (1848/9?–1924) with a book and lyrics by J. Cheever Goodwin (1850–1912). It had numerous revivals and tours, and ran at Niblo's Gardens, where *The Black Crook* had run.

The story, if one can call it that, follows the vicissitudes and travels of the lovers Evangeline and Gabriel (another of the many trousers roles featured in comic operas and musicals of the period), until they are reunited happily ever after at the end. Evangeline visits the Wild West, where she dances with a heifer, played by two actors inside either end of a cow costume, in the most popular number in the show. She is also followed at one point by a lustful whale, and the story takes her to Africa, and more adventures. A featured, ubiquitous character was the Lone Fisherman, much loved by audiences, who found his taciturnity hilarious: he never said much, but he was periodically there, making a quick entrance, peering through his telescope, then exiting.

Hick buffoon characters with supposed Yankee characteristics, the ancestors of vaudeville ethnic characters, were very popular. One of the most beloved was Solon Shingle, a Yankee lawyer in *The People's Lawyer* (1839) by Joseph Stevens Jones (1809–1977). Even more wildly popular was the character of Mose the Fireboy in Benjamin A. Baker's (1818–1890) *A Glance at New York* (1848). Mose was such a beloved folk hero that more plays and "penny novels" were written incorporating him as a character. Like Paul Bunyan, he was gigantic and exceptionally strong. He had flaming red hair and was fierce and unflinching in a fight. He may have been based on Moses Humphreys, a printer and a leader of one of the private fire companies in the Five Points, the rough and ready area of New York depicted in Martin Scorsese's film *The Gangs of New York* (2002), which, however, takes place mostly in the 1860s. The part was created by the New York actor-manager Frank Chanfrau (1824–1884), who continued to play the role in other pieces, and made quite a career of it.

Mrs. Mowatt's *Fashion; or, Life in New York*

One of the best known social comedies was *Fashion; or, Life in New York* (1845) by Mrs. Anna Cora Mowatt (1819–1870), known usually as Mrs. Mowatt. The wealthy, extravagant socialite Mrs. Tiffany and her daughter Seraphina both fall in love with the attractive Count Jolimaître (French: pretty master), who is actually a jack of all servants' trades in disguise, and quite the con man, complete with a fake French accent. He wants to marry Seraphina for her money, but he is unmasked by Adam Truelove, an old family friend, who also helps the family restore their fortunes, before the bankruptcy due to the pretentious Mrs. Tiffany's careless spending can ruin them.

The ending is unusual and particularly heart-warming. As Mr. Tiffany says, "Guilt ever carries his own scourge along," so instead of being hauled off to jail to await trial for fraud, Jolimaître agrees quite happily to marry Mrs. Tiffany's French maid, Millinette, who comes complete with the cutest of French accents. She has adored him ever since she knew him in Paris, where, among other things, he was a cook and, before coming to America, valet in an aristocratic household; and she has kept his secret. As he says contritely and cheerfully, "Well, then, I do confess I am no count, but, ladies and gentlemen, I may recommend myself as the most capital cook," and he enumerates his culinary specialties, whereupon Mr. Truelove, hoping Jolimaître will aspire to the title of "honest man," volunteers, with the help of Mrs. Tiffany, to find him a position as cook in a great household, for, says he, "Better turn stomachs than turn heads!"

Mrs. Tiffany's new employee Zeke, whom she renames Adolph, is an African American servant dressed in livery, and with a thick, stereotypical dialect. He is one of the first in a long line of comic stereotypes, but the character himself is real enough and quite delightful. And by contrast with his humanity and humor, Mrs. Tiffany is shown up as the snob she is. Zeke is a free man, slavery having been finally outlawed in 1841 in New York state, after a series of laws gradually eliminated it. The embarrassing portrait, from today's point of view, can actually be perceived as anti-racist, as contrasted with the pretentiousness and snobbery of Mrs. Tiffany.

The opening scene is between Zeke and Millinette, and it is typical of old French comedies of manners, where the servants opened the play by expository gossiping about their masters. At one point, Millinette has an aside to the audience: "I not comprend one word he say." This is quite funny, considering her obviously heavy, sometimes incomprehensible accent, as written throughout the play by Mrs. Mowatt.

Later in the scene, when Mrs. Tiffany has come in, she asks Zeke to bring her a "fow-tool," which is how she mispronounces the French word fauteuil (armchair), even after hearing Millinette say the word in answer to her question, "Millinette, how do you say arm chair in French?" Zeke is mystified. Says he, "(*looking about him*) I habn't got dat far in de dictionary yet. No matter, a genius gets his learning by nature." And he brings her a small table. Naturally, she lambasts him, and of course he then brings her an armchair.

The highfalutin, hoity-toity Mrs. Tiffany is the hostess with the mostess (she thinks). This Archie Bunker of her day has studied the text "French without a Master" for a week, so that she can converse with the count "in the court language of Europe," because "a woman of refinement and of fashion can always accommodate herself to anything foreign!" She has this to say to Millinette about Zeke, and it speaks ironic volumes. Remember that she is speaking to her maid, who is a "foreigner": "I am rather sorry he is black, but to obtain a white American for a domestic is almost impossible; and they call this a free country!" (This is twenty years before the Civil War and emancipation.) And she asks Millinette to suggest a new name for Zeke, which she adopts. She will call him Adolph, because his real name is unacceptable: "Ezekiel, I suppose Zeke! Dear me, such a vulgar name will compromise the dignity of the whole family." The humor here may be laid on with a trowel, but Mrs. Mowatt's satire of such awful attitudes rings true.

Her fascinating *Autobiography of an Actress, or, Eight Years on the Stage*, published in 1858, is a mine of information about the period and its theater. Her decision to do public poetry readings and, especially, to go on the stage, where she made a reputation in Shakespearean roles, was considered shocking in the New York of her day. Not only was theater thought disreputable and déclassé, the haunt of unsavory denizens of what was almost looked upon as the underworld, but in addition, Mrs. Mowatt was a member of high society, and of impeccable American Revolutionary War descent. It was partly due to her that theater began to be considered a respectable pursuit and a worthy profession. Even the upper classes could now attend performances with impunity, dressed in their glittering best. For almost a century and a half, in fact, one dressed for the theater in formal clothing. Mrs. Mowatt, as she was listed on playbills, acted for only eight years before retiring from the stage due to tuberculosis, a lifelong plague, but in that time she made her mark as a refined, sensitive interpreter of Shakespeare and modern plays.

For more information, read also *The Lady of Fashion: The Life and the Theatre of Anna Cora Mowatt* (Charles Scribner's Sons, 1954) by actor, soldier, diplomat, and professor of English Eric Wollencott Barnes (1907–1962).

Tom Taylor's *Our American Cousin*

Tom Taylor (1817–1880) was an English dramatist, known for his historical verse melodramas, burlesques, realistic comedies, and prose melodramas, the most popular of which was *The Ticket-of-Leave Man* (1863). His plays had quite a vogue in the America of the Civil War era. *Our American Cousin* (1858) is his best known play, for the most unfortunate of reasons: it was the farcical comedy of manners Abraham Lincoln (1809–1865) was seeing when he was assassinated. It starred the English-born actor-manager Laura Keene [Mary Frances Moss] (1826–1873) as Florence Trenchard, daughter of the aristocratic Trenchards, awaiting the arrival of their rich, previously unknown American cousin, whom they presume will help them out of their financial difficulties, since the family is heavily in debt. But Asa Trenchard is an imposter who hopes to bilk them out of the fortune he does not know they no longer possess. That briefest of plot throughlines already gives you an idea of the characters' superobjectives, objectives, obstacles, and actions.

In greater detail, the story unfolds as follows: We are in the drawing room at Trenchard Manor, where there is a table spread for luncheon, and from the servants' gossip, we learn that the Trenchard family cannot pay its bills, and is being dunned by creditors. Lord Edward, his sensible daughter Florence (our leading lady), and their guests assemble, and we meet the pompous Captain De Boots, the imperious gold-digger Mrs. Mountchessington, and her demure daughter Augusta, whom she wants to marry to the dimwitted, wealthy Lord Dundreary. She is suspicious of Florence, whom she thinks is also after Dundreary. Mrs. Mountchessington's daughter Georgina is sick and stays in her room, but when she enters, we see that Dundreary is enamored of her. The Trenchards receive a letter from Lord Edward's son, Ned, who has been in America, informing them that Lord Edward's uncle Mark Trenchard has died. He had quarrelled with his daughter over what he considered her bad marriage, and had gone to the States to find a lost branch of the family to whom to leave his wealth. He had not even wanted to know his granddaughter, Miss Mary Meredith. The Trenchards can expect Asa, one of the American branch of the family, to arrive in England to collect his inheritance. This brash Yankee soon shows up, and the farcical complications, and ins and outs of relationships, follow hard and fast. Mrs. Mountchessington, thinking Asa Trenchard wealthy, wants him to marry Augusta, as we shall see in the excerpt presented below. Mark Trenchard has left his fortune to his granddaughter Mary after all; she is the owner of a dairy, and a very competent, industrious young lady. Finally, Mrs. Mountchessington manages to marry off both her daughters, to Dundreary and De Boots. Florence will marry Harry Vernon, the love of her life, who has succeeded in securing a commission as captain in the Royal Navy, thanks to Dundreary's influence. And Asa, exposed as the fraud he is, is left high and dry.

In the original Broadway production, a great success at Laura Keene's Broadway theater, Joseph Jefferson (1829–1905), a founding member in her company, played Asa Trenchard, but he did not tour with the production to Ford's Theatre in Washington, DC, since he had already left her theater company. She had opened her New York theater in 1857, and Jefferson, who thought she usually had poor taste in plays, nevertheless admired her in other ways. He has this to say in his *Autobiography* (Century Company, 1889):

> As an actress and manager, Laura Keene was both industrious and talented. If she could have afforded it, no expense would have been spared in the production of her plays; but theatrical matters were at a low ebb during the early part of her career, and the memorable panic of 1857 was almost fatal to her.

The short-lived Panic of 1857 was one of those periodic economic and financial crises that beset the capitalist world. But brief as it was, Jefferson informs us that many banks went out of business: "Long rows of despairing depositors stood in lines eagerly besieging their delinquent trustees." In the theater, the payment of salaries was deferred: "The bands struck with one accord, and as usual got their money; the actors revolted and as usual did not get it. The public despondently stayed at home, the theaters were empty..." Almost needless to say, there were no actors' unions in those days: Actors' Equity Association was not founded until 1913.

This "memorable panic" was precursive of worse episodes to come, among them the worldwide crisis of 1873 during Reconstruction after the Civil War; and the depressions of 1893 and 1929, which saw the beginning of the Great Depression of the 1930s.

During the first reading in the green room of *Our American Cousin*, Jefferson tells us that E. A. Sothern [Edward Askew Sothern] (1826–1881), who was to play Lord Dundreary:

…sat disconsolate, fearing that there was nothing in the play that would suit him; and as the dismal lines of *Dundreary* were read he glanced over at me with a forlorn expression, as much as to say, "I am cast for that dreadful part," little dreaming that the character of the imbecile lord would turn out to be the stepping-stone of his career.

Indeed, Lord Dundreary and his "Dundrearyisms"—wordplay, descended as it were from the malapropisms of *The Rivals*—proved immensely popular. And his huge drooping sideburns—a word that owes its origin to those sported by the industrialist, politician, and Civil War general Ambrose Burnside (1824–1881)—came to be called Dundrearys. When the play opened in London in 1861, after having run in New York for 150 nights (quite a good run in those days), he played the role for a record 496 performances.

Sothern spoke with a drawl and with the lisp and initial "r" pronounced as "w," both indicated in the script, and came up with endless ad libs and gags, padding his part without a qualm, and he was allowed to do so. When he had complained originally about the small role, Jefferson (if the story is not apocryphal) said something to him that later became famous: "There are no small parts, only small actors." Among the celebrated Dundrearyisms, which are aphorisms, silly riddles, and new proverbs made from cobbling together two old ones, the most famous is, "Birds of a feather gather no moss." The part was so well received that it gave rise to a number of sequels, in some of which Sothern repeated his triumphant characterization.

The part of Asa Trenchard, Jefferson tells us, was a turning point not only for Sothern, but also for Laura Keene and for himself. A brash young actor, he made a great success in the part, but managed at the same time to alienate Laura Keene by his lack of discipline, a fault he later rectified. Eventually, by the end of that first season, they were reconciled, but he decided to leave the company and asked her permission to mount a production of *Our American Cousin*, "Which I decline to give. The play is my property, and you shall not act it outside of this theater."

In act 3, scene 2, Mrs. Mountchessington has been advising her daughter, Augusta, to choose between De Boots and Asa Trenchard, either of whom would make a good match, but Asa is richer, and therefore preferable. Augusta has agreed to consider him for a husband, and Asa, seeing through everything, says to Mrs. Mountchessington, "You sockdologizing old mantrap!" On that line, Booth pulled the trigger, barely heard amid the raucous laughter of the audience, just as the assassin had expected.

Joseph Jefferson and *Rip Van Winkle*

Joseph Jefferson was famous for his comic roles, just as Edwin Booth was for playing tragedies. Jefferson's theory of acting was that actors should live in the parts they played, as his *Autobiography* makes clear—a point of view that would later be called Stanislavskian. He believed in the thorough study and analysis of a role, although he relates that for his most famous role, Rip van Winkle, he was so excited and enthusiastic at the prospect of playing the part that he began by dressing for the role, to see what he would look like. A 1902 silent outdoor scene of him as Rip is available on YouTube, and he recorded the scene where he sees the men with the keg in the mountain.

The play was a sentimental comedy, with a tear-jerking ending. The version Jefferson used was written by Dion Boucicault (1820–1890), and opened first in London in 1865, several months after Lincoln's assassination, then in New York in 1866. Jefferson was constantly revising it, after having also performed an earlier version of the story, in Washington, DC in1860, before enlisting Boucicault's services.

When Rip returns from his twenty-years sleep after having been drugged by the ghostly spirits of Henry Hudson and his crew, playing at ninepins that create thunder in the Catskills, nobody in the village of Falling Waters, NY recognizes him. Jefferson delivered the poignant line, "Are we so soon forgot when we are gone?" and was much acclaimed for that moment. His daughter does recognize him, and all is set to rights, as he regains his home and family. The play spoke volumes to audiences in the aftermath of a chastened and punished country, profoundly changed by the Civil War.

On "the art of acting" in general, Jefferson has this to say:

> I have seen impulsive actors who were so confident of their power that they left all to chance. This is a dangerous course, especially when acting a new character. I will admit that there are many instances where great effects have been produced that were entirely spontaneous, and were as much a surprise to the actors who made them as they were to the audience who witnessed them; but just as individuals who have exuberant spirits are at times dreadfully depressed, so when an impulsive actor fails to receive his inspiration he is dull indeed, and is the more disappointing because of his former brilliant achievements. In the stage management [the period term for "direction"] of a play, or in the acting of a part, nothing should be left to chance, and for the reason that spontaneity, inspiration, or whatever the strange and delightful quality may be called, is not to be commanded, or we should give it some other name. It is, therefore, better that a clear and unmistakable outline of a character should be drawn before an actor undertakes a new part. If he has a well-ordered and an artistic mind it is likely that he will give at least a symmetrical and effective performance; but should he make no definite arrangement, and depend upon our ghostly friends Spontaneity and Inspiration to pay him a visit, and should they decline to call, the actor will be in a maze and his audience in a muddle.

English and French Comic Opera

Comedy in the nineteenth century took many forms that are now forgotten (some are discussed below), but many of the comic operas of the period have proved popular and enduring, like certain of the era's drawing-room comedies. The well loved satirical comic operas and operettas of the century have lasted not only because of their witty libretti but particularly because of the effervescent, memorably tuneful scores by such internationally renowned composers as Johann Strauss II (1825–1899) in Vienna, Sir Arthur Sullivan (1842–1900) in London, Hervé and, above all, Jacques Offenbach in Paris.

Offenbach's first megahit was *Orphée aux enfers* (Orpheus in the Underworld), with a brilliant score. It turns on its head the myth of deep, faithful married love embodied in Orpheus, Father of Music, and his wife Eurydice: the two can't stand each other, and each is unfaithful. At the same time the piece is a thinly veiled, scathing satire of the political regime and the prevailing sexual mores. The narcissistic, lustful Olympian gods and goddesses are portrayed as hypocritical hedonists—the philandering Jupiter is meant to be Napoleon III. And the characters even do a suggestive "Galop infernal" in Hades—to the tune famously known as the "can-can."

When the piece premiered in Paris in 1858, some critics lambasted Offenbach because he and his librettists, Ludovic Halévy (1834–1908) and Hector-Jonathan Crémieux (1828–1892), had dared to satirize classical mythology, then regarded with almost religious awe. The "prince of critics" Jules Janin (1804–1874) seemed particularly outraged at this "profanation" of "sainte et glorieuse antiquité" (holy and glorious antiquity). Overt anti-Semitism also played a part in the reactions of some: How dare these upstart Jews, these alien outsiders scoff at ancient Greece, the birthplace of "our" civilization? (Crémieux was Jewish, Offenbach was a Jewish convert to Catholicism, and Halévy was born into a family of converted Jews.) Wondering what all the fuss was about, the public flocked to the Théâtre des Bouffes-Parisiens, and a hit was born.

A Summary of Techniques for Performing Comic Opera

1. The tempo, or rhythm of the music as indicated in the time signature and the tempo set by the conductor set the limits of how much time you are allowed to take in playing the actions. You must time them with the music.

2. The melody, which provides the emotional subtext for the words, tells you how to express the emotions. You can play with it, or against it, depending on your interpretation.

3. Singing is an action, just as speaking is. A song is part of the character's action, used to advance the story as much as dialogue does.

4. Patter songs, such as those in Offenbach's or Gilbert and Sullivan's comic operas, must be sung with crisp, clear diction; and a steady rhythm. Many of them are character songs, which are numbers in which a character introduces him- or herself, so play them for real. Use the introductory music to these songs to convey something about the character to the audience, whether it be the prissiness and queasiness of Sir Joseph on board the H.M.S. Pinafore, feeling slightly seasick during the lead-up to his song, "I am the monarch of the sea"; or the Lord Chancellor gravely making his first entrance to the strains of a minor-key fugue in *Iolanthe*, nodding to left and right, greeting peers, some individually, like a president entering the chamber to deliver the State of the Union address.

5. Take dance classes, and learn at least elementary dance techniques.

6. The same internal and external acting techniques should be used to play the characters in musical pieces as in spoken material. Use your imagination to project yourself into the given circumstances. Find the objectives (what the character wants at any given moment; as well as overall), obstacles (what's in the character's way), and actions (what the character does to get what he or she wants).

7. For dialogue, the timing of jokes and laughs is an essential skill. You will also need to be able to do various kinds of comedic movements and takes (see chapter one).

Performing Comic Opera with Authentic Style; Offenbach; Gilbert and Sullivan

The brilliant opera singer Lotte Lehmann (1888–1976), sets forth a way of singing that is also a way of acting the sung line. Her method takes account of how the language would be spoken. Lehmann says in her book on Lieder, *More Than Singing: The Interpretation of Songs* (Boosey and Hawkes, 1945), that "a phrase must always have a main word, and with it a musical highlight." Furthermore, "every phrase must be sung as a sweeping line, not just as a series of words that have equal weight and no grace." This technique enables you to carry out an action in the same way that spoken utterances do.

In acting terms, sung words can be treated like spoken words: they have intentions and subtextual meanings. The idea that the meaning of the text should be clear, and that the acting should be full of passion, is by no means new. Eighteenth-century Italian singing teachers had a motto, "Chi pronuncia bene, canta bene": Who pronounces well, sings well. They meant that if a singer has good, clear diction and excellent articulation, he or she can sing well. Without excellent pronunciation and enunciation (in any language), there is no chance. As with speaking on stage, excellent diction is paramount importance: the words must be understood.

The famous opera baritone, Manuel García (1805–1906), son of the renowned Spanish tenor of the same name, was a teacher of bel canto technique, which he had originally learned from his father. In 1840, he wrote an important manual, *Traité Complet de l'Art du Chant* (Complete Treatise on the Art of Singing). An abridged version was published in English as *Hints on Singing* (Ascherberg, Hopwood, and Crew, Limited), and released in a "new & revised edition" in 1894. It is in the form of questions and answers, illustrated with numerous musical examples. "Part II" of the *Hints* is entitled "Singing Coupled with Words." García answers the question, "Of what importance are words to melody?" in the following way:

> To express any particular feeling or idea, we must make use of words. Hence the importance for the singer of delivering these with the utmost distinctness, correctness, and meaning, under the penalty of losing the attention of the audience [if this advice is not followed].

He then goes on to analyze vowels and consonants in a very technical way. But you will notice that he attaches importance to the "meaning" of the text, and this involves subtext and interpretation. To the question, "How can a singer transmit his emotions to the audience?" he answers: "By feeling strongly himself." This is essential advice today, as it was when he wrote it.

It was a principle clearly understood and applied by singers such as, Juliette Simon-Girard (1859–1954), who had worked with Offenbach, and created the title roles in *La fille du tambour-major* (The Drum-Major's Daughter; 1879) and *Madame Favart* (1878) for him. In 1903 she went into the recording studio to sing into the acoustic horn. She recorded one of the great numbers from the tuneful *Madame Favart*, the "Ronde des vignes" (Grapevine Rondo). You can hear it on a CD, *La Grande Époque: Rare Recordings of Delmas, Héglon, Lafitte. Simon-Girard* (Pearl GEMM 9113; 1994).

One can actually hear in Madame Simon-Girard's recordings that she knows she is funny, but she sings everything very seriously, with a sense of humor and comedy. And she knows that comedy is a serious business! Listening to her is a delight. She allows us to participate, to connive in the comedy, to share her point of view. She is very giving. That is another great performer's secret: Give to the audience. Let them in. Love them.

Offenbach, like W. S. Gilbert, staged and directed most of his own productions. What he demanded from his singers, and what we hear in Simon-Girard's recordings, was superb singing, and a true sense of droll, tongue-in-cheek comedy, which he had himself in abundance.

Aside from perfect vocal technique that included the ability to sing bel canto, Offenbach also wanted peak energy and great comic timing from his performers. No laid-back playing: the attitude must be up and forward, thrusting outward to the audience. During rehearsals for a revival of the brilliant political satire that also lampoons serious opera, *Les Brigands* (The Brigands; 1869)—W. S. Gilbert published an English translation in 1871, although it was not performed until 1889—things were not going well. The irate composer-director began gesticulating furiously with his cane while the finale was being gone through. He finally got the great energy and driving tempi he wanted, but at the same time he broke his walking stick. "Well," he exclaimed, "I may have lost my cane, but at least I've found my finale!"

His performers had to be able to speak dialogue like actors, not like opera singers who intone lines by placing everything in the same forward area of the mask, as they had to do when singing. Listen, for instance, to the recent recording of the one-act romp, *Le Financier et le Savetier* (The Financier and the Shoemaker; 1856; available on a CD from Accord; ASIN B000LSA7W2), based on *Le Savetier et le Financier*, a fable by the seventeenth-century poet, La Fontaine (1621–1695). The recording, beautifully conducted by musicologist and Offenbach expert Jean-Christophe Keck, fulfills all of these requirements: the singing is superb, and the dialogue spoken in a real way. There is also a series of Offenbach recordings made for French radio by the ORTF back in the 1950s and '60s that have captured the style perfectly. Many are available on CD.

For the authentic old style of Gilbert and Sullivan performances, listen to the 1993 CD *The Art of the Savoyard* (Pearl; ASIN B000000WYL). You can hear some of the first generation, including Richard Temple (1846–1912) and the infinitely droll Rutland Barrington (1853–1922). The immediate successors to the originator of most of the leading comedian "patter-song" roles, George Grossmith (1847–1912) also worked with Gilbert and made recordings: listen to Charles H. Workman (1873–1923), Walter Passmore (1867–1946; he created the role of Grand Duke Rudolph in *The Grand Duke* in 1896), and Sir Henry Lytton (1865–1938). He had first worked with Gilbert and Sullivan in the original production of *Princess Ida* and later was celebrated for doing the "patter-song" roles in the 1920s and '30s. All of these people, who had had the benefit of Gilbert's demanding, meticulous stage and character direction and Sullivan's musical direction, were magnificent, and had of course a perfect sense of the necessary tongue-in-cheek comic delivery and general manner of serious comedic playing.

After the generation that worked with Gilbert, we have recordings of the complete scores of the comic operas with Martyn Green (1899–1975). He is superb and his diction is magnificent. He still has his predecessors' sense of droll, restrained comedy. But he also

brought something to the roles that was unique to him: a real interpretation of each character that differentiates one from another, so
that, for instance, the patter songs do not all sound alike, but rather,
each belongs to its particular character. His successor, Peter Pratt
(1923–1995) is very droll in the recordings he made, particularly
because he had the same kind of dry voice that Lytton, Passmore, and
Barrington had. He too was a real actor, and differentiated each role.
John Reed (1916–2010) assumed the roles in 1959, having understudied Peter Pratt for eight years. I feel that he had lost the sense of
authentic style, despite his good diction and rather dry delivery. With
his campiness, he was nevertheless very popular with audiences, to
whom he sometimes played up outrageously, practically asking for
laughs by using a squeaky voice on certain words, rather than playing
the character for real. And the dialogue included in his recordings
sounds disappointingly "operatic." Do not take it as a model!

Stanislavsky in Gilbert and Sullivan's *The Mikado*

Long before the Moscow Art Theatre was even dreamed of, and when
he was still basically an exceptionally talented amateur, mounting productions at the Alekseev family theater, Stanislavsky played Nanki-Poo
in the 1887 Russian premiere of Gilbert and Sullivan's *The Mikado*. The
production was directed by Constantin's brother, V. S. Alekseev.

Even in those days, when he worked in the office at the family factory during the days, and labored on the play during evenings and on
weekends, he was thorough and thoughtful in his preparations, betokening the system yet to come. He and the company, known as the
Alekseev Circle, immersed themselves in everything Japanese. They
even invited a family of Japanese acrobats, who had been appearing with the circus, come to live with them, "They proved to be very
decent and were of great help," he tells us in *My Life in Art*.

As Stanislavsky describes it, the company really were absorbed
completely in learning about Japanese ways of dealing with accessories, and moving. The Alekseev family's Japanese guests taught them
everything they needed to know, much as Gilbert himself had done

with his own company, inviting Japanese people from the exposition in Knightsbridge to rehearsals of the original production. You can see the rehearsal process accurately recreated in Mike Leigh's brilliant film, *Topsy-Turvy* (1999), which is about the making of this comic opera.

The Japanese acrobats working with Stanislavsky and the company:

> …taught us all the Japanese customs, the manner of walking, deportment, bowing, dancing, handling a fan. It was good exercise for the body. On their instructions, we had Japanese rehearsal costumes with obis made for all the actors, and we practiced putting these on. The women walked all day with legs tied together at the knees, the fan became a necessary object of everyday life. We got the Japanese habit of talking with the help of a fan,

The Alekseev Circle had special classes in Japanese dancing and learned "how to turn rhythmically on our heels, showing now the right, now the left profile." They learned how to fall "like gymnasts" and "how to jump, coquettishly lifting our heels." When it came to working with the fan: "We learned to juggle with a fan, to throw it over a shoulder or a leg, and what is most important, mastered all the Japanese poses with the fan…"

The highly stylized production must have been most impressive, and even thrilling, resembling Japanese theatrical forms in some ways. Stanislavsky's faithfulness to the Japanese setting no doubt made for a wonderful show. What he seems to have left out of the equation, however (at least in writing about this production), is that *The Mikado* is not about Japanese society or mores. It has nothing to do with the actual Japan. No such characters as those in this wry satire ever existed in that far-off land. They did appear to exist because of the stylized portrayals in Japanese imports to Europe seen in prints, and in drawings on porcelains, textiles, and fans. But rather than parodying anything Japanese, this comic opera guys the Victorian love affair with images of "exotic" Japan, and is first and foremost a satire of Victorian English sexual attitudes and the class structure. It also spoofs Victorian melodrama, a theme that would be taken up again by Gilbert and Sullivan in their next piece, *Ruddigore*.

On the other hand, it cannot be denied that there is a racist aspect to the libretto, which retails the picture of Japanese culture as essentially savage and barbaric—for instance, when it comes to the Mikado himself. The august ruler is given to cruel, bizarre, and horrible punishments that "fit the crime," such as boiling in oil. And the general picture of people with such different ways of dressing, moving and behaving, as well as the yellow-face makeup can be perceived as caricatural. The ambiguous love of Japanese imported objects combines with a view of the Japanese themselves as barbaric and primitive, and this overlays Gilbert's satire of English ways. There is no respect paid in this imperialist age, with its automatic assumption of European superiority, to the greatness of other cultures: One is European—and in England, English—or one is not; and if one is not, one is not completely civilized, when one is civilized at all. Josephine Lee has gone into all these aspects of *The Mikado* in detail in her very interesting book, *The Japan of Pure Invention: Gilbert and Sullivan's The Mikado* (University of Minnesota Press, 2010).

In a production starring Eric Idle as Ko-Ko, directed by Jonathan Miller, and performed on stage in London (where I saw it), then taped for television in 1987, the satire of English customs and mores is eminently clear, as you can see in the DVD of the television broadcast. The costumes and abstract sets are pure Georgian England, and the setting is a 1920s seaside resort. Pooh-Bah, the quintessence of snobbery, is dressed in a gray morning coat and top hat, and sports a monocle and cane; he seems very old-school Edwardian. The Chorus of Japanese gentlemen is in correct morning dress as well. Although Japan seems merely incidental, and Edwardian-Georgian England central, there is still an inescapable racist aspect to the proceedings, as when, for instance, the gentlemen during the opening chorus, pull the corners of their eyes wide as they sing, "If you want to know who we are, / We are gentlemen of Japan." But this can also be seen as mocking racist stereotypes and the people who retail them. The gesture is done as a sort of wink at the audience, as if to say, "Of course, we are

Edwardian-Georgian gentlemen of England, not really Japanese at all: that should be obvious."

English Comedy Genres: Extravaganzas, Pantomimes, Farce, Burlesque, Comedy of Ideas, Drawing-Room Comedy

Comedy in England in the nineteenth century took many forms that are now forgotten. The three most popular and enduring genres were the pantomime, the farce, and the drawing-room comedy.

People also flocked to the now outmoded "extravaganza," an elaborate, spectacular show with a large cast. Transformed into a simple variety show, the genre still exists in certain venues, such as New York's famed Radio City Music Hall, and it was a relative of the Follies so popular in the 1920s. Beginning in the early 1830s, these eclectic pieces were a form of light comic burlesque with music, but with less emphasis on broad parody and more on musical and dance entertainment, and whimsical stories based on legends and fairy tales. In fact, the extravaganza was a direct precursor of the pantomime. One of its major practitioners was James Robinson Planché, the scripts of whose extravaganzas distinctly resemble the jumbles of George Colman "the Younger"; for instance, both their versions of the Bluebeard story are nearly identical. Planché also wrote his memoirs, which are an excellent source for studying the period.

British pantomimes, which were spectacle extravaganzas especially popular during the Christmas season, as well as parodies and burlesques with silly punning titles, were highly popular throughout the century. H. J. Byron churned out dozens of such plays, among them the Christmas pantomime *Robinson Crusoe, or, The Harlequin Friday and the King of the Caribee Islands* (1860) and the burlesques *Bluebeard from a New Point of Hue* (1860), *Aladdin or the Wonderful Scamp* (1861), and *Esmeralda, or, The Sensation Goat* (1861), the latter three, and many more, in doggerel rhymed couplets. W. S. Gilbert and H. J. Byron collaborated on several pieces, including a travesty with the ludicrous title *Robinson Crusoe; or, The Injun Bride and the Injured Wife* (1867). The Victorians were nothing if not silly, when it came to their taste in comedy. These burlesques, pastiches, and parodies were all farcical in nature, as well as travestying well known stories, operas, and plays.

But as the nineteenth century entered the more puritanical age of Queen Victoria (1819–1901), whose reign began in 1837, actors (looked on askance in previous centuries as well) and theater, except for most of Shakespeare (not all) was increasingly looked down upon by the staid middle class, even though they were its chief customers. As a result, theaters were simply given other names, such as Thomas German Reed's "Gallery of Illustration," for which Gilbert and Sullivan each wrote pieces with other collaborators, among them Frederick Eames Clay (1838–1889). Although largely forgotten today, Clay was a very highly regarded composer of songs and musical theater pieces, including four he wrote with Gilbert, among them, *Ages Ago* (1869), an early version of what became Gilbert and Sullivan's *Ruddigore*; and *Princess Toto* (1875), for which they had high hopes, but Gilbert is not at his best, and the score, though pleasant, is uninspired. Clay also worked on the English version of the American musical, *The Black Crook*, a musical comedy-extravaganza with an eclectic score consisting of songs by a number of contributors, arrangers, and adapters, with one of the worst books ever written for a musical comedy—"an Original Magical and Spectacular Drama in Four Acts"—by Charles M. Barras (1826–1873). It opened in New York at Niblo's Garden on Broadway and Prince Street in 1866, and ran for 475 performances, a record in those days; and it had at least fifteen revivals. Clay was a great friend of Arthur Sullivan, and introduced him to Gilbert.

Thomas German Reed (1817–1888) was an English theater manager, producer, and the composer of several comic pieces to early libretti by Gilbert and by F. C. Burnand (1836–1917), the future editor of the humorous periodical, *Punch*. In 1855, Reed and his wife, multi-talented contralto, Priscilla Horton Reed (1818–1895), founded and ran German Reed's Gallery of Illustration, producing clean, decorous comic operettas by Frederick Clay, Alfred Cellier (1844–1891), Sullivan, Edward Solomon (1855–1895), and others, in which Mrs. Reed performed, and there was no sexual innuendo permitted. Love stories there might be, but they didn't include sex.

You could take the whole family and never fear that the children would hear a word about sex. They might be treated to bigotry and imperialistic chauvinist sentiments, but no prurient libidinous innuendo would ever taint their innocent ears. The word "gallery" was chosen to avoid the not quite respectable word "theater," associated with cheap burlesques and sexual innuendo, and therefore offensive to Victorian sensibilities. The repressive attitude to sex, to actors and to the theater would be somewhat but not completely different thirty years later.

Among the particularly popular comedies was the phenomenally successful *Charley's Aunt* by Brandon Thomas, which opened in London in 1892 and ran for a record-breaking initial run of 1466 performances. The previous London record of 1362 performances had been held by the comedy *Our Boys* by H. J. Byron. *Charley's Aunt* was filmed and adapted for television many times. One of its most notable versions was the 1941 movie, a vehicle for Jack Benny. Translated into many languages, the play has had revivals worldwide, including many in New York and London. In 1948, it was musicalized as *Where's Charley?*, with a book by George Abbott and music and lyrics by Frank Loesser; it ran for 792 performances. The famous line from the play, which became a catchphrase, is repeated by different characters: "Brazil...where the nuts come from."

A late nineteenth-, early twentieth-century genre, the "comedy of ideas" is a play that revolves around a debate concerning ideas of politics, philosophy or religion, and the like, but in a humorous way. Characters often represent different points of view in the debate, as they do in the plays of George Bernard Shaw, whose plays exemplify a genre that was at one point highly appreciated. But its popularity was ultimately short-lived, and few write comedies of ideas nowadays. Light comedy, drawing-room comedies, and farce are far more popular with audiences. Shaw's way of writing seems not only dated, but tedious, particularly when his ideas on morality and sexuality are themselves dated, having been surpassed by changes in attitudes, mores, and manners.

In the mid-nineteenth and early twentieth centuries, a brand of humor came to the fore that had been around for centuries: ethnic humor. It had already existed in the stereotyping of national characteristics in Shakespeare's day, where we find the cliché of a Frenchman in Dr. Caius in *The Merry Wives of Windsor* and the Welsh, Scottish, and Irish stereotypes in *Henry V*.

Music hall in England and its American counterpart vaudeville, the nineteenth and twentieth century's popular entertainment form, featured—along with standard comedic, musical, and acrobatic acts—"dialect comedy" acts that presented stereotyped ethnic characters, usually ludicrous and generally unattractive. The acts were comic turns or routines in which the performers used accents that were considered funny, and played on stereotyped character portrayals of various ethnic groups. They played to the racist and ethnic prejudices and unconscious sexual fears and conflicts of many members of the audience. Among the most usual in America were Irish, Yiddish, and Italian, all three immigrant groups of low status when they arrived and before they were assimilated into mainstream culture. But the worst such acts were those where white performers in blackface played and parodied African Americans, the acts being an outgrowth of the minstrel shows, popular on both sides of the Atlantic.

In a minstrel show, the Bones, also called Brudder [Brother] Bones was the performer who sat on the end of the semicircle of minstrel singers and kept time by playing a pair of "bones": a rhythm instrument consisting of two bones that were clacked together, or, more usually, two bone-shaped sticks of wood. He and the Tambo—the performer who sat on the end of the semicircle opposite the end where the Bones sat, and played the tambourine—exchanged witty sallies and repartee with the Interlocutor, the performer who sat in the center of the semi-circle and served as both presenter (master of ceremonies) and straight man in comedic exchanges. Some African Americans did these sorts of acts as well, in the obligatory blackface makeup that ironically made them acceptable to the white audiences in the segregated theaters: it was often the only work they could get.

Scene Analysis: English Drawing-Room Comedy: Oscar Wilde's *The Importance of Being Earnest*

The subgenre of the drawing-room comedy is epitomized in the four full-length plays by Oscar Wilde (1854–1900) that were all written and performed in the last decade of the nineteenth century. The most popular and well known remains the often revived *The Importance of Being Earnest, A Trivial Comedy for Serious People*. As Wilde said in an interview in the St. James's Gazette on January 18, 1895, shortly before the play's opening, "It is exquisitely trivial, a delicate bubble of fancy, and it has its philosophy." When the anonymous reporter quizzed him, "Its philosophy?" Wilde replied, "That we should treat all the trivial things of life very seriously, and all the serious things of life with sincere and studied triviality." He had no "leanings towards realism," he said: "Realism is only a background, it cannot form the artistic motive for a play that is to be a work of art." And this whimsical play is in fact set against realistic backgrounds.

One of the funniest things in the play is indeed that trivial matters, such as the cucumber sandwiches in act 1, are treated as if they were the most important things in the world, and serious matters, such as monogamy, are treated as trivial and almost unimportant, if not beside the point. And as Brian Bedford said in a *New York Times* interview on January 5, 2011, publicizing the new production of *The Importance of Being Earnest* that Bedford directed and in which he also played Lady Bracknell, "What makes it funny is the seriousness."

The play was a phenomenal success when it opened on February 14, 1895 at the St. James's Theatre in London, on the eve of the libel suit instituted by Wilde against the infamous Marquis of Queensberry (1844–1900), who had shown up at the theater with a bouquet of rotten vegetables, but had been denied admittance. The enraged Queensberry objected to Wilde's relationship with his son, Lord Alfred Douglas (1870–1945), and was determined to hound Wilde in every way he could. On February 18, he left an insulting card at Wilde's club, and on April 3, the trial began. It would result in Wilde's arrest for "gross indecency," two more trials, and a guilty verdict that got him sentenced to two years at hard labor. He never fully recovered, and two years after his release he died in Paris, where he had gone to escape the terrible opprobrium and persecution to which he had been and would certainly have continued to be subjected.

Despite its joyful reception by critics and public alike, this enchanting comedy was forced by the scandal over his homosexuality to end its run early, and closed after only eighty-six performances. Wilde would write no more for the stage.

During rehearsals, Wilde coached the actors in the style of acting his play required: a sense of earnestness (appropriately), and a seriousness of delivery of his witty lines, pronounced with excellent diction and superb articulation. The pace had to be fast, but not so fast that the pointed jokes were lost. Pauses were eschewed. The audience could laugh, but never the characters.

Picture a beautiful, sunny day in old London Town, a day of bubbling good spirits. No comedy ever starts on a gloomy, rain-soaked day. In the opening scene, the sun is shining through the sheer lace curtains of the windows, plush velvet drapes drawn to the side and fastened. We are in the morning room of Algernon Moncrieff's flat in Half Moon Street, not far from Piccadilly and Green Park, in the Mayfair area of London. Wilde tells us that "the room is luxuriously and artistically furnished"— the street is not far from the Royal Academy of Art—which is to say that it is furnished in the latest Victorian fashion, no doubt with overstuffed armchairs and endless bibelots and porcelain figures adorning every tabletop and the mantelpiece that was ubiquitous, since there was no central heating. In the eighteenth century, Mayfair was a fashionable address, but by the 1890s, when the play is set, the area was already becoming what it is today: more a financial than a residential neighborhood. It is where Algernon can afford to live, as opposed to the more fashionable Grosvenor Square. The nearest railway terminus, which will play a pivotal role in the plot, is Victoria Station.

Algernon is a debonair, urbane sybarite, and a worldly man about town, born to wealth and raised to think very highly of himself because of his social class. He is preparing to receive his Aunt Augusta, who is Lady Bracknell, and her daughter, his cousin Gwendolen Fairfax, for tea, complete with cucumber sandwiches, which he munches as he talks with his friend "Ernest" Worthing, who is in love with Gwendolen and wants to marry her. He has arrived from his country estate expressly for the purpose of proposing to her. But Algernon will not hear of the match until "Ernest" explains the inscription on a cigarette case he had inadvertently left in Algernon's flat on his last visit: "From little Cecily, with fondest love to her dear Uncle Jack." "Ernest" admits that he is the guardian of a young lady who lives on his country estate, and that when there he goes by the name of John or Jack, and uses a fictitious, troublesome ne'er-do-well brother named Ernest as an excuse to go to London, to get him out of the perpetual scrapes he has gotten into. And he refuses to tell Algernon where the country estate is. The astonished Algernon says that he has his own fictitious person, Bunbury, and that he claims that his friend needs him as a way of getting out of any obligation he wishes to avoid. His friend supposedly lives in the country, and Algernon frequently goes "bunburying." Lady Bracknell and Gwendolen now arrive, and Algernon manages to get his formidable aunt out of the room, to give "Ernest" an opportunity for proposing to Gwendolen. She accepts, and she is so enamored of his name, "Ernest," that he resolves to have himself rechristened as Ernest at the first opportunity. When Gwendolen announces her engagement, Lady Bracknell is appalled, particularly when she learns that "Ernest" is of unknown parentage, and she forbids the marriage, and any further contact between the two. Surreptitiously, Jack gives his country address to Gwendolen, and Algernon, overhearing them, writes it down on his shirt cuff.

In the second act, we go to Jack's country estate, the Manor House, Woolton, Hertfordshire, and there we meet Cecily and her prim governess and tutor, Miss Prism, who tries to get the girl to study harder and to take things more seriously. The local rector, the Reverend Dr. Chasuble, pays a call. He is in love with Miss Prism, who shyly returns his affections. Now Algernon arrives, and passes himself off as Uncle Jack's scapegrace brother, Ernest, much to the delight of Cecily, who falls in love with him instantly, and much to the wary disapproval of Miss Prism. Cecily, like Gwendolen, adores the name "Ernest," and Algernon privately arranges with Dr. Chasuble to have himself rechristened by that name. Jack shows up in deepest mourning, because his brother Ernest, a victim of his wild ways, has just died of a severe chill in that capital of vice, Paris. Naturally, he is astonished and furious to find Algernon there, and has to pretend to be overjoyed. They go into the house, and Gwendolen, who has run away from London arrives. The two young ladies confront each other, when each learns that the other is in love with "Ernest."

When Gwendolen and Cecily meet for the first time, their behavior as they size each other up, and as each takes the other for a rival, is passive-aggressive. But after a certain point, this gives way to outright aggressiveness. Passive-aggressive behavior, which can be terribly annoying, not to say maddening in real life, is something of which we are all guilty at those times when we do not dare to express our true feelings. Those feelings emerge anyhow in some way, and on stage the incongruity between what we see the character feels and the manner in which he or she dares to express those feelings can be hilarious. When Basil Fawlty, the hotelier played by John Cleese in the television series *Fawlty Towers*, mutters so that only he and we hear his passive-aggressive remarks about his wife, we guffaw: "Drive carefully, dear," he mumbles as Mrs. Fawlty drives off, out of earshot. And he says this under his breath, with a rising intonation at the end, and with such obvious venom and hostility that we know he means the opposite. W. C. Fields, often an unhappily married husband in his films, is always muttering under his breath, as a passive-aggressive way of dealing with his anger.

CECILY. [...] May I offer you some tea, Miss Fairfax?
GWENDOLEN. (*With elaborate politeness*) Thank you. (*Aside*) Detestable girl! But I require tea!
CECILY. (*Sweetly*) Sugar?
GWENDOLEN. (*Superciliously*) No, thank you. Sugar is not fashionable any more.

(CECILY *looks angrily at her, takes up the tongs, and puts four lumps of sugar into the cup.*)

CECILY. (*Severely*) Cake or bread and butter?

GWENDOLEN. (*In a bored manner*) Bread and butter, please. Cake is rarely seen at the best houses nowadays.

CECILY. (*Cuts a very large slice of cake, and puts it on the tray*) Hand that to Miss Fairfax.

(MERRIMAN *does so, and goes out with* FOOTMAN. GWENDOLEN *drinks the tea and makes a grimace. Puts down cup at once, reaches out her hand to the bread and butter, looks at it, and finds it is cake. Rises in indignation.*)

GWENDOLEN. You have filled my tea with lumps of sugar, and though I asked most distinctly for bread and butter, you have given me cake. I am known for the gentleness of my disposition, and the extraordinary sweetness of my nature, but I warn you, Miss Cardew, you may go too far.

CECILY. (*Rising*) To save my poor, innocent, trusting boy from the machinations of any other girl there are no lengths to which I would not go.

GWENDOLEN. From the moment I saw you I distrusted you. I felt that you were false and deceitful. I am never deceived in such matters. My first impressions of people are invariably right.

CECILY. It seems to me, Miss Fairfax, that I am trespassing on your valuable time. No doubt you have many other calls of a similar character to make in the neighborhood.

Here are some possible choices for each character:

1. **Superobjective:** *Gwendolen:* To get married and be happy; to enjoy life. *Cecily:* To get married and be happy; to assert myself and have everything and everyone around me be aboveboard and honest; to get to the bottom of life's mysteries.

2. **Throughline of action:** *Gwendolen:* I deal with all the obstacles in my path, including anyone who stands in my way. *Cecily:* I deal with each person in turn, and I make sure I comes out on top.

3. **Counter-throughline:** *Gwendolen*: I have to be wary of every-one, and in this scene, I believe I have met my rival, and I have to deal with her. *Cecily*: I am an innocent, and in this scene, I mistake the reason for Gwendolen's visit, and thinks she is a rival.

4. **Adjectives describing the character:** *Gwendolen*: Imperious, self-assured, suspicious, perceptive, narcissistic. *Cecily*: Forthright, honest, suspicious, vindictive, serious.

5. **Point of view:** *Gwendolen*: I am a very good and superior person, quite sophisticated, and very kind to everyone, but I allow nobody to take advantage of me. *Cecily*: I am sincere and good-hearted, and I am very perceptive, even though others may think of me as naïve because I have led a sheltered life here in the country, and nobody is going to get the better of me.

6. **What is the main event in the scene?** Taking tea, as a way of getting to know each other, and sizing each other up.

7. **Where does the scene take place?** On the lawn near the house.

8. **What are the other given circumstances—time of day; weather; your physical condition?** It is the afternoon of a hot but pleasant summer day. Both young ladies are feeling well, but Gwendolen is a bit tired after her railway journey.

9. **What do you want—your objective?** Each wants to find out what the other wants. Cecily serves tea and Gwendolen politely accepts it. Perhaps Cecily wants to get Gwendolen to leave as soon as possible.

10. **What is in the way—the obstacle?** As they size each other up, each is the obstacle for the other. The question is whether the other person is really telling the truth. Each wants to maneuver the other into revealing the truth.

11. **What does your character do—your actions?** The words actually tell you specifically what is going on: Cecily offers tea, and Gwendolen accepts. Cecily serves, and deliberately does the opposite of what Gwendolen wants. They confront each other.

12. **Do you attain your objective by the end of the scene?** Yes, for both characters.

In act three, all problems are happily resolved, and the loving couples can be married. Wilde's final stage direction is "Tableau," a typical period convention. A tableau, from the French for "picture," is short for *tableau vivant*: a living picture. As Victoria parlor entertainment, tableaux vivants were like living, three-dimensional paintings, formed by people freezing in poses or attitudes, singly and in groups. In the theater, the tableau was a silent stage picture formed by the actors, indicating the opening or climactic action in a scene. It gave time for the audience to react and for the applause to begin as the curtain was falling at the end of a play; it would rise again immediately for the curtain call.

It is wonderful if a comedy's happy ending actually is a punch line. That is the most satisfying of all happy endings. Send 'em out laughing! At the very close of the play, Lady Bracknell, having discovered that Jack is not an orphan with unknown parents, but is really her nephew, Earnest, says, as he is embracing Gwendolyn, "My nephew, you seem to be displaying signs of triviality." He replies, "On the contrary, Aunt Augusta, I've now realized for the first time in my life the vital Importance of Being Earnest!"

XIII

Farce and Comedy in the Twentieth and Twenty-First Centuries: The Reality of Absurdity, or The Absurdity of Reality

Movement, Clothing, and Manners

Over the course of the twentieth century, not only did clothing itself become more comfortable and casual, but also what was required on formal occasions underwent a sea change. However, the dress of the late twentieth century being so close to our own in the twenty-first, there is little to be said that you don't already know about how clothing conditions movement. On the other hand, military uniforms, such those used in Neil Simon's *Biloxi Blues*, and the stiff attached collars and cravats worn by men earlier in the century, as well as the long gowns women wore, make a difference in how freely you can move. Cumbersome, hampering clothing can add to the fun in a bedroom farce, such as those by Feydeau, who was still writing at the turn of the century.

During the 1920s–40s, when going out of the house, women carried purses and wore gloves and hats, sometimes quite ornate, with feathers or small birds, and little veils that descended to cover the face. The length of women's skirts varied with the decade, and the costume of the Roaring Twenties Jazz Age "flapper" was distinctive:

tight-fitting, short sheath skirts, ending in fringes. Floor-length gowns and dresses were now worn only on formal occasions. Beautifully draped suits and dresses, sometimes with pleated sleeves, and stylish silhouettes emphasizing the graceful curve of the body were now the norm. Ornaments could include large bows or ribbons, and brooches to set off the color of the fabric. Necklaces, bracelets, and earrings, as well as finger rings, were all very popular. In the era of Coward's comedies, graceful movement in such clothing was a constant.

From the 1910s through to the end of World War Two and beyond, men often wore the double-breasted jacket, with its armhole cut high and small, and the sleeve wider at the top, with the jacket as a whole remaining close to the body, and the arms free to move without any binding effect. The starched, detached collars of the 1920s gave way by the 1930s to already sewn on, attached collars, which were much easier to wear; comfortable undershirts were always worn as well. In America, the first men's trousers with a zip-up fly, replacing the buttoned fly, were introduced by Hart Schaffner & Marx in 1936.

Upper-class Englishmen often wore ties with their regimental or school stripes, and therefore had a small selection; that would change as patterns became more attractive and elaborate. In the '20s, the three-piece tweed outfit of jacket, vest, and knee-length knickerbockers with knee-length socks, two-tone shoes, and a cap was popular for country wear. With a sweater and shirt instead of the jacket and vest, and with the knickerbockers wider than they were for walking down a country lane, or hunting, this was the obligatory golf outfit. The three-piece single or double-breasted suit, called a business suit in the United States and a lounge suit in Great Britain, with the vest worn with its lowest button unbuttoned, and a pocket watch on a chain, was the usual wear until the 1950s, when the two-piece, single-breasted suit replaced it.

For twentieth-century comedies of manners, such as those by Coward, and for the niceties of social conduct, table manners, and expected polite behavior in all situations, read the *Etiquette in Society, in Business, in Politics, and at Home* by Emily Post (1872–1960). The book, first published by Funk and Wagnalls in 1922, has gone into seventeen revised editions and is still in print. Her guiding principle is a good lesson for performing comedy of manners:

> Manners are made up of trivialities of deportment which can be easily learned if one does not happen to know them; manner is personality—the outward manifestation of one's innate character and attitude towards life.

Her advice still applies today, in our more casual age, even when women are informally dressed without gloves and hats, and men no longer have to wear cravats to fine restaurants, although a jacket is often de rigueur.

This informality in dress and manners also appears in the proliferation of comedy in Europe and the Americas in the twentieth century as never before, in the new media of radio, film, and from the late 1940s on, television. In the United States, amateur community theater flourished, along with numerous professional hit Broadway comedies and musicals, often performed on national tours and throughout the summer months in stock theaters. And comedy clubs, cabarets, and nightclubs grew apace, as did resort hotels, where the new art of stand-up comedy was practiced by individual comedians, many of whom in the 1920s through the 1940s were well known from vaudeville and went on to perform in films and television sitcoms.

French Boulevard Farce Continues: Flers and Caillavet's *L'Habit vert* (The Academician's Green Coat)

After 1900 and up until about 1940, the most widespread form of popular entertainment in Paris was the vaudeville-style revue, with its dances, serious and comic songs, and comic sketches. And there were many successful authors of light comedy and farce. Most notable were Marcel Proust's friends, Robert de Flers (1872–1927) and Gaston de Caillavet (1869–1915), nicknamed "The Lords of Laughter." Their plays dominated the Paris theater in the period preceding World War One.

One of their greatest hits was *L'Habit vert* (The Academician's Green Coat; 1912), a satire of the stiff pomposity that prevailed at the Académie Française and of the haughtiness, overweening pride, and narcissism of the aristocracy. At this point in history, the European aristocracy was at the top of the social scale, and even in a republic like France was treated with great deference by all social classes. Although this social aspect makes many plays from the era seem dated, the universal themes of Flers and Caillavet make their humor not only accessible but also still hilarious, like that of Molière.

The Duchess de Maulévrier, the American-born wife of the Duke de Maulévrier, director of the Académie Française, carries on an affair with her two-timing lover, Count Hubert de Latour-Latour, who is also involved with a chorus girl, who leaves him. Hubert is charming, but as ignorant as the day is long. He is working on publishing a journal written by one of his illustrious ancestors, for he is of ancient lineage. His secretary, Brigitte, the goddaughter of the president of the Republic, is in love with him, and she does all the work. When Latour-Latour and the duchess are discovered in flagrante by the duke and other voting members of the Académie, Brigitte, who has just come back in and discovered them as well, tells them that he was merely pleading with the duchess to intercede with the duke for a nomination to the vacant chair at the Académie. She then quits her job, and disappears, nowhere to be found. As it turns out, the members are looking to fill the vacancy with someone like Latour-Latour, who has written nothing, and is therefore no threat. One of them, General Boussy de Charmilles, has only one criterion for choosing a new "Immortal": "No generals!" Latour-Latour is inducted. During the reception ceremony, the duke begins reading aloud a love letter that the duchess had written and stuck inadvertently between the pages of his ceremonial speech of welcome. As soon as he realizes what he is reading, he is furious, and pandemonium ensues as everyone flees the chamber. But he is prevailed upon to continue his speech for the honor of the Académie, and the report is given out that he had momentarily suffered from heat prostration on this unusually hot day, so everyone returns, and the ceremony resumes. The duchess falls in love with the duke all over again because of his noble behavior, and breaks off the affair with Latour-Latour. In any case, Latour-Latour has been madly in love with Brigitte ever since she had fled. She has returned especially to attend the ceremony, and she now accepts his proposal of marriage.

The characters are incisively drawn. The duchess speaks French with "un fort accent américain," and quite inexactly, and she is guilty of malapropisms. When she is told that the duke's speech has been written in the manner of Louis XIV, she exclaims, "Yes, a perfect seventeenth-century pistachio!" (In French, the word "pistache" is much easier to mistake for "pastiche.") Her French is so funny and outlandish that sometimes the other characters have no idea what she is saying. Her friend and former lover, Parmeline, remarks that whenever she is attracted to someone, her accent gets thicker. There were a number of American heiresses who married into the French aristocracy, and one wonders if Flers and Caillavet had any particular people in mind.

The character of the pompous, smug, self-satisfied, and very right-wing duke, who must always have the final word of authority, is no doubt based on people the authors knew. The set-up is perfect: At the opening of the play, he enters to find a servant whistling as he sets out armchairs in the drawing room with the duke's portrait over the mantelpiece, in the duke's manor house at the seaside resort of Deauville. The duke has the first line of the play: "You allow yourself to whistle in here?"

"I beg Monsieur le duc's pardon. I thought there was nobody in this room," replies the servant.

"There was my portrait," says the duke. "You are no longer in my employ. Get out!"

The duke has a catchphrase that serves him on all occasions: "Je me porte bien" (I'm doing fine). He doesn't read newspapers, and when his secretary, who has arrived to go over the morning mail, says he thinks the duke might know what is going on anyway, he who is always unanswerable and brooks no contradiction replies, "Monsieur Laurel, nothing is going on. Nothing has gone on in France for eighty years. I mean since the fall of the legitimate monarchy." He is referring to the revolution of 1830, which overthrew Charles X, youngest brother of Louis XVI and the last of the elder Bourbon line. Charles X was succeeded on the throne by Louis-Phillipe of the younger Bourbon branch—their cousins, the Orléans family—whom the old-line duke considers beneath contempt and illegitimate. Louis XVI's cousin, Philippe d'Orléans, known as Phillipe Égalité, had voted to have him guillotined during the French Revolution.

The plays of Flers—an aristocrat fond of satirizing his social class—and Caillavet also sometimes have typical characters and jokes that show us the endemic, institutional anti-Semitism of the day. It is worth remembering that Caillavet was of Jewish background, and that this sort of ethnic humor was unfortunately acceptable to the audiences who had just lived through the Dreyfus Affair (1894–1906). Alfred Dreyfus (1859–1935), the only Jewish officer on the army general staff, was falsely accused of spying for Germany, condemned, imprisoned on Devil's Island, and later completely exonerated. The case divided the country into Dreyfusards and Anti-Dreyfusards, and awakened the latent anti-Semitism of some of the population. Both Caillavet and Flers, along with Emile Zola, Proust, and Anatole France, were among the famous Dreyfusards—supporters of Dreyfus, who maintained his innocence and clamored for his acquittal.

Other authors besides Flers and Caillavet were much appreciated before and during World War One. After the war, in the 1920s and '30s, Sacha Guitry (1885–1957), continuing to write his light comedies and melodramatic dramas, knew his greatest triumphs. In 1919, his hit farce was *Le mari, la femme, et l'amant* (The Husband, the Wife, and the Lover). With a title like that, the transparent plot was predictable, but the play's insouciant wit and charming dialogue ensured the success of this light, relaxing entertainment.

Having made up his quarrel with his famous actor father, Lucien Guitry (1860–1925), Sacha wrote a delightful comedy in 1920 for both of them to star in, *Mon père avait raison* (My Father Was Right). In 2009, it had a brilliant Parisian revival, which I had the pleasure of seeing. Many of his other plays have also been successfully revived in the last decade. And the plays of Louis Verneuil (1893–1952), so popular in the 1920s, were internationally successful, and many were translated into English and had good Broadway runs. They were also adapted for the screen, in several languages.

The boulevard theater has continued to flourish to this day, with many new plays. Neil Simon has been translated into French, and his hit plays are just as funny as they are in English. Still very popular, the farces of Feydeau, Labiche, and Courteline are frequently revived.

Tradition Expands: British Sex Farce Comes Alive!

Anyone walking through London during the 1960s and '70s would have been treated to such titles on theater marquees as *No Sex Please, We're British*; Marc Camoletti's *Boeing, Boeing* (1962), translated from the French by Beverly Cross; Kenneth Tynan's *Oh, Calcutta!* (1970; Off-Broadway, 1969) and other sex farces too numerous to mention. Just as French boulevard sex farce continued to be popular, and was now considered classic enough to be performed by the august Comédie Française, the home of classic tragedy and comedy, so bedroom humor dominated British theater. Some of it was imported to the United States, or, in the case of *Oh, Calcutta!* from New York to London, but some was so dependent on the culture of the British Isles and specific laws regarding sexual matters that it was not for American audiences, who would either not have understood, or, even if they had, would not have found certain plays amusing.

Pornography on stage and screen also proliferated, but that was not considered comic, although it had its comedic side. After a time, one could only laugh at the ubiquitous pool boy being accosted by the mistress of the house, in what was the only smidgen of a plot in these films. And many of them didn't even pretend to have that much plot. On the other hand, sexual innuendo of the kind offered by Mae West, with her salacious, lascivious attitude and double entendres, was intended to arouse at least the knowing smiles of the audience.

Burlesque, a form of musical theater that combines comedy sketches, musical numbers, and ladies who strip for the audience in burlesque houses, always featured comics and such actors as Phil

Silvers, the top banana who went on to have his own hit comedy television series, *Sergeant Bilko*, and to play on Broadway and in films.

No Sex Please, We're British by Anthony Marriott (b. 1931) and Alistair Foot opened in London's West End in 1971 and ran for more than eight years, despite universal pans from the critics. It proved less popular on Broadway, to say the least, and closed in 1973 after only sixteen performances. The convolutions of the British laws about pornography were not only unreal to the American public, but the whole play was also simply too frantic, needlessly complicated, inconclusive, and much too silly—much ado about nothing. Yes, Virginia there is such a thing as being *too* silly, even for farce. There is no point of view with which we can identify, and the target of the satire is unclear. Do the authors disapprove of the law or not, and does that even matter? Also, the characters are not interesting and there is not even a single quirky one among them. Suffice it to say that the authors had to have done something right, since the play had such a long London run.

Theater of the Absurd

Theater of the Absurd began in Paris in the 1950s with the plays of Beckett and Ionesco, and continued into the next decade. This was an era when the ideas of Freud, Berthold Brecht (1898–1956), and Karl Marx (1818–1883), and the writings of the Irish novelist, short-story writer, poet, and playwright James Joyce and of Marcel Proust had great importance in French intellectual life, and enormous influence on playwriting. World War Two had ended in 1945, leaving the world in a state of shock. Where could one look for meaning in such a world that had seen tens of millions killed—among them six million Jews, in the world's first attempt at genocide—and millions torn from their roots? For existentialist philosopher and playwright Jean-Paul Sartre (1905–1980), and the writers and philosophers who were also founders of this school of thought, Simone de Beauvoir (1908–1986) and Albert Camus (1913–1980), who had lived through it all, a new approach that took account of real circumstances and life as people experienced it was necessary. Sartre and de Beauvoir found part of the answer in the concept of engagement: Despite the fundamental absurdity of life, political engagment in humanitarian causes was necessary. Throw yourself into life, don't decline to be part of it, and by so doing, you can help change things.

"Theater of the Absurd" is a term coined by the English drama critic, playwright, theatrical scholar, and writer Martin Esslin (1918–2002), who used it as the title of a book, written in 1961, about playwrights Samuel Beckett, Harold Pinter, Eugène Ionesco, Jean Genet (1910–1986), and others. The term derives from the existentialist, Sartrian ideas that life is absurd, and that it only has the meaning we give it. Our choices in life are what determine who we are, but those choices, like the very idea of choosing, are absurd—that is, intrinsically meaningless. In other words, our choices only have the meaning we give them, if indeed we choose to give them any meaning. We may simply choose to exist, and not know why we have made the choices that would seem to determine where we are going in life. In any case, whether we choose or whether we do not—and not choosing is also a choice—life remains incomprehensible and, once again, absurd: it certainly doesn't have any meaning religion might give it. We are imprisoned within ourselves, and we try, but usually fail to find the common ground on which we can communicate with others. This philosophy underlies the absurdist plays, which are often done in a realistic style, and may have greater impact than if they were played in an abstracted, caricatural way. The latter style, too, can work for them however, as it has in productions of plays by Samuel Beckett.

Absurdist writing also reflects the influence of the surrealist movement in the arts, and of the silliness of the Marx Brothers, whose comedy routines in their movies are a sort of preabsurdist Absurdism, or perhaps a reductio ad absurdum. If you do these plays, keep the Marx Brothers and their ebullient enjoyment and zest for life in mind.

These qualities are quite useful for performing one of the first plays in the theater of the absurd movement, the often revived *Waiting for Godot* by Samuel Beckett, written in French and translated into English by Beckett himself. It was considered obscure and difficult to grasp when it was first produced, but now seems translucent:

its symbolism and paradigmatic situation are obvious. The play is also very funny, with lots of silly lines, wordplay, puns, and pathos. Clowning is by no means out of place. The objectives, obstacles, and actions for the actors are also eminently clear: Vladimir, affectionately nicknamed "Didi," and Estragon wait for Godot, with whom they have an appointment that seems perpetually put off to another time. Godot is supposed to offer them employment. Estragon's name means "tarragon" in French; tarragon is an aromatic herb, and Estragon, who has no means to wash himself, is no doubt highly aromatic. The two are probably homeless, they are always hungry, and they indulge in vaudeville-like dialogue and commedia physical clowning. The obsessive-compulsive, dictatorial Pozzo (a name very close to the Italian for crazy, "pazzo") and his obsequious, resentful, vindictive slave, Lucky pass through the scene twice, coming and going from someplace, and provide some distraction. Lucky talks a blue streak of what seems like nonsense, but it is a sort of history of Western philosophical ideas. Godot, who twice sends a boy to deliver a message, never does show up.

An important point is that none of the characters have any discernible background, no past lives that we are allowed into, so that we might know something more than what is presented on the surface. But would filling in background enable us to understand them further? Is not the idea itself absurd? Is not their surface presentation all we really know of other people anyway?

As an actor, you are free under the circumstances to invent almost any background you please, using yourself as the character in the way Lee Strasberg advocated. There is no other way to know what the characters are going through than to go through the actions. In other words, the only character on stage is really you.

Other playwrights who have written absurdist plays and plays with absurdist aspects are Edward Albee, Tom Stoppard, and Harold Pinter, whose work is discussed briefly below. Joe Orton added a gay sensibility to his absurdist plays; he was not afraid to treat the subject of homosexuality, until then generally taboo.

An Absurdist Farce: Ionesco's *La cantatrice chauve* (The Bald Soprano)

The theme of *The Bald Soprano*, an outrageous farce and one of the most famous of the absurdist plays, is that people are so terrified of life and so timid, that they live in the most limited, circumscribed way possible, dwelling on the banal and trivial details of their humdrum existences, and wasting their lives away in the process. This is what Karen Horney called in her analysis of neurotic lifestyles "shallow living": some people don't want to go deeply into anything, let alone themselves and their own personalities, because it might be too threatening. Society pressures people into conforming and they do so willingly rather than face fears about death, sex, freedom, and a disorienting knowledge of the uncaring or even threatening universe. Through shallow living and concentrating on the trivial and the banal, security is attained, but at what cost?

The Smiths are sitting quietly at home, trying to be calm and to ignore everything on the outside, despite what they read in the newspapers. The arrival of the Martins immediately creates tension, and events become more tense still with the arrival of the attractive fire chief, who threatens the happy, placid home with his erotic allure. And the constant intrusion of knowledge and unforeseen events threaten the security of the conformists.

Ionesco called his now classic one-acter an "anti-play." You might say its title is an anti-title: it really has nothing whatsoever to do with the play. But then, as he might ask, what has anything got to do with anything? Ionesco said that he wrote for the theater because he hated it. Is this a paradox, or simply an absurd remark? His anti-play has been running in Paris (Ionesco wrote in French) since it opened at the Théâtre de la Huchette, a pocket-sized theater, in 1950; I saw it there in 1963.

Ionesco's father was Romanian, and his mother was French, so he was naturally bilingual. He grew up in Paris, and at one point had wanted to learn English as a third language. The playwright was inspired to write *The Bald Soprano* by what he saw as the nonsensical, sometimes useless exercises on the Assimil language teaching records, so this hilarious play is full of inane non sequiturs. The story, which opens on "a long moment of English silence," concerns a group of very staid middle-class English people, the Smiths and the Martins, living placid, humdrum lives underneath which lurk emotional turmoil and repressed desires that will come to the surface as the play progresses.

The Smiths and their visitors, the Martins, talk of many things, and the Martins, talking to each other, comment on everything in a recurring line with variations, that became famous, "How curious, how bizarre, what a coincidence!" At one point, Mrs. Martin tells the assembled company of an extraordinary occurrence she had seen in the street when she was shopping for groceries: a man was down on one knee, and leaning over to tie his shoelaces! They are all astounded, and they say in unison, "Fantastic!" It doesn't take much to surprise them, apparently. But it would take a great deal to arouse them from their complacency and apathy. In their world, Ionesco tells us in a famous stage direction, "The clock strikes as much as it likes." And these repressed, middle-class people, tight-lipped and tight-assed and straight-laced, wouldn't dare to stop it, even if they wanted to! The fireman arrives to put out the fire. Is there one? There is an underlying, smoldering erotic fire. Farcical slapstick situations occur, with the fireman's hose playing a central role—a Freudian phallic symbol if ever there was one. The Smiths and the Martins repeat the same dialogue over and over, and they talk of Bobby Watson. "Which Bobby Watson?" Who is Bobby Watson, if he really exists?

The lesson here, once again, is that this extremely nonsensical farce must be played as if it is real and natural, and lived as you would live any other play. You must find the characters' superobjectives, throughlines, objectives, obstacles, and the verbal and physical actions they play. What seems illogical when you read it must become logical for you when you perform it.

The Anglophone World of Comedy: Broadway and the West End

The twentieth century produced brilliant British and American comic playwrights, among them the sensitive and hilarious Terence Rattigan

(1911–1977), with his comedies and dramas about English life; and the Americans: the genial, humorous, incisive John Guare (b. 1938); Wendy Wasserstein (1950–2006), with her bittersweet comedies and sensitivity to relationship issues; and Christopher Durang (b. 1949), a brilliant satirist who continues the absurdist tradition and brings to his writing a mordant sense of humor. His brilliant, wacky satire of Chekhov and of absurdist ideas, *Vanya and Sonya and Masha and Spike* (2013), is sidesplitting.

English farce writers include Philip King (1904–1979), whose masterpiece is the popular, silly *See How They Run* (1944). As the Bishop of Lax, uncle of the Penelope Toop, a former actress now married to the local vicar, in a dinner theater production of the play, I had to do a spit take (see chapter one): I poured and started to drink a glass of water, and sprayed it out all over the place when I was clapped on the back.

The play is set in the drawing room of the provincial vicarage of Merton-cum-Middlewick in the 1943, while World War Two was raging. And the complicated plot hinges on romance and espionage, as the vicar leaves for the evening, and an army officer who is a friend of Penelope arrives, along with her uncle the Bishop of Lax. Mistaken identity and hiding in closets are part of the proceedings.

The English playwright Michael Frayn's (b. 1933) *Noises Off*, first produced in 1982, and then mounted by innumerable amateur and stock companies, is a farce-parody. The play centers around a play within the play, a horribly bad sex farce called *Nothing On*. The term "noises off" refers to stage directions in which offstage sound effects are heard by the audience. The farce takes place mostly backstage, and the first act is a dress rehearsal, while the last two acts are set during two different performances. There are constant mishaps, and everything from props to lines is bungled, adding to everyone's sense of desperation as they try to cope with the endlessly unforeseen. Slapstick and knockabout abound as in classic commedia farces. Pandemonium and mayhem are the order of the day.

Five Major English Comedy Writers: Noël Coward (1899–1973), Harold Pinter (1930–2008), Tom Stoppard (b. 1937), Joe Orton (1933–1967), Alan Ayckbourn (b. 1939)

A preabsurd absurdist and lord of laughter and pathos, Noël Coward was surely one of the funniest writers of comedy in the twentieth century. He set a standard for elegance, insouciance, and optimism in his comedies of manners and light comedies that has stood the test of time. Even his sentimental side, evident in such films as *Brief Encounter*, based on his one-act play, is endearing and does not seem dated, despite the changes in sociocultural mores.

In *Private Lives*, marital discord is the stuff of comedy, and we laugh at what we might not find so funny in real life. The caustic exchanges of Amanda and Elyot are a riot, full of acerbic wit and cleverness. They have divorced, and as the play opens, they unexpectedly find themselves on adjoining balconies in a hotel in Nice, where they have gone on their honeymoons with their respective new spouses, Sybil and Victor, two dull people whom they each felt would be good for them, because of their placid temperaments, bland personalities, and supposed lack of desire to indulge in antagonistic arguments. Waxing nostalgic about their toxic marriage, Amanda and Elyot run away with each other to Paris, where they immediately resume their sniping. Sybil and Victor pursue them, and, by the end, they, too, are fighting with each other, as Amanda and Elyot head out the door.

I have seen three excellent stage productions: two on Broadway, in 1970 with Brian Bedford and Tammy Grimes, and 1983 with Elizabeth Taylor and Richard Burton as Amanda and Elyot, and one in London in 1975 with Maggie Smith and John Standing. The play still works like a charm. In a more serious vein, underlying the infectious light-hearted, but sometimes awful vituperation is the portrait of a generation emerging disillusioned and discontented from Victorianism, with its rigid values and class hierarchy, and not being quite sure what should replace them.

Coward indulged in a gentle satire of spiritualism while creating a fantasy comedy in which it is central. *Blithe Spirit* is another play about marital bickering. Charles Condomine, an author who is researching a new book, holds a séance in his home to gather material. Madame Arcati, a medium, conducts the séance, and manages to materialize the ghost of Elvira, Charles's first wife, who now proceeds to make life as difficult as possible for Charles and his second wife, Ruth. She tries to kill Charles by engineering an automobile accident, but Ruth dies instead. Charles summons the inept Madame Arcati for another séance, to exorcise Elvira, but, making mistakes as usual, she brings Ruth back. She then advises Charles to go away on a trip. When he leaves, both wives proceed to tear the place apart. But in the film ending, his car crashes, and he is killed, to live happily ever after with both wives.

The ditsy spiritualist medium was played to perfection by Margaret Rutherford in David Lean's 1945 film; she made a specialty of playing dithering confusion and nobody was more funny at being befuddled than she—quite a lesson in serious comedy: she was always genuinely confused and confounded, nonplussed and thrown by the slightest occurrence. These qualities made her a memorable Miss Prism in the 1952 film of *The Importance of Being Earnest*. The rest of the *Blithe Spirit* cast was equally perfect, with Rex Harrison as Charles, Kay Hammond as the ghost of Elvira, and Constance Cummings as Ruth.

Playing Coward requires a special lightness of touch and an involvement in the sometimes absurd mindset of the characters that few other comedies aside from those of Oscar Wilde demand. In many ways, Coward is close to Wilde: in tone, in feeling, in the paradoxical, witty expression of ideas, in the pleasure he takes in the English language, grammatically perfect and with a large vocabulary. But underneath the airy badinage is a seriousness that you as an actor cannot ignore, since the characters desperately want what they want, and try to conceal their desperation.

Sharing qualities of the theater of the absurd, and inspired by it, as well as by Coward's way with words and with play construction, certain works of Tom Stoppard, Joe Orton and Harold Pinter clearly show their influence, while going beyond them and creating work that is spontaneous and original in feeling. If much of Pinter's dialogue appears absurd in such plays as *The Birthday Party*, *The Homecoming*, and *The Dumbwaiter*, and is replete with his famous "Pinteresque" long pauses, that is because we seem to be listening in on conversations as we sometimes do on a bus or a train. We are in medias res, and we don't always know where the speakers are coming from, or what they have been through, or what their relationships with each other are. We are therefore mystified and intrigued as we gradually learn what is going on, if we do.

But as actors, you have to get inside the heads of the characters and find their motivations. And you have to know the history that led up to what we are witnessing, so that it makes sense to you, just as an overheard conversation makes sense to the people involved in it: They share a common basis, a shared history, and a premise on which they rely for sense and meaning.

As with Pinter, when you play Stoppard, you have to follow the same Stanislavsky system when analyzing and performing the characters. At the same time, you must be aware all the time of Stoppard's brilliant use of language, verbal twists and turns, wordplay, and puns. In *Travesties*, Lenin repeats the Russian word for yes, "da" so that it becomes the movement in the arts, "Da, da. Da, da." When I saw the original production, I howled with laughter at this Dadaist moment. Somehow, when you hear this rather obvious pun spoken from the stage, it is irresistibly funny, in the context of the scene, with Lenin on a library ladder and Tristan Tzara (1896–1963), founder of Dadaism, talking to him from the floor.

Stoppard writes screamingly funny intellectual comedy, trusting that his audiences are educated, and even if they do not have an academic background or a knowledge of the fields he is writing about, his plays remain accessible. Each of them is different and full of allusions to literature and the other arts, and each abounds in absurdist situations. *Travesties* is about Lenin in Zürich just before the Russian Revolution of 1917, where Tzara, and James Joyce were also staying. Stoppard, imagining them in scenes that never took place in reality, mixes in Dadaism and other absurdist avant-garde movements in the arts. All three were revolutionary and exerted a profound influence on the world, Joyce and Tzara in the arts, and Lenin in the political sphere.

Rosencrantz and Guildenstern Are Dead takes two minor characters in *Hamlet* and explores what their mindset might be, who they are, and who they hope to be, so that they become major in our eyes. Nobody familiar with this play will ever view *Hamlet* quite the same way again.

Rough Crossing is an adaptation of the Anglo-American P. G. Wodehouse's (1881–1975) *The Play's the Thing*. Wodehouse's apt, clever title is from a line spoken by the Prince of Denmark in act 2, scene 2 of *Hamlet*: "The play's the thing / Wherein I'll catch the conscience of the king."

Wodehouse wrote in all comedy genres, including farce, and *The Play's the Thing*, adapted from Ferenc Molnar's (1878–1952) *The Play at the Castle*, is one of the most delightful madcap farces ever penned. In Frank Hauser and Russell Reich's *Notes on Directing* (RCR Creative Press, 2003), the authors tell actors who have to play bad actors that the trick is to "remember only the words and their proper order and nothing else." This is perfect advice for the actor playing Almady in Wodehouse's sparkling, urbane farce:

The playwright Sandor Turai and his collaborator, the level-headed Mansky, arrive at a castle in Italy, where they are to rehearse their new operetta, being composed by young Adam, who is in love with the operetta's star, Ilona, who loves him in return. Their unexpected arrival, meant to be a nice surprise, turns out to be a terrible mistake, as they overhear their leading man Almady making love, or trying to make love to Ilona. Completely unmanned and devastated, Adam falls apart, and says he will never compose another note. To save the day and their project, Turai devises a plan: He and Mansky will convince Adam that Ilona and Almady were not making love, but rehearsing a passionate love scene from a French play by Victorien Sardou. Turai writes a script incorporating lines they overheard coming from the bedroom. Almady, an aging, lecherous ham, speaks no French, and has endless trouble with the numerous French names that the playwright, Sandor Turai, has deliberately included in order to trip up the actor, and to punish him further for his misdemeanor. In fact, Almady is obliged to concentrate so hard that he cannot pay attention to anything else. So it is in the side-splittingly funny rehearsal scenes that the advice provided by Hauser and Reich is perfect. It also involves playing opposites: You are playing against acting well, and deliberately acting badly. The plan works and everything ends happily, as it should in such a delightful comedy.

In the 1990 New Theatre of Brooklyn showcase production of Tom Stoppard's farce, *Rough Crossing*, based on the same Molnar comedy, I played a very oral character, Gal (Mansky in the Molnar piece), a man obsessed with food. In his review for the New York Times, Mel Gussow (1933–2005) characterized Gal as a "seaborne sybarite." The simplistic role is almost cartoon-like, but it is lots of fun, and quite entertaining. Stoppard's version involves rehearsals of a new Broadway musical that take place on board an ocean liner in one of the lounges, amply supplied with an appetizing buffet. I hovered round it, seldom straying far, eating from time to time, gazing with fondness at the delectable dishes, and occasionally putting in my oar with one-liners about what was going on in the rehearsals. In a later scene of mayhem, I entered our leading lady's cabin in the midst of the chaos, and seated myself at the table, oblivious to the pandemonium. And I gorged myself on the breakfast remains. "Is there any cream?" I said while digging into some pancakes and looking for the cream for my coffee; the line—irrelevant to the general situation, and coming out of left field—always got a laugh. Gal's one-track mind is perfect farce writing, and the obsession with food must be played absolutely for real, like Truffaldino's in Goldoni's *The Servant of Two Masters*. Incidentally, in rehearsal under Steve Stettler's wonderful direction, we found the play so hilarious that we were always cracking up. The danger for actors doing this is that the audience, who do not know the play at all, may not find it quite so funny, as they concentrate on figuring out what is going on. And indeed they didn't, at first. It took us time in performance to hit our stride and to adjust to the audience reactions.

Stoppard's *Arcadia* takes romanticism, romantic poetry, and the scholarly pursuit of mathematics and turns them on their heads. A contemporary couple is studying the life and work of a Victorian family, and we therefore go back and forth in time, turning our concepts of time on their head, in an absurdist fashion par excellence.

The absurdist, iconoclastic Joe Orton wrote comedies satirizing imperialism and English sexual attitudes. He was outspoken and exposed to public view what was usually hush-hush. Ronald Bryden, critic for the newspaper *The Observer*, called him "the Oscar Wilde of Welfare State gentility." For his amazing and tragic life story, see the film *Prick Up Your Ears* (1987), with Gary Oldman as Orton and Alfred Molina as his homicidal lover, Kenneth Halliwell.

His best known plays are *Entertaining Mr. Sloane* (1964), *Loot* (1966), and *What the Butler Saw* (1969). But just as hilarious is the lesser known one-acter in eleven scenes, *The Erpingham Camp*, an absurdist black comedy that updates the ancient Greek tragedy *Bacchae* (The Bacchantes) of Euripides, turning it into a farce. It was presented in 1967 on a double bill with *The Ruffian on the Stair*, as *Crimes of Passion*.

Scene 3 takes place in the director's office of a family holiday resort camp, where chaos reigns and rebellion ensues. Its latest revival was in 2009. The word "camp" is a double entendre, and refers to camp humor—a combination of pose, flip humor, and arch, ironic remarks, displaying a knowing attitude.

The Entertainments Organizer having died suddenly while on the job, Erpingham, owner and director of the resort, gives Chief Redcoat Riley, his principal deputy, formerly Ringmaster with a circus, "the chance of a lifetime," and places upon him the sash and badge of office, appointing him to take the Entertainments Organizer's place forthwith. When disaster ensues, he will be stripped of his decorations. The satire of imperialism in Erpingham's speeches is hilarious, even if the phenomenon itself is not. India had been independent of Great Britain since 1947, and Ireland since 1921, but for Erpingham, they might as well still belong to England.

ERPINGHAM. Serve us well, Chief Redcoat Riley. And my best wishes for the task ahead.
   (Music: "Land of Hope and Glory.")

[...] The courage and grit that founded Empires still stands. [...] ...we shall rejoice that, of our own free will, you were born an Englishman.

(*The music fades.*)

RILEY. I was born in County Mayo, sir.

ERPNGHAM. Ireland counts as England.

RILEY. Not with the Irish, sir.

This material must be played with gravity, as the music, "Land of Hope and Glory," tells us. The imperialists of the Victorian era and the twentieth century, when the British Empire fell apart, automatically assumed their own superiority, and the playing of Orton's satirical farce must reflect that attitude.

Returning to the tradition of realism, Alan Ayckbourn is in some ways the British Neil Simon. Like Simon, he has a facile way with dialogue that flows and abounds in laughs at the witty sallies, rejoinder, and repartee. And, again like Simon, he keeps the audience smiling throughout. His romantic comedies sometimes have a tinge of bitterness to them that does not, however, make them in any way unpalatable. On the contrary, they are engrossing throughout. In *Absurd Person Singular*, he took the upsetting story of a young girl's constant attempts to commit suicide, and made it a subject for a farce that plays upon our fears and arouses laughter that helps to overcome our potential trauma, in the Freudian mold. The play was successfully adapted for television, like a number of his other plays, such as his romantic comedy trilogy *The Norman Conquests*, which people on both sides of the pond enjoyed immensely.

Ayckbourn also continues the tradition of British sex farce, turning it on its head in such plays as *Bedroom Farce*, another play successfully adapted for television. In this Feydeau-inspired play about four couples in three bedrooms, we never see one couple's bedroom, and nobody actually has a love affair in any of the bedrooms, which are the scene of lovers' tiffs, quarrels, rows, and reconciliations that may not last. While the situations may be absurd, as in all farces, they are not absurdist in any philosophical or existential sense of the word.

Two Americans: Edward Albee (b. 1928), Neil Simon (b. 1927)

Albee and Simon are at opposite ends of the scale: Edward Albee writes sometimes absurdist, tricky, symbolic comedies, and Neil Simon always writes true-to-life, realistic plays. But they are similar in that both deal with human foibles rather than politics, and are often satirically pointed almost in the manner of Molière. Both can be very funny, and Simon is the master of rolling-in-the-aisles mirth.

Albee's one-act *The Zoo Story* is not a comedy, and he has his very serious side, but his comedy-dramas contain ironic moments and memorable characters, such as those in the ironic and bittersweet *Who's Afraid of Virginia Woolf?* I was a college student when I saw the original 1962 Broadway production with Uta Hagen and Arthur Hill, and I was bowled over. The play was so new and fresh and brilliant and funny, and it reflected so well the personalities of some people on the staff whom I actually knew at school, as well as its ambience, that it was a revelation. Here at last was a new voice in the American theater, and a magnificent one at that.

George is a shy, introverted professor of history at a small college, and he is married to the brassy, vulgar, acerbic Martha, daughter of the college president. Their last name is probably not Washington, and they could not be farther from being the mother and father of their country, as you will see. As the play opens, they are returning extremely drunk from a party given by her father, and Martha announces that she has invited a new young faculty member, Nick, and his wife Honey for after-party drinks. George is not happy, and they tear into each other, as they continue to do even after their guests have arrived. And they manage to lambast Nick and Honey as well. Eventually, to exact further revenge by causing Martha more pain, George talks about his and Martha's dead child, a fiction they have invented, since they could not actually have a child. But we only learn this gradually. As the play ends, George and Martha, disillusioned and knowing they only have each other, will continue life together without the imaginary crutch that has kept them going all these years.

There are other great twentieth-century American writers of comedy, among them Paul Rudnick, Larry Gelbart, Murray Schisgal, and, earlier, Kaufman and Hart, whose *The Man Who Came to Dinner* is discussed in chapter four.

Neil Simon is the premier master from whom many contemporary masters of comedy learned how to write. He began his career writing for some of the greatest comic actors and comedians of the twentieth century. In the 1950s, he wrote jokes and skits for Sid Caesar and *Your Show of Shows*, as did Woody Allen. All this was grist for his comedic mill, and he went on to write his famous comedies, some of which are so funny, that you laugh at every other line, and can't stop laughing all the way through. His plays are based in a psychological reality that we all recognize and identify with. This kind of writing demands realistic playing using the Stanislavsky system, which was basically designed for realistic and even naturalistic plays. Simon's plays also demand all the comedic techniques detailed earlier in this book.

In vaudeville, the overdone "doctor act" was overtly sexual, a salacious routine in which a ludicrous, usually myopic doctor examines patients with the help of a particularly buxom nurse, while constantly looking down the bosom of her scanty uniform. This turn is exemplified in the play and film of Neil Simon's hit Broadway comedy, *The Sunshine Boys* (1972; film, 1975), in which two retired vaudevillians, who broke up their act because they didn't get along and ended up hating each other, come out of retirement to recreate their doctor act for a television special.

In a real-life variant, an actual doctor act performed by the American vaudeville comedy team Smith and Dale, "Dr. Kronkheit and His Only Living Patient," was filmed in *Two Tickets to Broadway* (1951). The name "Kronkheit" was from Yiddish and German (*Krankheit*) for sickness, or disease. You can see Smith and Dale on YouTube.

Another of Simon's comedies, perhaps his most famous, since it also gave rise to a hit television series, is *The Odd Couple* (1965; film, 1968; television series, 1970–1975), which is about the obsessively neat Felix who has separated from his wife and comes to stay with his obsessively sloppy friend, the sportswriter Oscar. The two of them are at odds from day one.

Neil Simon, who writes in all comedy genres, has written some farces, including *Plaza Suite* (1968), which tells three stories in three acts, and *Laughter on the 3rd Floor* (1993), which is the endlessly complicated story of writers for a television show. All the hallmarks of farce, including knockabout physical comedy, are used to tell stories of marital complications and love affairs.

Simon also wrote plays based on the Russian literature he admires, notably *The Good Doctor*, which dramatizes short stories by Chekhov. But most of his plays are based on aspects of his own life. He is a master at constructing plays and engineering laughs. He had written so much for television that his skills enabled him to adapt many of his stage plays for the screen, in superb movie and television versions. He knows how to set up a joke like nobody else, which is why he serves as an ideal model to writers of comedy in all media. And for actors, his jokes practically play themselves.

Part Three

Comedy on Camera

Introduction

Performing Comedy on Screen

I f you want to do comedy in the media, watch comic films and television sitcoms. You can learn a great deal by viewing them with an analytical eye, and by studying the work of the great film and TV comedians discussed in chapters fourteen and fifteen.

To see how the directors have set up the laughs, notice how each scene is edited from takes done at different angles. (Of course, the word "takes" refers here not to the comedic takes detailed in chapter one, but to each continuous photographing of a scene or part of a scene.) And notice which take was used when the laugh lines are there. Often, it will be a close-up, or a medium two-shot.

Notice as well the actors' timing, and learn from them how to play fully each of the many takes that may be required in a scene. Very important: Treat each take as a complete scene in itself, with a beginning, middle, and end. That way the take can be edited into the final cut of the scene. This requires great skill and dexterity, and a sense of continuity: You have to repeat each physical position and/or gesture each time, for each take and for each angle. The angles are shot in a series of takes. Continuity is so important that it is overseen on every set by someone who pays attention only to it, and can tell you how full that glass of milk was in the last take, and whether you gestured with your right hand or your left.

The finalized scene is put together by the director, photographer, and editor piecemeal from the various takes, and is therefore not one continuous performance of yours with no breaks. You usually do not have to sustain a performance through a scene, except in the master shot, which will be broken up in the editing process, as the different takes are inserted. Instead, you have to sustain the performance only for each take, which could be a page of script, a line or two, or a physical comic bit.

Television is less complicated because there are always fewer takes and fewer angles, but you have the same obligation as an actor to repeat the same movement, gesture, and position physically every time you do the scene.

There are formulaic scenarios and characters in TV sitcoms. Scott Sedita has delineated the characters in his masterful book, *The Eight Characters of Comedy: A Guide to Sitcom Writing and Acting* (Atides, 2006). Knowing in depth the type you are playing facilitates your job enormously. You must individualize and personalize whatever type you are playing, and not make the character a cliché or stereotype, but a living person, with real goals and desires.

Similarly, in the old studio system days in Hollywood, some actors made a specialty of playing certain types. The stable of character actors always brought the same personality and attitude or point of view to whatever role they played:

Franklin Pangborn (1889–1958) is always prissy and effete. He is very ordered in his gestures, compulsively neat, and slightly fey, in that closeted, stereotyped way gay people were so often portrayed in early cinema. He could be a hotel clerk, a salesman in a department store, a film director or producer, or any number of other roles, but he was always the same kind of compulsive, fussy personality, and was always disapproving when people weren't as neat and tidy as he was: he looked down on them, in fact.

Edward Everett Horton (1886–1970) was always frantic, fussy, discombobulated and slightly taken aback in all the high society characters he played in many films, including Fred Astaire / Ginger Rogers musicals, such as *The Gay Divorcee* (1934), *Top Hat* (1935), and *Shall We Dance* (1937). He often didn't seem to know quite what to make of things, but he had his ideas on what should and shouldn't be done nevertheless. He was frequently paired with the earnest, perpetually slightly surprised Eric Blore (1887–1959). For both of them, coping with circumstances was difficult, and they both embodied the idea of behaving like grown-up children. But they did not think they were behaving like children, immaturely—such people never do in real life: this behavior apparently came naturally, automatically, and unconsciously to them as they interpreted their characters. (For more on this topic, see chapter one under "Two Techniques: Behaving Like a Child…").

For today's comic character actor, the lesson to be learned is that a specific personality and specific character attitudes and points of view can be a desirable passport to a career, especially when these things are natural, real, and not obviously and annoyingly put on and indicated in order to be funny. Some more examples:

Brilliantly vapid, vacuous, yet motherly, Mary Boland (1880–1965) was usually slightly discombobulated and sometimes hysterical, as she is in *Pride and Prejudice* (1940), in which she plays Mrs. Bennett. See her in *Three Cornered Moon* (1933), as Mrs. Nellie Rumplegar, a pixilated socialite whose family has lost all its money in the stock market crash of 1929. Her daughter, the picture's star, is played by the versatile Claudette Colbert (1903–1996), who could play both comedy and tragedy with equal success. Don't miss her in *It Happened One Night* (1934) and *The Palm Beach Story* (1942).

Styles of film comedy vary tremendously, as the examples given throughout this introduction and the next two chapters demonstrate. You can enjoy everything from physical, slapstick farce to more genial romantic comedies. Among the latter is *Pillow Talk* (1959), starring the ruggedly handsome Rock Hudson (1925–1985) and the beautiful, charming Doris Day (b. 1924), who made many comedies and musical films, and had her own television sitcom series, *The Doris Day Show* from 1968 to 1973. The story of *Pillow Talk* has echoes in the sex comedy *Down With Love* (2003), starring Ewan

McGregor (b. 1971) and Renée Zellweger (b. 1969), showing once again the ubiquity of the age-old plots in which a would-be lover disguises himself to win the woman of his dreams. Incidentally, the brilliant comic actor Tony Randall (1920–2004), known for his role as Felix in the television series based on Neil Simon's *The Odd Couple* (1970–1975), makes notable appearances in both films. Zellweger, a versatile performer in both drama and comedy, is also very funny in such delightful comedies as *Nurse Betty* (2000) and *Bridget Jones's Diary* (2001). The brilliant, naturalistic actor Edward G. Robinson (1893–1973), known for his dramatic roles and, earlier in his career, for playing gangsters, shines comedically in Frank Capra's charming romantic comedy *A Hole in the Head* (1959) as Mario Manetta, the brother of Tony Manetta, played by Frank Sinatra (1915–1998), a great actor who could do drama and comedy equally well. They all play it for real—I cannot emphasize enough that that is the secret to playing comedy.

It is a good idea to analyze the plot of any film script you are working on, so that you really know where your character fits into the story (see chapter two). That way, you can keep things simple, and your work will be that much clearer. There are certain contemporary stories used over and over again, such as stories of self-discovery. Among them is the romantic comedy plot in which a staid married couple whose marriage is in difficulty reexamine their relationship in light of their encounters with eccentric, zany characters and in sometimes bizarre situations. One example among many: *Wanderlust* (2012), starring Paul Rudd (b. 1969) and Jennifer Aniston (b. 1969).

All the films and television shows mentioned in this book are available on DVD. The annotated appendix of major comedy film writers and directors should prove particularly helpful in furthering your cinematic knowledge. Some noted filmmakers and screenwriters, among them Neil Simon, Marcel Pagnol, and Sacha Guitry, are included on the list of twentieth-century playwrights, since they wrote a great many stage works; the theater made their reputations before they ever started working in film.

A Summary of Techniques for Playing Comedy on the Film and Television Screen

The difference between performing comedy on stage and on screen consists mainly of three things:

1. **Keep energy internal**: In the case of verbal or physical comedy, all your reactions have to be internal and real, with focused energy kept inside, and not projected energetically outward as on stage, although in some superficial slapstick children's shows, the opposite of such a technique is demanded, namely indication and slapstick, which is often badly done and very unfunny. Even an extravagant gesture should not be done with projected energy, as it is on the stage. The camera reads everything you do, and externally projected energy does not work. Watch Jackie Gleason or Lucille Ball at their most extravagantly external in gesture and facial expression, and you will see that they nevertheless focus their energy from within. This internal focus keeps the extravagance real and therefore convincing.

2. **Fill pauses with focused internal energy**: You are not usually performing for an audience, except in the case of TV sitcoms shot before a live public. So ordinarily you don't have to time out laughs in the same way, but you do have to pause, and to fill the pause, concentrating on your objectives. It is the director and editor who will cut and hold in the right places, as Billy Wilder did in the now classic comedy, *Some Like It Hot*. He explains as much and more about film comedy in an instructive extra on the DVD, an interview in which he talks about how he lights comedy scenes, as opposed to dramatic scenes.

3. **Speak naturally**: You do not have to project your voice. The sensitive mikes pick up even a whisper. Talk to the person you are addressing as you would in a real room or other setting—he or she is right there, after all—as opposed to

talking to the person next to you as if he or she were a mile away, as you often must do on the stage. Again, this is a question of how you focus your energy, in this case the necessary vocal energy to carry your intentions without projecting them vocally.

Build the character from the inside out, as you would in the theater: Deal with the character's thoughts and mindset, and determine the superobjectives, objectives, obstacles, and actions, all of which you will have to do before actual rehearsals begin, since there is so little time, either in film or in television. You can still assiduously prepare the scripts on your own, even using cue sheets or sides. The objectives and actions will be adjusted in the course of rehearsals. Meanwhile, you will have given yourself a firm basis on which to proceed.

You also need to know about the specific techniques required when playing in front of the camera. The techniques listed below apply both to television work, and to making film comedies, where there may be more complicated camera angles and location shots, since film expands considerably on the possibilities available for television sitcoms. Television is usually more limited in both budget and scope, so production values are not high for sitcoms, confined as they are to half-hour episodes. But a half hour in television essentially means twenty minutes, since every act or scene ends with a climax leading directly to the commercial breaks. So the television comedian has much less material to deal with than the film comedian, who is involved in telling a longer story. This is akin to performing a comedy on stage, but with the usual scenes shot out of sequence and done on retakes from different camera angles.

Here are more crucial pointers:

1. Familiarize yourself with all the technical aspects of the studio, including the different kinds of mikes, from body mikes to booms, that are used on shoots. Know the technical procedures, such as the use of the clapboard to mark the

beginnings and ends of takes. And learn the different camera shots and angles, which you will find conveniently listed in *Blumenfeld's Dictionary of Acting and Show Business* (Limelight, 2009).

2. Be aware of your relationship to the camera, and of which shot is being done (long shots, medium shots, or close-ups), so that you know how the shot is framed, which will partly condition how you make gestures—widely or close in—that may have to be repeated in other kinds of shots.

3. Keep gestures to a minimum, and only be extravagant with them when the script calls for that, or when you are so directed.

4. Be aware of your positioning vis-à-vis the other characters, and whether they are in or out of the frame when you talk to them. This conditions where you look.

5. Do not look directly into the camera unless you are directed to do so. You may be told to look to right or left of the camera, or above or below it, so the director can get a particular angle. In a close-up, with the camera right in your face, there may be a piece of tape on the side of the lens where you will be directed to look.

6. The internal (psychological) and external (physical) actions should be clear from the script, and as you will be shooting in short increments, you can perfect your playing of them.

7. During rehearsal and shooting, avoid indicating. And that includes mugging—making faces—for the camera. In the broadest of farces, you may be directed to do just that, but if you do not have to, then don't!

8. Use such comedy techniques as the different takes listed in chapter one. When you are shooting in front of a live audience, you can also use techniques of timing laughs.

9. Remember that the camera picks up even a momentary passing thought or the flicker of an eyelash, so the more you have a real internal life going on for the character, the better will be the performance. The camera sees unreality as unreal, just as it sees reality as real. A false reaction can immediately

falsify your entire performance, just as a poorly done accent can.

10. Stay focused and concentrated. Even though there is silence in the studio once the warning bell has sounded and the stage manager has told everyone to settle, there is still a lot of activity going on, much of it by the technicians who are moving boom mikes as you move, or cameras that follow your blocking. You have to ignore the mike and the camera, and act as if they were not there, which they are not, from the character's point of view: they don't exist.

11. Be as spontaneous and organic as possible in the circumstances.

12. Play the moment as it occurs. Do not anticipate.

13. I repeat: Do each take as if it were the entire scene, with a middle, beginning and end, even though you know there is more to the scene. That way the film can be edited, and each scene feels complete.

14. If cue cards or a teleprompter are provided, and you need to use them, learn to read from them without appearing to do so, by keeping them in your peripheral vision.

15. Always hit your mark, which is a spot indicated on the set somewhere in front of the camera by spike tape, chalk or other means, where the actor is to stand or move to; hence to "hit the mark": to arrive at the correct designated spot.

16. During the shooting process, you will hear directions given to technicians, and their responses, and you should know what they mean. You will also hear the directions meant for actors, which you must obey:

    A. **Action!** Start acting! This is used during both rehearsals and takes, and is often preceded by the warning word "and," followed by a brief pause: "And… action!"

    B. **Answer back to the camera!** Look directly into the camera lens when you speak! But as stated above, you should otherwise avoid looking at the camera.

C. **Approach!** An instruction from the director to the cameraperson, meaning, "Move the camera toward the subject being photographed!" Also heard as "Come in!"

D. **Back to one!** Return to your starting positions: we are going to do another take right away! A film director's command to both actors and technical personnel; also heard as "**Resetting back to one!**"

E. **Check the gate!** For technicians: Look into the camera lens frame in order to make sure no dust or dirt has gotten into it that might have interfered with the clear taking of a shot! In film and filmed television commercials or programs, this is the director's instruction, and is usually carried out by the first assistant cameraperson; it is often the last technical job done before moving on to the next take.

F. **Clear yourself!** Move so we can see you through the camera without interference! In film, this is a direction to an actor to move so as not to be partially hidden, e.g., if something is casting an unwanted shadow on the actor's face.

G. **Cut!** Stop the action! This is a direction to both crew and actors.

H. **Cut and hold!** Actors, stop what you are doing, but don't move off your marks, and maintain your positions! Crew, put your equipment on pause! In film, this direction is usually given when there is a technical glitch that is expected to be solved quickly and expeditiously, so that shooting can resume immediately.

I. **Give me a banana!** Walk in a single, continuous, gentle curve that makes a semicircle! A director's instruction to an actor who must walk in front of the camera.

J. **Hit the lights!** For technicians: Turn on the illumination!

K. **Hit the mark!** The direction to a film or television actor to arrive at a designated spot. Also heard as "Hit your mark!"

L. **Hit your mark and say your lines!** Speak as soon as you arrive at the mark!

M. **In five...four...three...two...[one]!** The command in a television taping or digital shoot for the actors to begin performing, usually accompanied by a hand cue: the word "one" is not said; sometimes preceded by the words **"We're on."**

N. **Into positions!** Get on your marks! A direction to actors to go to their starting places, or to assume opening poses, because shooting is about to start. Also heard as **"First positions!"**

O. **Marker!** The word said aloud by the person operating the clapboard at the beginning of a take, before banging the boards together.

P. **Mark it!** The director's or, more usually, the director of photography's instruction to the clapboard operator, who has written the take and scene number and other relevant information on the clapboard, to bang the boards of the clapboard together to make a sound at the beginning of a take; and at the end of a take just after the director has said **"Cut!"**

Q. **Quiet on the set!** Direction to everybody to be absolutely silent, preparatory to the beginning of shooting.

R. **Settle!** A command meant for everyone, and shouted when a warning bell has sounded, and shooting is about to begin.

S. **Sit into the shot!** After you hear the cue "Action!" move in and sit down on the designated mark! A direction to actors to move from off-camera into camera range, and to sit down in the place on which the camera is focused as the take begins, e.g., a sofa.

T. **Slate it!** A direction to the operator of the clapboard given at the beginning of a take: Hold the slate up in front of the camera so we can see it clearly! Similar to

"**Mark it!**" Actors also "slate" for auditions, that is, they state their names and any other information requested before beginning to act, at the command "Action!" from the casting director.

U. **Stand by!** Get ready! A warning direction or instruction from the stage manager or assistant film or television director to technicians or actors to be prepared on the command "Action!" or "Go!" to do what comes next.

V. **We're clear!** The cameras are off and we are not broadcasting! This announcement is made during a live television broadcast, such as a talk show or *Saturday Night Live*, to the personnel in the studio at the beginning of a commercial break, and at the end of the show.

W. **Wind it up!** A hand cue consisting of rolling the index finger in forward circles, indicating to the performer on a television show that the moment to end that part of the broadcast is rapidly approaching, and that the performer should bring things to a satisfactory conclusion. The hand signal is often followed by drawing a finger across the throat—the hand cue for **Cut!**

X. **Your back is facing the camera!** Turn around and position yourself so that we see your face! An indication from a director to actors; also heard as "Your back is to the camera!"

Y. **You're off!** You are no longer on the air! The broadcast has stopped and the performer may move and speak freely.

Z. **You're on!** The indication that a broadcast is beginning, meaning, "You're on the air: start talking!"

When the director says, "Action!" start talking! And, to emphasize what cannot be emphasized enough, remember these two elementary rules:

1. Listen and respond. You have to listen not only to the words, but also, importantly, to the intentions.

2. Mean what you say. You are going after an objective, something you want and need, so you have to immerse yourself wholeheartedly in the situation and the given circumstances.

And one more thing: Have fun!

XIV

Lessons and Tips from the Great Film

and Television Actors

How did they do it? Why do we find them so funny?
The film and television actor-comedians discussed here had supreme comic ability and superb senses of humor. And they always lived in the moment: Their minds were not elsewhere as they concentrated on the situation, on what they were living through. You can see this in their eyes. And they knew how to listen, and how to respond not only to the words they heard, but also to the intentions underneath them—the subtext. They did what Stanislavsky said actors must do: they found their own system of working, based in logic, in following the script, in using their imaginations to immerse themselves in the given circumstances, and in understanding their characters' psychology and behavior. And their timing was superb. Many of them had stage experience in both vaudeville and plays. And many of them also acted serious roles, surprising the public so used to seeing them in comic parts. First and foremost, they were great actors, most of them known for serious as well as comic roles. And they knew the secret of playing comedy that you have now heard many times: to be funny, you have to be serious.

Secondly, they had very individual, fully realized personalities, often with distinctive voices. Each actor was unique. They were instantly recognizable and, most importantly, sympathetic and likable.

Among them was Jean Arthur (1900–1991), with the trademark occasional quirky squeak in her voice, a superb actress who was the virtual queen of screwball comedies, a genre that includes *Mr. Deeds Goes to Town* (1936), in which she co-starred with Gary Cooper (1901–1961); Kauffman and Hart's *You Can't Take It With You* (1938), co-starring James Stewart (1908–1997), and an all-around wonderful cast; *Bringing Up Baby* (1938), co-starring Cary Grant (1904–1986), with his admirable sense of irony, and Katherine Hepburn (1907–2003). Grant and Hepburn co-starred as well in romantic comedies such as *The Philadelphia Story* (1940), with James Stewart as part of a romantic triangle. Stewart also starred in the political comedy *Mr. Smith Goes to Washington* (1939) and the enduring Christmas classic comedy *It's a Wonderful Life* (1946). He is notably endearing in the romantic comedy *The Shop Around the Corner* (1940), co-starring the warm, delightfully bemused Margaret Sullavan (1909–1960) and the inimitable Frank Morgan (1890–1949)—a great actor best known as the wizard in *The Wizard of Oz* (1939)—ringing all the changes in his role, from curmudgeonly anger and pomposity to sadness and sympathetic kindness.

And let us not forget Myrna Loy (1905–1993), sensible and zany in *Mr. Blandings Builds His Dream House* (1948), co-starring Cary Grant; and as the sophisticated Nora Charles in the urbane comedy detective *Thin Man* series, beginning with *The Thin Man* (1934), co-starring William Powell (1892–1984). He is also notable in the screwball comedy *My Man Godfrey* (1936), co-starring Carole Lombard (1908–1942), and in the title role of *Life with Father* (1947). Myrna Loy's delightful autobiography, written with James Kotsilibas-Davis, *Myrna Loy: Being and Becoming* (Alfred A. Knopf, Inc., 1987) is very much worth reading.

The actors were lovable even when they were ditzy and bossy, like the vivacious, matronly Mary Boland (1880–1965), in so many of her pixilated roles—see her in *There Goes the Groom* (1937), *The Women* (1939), and *Pride and Prejudice* (1940); or like the sweet-tempered, whimsical, and often very funny Spring Byington (1886–1971) in such films as *You Can't Take It With You*, *When Ladies Meet* (1941) and *In the Good Old Summertime* (1949); or curmudgeonly and also endearing, like W. C. Fields, or Walter Matthau in many of his roles.

The multi-talented Clifton Webb (1889–1966), a superb actor who had had quite a distinguished show business career before he made movies, is hilarious, delightful, funny, cynical, acerbic, and curmudgeonly even in some of his serious dramatic films, such as *Laura* (1944) or *The Razor's Edge* (1946); see him as the outrageous babysitter Mr. Belvedere in the comedy *Sitting Pretty* (1948). Do read his amusing biography, written with David L. Smith, *Sitting Pretty: The Life and Times of Clifton Webb* (University Press of Mississippi, 2011.) He is deliberately, hilariously a curmudgeon at times. Curmudgeons suffer, as we have seen, and this makes them both sympathetic and funny.

These comedian-actors, and so many more radiated charm and enthusiasm, and they all came across as genuine, real people. And they all came across as nice people, too, not malicious or nasty. They had lots of fun, and this communicated itself to the public. Often, they were put upon in the problematic situations in which they either found themselves, or got themselves into. And this, too, along with their senses of humor and irony, made the audience like them, and identify with them.

The Silent Film Comedians: Buster Keaton, Charlie Chaplin, and Harold Lloyd

Buster Keaton was one of those actors who grew up with physical comedy techniques. He was from a vaudeville family. As he tells us in his autobiographical memoir, *My Wonderful World of Slapstick* (Doubleday, 1960), "Oddly enough, I cannot remember Pop teaching me anything. I just watched what he did, then did the same thing. I could take crazy falls without hurting myself, simply because I had learned the trick so early in life that body control became pure instinct with me." Keaton made wonderful comic films, and had no peer in the art of deadpan. One of the main things to learn from watching Keaton is that the way to play deadpan is to keep reactions on camera internal: they will be reflected in your eyes, and the camera will pick them up. Many of the characters Keaton plays don't dare show how they are feeling, and his attempt to repress the expression of emotion is part of what makes him so funny.

Sir Charles Spencer Chaplin] (1889–1977) the English actor, writer, satirist, producer, director, and composer known as Charlie Chaplin, was interviewed in March, 1915 by Victor Eubank for *Motion Picture Magazine*. The interview is reprinted in full by editor Kevin J. Hayes in *Charlie Chaplin Interviews* (University Press of Mississippi, 2005). Chaplin has this to say about playing comedy, and how he approached it:

> "It really is a serious study," he said, "although it must not be taken seriously. That sounds like a paradox, but it is not. It is a serious study to learn characters; it is a hard study. But to make comedy a success there must be an ease, a spontaneity in the acting that cannot be associated with seriousness."

He made a thorough study of all his characters, sometimes basing them on real-life models. When he played a barber, he tells us, he went to have his hair cut and not only studied the barber while he waited, but "followed him home that night," observing everything he did: "I wanted to know all his little idiosyncrasies."

When the camera turns, Chaplin informs us, there is almost no time to think, and "you must act on the spur of the moment." This requires thorough advance preparation, but Chaplin, who prepared the character, did not prepare what he was actually going to do: "I try to lose myself. I am the character I am representing, and I try to act just as I have previously thought the character would act under the same circumstances." (This sounds almost like an anticipation of Lee Strasberg's Actor's Studio Method.) This improvisational way of working, which harks back to the old commedia days when actors improvised based on a scenario, was all very well in the silent film days, but once talkies came in, the dialogue had to be adhered to, and preparing a character for a film became more like readying a character in a stage play. While improvisation may have gone out the window in most but by no means all cases of making comic films, the feeling of spontaneity and everything else he says about acting comedy continue to be essential.

Chaplin's distinctive "Little Tramp" character was inspired by Max Linder (1883–1925), the innovative French comic actor who preceded him. Chaplin adopted a number of character traits and comedic techniques from Linder, who can be seen on DVD in his silent films. Linder also had a great influence on Buster Keaton and Harold Lloyd (1893–1971). Max Linder was the originator of the film style of slapstick, and created a persona that became very well known worldwide, that of a dandy dressed to the nines in top hat and tails, and carrying a cane which he flourished. Chaplin appropriated the cane and made his own, using it in a variety of ingenious ways. He tells us that using the cane was spontaneous on his part, born of a serendipitous incident, but it was obviously at least unconsciously inspired by Linder. Observing Chaplin and Linder's use of this prop is a lesson in how to personalize and particularize a prop. The cane is an extension of the person, who uses it to express a variety of feelings, from insouciance to tension.

Harold Lloyd, too, was a master of specificity. In a famous scene in *Safety Last* (1923), he wasn't hanging from just any clock—that clock high above the street had specific attributes. The silent film did not have all the sound effects we would hear nowadays, of course, but you don't need them to find the scene riveting. In imminent danger of falling into the street below, Lloyd was hair-raising, and we are terrified for him, yet we also laugh at his unusual predicament. We just know he is going to make it safe and sound to the ground. His attitude tells us so. Every moment, every move Lloyd makes is specific, and done with precision and flair. Straight-faced, wide-eyed, he did his own stunts, for real. He is also a lesson in how to play naively, innocently, and with complete involvement in the circumstances.

The Early Talkies Comedians: The Marx Brothers, Laurel and Hardy, W. C. Fields, and Mae West

The Marx Brothers made a series of satirical, iconoclastic comedies that even incorporated certain surrealistic elements, and made fun of theatrical conventions, as in the anti-war travesty *Duck Soup*

(1933), which also includes the famous mirror routine with Harpo and Groucho. Their early films included their younger brother Zeppo [Herbert Marx] (1901–1979) as the romantic lead, but the trio of comedians consisted of Groucho [Julius Henry Marx] (1890–1977), who wrote memoirs and had a popular long-running television show, *You Bet Your Life* (1950–1961); Harpo [Adolph Marx] (1888–1964), the silent mime comedian; and Chico [Leonard Marx] (1887–1961), with his Italian accent. Their comedy has an improvisational feel to it—in certain films much of it was in fact improvised—and the brothers are a lesson in concentration and focus, as in that famous mirror routine. That routine, while thoroughly worked out, is anything but mechanical: as Groucho tries to catch Harpo, we see him thinking up what he can do next to surprise Harpo, which Harpo quite unaccountably always anticipates, hence the hilarity of their playing.

Among their most popular films is a satire of snobbery and social hierarchy set against the background of shady dealings and a love story, *A Night at the Opera* (1935), by George S. Kaufman and Morrie Ryskind. The scene where everybody piles into an already crowded ship's cabin is justly famous. Worth noting is the performance of the super-serious, dignified grande dame Margaret Dumont (1882–1965) as the society hostess Mrs. Claypool, hilarious in her non-plussed discomfiture. The Marx Brothers improvised around the script as the camera rolled, much to her surprise, and her consternation is therefore real. Dumont was also in *Duck Soup* and several other Marx Brothers films, as well as many other movies.. And the staid, distinguished Sig Ruman—[Siegfried Albon Rumann] (1884–1967; he emigrated from Germany in 1924)—a superb comic and dramatic actor who appeared in one hundred twenty-eight projects, is a riot as the splenetic, stuffy opera manager Gottlieb, one of his most famous performances.

The Marx Brothers exemplify acting in farce, as they guy the establishment and the socioeconomic system. They were not afraid to be wacky and to let themselves go. They provide great lessons: Let yourself go with the flow. Be spontaneous and enjoy the serendipitous. And if you are in a farce, do it at top speed.

Laurel and Hardy, the comedy duo of Stan Laurel [Arthur Stanley Jefferson] (1890–1965), from England, and Oliver Hardy [Oliver Norvell Hardy] (1892–1957), made one hundred eighty-seven films and shorts. Laurel, the eternally put-upon, hapless bumbler and sad-sack, always exasperated the overwrought, overweight Hardy, with his toothbrush mustache, and his catchphrase, "Here's another fine mess you've gotten me into." Comedian-singer Eddie Cantor (1892–1964) said of them, "It's their seriousness that strikes me. They play everything as if it might be Hamlet or Macbeth." Among their funniest films are *The Music Box* (1932), *The Devil's Brother* (1933; a version of Auber's opera *Fra Diavolo*), *March of the Wooden Soldiers* (1934; original title: *Babes in Toyland*), *Bonnie Scotland* (1935), *Sons of the Desert* (1935), *Way Out West* (1937), *The Flying Deuces* (1939), and *Nothing But Trouble* (1944).

Each of the partners was always specific in his playing, even though their characters became formulaic. The lesson is in that very specificity, even if you are playing a well known type. Be real and individual, and do not play mechanical clichés. And they were perfect examples of adults behaving like children (see chapter one). Their pioneering comedy partnership was also the important role model for all the comedy partnerships that followed them, such as those of Martin and Lewis, Abbott and Costello, and even Jackie Gleason and Art Carney in *The Honeymooners* TV series.

W. C. Fields [William Claude Dukenfield] (1880–1946) began his career as a vaudevillian, and his physical comedy is a supreme lesson in dexterity and in infusing nonsense with reality. Fields was a master of the inappropriate response, one of the things that makes his comedy so hilarious. He professed to hate children, and perhaps he really did. The way he behaves with them is very funny, because it is so completely lacking in compassion, empathy, or understanding. His performance in *The Bank Dick* exemplifies his attitude that children are dangerous little animals who might bite if you are not careful. And his reactions are always very real, understated, and internal. Like Keaton, the character he plays is afraid of the consequences of expressing himself too openly, and this is a very galvanizing motivation. His characters often mumble under their breaths in a passive-aggressive way that would also be that of John Cleese in *Fawlty Towers.*

Including a certain amount of improvisation, *My Little Chickadee* is a great classic, starring him and Mae West (1893–1980), and featuring a very young Margaret Hamilton (1902–1985), hilarious as a dour, tight-lipped puritanical spinster who disapproves of West and doesn't quite know what to make of Fields. This was apparently the case in reality, and as the camera rolled, her quizzical nonplussed looks are true spontaneous reactions, and extremely funny as a result of her not knowing what to expect.

Fields's dour persecution complex is rib-tickling, and a lesson to all actors in how to play someone who is put upon and reacts with passive-aggressive anger. The film is set in the American west in the late pioneer era of the 1880s, and Fields plays a shabbily genteel con man, whose behavior is repressed and falsely polite, as he apes the stylish manners of a gentleman, without quite capturing a gentleman's style of behavior—the effect of incongruity is very droll.

A mistress of the double entendre, Mae West, with her distinctive character and campy humor, was known for her sexual allusions, and her raised, sexy eyebrow, even when she wasn't saying something overtly sexual. She began as a vaudeville performer, and went on to write plays and screenplays as vehicles for herself, including *I'm No Angel* (1933), *She Done Him Wrong* (1933)—the title is a slangy sexual allusion—*Go West Young Man* (1936), and *Klondike Annie* (1936). In *Night After Night* (1932), she had one of her most famous lines: A hatcheck girl admiring her expensive jewelry exclaims, "Goodness!" To which Mae West replies, "Goodness had nothing to do with it." Another famous line occurred in *She Done Him Wrong*: "Is that a gun [often misquoted as "pickle"] in your pocket, or are you just glad to see me?" And in *I'm No Angel*, she said lazily to her maid, "Beulah, peel me a grape." When you watch her, you can see she knows she is funny, but her goal is not to be funny, but to exude sex, and to be seductive, verbally and physically, to her acting partners.

The Mid-Twentieth Century: The Three Stooges, Danny Kaye, Jerry Lewis, Walter Matthau, and Jack Lemmon

For brilliant slapstick, see the many shorts made by the Three Stooges, originally a comedy vaudeville act whose trio varied over the decades. The originals were played in film by Moe Howard [Moses Harry Horwitz] (1897–1975) as Moe, the leader of the group; Larry Fine [Louis Feinberg] (1902–1975) as Larry; and Shemp Howard [Samuel Horwitz] (1895–1955) as Shemp. Later on, they were Moe, Larry, and Curly, played by Curly Howard [Jerome Lester "Jerry" Horwitz] (1903–1952). Some of their physical routines are discussed in chapter one. They were known for their comically sadistic treatment of each other and for constantly arguing and bickering and losing their tempers.

Danny Kaye's [Daniel David Kaminski] (1913–1987) thirty-three screen projects are works that display his genius. They include *The Secret Life of Walter Mitty* (1947), *The Inspector General* (1949), *On the Riviera* (1951), and the satirical film that parodies medieval costume epics, *The Court Jester* (1955). He was a superb singing comedian and actor, and a brilliant technician. Just looking at how he moves his jaw when he articulates is a lesson in itself, and his rubber-faced and genial joviality show the comic spirit that should be infused into every portrayal.

Jerry Lewis [Joseph Levitch] (b. 1926) is another quirky comedian, with a deliberately odd, whiny, nasal, put-on voice that works for some, and that many have found irresistibly comic, especially when combined with his rubber-man, plastic gait and odd gestures. He seems to inhabit his characters, behaving overtly like a child. Many of his characters in the old films are nerds, despite the quirkiness that seems rather unreal at times. And he is an excellent actor of serious roles as well. Even the absurdist unreality of some of his films is real to him. And he is living proof of what he maintains: to be a good comedian you first have to be a good actor.

Another amazing comic actor, who embodied all the comedic techniques and qualities discussed here, was Walter Matthau (1920–2000). His hangdog look and mournful expression were part of his persona in almost every part he played: they came with the territory. And his single-minded sense of purpose, never overdone, but played for real every time, was one of the things that made his characters so memorable, as if he were saying, "Life is earnest, life is real, life is a crock! But you gotta deal with it somehow. What am I gonna do?"

In *The Fortune Cookie* (1966), Matthau plays Willie Gingrich, a brash shyster lawyer, with a sloppy office filing system reminiscent of W. C. Fields's in *Man on the Flying Trapeze*. Matthau's performance is perfection: a detailed rounded character who is always thinking on his feet, and in the worst possible con man way. You can see and hear him conniving silently—this is the advantage of the subtlety permitted by the camera—and watch those crooked wheels turning, as he convinces Jack Lemmon (1925–2001), another superb comic actor, to go along with a scheme to defraud an insurance company. In lesser hands, these characters would have been one-dimensional cardboard obsessive-compulsives, but in the hands of these actors, they took on many dimensions.

A naturally kind and gentle man, by all accounts, Matthau specialized in playing curmudgeons, as he did in *The Sunshine Boys* (1975), where he was perfectly cast as retired vaudevillian Willy Clark opposite George Burns (1896–1996) as Al Lewis, his former vaudeville partner. It featured a variation of the overtly sexual, overdone "doctor act," a salacious vaudeville routine in which a ludicrous, usually myopic doctor examines patients with the help of a particularly buxom nurse, while constantly looking down the bosom of her scanty uniform. You can see an authentic variant in the American vaudeville comedy team Smith and Dale's (Joe Smith [1884–1981] and Charlie Dale [1885–1971]) "Dr. Kronkheit and His Only Living Patient," filmed in *Two Tickets to Broadway* (1951). The name "Kronkheit" was from Yiddish and German (*Krankheit*) for sickness, or disease.

In Neil Simon's *The Odd Couple* (1968) he played the slob, Oscar Madison, opposite Jack Lemmon as the compulsively neat and tidy Felix Ungar. Both films are worth looking at, not only for the laughs, but also, once again, in order to observe and learn from the seriousness of the acting.

Billy Wilder's *Some Like It Hot* is often considered the greatest film comedy. Indeed, it is quite wonderful. Lemmon, as Jerry, is forced to disguise himself in drag, along with his pal Joe, played by Tony Curtis [Bernard Schwartz] (1925–2010). In order to escape some gangsters, they pretend to be part of a band of girl musicians, starring Sugar Kane Kowalczyk, played by Marilyn Monroe (1926–1962), who could be supremely funny. . The convoluted plot rolls inevitably to its happy end, with one of the funniest lines ever penned: rubber-faced comedian Joe E. Brown (1892–1973), as the millionaire Osgood Fielding III, has fallen in love with the disguised Jack Lemmon, and proposed marriage. When Lemmon reveals his true gender, Brown glances at him insouciantly, and says, "Well, nobody's perfect."

A Comic Innovator: Woody Allen

Modern comedy is unthinkable without the films of the prolific Woody Allen [Allen Konigsberg] (b. 1935), who wears many hats: actor, screenwriter, playwright, satirist, director, film producer, composer, and author of books. Allen's persona is that of the nebbish who seems incapable of accomplishing anything, but who nevertheless manages to do a great deal. He often plays the put-upon loveable loser, with whom we immediately sympathize. Among all his hilarious movies, one of the funniest I have ever seen is *Small Time Crooks*, in which Allen plays Ray, a small-time crook who enlists the help of his other ex-jailhouse friends in a scheme to tunnel into a bank so they can rob it. He rents a vacant pizza parlor next door to the bank as a cover, and starts a cookie business, because his wife can't make pizza, and the affair proves so lucrative, that they become wealthy. On the way, the twists and turns of the farcical plot are sidesplitting. Not only is Allen himself hilarious, but the entire cast he has assembled is pure genius. Tracey Ullman (b. 1959) plays his delightfully acerbic but loving wife, who bakes the cookies, and Elaine May (b. 1932) as Ullman's ditzy relative is out of this world. The film is quite a lesson in making the most absurd circumstances real and convincing.

Allen's point of view about comedy was expressed in his usual lively manner in an interview in Larry Wilde's *Great Comedians Talk About Comedy* (Executive Books, 2000), in which Allen says that the material the comedian has to work with, whether good or bad, depends for its effect on the personality and expertise of the comedian. Once you have what he considers the intangible quality of being funny, you work at the craft, and you develop it into your own individual art. This is your obligation. Beyond that, a career in show business is "a combination of hard work and luck." You can help your luck along by discipline and by doing the arduous work, and sticking with it. Like so many other authorities on the subject of humor, he believes that suffering and emotional privation are at the root of comedy.

Woody Allen exploits the relationship between sex and laughter in the romantic relationships he portrays. Perhaps his apparently needy inhibited persona invite and arouse the maternal instinct in the women he is involved with as a character in his films. It is a mask for his repressed aggression. This is another lesson: Inhibition can be funny, especially when it is carried too far, and the release of inhibition, which also relieves our tension, can cause us to laugh.

Another way in which he maintains spontaneous acting in front of the camera is not to reveal the entire script to the cast, except piecemeal on a need-to-know basis. In any case, he is constantly rewriting it, as developments occur to him. When he directs a scene, as I discovered when doing background work in *Zelig*, he does not even tell the extras exactly what the scene is about, but directs people to carry out actions, sometimes in particular ways with particular attitudes. He also picks extras out of the crowd to do certain bits, either alone or in pairs or groups, and these may or may not wind up in the final cut. You have no idea what you are actually doing the actions for, but you still have lots of fun doing them.

Allen directed *Bullets Over Broadway,* and Diane Wiest (b. 1948) is a riot as Helen Sinclair, an aging star actress in a Broadway play written by David Shayne, a novice, played perfectly by John Cusack (b. 1966). Warner Purcell (the versatile Jim Broadbent [b.1949]), a lecherous actor in the show, and his eating disorder, are also a scream, as is

Chazz Palmintieri (b. 1952) as Cheech, the gangster detailed to watch rehearsals of the show, in order to chaperone Olive Neal (Jennifer Tilly [b. 1958]), the ditzy girlfriend of Nick Valenti (Joe Viterelli [1937–2004]), playing the don who has invested in the show on condition that she play the lead. The specificity of each moment, and the reality of the stereotypical characters, many based on deliberate clichés that the actors have made real and individual, constitute a study in themselves, if you can stop laughing long enough.

Another Comic Genius: Mel Brooks

A comic genius of a different sort, equally as important as Woody Allen in the development of modern comedy, is the effervescent, ebullient Mel Brooks, who brings a gusto and an enjoyment to everything he does. Born Melvin "Mel" Kaminsky in 1926, Brooks, like Allen, wears many hats: actor, comedian, writer, satirist, composer, lyricist, director, and producer. He began his writing career in television comedy shows, and did five comedy albums in the *2000 Year Old Man* series (1961–1998), created and written in collaboration with Carl Reiner. Brooks played a wry, hysterically funny character with a Yiddish accent, although he was born before Yiddish was ever dreamed of.

Brooks is not afraid to be outrageous, or vulgar, and to poke fun at the sacrosanct. He is responsible for one of the funniest puns I ever heard. In the film he wrote, directed, and starred in, *The History of the World: Part I*, during the sequence about the Spanish Inquisition he has a riotously funny song and dance sequence done by the monks who are Inquisitors. In talking about the Grand Inquisitor, Tomás de Torquemada (1420–1498), who was a monster, Brooks says, "He was so stubborn you couldn't Torquemada anything!" It is only because the Inquisition is so remote in time that we can even begin to find this funny. On the other hand, Brooks's remake of *To Be or Not To Be* is perhaps less funny than the original, because the script adds plot elements that muddy the original waters and that make it too *angepatscht*, a Yiddish word that means messy, as with a wall on which the paint has been thrown any old way.

Many people find Brooks's original film of *The Producers*, starring Gene Wilder (b. 1933) and Zero Mostel (1915–1977), and the 2001 Broadway musical (it ran for 2535 performances, including previews, closing in 2007), and the 2005 film made from it hilarious, but for others, despite its immense popularity, it remains a trivialization of the events of World War Two.

One of the many lessons Brooks has to teach is that of exuberance. And because he is unique, you can also learn the value of being yourself, and not being afraid to be original.

When it comes to writing as well as performing and directing, Mel Brooks is a genius, having written the projects mentioned here and many more. In an interview in Mike Sacks's *Poking a Dead Frog: Conversations with Today's Top Comedy Writers* (Penguin, 2014), he tells us that he always starts with characters, and then finds a story to fit them into: "Everything I've ever done, I've started with characters." For *The Producers*, he started with the accountant (played by Gene Wilder), a man of dreams who loves theater. From there, Brooks tells us, "I knew I needed a producer, a reprehensible producer." And so the story grew and developed in a natural way, as Brooks allowed free rein to his comic imagination.

Some More Contemporary Comedians: Billy Crystal, Leslie Neilson, Will Ferrell, Albert Brooks, Jim Carrey, Christopher Guest

Billy Crystal (b. 1948), exuberant and obviously enjoying himself, is worth studying in his often sardonic comedies, among them *Throw Momma from the Train* (1987), a takeoff of Hitchcock's chilling classic *Strangers on a Train* (1951); *Analyze This* (1999) and *Analyze That* (2002), and the romantic comedies *When Harry Met Sally...* (1989) and *Forget Paris* (1995). He is evidence of one of the great principles of comedy playing: Enjoy yourself! The audience will be on your side instantly, and will have a great time, which is, after all, what they are there to do.

Leslie Nielsen (1926–2010) began his career as a serious actor, but later switched to comedy, in which he excelled. He made parodies of disaster movies, such as *Airplane* (1980) and the *Naked Gun* series

(1988, 1991, 1994), takeoffs on James Bond. And he played every role with the utmost seriousness, and a certain deadpan that did not preclude a twinkle in the eye.

Among contemporary comedians who combine a sense of the ridiculous with a seriousness of purpose is Will Ferrell (b. 1967), superb at playing the inane and the fatuous. He is always the dumb one, convinced he knows more than anyone else. And this is the way to play such characters: with a sense that they are right and the world is wrong. Among his seventy-seven screen projects, as of this writing, outstanding are *Elf* (2003), an inane, hilarious spoof in which Ferrell plays Buddy, a deluded, child-like psychotic who is convinced he is one of Santa's elves. James Caan (b. 1940), brilliant in serious roles, proves himself a superb comedian as Ferrell's exasperated father, nonplussed when Ferrell suddenly shows up one day out of the blue. *Talladega Nights: The Ballad of Ricky Bobby* (2006) parodies the world of high-speed racing; and *Blades of Glory* (2007) is a satire of the ice-skating world, also starring the supremely funny Will Arnett (b. 1970) as Ferrell's rival, who manages to be straight-faced and smiling at the same time.

The films of Albert Brooks [Albert Lawrence Einstein] (b.1947; American), actor, director, screenwriter, and satirist, are charming and have great appeal. Brooks has done thirty projects as of this writing, and has appeared in several of his own films, which he wrote in collaboration with others, and/or directed, including *The Muse* (1999), about a delusional young lady, played perfectly by Sharon Stone (b. 1958), whom screenwriter Steven Philips (Brooks) accepts for a very long time as being an actual muse, inspiring him to write screenplays; and *Mother* (1996), co-starring the inimitable, delightfully funny Debbie Reynolds (b. 1932), so wonderful in the spoof of Hollywood at the dawn of talking pictures, *Singin' in the Rain* (1952), with Gene Kelly (1912–1996) and Donald O'Connor (1925–2003), both of whom were not only magnificent dancers, but also great comic actors. A lesson in comic technique, timing, and the playing of the character's inhibitions (she is always worrying about what the neighbors will think), Reynolds's performance as his mother, whom he comes to stay with in order to work out certain psychological problems in their relationship, is hilarious. Brooks's *The Scout* (1994), which he co-wrote with Andrew Bergman—the film was directed by Michael Ritchie (1938–2001)—stars Brendan Fraser (b. 1968), known for his heroic roles (the series of *Mummy* pictures; *Quiet American*), who is very funny as the world's greatest baseball player, Steve Nebraska, an unaware, repressed neurotic, with psychotic tendencies. Diane Wiest is hilarious as Dr. H. Aaron (remember Hank Aaron?), his psychotherapist, roped into the job by Brooks as Al Percolo, the constantly mistaken scout who discovered and mentors Nebraska for the Yankees. Nebraska cannot sign his contract until he has been vetted by a psychologist, and he may be certifiable. Everything works out perfectly in the end, and Brooks, who has become Nebraska's friend, is vindicated. This is just the kind of project where a study of psychology is useful, and even necessary. Brooks has an earnestness and a forthright approach to reality in all of these wry, tender, and heartwarming comedies about people who aspire to learn about themselves and to achieve something.

Jim Carrey [James Eugene Carrey] (b. 1967) and his physical comedy do not appeal to everyone, but he is superb and provides a great lesson to actors in how to make clowning absolutely real. He is Mr. Rubberface, as opposed to Mr. Deadpan. He is not subtle. He overdoes it deliberately and outrageously, but he obviously believes everything he does, and is completely committed to and involved in being the character and the actions he plays, so that everything works beautifully. His forty-three films include *Dumb and Dumber* (1994), *Ace Ventura: The Pet Detective* (1994), *Ace Ventura: When Nature Calls* (1995), *The Cable Guy* (1996), *The Truman Show* (1998), *Me, Myself, and Irene* (2000), *How the Grinch Stole Christmas* (2000), *Bruce Almighty* (2003), and *Yes Man* (2008).

Christopher Guest (b. 1948) is a great American actor, screenwriter, director, composer, and musician, known for his mockumentaries. His mockumentaries, most of them co-written with Eugene Levy (b. 1946), who acts in them, along with Guest, provide lessons in every technique of reality in comic acting: specificity, seriousness, and what we find funny about obsessive people, who seem to see nothing beyond their particular interest, so that the rest of the world does not exist, and everything revolves around them, protecting them from harm and from disturbing self-knowledge. Notice how seriously the characters take themselves, how the actors adopt the characters' mind-set and one-track concentration on an objective. They can go haywire over a dog's missing toy in *Best in Show* (2000), or wax tearfully nostalgic about their old folk-music days in *A Mighty Wind* (2003), or channel all their energy into doing a truly terrible community theater show that they are convinced is Broadway-bound under the leadership of Guffman (played by Guest, who is a riot) in *Waiting for Guffman* (1996). And in every case, what they do with such commitment has absolute reality to it.

English Film and Television Comedy

If you want to see brilliant comedy technique that will knock your socks off, watch some of the British television sitcoms and film farces from the last century. Nobody could be funnier than the naturally funny actors in them. And they are hilarious, lessons in supreme comic timing and the greatest real reactions in the business. The scripts, too, were sheer genius.

The Ealing comedies, named for London's Ealing Studios in which they were made, include those starring the magnificent, versatile Sir Alec Guinness (1914–2000), one of the greatest English actors of both stage and screen of the last century. Everything he did in both his serious and comic roles is worth studying. He played his comic roles as really, as specifically, and as seriously as he did his dramatic and tragic roles. Among his most hilarious films are *The Lavender Hill Mob* (1951), where his partner in crime is Stanley Holloway (1890–1982), with his forthright manner and wonderful Cockney accent; *The Ladykillers* (1955), *The Horse's Mouth* (1958), and *Kind Hearts and Coronets* (1949), in which he played eight roles in a tour de force for which he was much acclaimed.

Also notable was Peter Sellers (1925–1980), a versatile English character actor and extremely funny comedian. He is known for his creation of the bumbling and klutzy Inspector Clouseau, complete with a hilarious fake French accent, in the *Pink Panther* series of films, and for many other leading roles. In 1959 alone he made three films, *The Mouse That Roared* and *Man in a Cocked Hat*, both satires about international politics, and a satirical comedy about class relations in industry, *I'm All Right Jack*. It also starred the ingratiating, genial Ian Carmichael (1920–2010), naïve and charming as Stanley Windrush, the eager scion of a factory owner who decides to learn first hand about working class life by going to work in the family factory. Sellers plays Fred Kite, the Marxist union leader, complete with Cockney accent. He is a riot! So are Irene Handl (1901–1987) as his wife, complete with her wonderful Cockney accent and comforting maternal air; Terry-Thomas (1911–1990), with his trademark moustache and toothy smile showing the gap in his front teeth, and his posh accent, as the eternally flustered Major Hitchcock; John Le Mesurier (1912–1983), perfect as an obsessive-compulsive time-and-motion-study man with a one-track mind and a nervous tic; Miles Malleson (1888–1969) as Windrush, Sr.; and the rotund, earnest Margaret Rutherford (1892–1972) as Stanley's skeptical Aunt Dolly. All of them appeared in many other supremely funny movies, in the golden age of British satirical film comedy, and all of them are object lessons in how to do it.

In 1964, the English revue *Beyond the Fringe* came to Broadway, and regaled audiences with its political and artistic satire. It was a sort of ancestor of the surrealistic television series *Monty Python's Flying Circus* (1969–1974). Then there was *Fawlty Towers* (1975–1979) with Monty Python's John Cleese (b. 1939) leading the way as the frantic, hysterical hotel owner, Basil Fawlty.

Mapp and Lucia (1985–1986), the TV series based on the satirical, whimsical *Lucia* series of novels by E. F. Benson (1867–1940), starred Prunella Scales (b. 1932) as Mapp; she had played Mrs. Fawlty, Basil's shrewish, but logical wife. Her co-star was the whimsical, supremely amusing and versatile Geraldine McEwan (b. 1932) as Emmeline "Lucia" Lucas—she would later play Miss Marple in the TV series *Agatha Christie's Marple* (2004–2007).

Another great actor and comedienne is Penelope Keith (b. 1940), whose upper-class drawl is funny in itself. She had starred in her own very sitcom series, *To the Manor Born* (1979–2007).

The political satire of the TV series *Yes, Minister* (1980–1984) and its sequel, *Yes, Prime Minister* (1986–1987), was very funny and beautifully observed. So was much of the four-part historical *Blackadder* (1983–1989) series starring Rowan Atkinson (b. 1955), Tony Robinson (1946), and Hugh Laurie (b. 1959). The eighteenth century and Regency, and the World War One series were perhaps better and wittier than the earlier medieval and Elizabethan series that traced the rise of the Blackadder family of highly placed servants to the dimwitted monarchs and the Prince Regent, and of Blackadder's accompanying dogsbody and whipping boy, Baldrick, played by Tony Robinson. Stephen Fry (b. 1957) played an obtuse general in the World War One series that sends up the military mentality. He and Hugh Laurie played the butler and his employer, respectively, in a *Jeeves and Wooster* (1990) series based on the Wodehouse stories.

Even the terrible vulgarity and political incorrectness of *Are You Being Served?* (1972–1985) has lessons to teach. The ensemble cast went all out. And the nice thing about the modern technological age is you can see all of them all over again: they are available on DVD.

Tim Curry (b. 1946) is a versatile actor, whose specific playing of characters and ability to let himself go and do whatever outrageous things a role may demand is legendary. He could play a gender-bending role in *The Rocky Horror Picture Show* (1975), but was also a brilliant Mozart, written with ahistorical inaccuracy, but with great comedy, in the Broadway production of Peter Shaffer's (b. 1926) historical comedy *Amadeus* (1980), filmed in 1984, with Tom Hulce (b. 1953) as Mozart.

Among contemporary, notable British comedians who have appeared in both in television and movies is Ricky Gervais (b. 1961), master of the understatement and of so-called underplaying. He invests every character he plays, including himself in his solo stand-up act, with a dry ironic sense of right and wrong, and a smile plays about his lips, especially when he feels insulted or put down in some way, as in his brilliantly observed series *Extras*

(2005–2007), about background players in film and television; and *The Office* (2005–20013), with its American offshoot starring Steve Carrell (b. 1962) and a wonderful cast.

French, Italian, and Mexican Film Comedy

French, Italian and Mexican comedy are also riotously funny. Louis de Funès [Louis Germain David de Funès Galarza] (1914–1983) was one of the funniest stage and screen comedians who ever existed. His trademark was being constantly nonplussed, and reacting with restrained fury, muttering, incoherent sounds, and manic shaking of the head. He always seemed to be about to fly off the handle, but he kept all this controlled and within bounds, so that it was never overdone and was always real. See him in *Le tatoué* (The Tattooed Man; 1968), in which he plays a wealthy art collector who covets, to the point of desperation, a tattoo done by Modigliani on the back of a man, played hilariously by Jean Gabin (1904–1975); *Les aventures de Rabbi Jacob* (1973), a very, very funny, laugh-out-loud film in which he plays a kind of French Archie Bunker, forced to disguise himself as a Hasidic rabbi; and in *La soupe aux choux* (Cabbage Soup; 1981), in which farting is humor; *L'aile et la cuisse* (The Wing and the Thigh; 1976), in drag as a restaurant reviewer, and so many more.

Don't know if you're coming or going? Don't know which way is up or down? In real life that could be a tragedy, but on the stage, it's a farce. Discombobulation and massive confusion are at the heart of *Oscar* (1967), a classic film of madcap, screwball genius, equal to any by Feydeau. Based on the hit play of the same name, *Oscar* stars de Funès reprising his stage role. Poor man! Troubles pile on his head so fast that he scarcely knows what he is doing as he tries to keep everything straight in his mind. Who is who? Who wants what from whom? Who is his real daughter? Who is his wife? Who loves whom? Does his former maidservant, now married to a baron, really have to act like a snobby baroness to the manor born, and insist that he kiss her hand?

De Funès plays Bernard Barnier, a rich businessman who leads a tranquil life, at home with his daughter Colette and his wife. To stay in shape, he exercises regularly with his trainer, Philippe, who is not terribly bright, though he is exceptionally strong. The Barniers have three servants: Bernadette, the maid; Oscar, the chauffeur; and a young manservant. One fine morning, Christian Martin, Bernard's confidant and business associate arrives to inform him that…But, no, I will not tell you the rest of the plot. It would ruin your enjoyment. Suffice it to say that this has got to be one of the funniest films ever made.

De Funès's predecessors, Bourvil [André Robert Raimbourg] (1917–1970) and Fernandel [Fernand Joseph Désiré Contandin] (1903–1971), are still revered and enjoyed. Fernandel's acting, always wonderful, is a superb lesson in taking the character's situation as absolutely real and experiencing the pain. A perfect example is his performance in the title role of *Le Schpountz* (1938), Marcel Pagnol's (1895–1974) film about a man who dreams ardently about being a romantic leading man, and who is eventually happy to learn that he is a comic genius. Why? Because he plays everything, even the most absurd situations, for real. The title was unaccountably translated as *Heartbeat*, but the word "schpountz" means something like patsy, fall guy, or cluck.

One of the greatest performers of his era, Louis Jouvet (see chapter five), was not only a brilliant stage and screen actor in both drama and comedy, but also a marvelous human being, who hated intolerance and bigotry of every kind, and brought this to bear in his work, in which he displays a profound, intuitive understanding of psychology. When he acted in films, he was uncannily real and completely convincing. In 1947, he played the astute, humane Detective Antoine in Henri-Georges Clouzot's *Quai des Orfèvres* (the address of the main Paris police prefecture); and it is almost hard to believe he is acting, so astoundingly natural is he. Every moment is spontaneous, alive, and so real that it is as if one were watching a newsreel of actual events.

In comedy, he is equally alive and completely different as the wily, conniving Mosca in the film adaptation of Ben Jonson's ironic *Volpone* (1936), which features a who's who of the great French actors of the period, including Harry Baur (1880–1943)—don't miss him as Jean Valjean in *Les Misérables* (1934)—Fernand Ledoux (1897–1993)), and Charles Dullin (1885–1949; he is also in *Quai des Orfèvres* and plays

Thénardier in *Les Misérables*), all of them brilliant. Jouvet is smooth and controlled as Mosca, and incisive and direct in his movements, sporting a jaunty Renaissance hat with a long front peak. His sense of the period and his comic timing are perfect. In fact, this is true of all the actors in the film.

And Jouvet's performance as Jules Romains' (1885–1972) Dr. Knock in the cinematic adaptations of the play, *Knock*, which he filmed twice, in 1933 and 1951, is pricelessly funny. Knock is a quack doctor who takes over a practice in a small country village, where he hoodwinks his gullible, sometimes hypochondriac patients, until he gets his comeuppance.

Federico Fellini (1920–1993), the Italian director and screenwriter made fifty-two films, many of them sardonic comedies with a touch of surrealism (see appendix two). His films are wry, deliciously deep, and sometimes sentimental in their comedy, providing his unique vision of the world and its vagaries, its quirks, and fantasies.

The endearing Mexican Cantinflas [Fortino Mario Alfonso Moreno Reyes] (1911–1993), who acted in fifty-one films, among them *El bolero de Raquel* (1957) and *Pepe* (1960). The manically energetic Italian comic actor Roberto Benigni [Roberto Remiglio Benigni] (b. 1952) has made thirty films as of this writing. Both actors provide wonderful lessons in comic acting, and in the individuation of personality that makes each distinctive.

Some More American Films to Learn From

William Wyler's (1902–1981) classic madcap romantic farce, *How to Steal a Million* (1966), stars Audrey Hepburn (1929–1993) as Nicole, the daughter of a genius art forger Bonnet, played by Hugh Griffith (1912–1980), and Simon Dermott, played by Peter O'Toole (1932–2013), who falls in love with her. In order to prevent her father's being arrested, Nicole must steal the Cellini Venus, which he has forged. Dermott agrees to help her. The characters include the obsessive Eli Wallach (1915–2014) as Davis Leland, a wealthy industrialist who is in love with Nicole, and desperately wants to own the Cellini Venus; and Marcel Dalio [Israel Moshe Blauschild] (1900–1983; he plays the croupier at Rick's in *Casablanca* [1942]) as Senor Paravideo, who is falling all over himself to purchase a gorgeous Van Gogh from Bonnet, who has painted it himself. The scenes in the museum, where the guards are frantic when a false alarm is set off by Dermott, are a lesson in frenzied farce playing. And the scenes at Bonnet's home and at the Ritz are expertly done and a lesson in absolute commitment to the given circumstances and objectives of the characters. These people want what they want with a vengeance and a desperation that is belied by their sometimes calm or hail-fellow-well-met demeanors.

In the film *Fatso* (1980), Dom DeLuise's (1933–2009) performance as Dominick DiNapoli draws tears of laughter from the audience. Mel Brooks's wife, the brilliant Anne Bancroft (1931–2005), who also directed and wrote the film, is wonderful, too, as Antoinette. The film's opening sequences deal with an intrinsically horrible situation, the funeral of Dominick and Antoinette's obese nephew, who died prematurely. Nobody could laugh at this terrible situation, but audiences can laugh at the reactions of the mourners, because they are so preposterous and out of keeping with the situation. At the same time, those reactions are genuine, and deeply felt.

Bancroft's pain at the premature death of her vastly overweight nephew is actually funny, believe it or not, partly because every time we think she has calmed down, she starts up again, wailing and screaming, almost too much—an instant reversal of emotion that is a perfect example of the instant switch (see chapter one).

The comedy builds. It continues in the cemetery, where Dominick, weeping and looking to the heavens, wants to dispose of the coat he is carrying, and automatically, unthinkingly drapes it on the outstretched arm of a woman mourner, who happens to be passing by. She walks off, apparently not even noticing that it is there. He continues weeping to the heavens. Absurd as the moment is, it is played absolutely for real.

Dominick, somewhat of an emotional sentimentalist, works in his family's greeting card shop. He is a man of compassion, and he can empathize with everyone. As he is showing birthday cards to a customer, he reads the saccharine, banal greeting poems aloud, and after a line or two, starts weeping, so much do they affect him. The scene is very funny, because DeLuise does this, as he does everything, with absolute conviction. He plays the actions fully and really. He means everything he says, even when what he says is patently ridiculous to the rest of us.

Dom DeLuise's psychologically astute portrayal of the desperately food-addicted Dominick is beautifully observed. He calms down every time he eats, and gets involved in the taste of the food, to the exclusion of everything around him. He cooks mouthwatering dishes and eats them with such single-minded commitment and such reality that we cannot help but laugh, as we almost salivate along with him. You can practically taste the food yourself. He has to choose between his girlfriend and his passion for eating. See the film to find out what he decides.

Gender-bending is the underlying theme of *Victor Victoria* (1982), a farce with a plot in which the confused characters learn as much about themselves as about each other. It was adapted in 1995 as *Victor / Victoria*, a hit Broadway musical that ran for twenty-five previews and seven hundred thirty-four performances. Both were directed by Blake Edwards and starred his wife, the silver-voiced, exceptionally beautiful Julie Andrews (b. 1935). Her co-stars were James Garner (1928–2014) and the jocular Robert Preston (1918–1987), who cracked up during his final song and dance number, as Edwards let the camera roll—one of the most spontaneous and real moments in comic films. Among its many lessons, this movie shows the necessity of exploring a character's sexuality, and the feelings about other people's sexuality. Homophobia is exposed as the stupid, bigoted insecurity it is, and the glory of sexual enjoyment is given full play. Be yourself, and live your life without caring what other people think of your sexuality! One of the questions to ask yourself whenever you prepare a role is how your character feels about sex, both his or her own and other people's, and how this plays out in the script.

Married to the Mob (1988) is a hilarious satire of the innumerable gangster and Mafia films. The cast is brilliant, with Dean Stockwell (b.

1936), who is wonderful in both drama and comedy, as the Mafia boss Tony "the Tiger" Russo; Matthew Modine (b. 1959) as Mike Downey, an FBI agent trying to bring him down; and Mercedes Ruehl (b. 1948) as Connie Russo, Stockwell's wife. The supremely funny Alec Baldwin (b. 1958) plays Mafioso "Cucumber" Frank de Marco, and Michelle Pfeiffer (b. 1958) is Angela de Marco. The whole cast is perfect, and their dramatic experience shows in their serious playing of every scene. They play the gangsters as really as they would in the *Godfather* films of Francis Ford Coppola (b. 1939).

Jonathan Lyn's (b. 1943) *My Cousin Vinny* (1992) became a comedy classic almost from the moment of its release, and all the performances are brilliant, both those of its stars, Joe Pesci (b. 1943) as Vinny Gambini and Marissa Tome (b. 1964), as Mona Lisa Vito, his fiancée, who won an Oscar for Best Supporting Actress, and of everyone in the supporting cast as well. Ralph Macchio (b. 1961) plays Bill Gambini and Mitchell Whitfield (b. 1964), Stan Rothenstein, the earnest defendants wrongfully on trial for murder in this comedy of mistaken identity. The trial takes place in the courtroom of Judge Chamberlain Haller, played with royal dignity by Fred Gwynne (1926–1993). The able, conceited prosecuting attorney is brilliantly played by Lane Smith (1936–2005), and the stuttering Public Defender is painfully acted by Austin Pendleton (b. 1940). Each of them is a lesson in both individual character and ensemble playing, as well as in their total commitment to the given circumstances. Dale Launer (b. 1952) wrote the hilarious script, full of wry satirical comedy that sends up northern attitudes about the south, and also sends up southern attitudes.

Another brilliant comic performance, among many she has done, is Reese Witherspoon's (b. 1976) as Elle Woods in *Legally Blonde* (2001). She plays Woods as the stereotype of the dumb blonde, and appears to be vapid and superficial, which is a stupid stereotype. I mean, it's really dumb, even for a stereotype. Reese Witherspoon has not only stunning good looks, but also tremendous charm, and she is a brilliant actor as well. And the character she plays is also brilliant, masking her intelligence under what seems like a superficial interest in fashion and in the color pink. People look at her, as she opens her eyes wide, and think they can manipulate her. And every time, she shows them that she knows what they are up to. Their cynical ploys don't work on her! She is too smart for them. One of her techniques, arising organically no doubt out of playing the moments, is to mask what she knows with a charming smile, while she hurls verbal zingers at those who would abuse her. This is a great use of the all-important technique of playing opposites.

Along with those just mentioned are the charming romantic comedy with its theme of women's rights, *Baby Boom* (1987), starring Diane Keaton (b. 1946), also notable in many other comedies, including several for Woody Allen, and playwright and actor Sam Shepard (b. 1943) as the Vermont veterinarian she falls in love with; *Coming to America* (1988) and many others starring the prolific and hilarious Eddie Murphy (b. 1961); and *Midnight Run* (1988), starring Charles Grodin (b. 1935) and Robert De Niro (b. 1943), both of whom are excellent in serious and comic roles.

Don't forget *The Monster-in-Law*, the classic farce with Cameron Diaz and Jane Fonda discussed in chapter four; or the riotous satire of the fashion industry and fashion magazines *The Devil Wears Prada* (2006), directed by David Frankel (b. 1959), and written by Aline Brosh McKenna (b. 1967) and Lauren Weisberger (b. 1977), based on her novel. Meryl Streep (b. 1949; supreme in both comedy and drama) is beastly and adorable and sympathetic as Miranda Priestly, the imperious editor-in-chief; Stanley Tucci (b. 1960) as her amanuensis Nigel, the soul of kindness underneath his veneer of professionalism; Anne Hathaway (b. 1982) as Andy Sachs, the naïve newcomer to the organization; and Emily Blunt (b. 1983), adorable as Emily, the defensive, snobbish secretary who would be obnoxious if we didn't sympathize with her because we see immediately what she is up against (Streep, for one thing) in this mad, dog-eat-dog world.

And don't miss Meryl Streep as Julia Child (1912–2004) and Stanley Tucci as her husband, diplomat Paul Child (1902–1994), in the delightful romantic culinary comedy, Nora Ephron's *Julie and Julia* (2009), with Amy Adams (b. 1974). She is charming as the food blogger who decides to cook her way through Julia Child's classic masterpiece *Mastering the Art of French Cooking*. If you like good food, you will love this film.

XV

The Television Sitcom Then and Now:
The Vaudeville Skit Comes of Age

Television sitcoms are the descendants of vaudeville comedy sketches, the humor of which is ultimately derived from ancient Greek comedy. Pure vaudeville was transferred very early to the television screen, with Milton Berle (1908–2002), for instance, in *The Buick Berle Show* in the 1950s; and Ed Wynn, who had appeared in the Ziegfeld Follies, hosting TV variety shows starting in 1949.

You see a lot of shtick, which was a vaudeville staple, on television sitcoms, and it can be very funny. Shtick—a Yiddish word, meaning a piece, or bit of something—is show business slang for a bit of comic business, or a comic routine. Shtick can be anything from a particular intonation pattern, a catchphrase, gesture, gimmick, or distinctive movement that an actor or comic has made his or her personal trademark.

As Alice Spivak points out in the book we wrote together, *How to Rehearse When There Is No Rehearsal: Acting and the Media* (Limelight, 2007), working in television sitcoms is a bit closer to working in the theater than working in either films or other television programs, because the shows are taped in front of live audiences after having been rehearsed, for almost a week. On the other hand, the rehearsals are more for the camera and the writers than for the actors, and the writers work hard, constantly rewriting the dialogue. The daily rehearsals are attended by almost everybody connected with the project, including the producers and casting directors. As an actor, you have to justify blocking that often accommodates the three cameras used, but seems to have little characterological justification. In the broadcast show, the laughter comes from a prerecorded laugh track, mixed in with the audience laughter recorded at the taping.

Much of the rehearsal time is spent looking for what everybody at the rehearsals thinks are the funniest line readings:

> What passes for rehearsal, including searching for the funniest line readings, is done by teamwork. All the people watching rehearsals have their say, and the actor has to try out each line reading until there is a consensus of opinion. It is only when the actor is the star *and* the producer that he or she has the final word.

The early television situation comedy—a phrase conveniently shortened into one word: sitcom—featured several other comedians already well known for their stage vaudeville routines, and then for their radio shows. Jack Benny (1894–1974) in *The Jack Benny Program* (1950–1965; popularly known as *The Jack Benny Show*), and George Burns (1896–1996) and Gracie Allen (1895–1964) in *The George Burns and Gracie Allen Show* (1950–1958) are two more cases in point. These performers went from vaudeville, to early talk films, to radio and then on to television. In that medium, the vaudeville routines were eventually formatted into half-hour shows. They had perfunctory, but amusing plots, revolving around situations that required immediate solutions to problems. The comedy depended on how the particular characters, established since the days of vaudeville, dealt with the situations. The material to be performed actually takes about twenty-two minutes, the rest of the half hour being devoted to commercials.

Each of the comedians mentioned above was individual, distinctive, and memorable, and each had a gimmick, which in the case of a comedian or comic actor is a memorable, simple device or personal characteristic for which the actor becomes known. It is indelibly associated with the persona the actor assumes, and is expected by the audience, particularly in the case of television sitcoms, but it can be equally useful in films or on stage. The outrageous British music hall comic and television actor and personality, Frankie Howerd had a very simple one: his trademark "Ooh!" (opening his eyes in blank surprise) of incredulity, and he would turn to the audience sometimes as well, after he had said it, implicitly asking them to be on his side. Few can get away with such obvious gimmicks, but he was so naturally funny that what he did was accepted. You can see him in a cameo role as a fruit vendor with a runaway horse and cart in *The Ladykillers* (1955), the Ealing comedy starring Alec Guinness.

Milton Berle's gimmicks were funny, mugging faces that he made, and he would walk on the inside edges of his feet. He also did takes directly into the camera, mugging and smiling at the audience as he reacted to some remark. And his shows had shtick bits that the audience expected, such as the makeup man who came on with a powder puff and patted Berle's face, from which clouds of powder would rise. Berle was a great actor, and as good in serious, straight roles as he was in comic ones. For him, acting is reacting, which is a well known theatrical saying. In his interview in *Great Comedians Talk About Comedy*, he tells us that he took acting very seriously. When it comes to comic timing, you have to have the courage to wait, he tells us. In other words, you might pause after a laugh line, because you know the audience will laugh, but you have to go on performing if they don't. Some comic actors time things technically: "If this is supposed to be funny shall I take three beats?" But that is not necessarily a good idea. Spontaneity is a much better approach, since the audience will respond differently each time.

George Burns's gimmick was that he sang badly (deliberately) in his hoarse voice, and he and his very charming wife Gracie would have exchanges in which she took everything literally, resulting in some howlingly funny moments. She was never sarcastic or mean-spirited, but always remained sweet and unaffected, although she could be condescending, not in a mean way, but in a condoling, sympathetic way. As Burns says, "Gracie thought everybody was out of step but her." And she was always feeling sorry for Burns and the other people she talked with, because they were too dumb to understand what was obvious to her, but to nobody else. As Burns says of her, "She was not a comedienne, she was an actress." Once again, it was her earnest attitude and the seriousness with which she delivered the literally incredible joke lines that made them funny. She did it all for real, and believed in the circumstances. And she did not do things mechanically, which Burns decries in other comic actors, whom he does not name in his interview in *Great Comedians Talk About Comedy*. They may have a perfect sense of timing and know all the tricks of the trade, but they are not funny, because they don't do things for real. They are not honest in their acting. And such people lack a personality trait that is essential for doing comedy: warmth.

Burns used a trademark cigar as not only a prop, but a gimmick. His technical way of holding for laughs and timing them so that he came in with his next line before the laughter had completely died down—which is the classic technique used in both stand-up comedy and plays—was to smoke his cigar until it was time to speak again.

Jack Benny had three gimmicks: his miserliness, his poor violin playing (he could actually play quite well), and his vanity about his age, which was perpetually thirty-nine—he was much older than that when he started using the joke, but it worked anyway. Early in his career, he had done an act with his violin, and even when the act later included more talking than violin playing, he stood there talking while he held the violin. This was very funny, because people expected him to play it, and paid extra attention to what he was saying. He never did play it, but the gimmick held people's attention.

In *Great Comedians Talk About Comedy*, Benny gives wonderful advice about how to perform, and among other things, he tells us he never wanted "to have a superfluous moment": he followed the principle that every gesture, every movement, every moment has to mean something. Every take, every look directed at somebody or something in his famous deadpan style had to have significance; that is one reason his sideways glances are so funny: each one is specific, in the context of a specific situation.

Benny's reputation for perfect timing was well deserved. According to him, the way he achieved timing was by talking slowly, and as if he were involved in a real conversation with a group of friends. During the conversation, he had to make points. He would stop and think for a second, seem to hesitate, and then start talking again. During every pause and whenever he hemmed and hawed, he appeared to be thinking: His way of dealing with pauses was to fill them with mental process. They were never empty, and they even worked on the radio. This was all very natural to him, but he also rehearsed assiduously, so that he could appear to be timing the pauses and the line readings spontaneously. As Benny tells us, some people who talk very quickly have great timing, but for him, talking quickly would have been impossible.

That individual sense of timing is one of the things each leading comedian brings to the parts in a sitcom, and, while the timing itself varies as each moment is played out, the basic idea of how the actor deals with timing does not. It's one of the things the audience expects. If Benny had suddenly started rushing through the script, the audience would not only have been nonplussed and found it difficult to follow, but would also have been displeased. In any case, given his established persona and the way of delivering lines that had become second nature to him, he couldn't have speeded through the material.

The iconic comedian Jackie Gleason (1916–1987) also began his career in vaudeville, and in a number of his television shows, he does vaudeville skits featuring various characters. He came up with a number of memorable tag lines. His first catchphrase was, "And awa-aa-ay we go!" and he said it as an exit line at the end of his opening monologue in his first television comedy variety series, *The Jackie Gleason Show* (1952–1959). It was accompanied by "traveling" music, and a soft-shoe shuffle with appropriate gestures. Another famous line was, "How sweet it is!" This was from the 1962 film, *Papa's Delicate Condition*, said when things went well, and the character he played was feeling mellow.

His megahit *Honeymooners* TV series began in 1955. Gleason played the Brooklyn bus driver, Ralph Kramden, the "Lovable Loser" on Scott Sedita's list of types in *The Eight Characters of Comedy*. He often ended the show with this phrase to his wife, Alice, the "Logical Smart

One," played for most of the series by Audrey Meadows (1922–1996): "Baby, you're the greatest!" He would take her in his arms, all problems resolved—until next week's episode. But the couple fought frequently. Ralph never hit Alice but he threatened her often enough, with "One of these days…one of these days…Pow! Right in the kisser!" and "Bang! Zoooom!" The latter phrase was accompanied on the second word with the gesture of one palm slapping down across the other and making an upward motion, and you knew he meant to send her to "The moon, Alice, the moon." When he disapproved of something she had said, Ralph would intone irately, "You're a regular riot!" especially when Alice had been sarcastic to him, particularly about his being overweight. Again, I want to stress the reality of the comedy, the truthfulness that gave rise to the phrases and the actions.

In the hit comedy series, *I Love Lucy* (1951–1957), Cuban-American bandleader Ricky Ricardo, played by musician and actor Desi Arnaz (1917–1986), was forever exasperated with his wife Lucy, played by Lucille Ball (1911–1989). He was Sedita's type of the "Logical Smart One" and she was the "Lovable Loser." He was the straight man, and she was the comedienne. His accent was his gimmick, and it got thicker the more exasperated he became, until finally he would burst into Spanish. Her gimmick was her zaniness, and she was always cooking up harebrained schemes, enlisting the help of her neighbor and sidekick, Ethel Mertz, the "Dumb One," played by Vivian Vance (1909–1979), often in order to get into show business, and perform in one of Ricky's shows. Ethel would fall afoul of her exasperated, irate, short-tempered husband, Fred, the "Bitch/Bastard," played by former vaudevillian, William Frawley (1887–1986). Of course, everything was always resolved satisfactorily by the end of each half-hour episode.

Theoretically, a situation comedy is one that depends more for its humor on the circumstances that the characters find themselves involved in, rather than on the characters themselves. But, as with *The Jack Benny Show*, *The George Burns and Gracie Allen Show*, *The Honeymooners* and *I Love Lucy*, since the same characters (the leads and their sidekicks) appear every week, much of the humor depends on the audience's familiarity with them, and the humor comes from how they get out of the scrapes they get themselves into. The audience has to like them, or they will go off the air, because nobody will watch. All these characters, even the bitch/bastard Fred Mertz, had that essential quality of warmth, and the audience loved them for it. They were loving and warm to each other even when they were at loggerheads, and everyone knew that their quarrels were not going to lead tragically to the divorce court.

Its origins in vaudeville skits, stand-up comedy, and Hollywood screwball comedies like *My Man Godfrey* (1936) forgotten, television sitcom evolved, and became more sophisticated. Such shows as *30 Rock* (2006–2013) are satirical as well as depending on character and situation. Political and social situations are slyly and cleverly dealt with, as opposed to the simple stories of most of the old comedies, which avoided much of anything approaching the controversial. The genial, soothing establishment family comedies of the 1950s, such as *Father Knows Best* (1954–1960) and *Leave It to Beaver* (1957–1963), were fun, but were at the same time unthreatening and tame. They were considered wholesome entertainment for the entire family. Not a "dirty" word was heard, no toilet was ever shown, and married couples never slept in the same bed, but only in the twin beds shown in their bedrooms, if we entered them at all. Any overtly sexual or political material was deliberately or perhaps unconsciously avoided, except in one or two controversial areas, such as teenage dating, for instance. That is, the possibility of sexual activity during teenage dating was considered controversial, if not taboo, and any such practice was of course warned against, if it was mentioned and then only obliquely. So even this material was eminently safe, which didn't make it less amusing and heartwarming, but did provoke a yawn or two, and a sneer at its unreality. Life as it was lived was not portrayed, but an idealized version of how it should be lived in the eyes of the staid and the socially conservative was. After all, striving after the ideal that most people did not experience in the bosoms of their dysfunctional families was something to aspire to.

But some of the best comedies of the period, such as *I Love Lucy* and *The Honeymooners*, had a kind of subversive, undermining influence, and were extremely funny in their implications about the comfort-able, settled nature of post-war American life. Indeed, in those two examples, dysfunctionality was the very stuff from which they were concocted, and we laughed at it, because, although the situations were absurd and outlandish, they were a truer reflection of what most of us were going through. What was supposed to be a durable, stable way of life was in reality replete with insecurity, which broke people forcibly out of their complacency and placidity.

The war was over, but the Korean War began a scant few years later, and the new horrors of McCarthyite anti-Communism witch hunts were about to emerge. Vietnam was not far off, nor was the so-called sexual revolution and the flower power, hippie drug culture that many conservative elements found threatening and unpalatable. And nowa-days in America, the shrill right wing and the so-called tea party have made civility in political discourse almost a thing of the past, so that the climate is ripe for more comedies parodying the tea party buffoons and ignoramuses, who have infused a brand of know-nothing popu-lism and ignorance of the constitution, often combined with absurd, destructive religiosity, into our cultural and political lives, whether we want them there or not. They have a right to free speech, like the rest of us, but their pronouncements are so many vague, frothy statements of narrow-minded, proto-fascistic nonprinciples that they are ripe for comedic interpretation, when they are not risible themselves.

In the last quarter of the twentieth century, favorite series included *Friends* (1994–2004) and *Seinfeld* (1990–1998), starring the affable Jerry Seinfeld (b. 1954); and we saw such comedies as *The Bob Newhart Show* (1972–1978), which dealt with feminism and other issues and starred actor and comedian, Bob Newhart (b. 1929), known for his sadsack, deadpan demeanor and dry delivery, as a psychologist, and *Newhart* (1982–1990), in which he played a transplanted New Yorker who owns and inn in Vermont.

The distinguished, prolific actor and comedian Bill Cosby (b. 1939), now sadly in such trouble over accusations of rape and sexual mis-conduct, was discovered by Carl Reiner, and had several hit television series. They included *The Cosby Show* (1984–1992), in which he played

Dr. Huxtable, head of a successful family in a major African-American series, one of the first shows to depict the milieu, no different than any other middle-class family of whatever ethnic background. In another hit series, *Cosby* (1996–2000), he starred as Hilton Lucas, forced into retirement. Both shows revolved around him and his family life. And the prolific Wanda Sykes (b. 1964) and Chris Rock (b. 1965), who have also worked together, are eloquent testimony to the genius of African-American comic actors, as is the wonderful writer and comic actor Richard Pryor (1940–2005). They were all preceded by another comic genius, Academy Award winner Hattie McDaniel (1892–1952), whose turn as a hired caterer / maid in *Alice Adams* (1935), although the film has racist overtones, is hilarious, and the best thing in the rather sentimental film. She appeared in ninety-five films and television series, including her own, *Beulah* (1952), based on her radio show (1947–1950). Most famously, she played Mammy in *Gone with the Wind* (1939), for which she won an Academy Award for Best Supporting Actress.

All in the Family (1971–1979), gave us memorable performances from everyone, revolving around Carroll O'Connor (1924–2001), who in real life was politically liberal, as the loudmouth bigot Archie Bunker; and *Archie Bunker's Place* (1979–1983), a spinoff in which Archie runs a bar. Among other guest stars was Sherman Hemsley (b. 1938), who appeared in fifteen episodes as George Jefferson, the character he played in his own series, *The Jeffersons* (1975–1978), about a noveau riche African-American family living in a luxury high-rise New York building.

Other popular sitcom series include *Golden Girls* (1985–1992), about four women who live together in Miami; *Wings* (1990–1997), concerning two brothers and their friends at the Nantucket airport; and *Will and Grace* (1998–2006), the first gay-themed sitcom, with Will, a gay man and his friend Grace, who is straight, and their campy friends.

All of these series, as well as the variety series *Saturday Night Live* (first season, 1975), which is still with us, were more socially aware and conscious of such movements as feminism, civil rights, and of changing mores generally than had been the case with the sitcoms of the 1950s, which tended to view society through rose-colored glasses.

As examples of the genre, however, they have something in common with the formulas used for those older sitcoms. For one thing, they all have a running cast of memorable, distinctive, appealing characters. The cast of regulars is supplemented by guest stars. An episode is usually a complete story, or sometimes part of a story that runs for two or more episodes. The writing is broad as always. And the acting is also broad but real, because the actors are committed to what they are doing and to the actions they are playing, as they have always been.

In contemporary sitcoms, where the writing varies tremendously and some shows can be extremely unreal and silly, the same formulas prevail. The acting remains broad (sometimes way overdone) in such popular sitcoms as *That '70s Show* (1998–2006), the vulgar sex comedy *Two and a Half Men* (2003–2014), *How I Met Your Mother* (2005–2014), *Mike and Molly* (first season, 2010), *Two Broke Girls* (first season, 2011), *The Millers* (first season, 2013), *The Big Bang Theory* (2007–2014), *Mom* (first season, 2013), *The McCarthys* (first season, 2014), and others. In shows designed for children, such as those on Nickelodeon and the Disney Channel, the young actors are asked to do the most unsubtle possible comic playing, with lots of shtick and a great lack of reality, hamming it up and using techniques they have sometimes barely mastered.

In any case, you must do what is required by the writing and by the director. Whatever you are doing, commit yourself to fulfilling the actions and filling each moment energetically, with as much gusto and enjoyment as possible.

Appendix One

Major Comedy Writers from Ancient Greece through the Twenty-First Century

Ancient Greece

Aristophanes (445–385 BCE; Greek) Eleven plays that we know of, exemplifying the Old Comedy, including *Hippes* (The Knights; 424 BCE); *Nephelae* (The Clouds; 423 BCE); *Sphekes* (The Wasps; 422 BCE); *Ornithes* (The Birds; 414 BCE); *Lysistrata* (411 BCE); *Batrachoi* (Frogs; 411 BCE).

Menander (343/342?–291/290 BCE; Greek) Unknown number of plays, probably more than one hundred, most lost, exemplifying the New Comedy; two major scripts survive: *Dyskolos* (The Grouch; 317 BCE)—nearly complete; and *Samia* (The Maiden from Samos; ca. 321/316? BCE)—about one-third complete.

Ancient Rome

Plautus (251?–184? BCE; Roman) Ca. twenty-one comedies, of which twenty survive intact, including *Asinaria* (Asses); *Miles Gloriosus* (The Braggart Warrior; ca. 205 BCE); *Stichus* (200 BCE); *Aulularia* (The Pot of Gold; 195 BCE); *Pseudolus* (191 BCE); *Rudens* (The Rope); *Amphytruo* (Amphytrion); *Menechmi* (The Two Menaechme); *Curculio*; *Casina*.

Terence (195?–159 BCE; Roman) Six surviving comedies: *Andria* (The Women of Andros; 166 BCE); *Hecyra* (The Mother-in-Law; 165 BCE); *Heautontimorumenos* (The Self-Tormentor; The Masochist; 163 BCE); *Eunuchus* (The Eunuch; 161 BCE); *Phormio* (161 BCE); *Adelphi* (The Brothers; 160 BCE).

Medieval Europe

See chapter eight for a discussion of anonymous French and English farces.

Sixteenth Century

Pietro Aretino (1492–1536: Italian) Six plays, including five prose comedies, among them *La cortigiana* (The Courtesan; written ca. 1526, produced 1537); *Il marescalco* (The Stablemaster; 1526/27); *Lo ipocrito* (The Hypocrite; 1545), based on Plautus's *Menechmi*, also the basis for Shakespeare's *The Comedy of Errors*.

Lodovico Ariosto (1474–1533; Italian) Seven plays, including *La cassaria* (The Strongbox; versions in prose, 1508, and verse, 1531); *I suppositi* (The Pretenders; versions in prose, 1509, and verse, 1528/31); *Il negromante* (The Necromancer; verse, 1520).

Thomas Dekker (1572–1632; English) More than forty plays both alone and in collaboration (exact number unknown; most lost), mostly tragicomedies and comedies, including *The Shoemaker's Holiday, or the Gentle Craft* (1599) and *The Honest Whore* (1604).

Giambattista Della Porta (1535–1615; Italian) Scientist, traveler, playwright; seventeen plays, including fourteen comedies, most in the genre of the commedia erudite (see glossary), among them *L'astrologo* (The Astrologer; 1570); *La sorella* (The Sister; 1588); *Il moro* (The Moor; published 1607).

Pierre Gringoire (1470–1538; French) Poet, actor, playwright; number of plays unknown; wrote pieces, many of them *soties* (literally, "stupidities"; see glossary), for the Paris theater company Les Enfants sans souci (The Carefree Children), including his most well known surviving trilogy of soties, *Le Jeu du Prince des Sots et de la Mère Sotte* (The Play of the Prince of Fools and Mother Folly; 1512).

Etienne Jodelle (1532–1573; French) Three plays, including the first classical comedy, an ancestor of *Tartuffe*, *Eugène* (1552), a satire of the clergy in which a priest seduces a married woman.

Ben Jonson (1532–1637; English) Thirty-six masques and nineteen plays, including fifteen comedies, among them *Every Man in His Humor* (1598), *Volpone* (1605–1606), and *Bartholomew Fair* (1614).

Pierre de Larivey (1540?–1611?; French) Seven surviving plays, including the comedies, *Les esprits* (The Ghosts; published, 1579); *La veuve* (The Widow; published, 1579); and *Les trompeurs* (The Deceivers; 1611).

Niccolò Machiavelli (1459–1527; Italian) Statesman, soldier, government official, diplomat, courtier, writer, translator; two plays, both major influences on European theater: *La mandragola* (The Mandrake [Root]; written 1513/1520; produced 1518?/1520; published 1524); *La Clizia* (Clizia; written 1520/1525; produced 1520; published 1525), adapted from Plautus' *Casina*.

William Shakespeare (1564–1616; English) Thirty-seven plays (and several more that are disputed), including tragedies, histories, problem plays (formerly categorized as comedies) that are tragicomic, ironic, and moralistic: *The Merchant of Venice* (1596–1597); *Twelfth Night, or What You Will* (1601); *Measure for Measure* (1603); *All's Well That Ends Well* (1606–1607); *The Winter's Tale* (1609–1610); and *The Tempest* (1610–1611); and comedies with happy endings, and elements of farce and sometimes of fantasy: *The Two Gentlemen of Verona* (1589–1591); *The Taming of the Shrew* (1590–1591); *The Comedy of Errors* (1594); *Love's Labor's Lost* (1594–1595); *A Midsummer Night's Dream* (1595); *The Merry Wives of Windsor* (1597–1598); *Much Ado About Nothing* (1598–1599); and *As You Like It* (1599–1600).

Nicholas Udall (1504–1556; English) Cleric, teacher, translator; one major farce, *Ralph Roister-Doister*, ca.1553/1562.

Seventeenth Century

Colley Cibber (1671–1757; English) Actor, playwright, memoirist; twenty-six plays, including Shakespearean adaptations, notably *Richard III* (1700; revised 1718), and original musical entertainments, burlesques, farces, and comedies, among them *Love's Last Shift, or The Fool in Fashion* (1696), the first of his fifteen comedies; *The Careless Husband* (1704); *The Lady's Last Stake, or The Wife's Resentment* (1707); *The Refusal, or The Ladies' Philosophy* (1721).

William Congreve (1670–1729; English) Seven performance projects, among them four comedies, all masterpieces: *The Old Bachelor* (1693); *The Double Dealer* (1693); *Love for Love* (1695); *The Way of the World* (1700).

Pierre Corneille (1606–1684; French) Thirty-four plays, including the tragedies for which he is best known, among them *Le Cid* (1636), and fifteen tragicomedies and comedies, among them his first play, *Mélite* (Melita; 1629); *L'illusion comique* (Theatrical Illusion; 1636); *Le menteur* (The Liar; 1643).

Florent Dancourt [stage name of Florent Carton, sieur d'Ancourt] (1661–1725; French) Actor, dramatist; ca. sixty plays, including *Le chevalier à la mode* (The Fashionable Cavalier; 1687); *La maison de campagne* (The Country House; 1688); *Les bourgeoises de qualité* (The Middle-Class Ladies of Quality; 1700); *Le galant jardinier* (The Gallant Gardener; 1704).

John Dryden (1631–1700; English) Poet, dramatist, translator, adapter, literary critic who wrote prolifically in many genres; Poet Laureate in 1688; eighteen plays, including heroic verse tragedies, and seven comedies, among them *The Wild Gallant* (1663); *An Evening's Love* (1668); *The Mistaken Husband* (1674). His farce, *Sir Martin Mar-all, or The Feign'd Innocence* (1667), one of the most successful plays of the century, was adapted from *The Blunderer* (1666), a translation of Molière's *L'Étourdi, ou les Contretemps* (The Scatterbrain, or The Obstructions; 1653) by William Cavendish, First Duke of Newcastle (1592–1676); Dryden also took material for this farce from a number of other sources. In his *Diary* entry for August 16, 1667, Samuel Pepys called it "the most entire piece of mirth, a complete farce from one end to the other, that certainly was ever writ. I never laughed so in all my life."

Tom Durfey (1653–1723; English) Called himself Thomas D'Urfey, and claimed to be of French descent; composer of five hundred songs, including ten for *The Beggar's Opera*; thirty-two plays, most of them comedies, among them *The Fond Husband* (1676); *The Virtuous Wife* (1689); *The Comical History of Don Quixote* (1694), based on Cervantes' novel, with music by Henry Purcell (1659–1695).

Sir George Etherege (1636?–1692; English) Diplomat, writer; three plays, all masterpieces: *The Comical Revenge* (1664); *She Would If She Could* (1668); *The Man of Mode* (1676).

George Farquhar (1677/78–1707; Irish) Seven plays, including *Love and a Bottle* (1698); *The Constant Couple, or a Trip to the Jubilee* (1699); *The Recruiting Officer* (1706); *The Beaux' Stratagem* (1707).

Molière [stage name of Jean-Baptiste Poquelin de Molière] (1622–1673; French) Actor, director, playwright; ca. thirty-seven plays, including *Les précieuses ridicules* (The Ridiculous Pretentious Ladies; 1659); *L'école des femmes* (The School for Wives; 1662); *Tartuffe ou L'imposteur* (Tartuffe, or The Imposter; 1664); *Dom Juan, ou Le festin de pierre* (Don Juan, or The Feast of Stone; 1665); *Le médecin* *malgré lui* (The Doctor in Spite of Himself; 1666); *Le misanthrope, ou L'arbitraire amoureux* (The Misanthrope, or The Arbitrary Lover; 1666); *L'avare, ou L'école du mensonge* (The Miser, or The School of Lies; 1668); *Georges Dandin, ou Le mari confondu* (Georges Dandin, or The Confused Husband; 1668); *Le bourgeois gentilhomme* (The Middle-Class Gentleman; 1670), a comédie-ballet with music by Jean-Baptiste Lully (1632–1687); *Les fourberies de Scapin* (Scapin's Deceitful Tricks; 1671); *Les femmes savantes* (The Learned Ladies; 1672); *Le malade imaginaire* (The Imaginary Invalid; 1673). His influence on English Restoration comedy was enormous; for one example, see above, under John Dryden.

Tirso de Molina (1571?–1648; Spanish) Playwright; eighty-two plays, mostly comedies, including the *comedia de capa y espada* (see glossary) *Don Gil de las calzas verdes* (Don Gil of the Green Breeches; 1615); *La villana de Vallecas* (The Peasant Girl from Vallecas; 1620); a Don Juan play: *El burlador de Sevilla y el convidado de piedra* (The Trickster of Seville and the Stone Guest; 1630).

Antoine Jacob de Montfleury (1639–1685; French) Playwright; son of the actor Montfleury (Zacharie Jacob; 1600?–1667), caricatured in Edmond Rostand's (1868–1918) *Cyrano de Bergerac* (1897); twenty comedies, among them *Le mari sans femme* (The Wifeless Husband; 1663); *L'école des jaloux* (The School for the Jealous; 1664); *L'école des filles* (The School for Girls; 1666); *La femme juge et partie* (The Litigant Who Was Her Own Judge; 1669); *Le comédien poète* (The Actor-Poet; 1674).

Philippe Quinault (1635–1688; French) Playwright, scenarist, librettist; collaborated with a number of famous composers, most notably Jean-Baptiste Lully, for whom he wrote ballet scenarios and operas; fifteen opera libretti and ballet scenarios; twenty-four plays, including the comedies *L'amour indiscret, ou Le maistre étourdi* (Indiscreet Love, or The Befuddled Master; 1654); *La comédie sans comédie* (Comedy Without Comedy; 1655); *La mère coquette, ou Les amants brouillés* (The Coquettish Mother, or The Confused / Quarrelsome Lovers; 1664).

Jean-François Regnard (1655–1709; French) Twenty-five comedies, including *Le joueur* (The Gambler; 1696); *Les folies amoureuses* (The Amorous Follies; 1704); *Le légataire universel* (The Sole Heir; 1708).

Paul Scarron (1610–1660; French) Novelist, poet, playwright; his widow became Mme. de Maintenon (1635–1719), mistress and later wife of King Louis XIV; known for his satiric verses and for his book, *Le roman comique* (The Comic Novel; written, 1651–1657), about a group of strolling players; six major satirical romantic comedies, including *Jodelet, ou Le maître valet* (Jodelet, or The Master as Valet; 1643); *Les trois Dorothées, ou Le Jodelet souffleté* (The Three Dorothys, or Jodelet Slapped; 1646); *L'écolier de Salamanque, ou Les ennemis généreux* (The Schoolboy from Salamanca, or The Generous Enemies; 1654).

Sir John Vanbrugh (1664–1726; English) Two plays, both master-pieces: *The Relapse, or Virtue in Danger* (1696), a sequel to Cibber's *Love's Last Shift; The Provok'd Wife* (1697).

Lope de Vega Carpio [Lope Félix de Vega Carpio] (1562–1633; Spanish) Playwright; three hundred seventeen plays in all genres, mostly comedies, including many in the genres of the *comedia de capa y espada* and the *comedia histórica* (historical play / comedy, loosely based on historical events); among his most famous works are *Fuenteovejuna* (The Sheep Well; 1611); the comedias de capa y espada, *La buena guarda* (The Good Guard; 1610); *El acero de Madrid* (The Waters of Madrid; 1606/1612); *El perro del hortelano* (The Dog in the Manger; 1613/1615).

William Wycherly (1641–1715; English) Four plays, all masterpieces: *Love in a Wood, or, St. James's Park* (1671); *The Gentleman Dancing-Master* (1673), *The Country Wife* (1675); *The Plain Dealer* (1676).

Eighteenth Century

Pierre Caron de Beaumarchais (1732–1799; French) Merchant, playwright; one opera libretto, *Tarare* (1787; music by Antonio Salieri

[1750–1825]); ten plays, including the *Figaro* trilogy: *Le barbier de Séville, ou La précaution inutile* (The Barber of Seville, or The Useless Precaution; written 1772; produced 1775); *La folle journée, ou Le mariage de Figaro* (The Mad Day, or The Marriage of Figaro; written 1775–1778; banned, 1779; produced 1784); *La mère coupable, ou L'autre Tartuffe* (The Guilty Mother, or The Other Tartuffe; 1792).

Alexandre-Louis-Bertrand de Beaunoir [penname of Abbé A. L. B. Robineau] (1746–1823; French) Often wrote under the pseudonym Madame de Beaunoir. His wife, Louise-Céline Cheval, Madame de Beaunoir (1766–1821) was also a writer, and he wrote several plays using her name; they probably collaborated on several as well. One-time priest; memoirist, historian, librettist, playwright; ca. two hundred one-act and full-length comedies, among them *Jérôme Pointu* (1781), which had a number of sequels, so popular did the character prove; *L'Écouteur aux portes* (The Listener at Doors; 1784); *Le Sculpteur, ou La femme comme il y en a peu* (The Sculptor, or The Woman Like Few Others; written by his wife, probably in collaboration with him; 1784); *Le Ramoneur prince, ou Le prince ramoneur* (The Prince Chimney-Sweep, or The Chimney-Sweep Prince; 1784); *Les frères amis* (The Friendly Brothers; 1788); *Le Danger des liaisons* (The Danger of Liaisons; written by his wife, probably with his help; 1798); *Fanfan et Colas, ou Les frères de lait* (Fanfan and Colas, or The Foster Brothers; written under his pseudonym, Madame de Beaunoir; 1822).

Pietro Chiari (1712–1785; Italian) Former Jesuit; novelist, librettist; rival of Goldoni and Count Carlo Gozzi; opposed Molière style of farce; in 1762 left Venice and went to Paris to be manager-director of the Comédie-Italienne; six tragedies and ca. sixty comedies, many in the comédie larmoyante style, including *La scuola delle vedove* (The School for Widows; 1749); *Il filosofo veneziano* (The Venetian Philosopher; 1753); *La sposa fedele* (The Faithful Wife; 1773).

George Colman "the Elder" (1732–1794; English) Barrister, theater manager, essayist, playwright; more than thirty plays, including the comedy of manners, *The Jealous Wife* (1761), based on Henry Fielding's (1707–1754) novel *Tom Jones* (1749); *The Clandestine Marriage* (1766), in collaboration with David Garrick; the farces *Polly Honeycombe* (1760) and *The Deuce Is in Him* (1763).

George Colman "the Younger" (1762–1832; English) Playwright, theater manager; inventor of the jumble (see glossary); more than thirty-six plays, comedies, libretti, including libretto to the anti-slavery opera *Inkle and Yarico* (1787), and burlesque jumbles, among them *The Review, or The Wags of Windsor* (1800); *Gay Deceivers, or More Laugh Than Love* (1804); *Who Wants a Guinea?* (1805); *The Quadrupeds of Quedlinburgh, or The Rovers of Weimar* (1811).

Philippe Néricault Destouches (1680–1754; French) Diplomat, government official, actor; twenty-three comedies, including his most successful, *Le Philosophe marié, ou Le mari honteux de l'être* (The Married Philosopher, or The Husband Ashamed to Be One; 1727) and *Le glorieux* (The Glorious One; 1732).

Charles Rivière Dufresny (1654–1724; French) Twenty-seven comedies for the Comédie-Française and the Comédie-Italienne, among them *L'esprit de contradiction* (The Spirit of Contradiction; 1700), a one-act play, considered his masterpiece; *Le double veuvage* (The Double Widowhood; 1702); *La coquette du village, ou Le lot supposé* (The Village Coquette, or The Supposed Apportionment; 1715); *La réconciliation normande* (The Norman Reconciliation; 1719); *Le dédit* (The Retraction; 1719).

David Garrick (1717–1779; English) Actor-manager; the most noted actor of his era, famous for his reforms in acting and theatrical presentation; father of modern realistic acting; manager of the Drury Lane; playwright; several Shakespeare adaptations, including *Catherine and Petruchio* (1754), from *The Taming of the Shrew*, and *Hamlet* (1772); twenty-three plays, mostly farces and comedies, including *The Lying Valet* (1741); *The Guardian* (1759); *The Clandestine Marriage* (1766), written in collaboration with George Colman "the Younger"; *A Peep Behind the Curtain, or The New Rehearsal* (1767); *The Irish Widow* (1772), a farce; *Bon Ton, or High Life above Stairs* (1775).

Carlo Goldoni (1707–1793; Venetian-Italian) One hundred thirty-three stage works, including tragedies, tragicomedies, forty-three opera libretti (of which four were in the opera seria genre, and the rest comic). More than one hundred of his pieces are comedies, some in French but most in Italian, many using features of the Venetian dialect, including *Il servitore de due padroni* (The Servant of Two Masters; 1745), also known as *Arlecchino* [Harlequin] *servitore di due padroni*; *Il bugiardo* (The Liar; 1750–1751); *La locandiera* (The Mistress of the Inn; 1751); and *I rusteghi* (The Rustics; 1760).

Oliver Goldsmith (1728/1730?–1774; Anglo-Irish) Novelist, playwright; two plays: the unsuccessful *The Good-Natured Man* (1768) and his masterpiece, the often-revived *She Stoops to Conquer, or The Mistakes of a Night* (1773).

Carlo Gozzi (1720–1806; Venetian-Italian) Memoirist, poet, literary theorist, playwright; thirty-three plays; known for his melodramatic fairy-tale tragicomedies, combining fantasy and commedia, including *L'amore delle tre melarance* (The Love of Three Oranges; 1761); *Turandot* (1762); *La donna serpente* (The Serpent Woman; 1762); *I pitocchi fortunati* (The Fortunate Beggars; 1763); *L'augellino belverde* (The Pretty Little Green Bird; 1765).

Ludvig Holberg (1684–1754; Danish) Polymath, historian, playwright; thirty-five plays, including *Jeppe paa Bjerget eller den forvandlede Bonde* (Jeppe of the Hill; or The Transformed Peasant; 1722); *Den politiske Kandestøber* (The Political Tinker; 1722); *Erasmus Montanus* (1723); *Den Stundesløse* (The Fussy Man; 1723); *Maskarade* (Masquerades; 1724); *De Usynlige* (The Masked Ladies; 1731).

Pierre-Claude Nivelle de La Chaussée (1692–1754; French) Invented the genre of the *comédie larmoyante* (lachrymose comedy);

twenty-one plays, including *Le préjugé à la mode* (The Fashionable Prejudice; 1735); *Mélanide* (1741); *L'école des mères* (The School for Mothers; 1744).

Alain René Le Sage (1668–1747; French) Novelist, playwright; one hundred thirteen plays, comic opera libretti, and comedies, including his two most famous comedies for the stage, *Crispin, rival de son maître* (Crispin, Rival of His Master; 1707); *Turcaret* (1709).

Jakob Lenz [Jakob Michael Reinhold Lenz] (1751–1792; German) Poet, playwright; adherent of the Sturm und Drang movement, but atypical in being unmelodramatic and more realistic; fifteen plays, most of them satirical comedies, including *Der Hofmeister, oder Die Vorteile der Privaterziehung* (The Tutor, or The Advantages of Private Education; written 1773; produced 1778); *Die Soldaten* (The Soldiers; written 1775; produced 1863); *Die Freunde machen den Philosophen* (The Friends Make a Philosopher; 1776).

Pierre Carlet de Chamblain de Marivaux (1688–1763; French) Thirty-five plays, including *La double inconstance* (The Double Inconstancy; 1723); *La fausse suivante, ou Le fourbe puni* (The False Serving Maid, or The Rascal Punished; 1724); *Le jeu de l'amour et du hasard* (The Game of Love and Chance; 1730); *L'école des mères* (The School for Mothers; 1732); *La mère confidente* (The Mother as Confidant; 1735).

Richard Brinsley Sheridan (1751–1816; Anglo-Irish) Member of Parliament, theater manager, dramatist; ten performance projects, including the opera libretto, *The Duenna* (1775), and the comedies *The Rivals* (1775); *The School for Scandal* (1777); *The Critic* (1779).

Nineteenth Century

James Albery (1838–1889; English) Author, dramatist; wrote ca. thirty-five plays, among them adaptations of English literary works (e.g. *Pickwick* [1871], adapted from Charles Dickens's *The Pickwick Papers*), and French comedies; farces and original comedies, include his two most successful plays *Two Roses* (1870), a comedy that ran for 300 performances at the Lyceum and was produced by Sir Henry Irving; and *Pink Dominoes* (1877), a farce that ran for 555 performances; among his other well-known works are the farce *Brighton* (1888) and the libretto to the one-act operetta, music by Alfred Cellier, *The Spectre Knight* (1878), a companion piece to Gilbert and Sullivan's *The Sorcerer* and later to *H.M.S. Pinafore*. His son, Sir Bronson James Albery (1881–1971), was a noted theater director and producer.

Emile Augier (1820–1889; French) Twenty-nine plays, most of them comedies, including *Le gendre de M. Poirier* (M. Poirier's Son-in-Law; 1854); *Le marriage d'Olympe* (Olympe's Marriage; 1855); *Le fils de Giboyer* (Giboyer's Son; 1862).

Henry Becque [Henri François Becque] (1837–1899; French) Journalist, playwright; known for the naturalism of his realistic comedies and dramas; one opera libretto and twelve plays, among them *L'enfant prodigue* (The Prodigal Son; 1868); *Les honnêtes femmes* (Virtuous Women; 1880); *Les corbeaux* (The Crows; aka The Vultures; 1882); *La Parisienne* (The Parisian Lady; 1885).

H. J. Byron [Henry James Byron] (1835–1884; English) Third cousin of poet George Gordon, Lord Byron (1788–1824); actor, stage director, theater manager, journalist, novelist, editor of humorous magazines, playwright; fifty-six burlesques, pantomimes—some in collaboration with W. S. Gilbert and others—and plays, mostly comedies, including *War to the Knife* (1865) and *A Hundred Thousand Pounds* (1866); the melodrama *The Lancashire Lass; or, Tempted, Tried and True* (1867). His greatest comedy hits, often revived, were *Dearer Than Life* (1867), *Married in Haste* (1875), and *Our Boys* (1875).

Anton Pavlovich Chekhov (1860–1904; Russian) Medical doctor; non-fiction and short story writer, playwright; seven full-length plays and ten farces, which he called "vaudevilles." His name will forever be associated with Constantin Stanislavsky and the Moscow Art Theatre, where his last three major plays premiered. Among his one-act farces are the monologue, *O vredye tabaka* (On the Harmfulness of Tobacco; several versions, written 1886 to 1903); *Myedvyed* (The Bear; The Boor; 1888); *Lyebednaya pyesna* (Swan Song; 1888); *Svadba* (The Wedding; 1889); *Predlozheniye* (The Marriage Proposal; 1890); *Yubiley* (The Anniversary; The Jubilee; 1891). His full-length plays include *Ivanov* (1887); *Chaika* (The Seagull; 1896; MAT premier, 1898); *Dyadya Vanya* (Uncle Vanya; 1899); *Tri sestri* (Three Sisters; 1901); *Vishnyovy sad* (The Cherry Orchard; 1904).

Georges Courteline [penname of Georges Victor Marcel Moinaux] (1858–1929; French) Thirty-one plays, most of them comedies, including *Boubourouche* (1893); *La paix chez soi* (Peace at Home; 1903); *La cruche, ou J'en ai plein le dos de Margot* (The Dolt, or I've Had More Than Enough of Margot; 1909), written in collaboration with the prolific Pierre Wolff (1865–1944).

Georges Feydeau [Georges Léon Jules Marie Feydeau] (1862–1921; French) Thirty-nine plays, including *Tailleur pour dames* (Ladies' Tailor; 1887); *Monsieur chasse!* (Monsieur Goes Hunting!; 1892); *Un fil à la patte* (Caught by the Heel; 1894); *L'hôtel du libre échange* (Free Exchange Hotel; Hotel Paradiso; 1894), written in collaboration with Maurice Desvallières (1857–1926); *Le dindon* (The Turkey; The Gull; The Pigeon; The Dupe; 1896); *La dame de chez Maxim* (The Lady from Maxim's; 1899); *Occupe-toi d'Amélie* (Keep an Eye on Amélie; 1908); *La puce à l'oreille* (A Flea in Her Ear; 1907); *Feu la mère de madame* (Madame's Late Mother; 1908); *On purge bébé* (Let's Get Rid of It!; Going to Pot; 1910); *Mais n'te promène donc pas toute nue!* (Stop Walking Around Stark Naked!; 1911). An expression from *La puce à l'oreille* has become famous as typifying the French farce: in the midst of the confusion in a hotel staircase, Raymonde, the wife of Victor-Emmanuel Chandebise, surprised to think that he is there, exclaims, "Ciel! mon mari!" (Heavens, my husband!). This is often confused with the line from Becque's *La Parisienne*, written twenty-two years earlier than the Feydeau farce: "Prenez garde, voilà mon mari!" (Watch out, there's my husband!)

Aleksander Fredro (1793–1876; Polish subject of Austro-Hungarian Empire) Aristocrat, political activist, playwright; forty comedies, including *Pan Geldhab* (Mister Geldhab; written 1818; produced 1821); *Sluby panienskie, czyli Magnetyzm serca* (Maidens' Vows, or The Magnetism of the Heart; written 1827; produced 1833); *Zemsta* (Vengeance; 1833).

W. S. Gilbert [Sir William Schwenck Gilbert] (1836–1911; English) Barrister, poet, playwright, stage director; sixty-nine plays, parodies, pastiches, and burlesques, including *The Pretty Druidess, or The Mother, the Maid, and the Mistletoe Bough* (1869), a satire of Bellini's *Norma*; and comic opera libretti, including the fourteen Gilbert and Sullivan pieces written in collaboration with composer Sir Arthur Seymour Sullivan (1842–1900), among them *H.M.S. Pinafore, or The Lass That Loved A Sailor* (1878), *The Pirates of Penzance, or The Slave of Duty* (1879), and *The Mikado, or The Town of Titipu* (1885), their greatest hits; plays include *Pygmalion and Galatea* (1871); *The Wicked World* (1873); *Sweethearts* (1874); *Engaged* (1877); *Brantinghame Hall* (1888); *Rosencrantz and Guildenstern: A Tragic Episode, in Three Tabloids* (1891), a satire of *Hamlet*, in which Brandon Thomas (see below) played Claudius in an 1892 revival.

Alexandr Sergeyevich Griboyedov (1795–1829; Russian) Seven plays, including the major verse comedy classic *Gore ot uma* (Woe from Wit; written 1823; published privately and circulated in1825; censored and banned; partial version published in 1833; finally published complete in 1861).

Ludovic Halévy (1834–1908; French) Novelist, known for *L'abbé Constantin* (1862), dramatized in 1887 by Hector-Jonathan Crémieux (1828–1892) and Pierre Decourcelle (1856–1926); playwright, librettist; wrote many projects in collaboration; libretto to Bizet's *Carmen* (1875), with Meilhac; libretti to Offenbach's *Orphée aux enfers* (Orpheus in the Underworld; 1858), *La chanson de Fortunio* (Fortunio's Song; 1861), and *Le pont des soupirs* (The Bridge of Sighs;1868), all with Hector Crémieux; libretti to Offenbach's *La belle Hélène* (Beautiful Helen; 1864), *Barbe-bleue* (Bluebeard; 1866), *La Vie parisienne* (Parisian

Life; 1866), *La Grande-duchesse de Gérolstein* (The Grand Duchess of Gérolstein; 1867), *La Périchole* (1868), and *Les Brigands* (The Brigands; 1869), all with Meilhac.

See also below, under Henri Meilhac: the works they wrote together comprise eight volumes.

Harrigan and Hart: Edward Harrigan (1845–1911; American) Actor, playwright, composer, theater manager; and **Tony Hart** [Anthony J. Cannon] (1855–1891; American), actor, writer, lyricist; team of writer-performers, famous for such comedies as *Old Lavender* (1877), *The Major* (1881) and *McSorley's Infatuation* (1882); best known for their highly successful *Mulligan Guards* series of burlesque musical plays, of which the first was *The Mulligan Guards' Ball* (1879), with music by Harrigan's father-in-law, David Braham (1838–1905), known as "The American Offenbach."

Alfred Jarry (1873–1907; French) Novelist, dramatist; two highly influential farces, both political, bitterly satiric, and precursive of surrealism and of the theater of the absurd: *Ubu roi* (Ubu King; written, 1888; produced, 1896); its sequel, *Ubu enchaîné* (Ubu in Chains; 1900).

August von Kotzebue (1761–1819; German) Two hundred twenty-seven plays (some in one act), adaptations, comedies, comic opera libretti, dramas, melodramas; comedies include *Die Indianer in England* (The Indians in England; 1789); *Die beiden Klingsberg* (The Two Klingsbergs; 1799); *Die deutschen Kleinstädter* (The German Small-Town People; 1802); *Blind geladen* (Loaded with Blanks; 1811), adapted for the English stage as *How to Die for Love: A Farce in Two Acts* (1812).

Eugène Labiche (1813–1888; French) One hundred seventy-two plays, comedies, farces, some written with collaborators; including *Le Chapeau de paille d'Italie* (The Italian Straw Hat; 1851), in collaboration with Marc Michel (1812–1868); *Le Voyage de M. Perrichon* (M. Perrichon's Trip; 1860).

Henri Meilhac (1831–1897; French) Librettist, playwright; wrote many projects in collaboration with Ludovic Halévy, see above; ca. eighty comedies, farces, and comic opera libretti, including the comedies *Les curieuses* (The Curious Women; 1864); *Fabienne* (1865); written in collaboration with Halévy: *Frou-Frou* (The Show-Off; 1869) and *Le réveillon* (The New Year's Eve Dinner Party; 1872), the basis for Johann Strauss's *Die Fledermaus* (The Bat; 1874).

Johann Nestroy (1801–1862; Austrian) Actor, playwright; eighty-three plays, including many folk dramas, among them *Der böse Lumpazivagabundus oder Das leiderliche Kleeblatt* (The Evil Spirit Lumpazivagabundus, or The Roguish Trio; 1833); comedies and farces adapted from French sources, original pieces, satires; often used the Viennese dialect; comedies include *Das Mädl aus der Vorstadt, oder Ehrlich währt am längsten* (The Lass from the Suburbs, or Honesty Is the Best Policy; 1841); *Einen Jux will er sich machen* (He Wants to Have a Fling; 1842); *Kampl, oder Das Mädchen mit Millionen und die Näherin* (Kampl, or The Millionairess and the Seamstress; 1852).

Alexandr Nikolayevich Ostrovsky (1823–1886; Russian) One of the most important Russian playwrights; fifty-four plays in all genres, including the tragedy *Groza* (The Storm; 1859), the fairy-tale fantasy *Snegurochka* (The Snow Maiden; 1873), and the comedies *Svoi lyudi—sochtyemsya!* (Our Own People—We'll Settle It!; A Family Affair—We'll Settle It Ourselves!; writtten1849; produced 1860); *Byednaya nyevyesta* (The Poor Bride; 1853); *Nye ve svoi sani nye sadyis!* (If It's Not Your Sled, Don't Sit On It; 1853); *Na vsyakogo myudryetsa dovolno prostoty* (Enough Stupidity for Every Wise Man; usually called Diary of a Scoundrel; 1886).

James Robinson Planché (1796–1880; English) Wrote, adapted, or translated one hundred seventy-six plays, extravaganzas, comedies, farces, burlettas, and opera libretti; among his extravaganzas, published in several volumes: *Blue Beard: A Grand Musical, Comi-Tragical, Melo-Dramatic, Burlesque Burletta* (1839), in collaboration with Charles Dance (1794–1863); *Harlequin and the Giant Helmet, or The Castle of Otranto* (a parody-adaptation of Horace Walpole's [1719–1777] novel [1764]; 1840); *The Discreet Princess, or The Three Glass Distaffs* (1855).

Victorien Sardou (1831–1908; French) Seventy-eight tragedies, melodramas, plays, and comic opera libretti, including *Le Roi Carotte* (King Carrot; 1872), music by Jacques Offenbach; the comedy *Piccolino* (1861), made over into a comic opera in 1876 in collaboration with Charles Nuitter (1828–1899), who also wrote libretti for Offenbach, Lecocq and other composers, and music by Ernest Guiraud (1837–1892), known for his work on Bizet's *Carmen* and Offenbach's *Les contes d'Hoffmann*; and the comedy *Divorçons* (Let's Divorce; 1880). He is best known nowadays for his melodramatic play *La Tosca* (1887), on which Puccini's opera was based.

Eugène Scribe [Augustin Eugène Scribe] (1791–1861; French) His works comprise seventy-six volumes, including one hundred seventy-four comédie-vaudevilles, thirty-five comedy-dramas, thirty-seven opera libretti and ballet scenarios, and eighty-six comic opera libretti; ca. four hundred twenty-five works in all, the exact number, including revised titles and those written in collaboration, impossible to determine, according to expert historian and biographer, Jean-Claude Yon in *Eugène Scribe: la fortune et la liberté* (Librairie A. G. Nizet, 2000); many were written in collaboration, and many were one-act pieces. His most notable comic plays include *L'ours et le pacha* (The Bear and the Pasha; 1820), written in collaboration with Xavier Boniface Saintine (1798–1865); *Le menteur véridique* (The Truthful Liar; 1823); *Le mariage d'argent* (Marriage for Money; 1827); *Bertrand et Raton* (Bertrand and Raton; 1833); *Le verre d'eau, ou Les effets et les causes* (The Glass of Water, or Causes and Effects; 1840).

Brandon Thomas [Walter Brandon Thomas] (1848–1914; English) Major comic actor; pamphleteer, songwriter, playwright; ten plays, among them his first great success, *Comrades* (1882); *A Highland Legacy* (1888); *Marriage* (1892); best known for his internationally successful three-act farce *Charley's Aunt* (1892).

Théodore-Ferdinand Vallou de Villeneuve (1799–1858; French) Opera librettist, serious dramatist, prolific comic playwright who often wrote in collaboration; known for his more than one hundred boulevard vaudevilles (farces; see glossary), including *Le premier prix, ou Les deux artistes* (First Prize, or The Two Artists; 1822); *La dette d'honneur* (The Debt of Honor; 1826); *Le bateau de blanchisseuses* (The Laundresses' Boat; 1832); *Voltaire en vacances* (Voltaire on Vacation; 1836); *Yelva, ou L'orpheline russe* (Yelva, or The Russian Orphan; 1840).

Oscar Wilde [Oscar Fingal O'Flahertie Wills Wilde] (1854–1900; Irish) Poet, aesthete, essayist; one novel, *The Picture of Dorian Gray*; eight plays, including four major comedies, *Lady Windermere's Fan* (1892); *A Woman of No Importance* (1893); *An Ideal Husband* (1895); *The Importance of Being Earnest* (1895).

Twentieth and Twenty-First Centuries

Edward Albee (b. 1928; American) Thirty-two plays as of this writing, among them his first play, the one-act tragic drama, *The Zoo Story* (written, 1958); the one-act satires, *The Sandbox* (1959) and *The American Dream* (1961); and the sardonic full-length, absurdist comedy-dramas, *Who's Afraid of Virginia Woolf* (1962; film,1966); *A Delicate Balance* (1967; film 1973); *The Lady from Dubuque* (1977); *Three Tall Women* (1990); *The Goat or Who is Sylvia?* (2002).

The Álvarez Quintero Brothers: Serafín Álvarez Quintero (1871–1938); **Joaquin Álvarez Quintero** (1873–1944) Prolific Spanish playwrights known for their sunny, sentimental comedies and one-act *sainetes* (farces); two hundred thirty plays, including *Las flores* (The Flowers; 1901); *La zagala* (The Country Girl; 1904); *Mañana de sol* (A Sunny Morning; 1905); *El genio alegre* (The Merry Heart; 1906); *El centenario* (The Hundred-Year Old; 1909); *La flor de la vida* (The Prime of Life; 1910); *La puebla de las mujeres* (The City of Women; 1912); *Fortunato* (1912).

Jean Anouilh [Jean Marie Lucien Pierre Anouilh] (1910–1987; French) Dramatist; forty plays; known for both his serious dramas, such as *Antigone* (1942), *L'Alouette* (The Lark; 1952), and *Beckett, ou l'honneur de dieu* (Beckett or the Honor of God; 1959; film,, 1964); and for his comedies, among them *Le bal des voleurs* (Thieves' Carnival; 1938); *L'Invitation au château* (Invitation to the Chateau; usually known as Ring around the Moon; 1947); *La valse des toréadors* (Waltz of the Toreadors; 1952).

Alan Ayckbourn (b. 1939; English) Seventy-four plays as of this writing, including his first great success, *Relatively Speaking* (1967); *How the Other Half Loves* (1969); *Absurd Person Singular* (1972; television adaptation, 1985); *The Norman Conquests* (1973; television adaptation, 1977), a trilogy; *Bedroom Farce* (1975; revival, 1978; television adaptation, 1980).

J. M. Barrie (1860–1937; Scottish) Novelist, playwright; forty-one plays including *Quality Street* (1901); *The Admirable Crichton* (1902); the perennially popular and often adapted *Peter Pan, or The Boy Who Would Not Grow Up* (1904); *What Every Woman Knows* (1908); *Dear Brutus* (1917).

Philip Barry (1896–1949; American) Twenty-two plays, including the comedies of manners, *Paris Bound* (1927; film, 1929); *Holiday* (1928; film, 1938); *Here Come the Clowns* (1938); *The Philadelphia Story* (1939; film, 1940; adapted as film musical, *High Society*, 1956).

Samuel Beckett [Samuel Barclay Beckett] (1906–1989; Irish) Lived mostly in Paris; wrote in French and English; novelist, playwright, essayist, critic, poet, short-story writer, nonfiction writer; friend and sometime amanuensis of James Joyce (1882–1941); Nobel Prize in Literature, 1969; eight novels; seven radio plays; twenty-three stage plays, absurdist comedies, and satires, including *En attendant Godot* (*Waiting for Godot*, his own translation; 1953); *Fin de partie* (*Endgame*, his own translation, 1957); *Krapp's Last Tape* (1958); *Happy Days* (1961).

Alan Bennett (b. 1934; English) Actor and prolific book, radio, television, film and stage writer of dramas and comedies; eighteen stage plays as of this writing; co-author of and performer in the satirical revue *Beyond the Fringe* (1960); author of the West End and Broadway hit *The History Boys* (2004; film, 2006), a comedy-drama; screenplay for the biopic *Prick Up Your Ears* (1987), based on the book by John Lahr (b. 1941).

Charles Busch (b. 1954; American) Playwright, screenwriter, actor, female impersonator, stage director; three screenplays and twenty-two stage plays as of this writing, among them *Vampire Lesbians of Sodom* (1984); *Theodora, She-Bitch of Byzantium* (1984); *Psycho Beach Party* (1987); *Die, Mommie, Die* (1999; film 2003); *The Tale of the Allergist's Wife* (2000); *The Tribute Artist* (2013).

Gaston Arman de Caillavet (1869–1915; French) Journalist, playwright; son of Mme. Arman de Caillavet [Léontine Lippmann] (1844–1910), salon hostess, mistress and muse of Nobel Prize-winning author and member of the Académie Française, Anatole France (1844–1924); collaborated with Robert de Flers (see below) on opera libretti and satirical and sentimental boulevard comedies, for which Caillavet wrote the hilarious dialogue.

Marc Connelly (1890–1980; American) Actor, playwright, lyricist; wrote seventeen books for musicals and plays, in collaboration or alone, including *Merton of the Movies* (1922); *To the Ladies* (1922); *The Deep Tangled Wildwood* (1923); *Beggar on Horseback* (1924), all four written with George S. Kauffman; *The Green Pastures* (1930).

See also below, under George S. Kaufman.

Noël Coward (1899–1973; English) Stage and screen actor, short story writer, novelist, diarist, lyricist, composer, playwright, songwriter, vocalist, cabaret performer; fifty-nine works for the stage and screen, including musical books; among his plays are *Fallen Angels* (1925); *Hay Fever* (1925; television film, 1984); *Tonight at 8:30* (1935), an evening of one-act plays, also done as a television series, 1991; *Private Lives* (1930; film 1931); *Design for Living* (1933; film, 1933); *Blithe Spirit* (1941; film, 1945), billed by Coward as an "improbable farce"; *Present Laughter* (1942).

Fernand Crommelynck (1886–1970; Belgian) Actor, journalist, playwright; known for his sophisticated, ironic comedies; eleven produced plays, among them *Nous n'irons plus au bois* (We Won't Go Back to the Woods; 1906); *Le sculpteur de masques* (The Sculptor of Masks; 1911); *L'agent Rigolo et son chien policier* (Agent Rigolo and His Police Dog; 1912); *Les Amants puérils* (The Puerile Lovers; written, 1913; produced 1920); *Le Cocu magnifique* (The Magnificent Cuckold; 1920), a "lyrical farce," considered his masterpiece; *Tripes d'or* (Golden Guts; 1925); *Chaud et froid* (Hot and Cold; 1936).

Russel Crouse (1893–1966; American) Actor, playwright, librettist, producer; ca. twenty plays and musical comedy books, many written in collaboration.

See below, under Howard Lindsay.

Eduardo De Filippo (1900–1984; Italian) Actor, poet, playwright, screenwriter; more than fifty plays and screenplays, including those adapted from his stage plays; his works include many one-act farces and full-length dramas and comedies, often in Neapolitan dialect; comedies include *Questi fantasmi!* (Oh, These Ghosts; 1946); *Filumena Marturano* (1946), filmed by Vittorio de Sica as *Matrimonio all'italiana* (Marriage, Italian Style; 1964); *La grande magia* (The Grand Magic; 1949); *Sabato, domenica e lunedì* (Saturday, Sunday, Monday; 1959).

Christopher Durang (b. 1949; American) Actor, playwright; fifty satirical dark, absurdist full-length and one-act comedies as of this writing, including *The Idiots Karamazov* (1974), co-written with Albert Innaurato (b. 1947); *The Nature and Purpose of the Universe* (1975), in which I created the roles of the Coach and the Pope; *A History of the*

American Film (1978); *Sister Mary Ignatius Explains It All For You* (1979; film, 2001); *The Marriage of Bette and Boo* (1985); *Beyond Therapy* (1981; film, which Durang felt had destroyed his play, 1987); *Durang / Durang* (1994), an evening of one-act plays; *Vanya and Sonia and Masha and Spike* (2013).

Jules Feiffer (b. 1929; American) Award-winning cartoonist, satirist. author, playwright, screenwriter, teacher; wrote twenty-five books, fifteen screenplays, including *Carnal Knowledge* (1971), directed by Mike Nichols; *Popeye* (1980), directed by Robert Altman; fourteen plays, including *Little Murders* (1967; film 1971); *The White House Murder Case* (1969); *Grown Ups* (1981).

Robert de Flers [Robert Pellevé de la Motte-Ango, marquis de Flers] (1872–1927; French) Fellow student and friend of Marcel Proust at the Lycée Condorcet; married Geneviève Sardou, daughter of Victorien Sardou (see above); member of the Académie Française; journalist, novelist, short-story writer; wrote thirty-nine libretti and plays, most in collaboration, among them twelve opera and operetta libretti, eight with Gaston Arman de Caillavet; twenty-three boulevard comedies, seventeen written in collaboration with Caillavet, among them, *Le Roi* (The King; 1908); *Le Bois sacré* (The Sacred Wood; 1910); *L'Habit vert* (The Academician's Green Coat; literally, The Green Outfit or Suit, referring to the French Academician's uniform coat; 1912), often considered their masterpiece. Flers devised the plots and characters, while Caillavet wrote the comic dialogue. Flers later collaborated on eight plays and libretti with librettist and dramatist, Francis de Croisset [Franz Wiener] (1877–1937).

Larry Gelbart (1928–2009; American) Radio, television, film, and stage writer; wrote forty-two projects, including the radio series *Duffy's Tavern* (1941–1951); television series *M*A*S*H* (1972–1982); Stephen Sondheim Broadway musical book, *A Funny Thing Happened on the Way to the Forum* (1962), co-written with Burt Shevelove (1915–1982); *Sly*

Fox (1976), a Broadway adaptation of Ben Jonson's *Volpone*; screenplay for *Tootsie* (1982), co-written with Murray Schisgal.

Simon Gray [Simon James Holiday Gray] (1936–2008; English) Diarist, memoirist; five novels; forty stage, film, and television plays and adaptations, including *Butley* (1971); *Otherwise Engaged* (1975); *Quartermaine's Terms* (1981).

John Guare (b. 1938; American) Playwright, screenwriter, librettist; sixteen plays as of this writing; known for his wry, rueful comedies, among them *The House of Blue Leaves* (1971); *The Landscape of the Body* (1977); *Six Degrees of Separation* (1990).

Sacha Guitry (1885–1957; French) Actor, film director, screenwriter, playwright; son of the great actor Lucien Guitry (1860–1925); career in decline after World War Two, because of his involvement with the Vichy government; officially absolved, 1947; thirty books; thirty-six screenplays, directed thirty-three films, in many of which he also acted, including *Le roman d'un tricheur* (The Story of a Cheat; 1936); *Les perles de la couronne* (The Crown Pearls; 1937); one hundred twenty-four stage plays, including *La jalousie* (Jealousy; 1915); *Mon père avait raison* (My Father Was Right; 1920; film, 1936).

Moss Hart (1904–1961; American) Theater director, librettist, playwright; known for his collaborations with George S. Kaufman (see below); books for Irving Berlin's *Face the Music* (1932) and *As Thousands Cheer* (1933), Cole Porter's *Jubilee* (1935); Richard Rodgers' *I'd Rather Be Right* (1937), book written in collaboration with George S. Kaufman, lyrics by Lorenz Hart (1895–1943).

Eugène Ionesco (1909–1994; Romanian-French) Thirty plays, most in the theater of the absurd genre, including the one-acters *La cantatrice chauve* (The Bald Soprano; written 1948; produced 1950), *La leçon* (The Lesson; 1950), and *Les chaises* (The Chairs; 1952); *Rhinocéros* (Rhinoceros; three acts; written 1957; produced 1960).

George S. Kaufman [George Simon Kaufman] (1889–1961; American) Forty-three plays and musicals, most in collaboration with various writing partners, including *Dulcy* (1921; film, 1940), with Marc Connelly (see also above); *A Night at the Opera* (1935), screenplay for the Marx Brothers, written in collaboration with Morrie Ryskind (1895–1985); *Once in a Lifetime* (1930; film, 1937); *Merrily We Roll Along* (1934); *You Can't Take It with You* (1936; film, 1938); *The Man Who Came to Dinner* (1939; film, 1942); *George Washington Slept Here* (1940), all with Moss Hart; *The Solid Gold Cadillac* (1953), written with Howard Teichmann (1916–1987).

George Kelly (1887–1974; American) Actor, producer, playwright; directed most of his own pieces; sixteen plays, most of them comedies, including The Faltering Words (1919); his most famous, *The Torchbearers* (1921) and *The Show-Off* (1924).

Howard Lindsay (1889–1968; American) Actor, director, producer, playwright; more than twenty-five plays and musical comedy books, most written in collaboration, notably with Russell Crouse; their plays and musicals include *Life with Father* (1939; film, 1948, starring William Powel [1892–1984] and Irene Dunne [1898–1990]; television series, 1953); its sequel, *Life with Mother* (1948), with both stage plays, adapted from the books by Clarence Day (1874–1975) starring Lindsey and his wife Dorothy Stickney (1896–1998) as Mr. and Mrs. Clarence Day; *State of the Union* (1945); book for Irving Berlin's *Call Me Madam* (1950; film, 1953), with both the stage and film versions starring Ethel Merman (1908–1984); *The Great Sebastians* (1956), starring Alfred Lunt (1892–1977) and Lynn Fontanne (1887–1983); book for Rodgers and Hammerstein's *The Sound of Music* (1959; film, 1965); *Mr. President* (1962). With Damon Runyon (1880–1946), he wrote *A Slight Case of Murder* (1935; film, 1938).

Frederick Lonsdale (1881–1954; English) Playwright, librettist; twenty-two plays and musical comedy books, including the West End and Broadway hit operetta *The Maid of the Mountains* (1914); known for his satirical comedies about upper-middle-class life, among them *Aren't We All?* (1923); *Spring Cleaning* (1923); *The Last of Mrs. Cheyney* (1925); *On Approval* (1927); *Once Is Enough* (1938).

Charles Ludlam (1943–1987; American) Actor, director, playwright; founded the Ridiculous Theater Company, 1967; known for his outrageous, campy sense of humor and satire; twenty-nine comedies, including *Conquest of the Universe, or When Queens Collide* (1968); *Eunuchs of the Forbidden City* (1971); *Camille* (1973); *Der Ring Gott Farblonjet* (1977), an adaptation of Wagner's *Ring* cycle; *The Ventriloquist's Wife* (1978); *The Mystery of Irma Vep* (1984).

David Mamet (b. 1947; American) Author, playwright, film director, teacher, essayist; thirty-four plays and eighteen screenplays as of this writing, including *Sexual Perversity in Chicago* (1974); *American Buffalo* (1975; film 1996); *Glengarry Glen Ross* (1984; film 1992).

W. S. Maugham [William Somerset Maugham] (1874–1965; English) Short story writer, novelist, playwright; successful in London and New York; thirty-two plays, including sixteen comedies, among them *Our Betters* (1917); *The Circle* (written 1919; produced 1921); *The Constant Wife* (1926).

Ferenc Molnár [Ferenc Neumann] (1878–1952; Hungarian-American) Journalist, memoirist, novelist, playwright; fled Nazis and emigrated to New York, 1940; twenty-nine plays, mostly comedies, many adapted for the American stage and/or screen; his plays include *A doktor úr* (The Attorney-at-Law; 1902); *Az ördög* (The Devil; 1907); *Liliom* (drama, 1909; the basis for Rogers and Hammerstein's 1945 Broadway musical *Carousel*); *A testör* (The Guardsman; 1910; a 1924 Broadway hit comedy and 1931 film, both starring Alfred Lunt and Lynn Fontanne; the plot was used as the basis for a completely transformed 1941 film version of the operetta *The Chocolate Soldier* by Oscar Straus (adapted from George Bernard Shaw's comedy *Arms and the Man*), with only his music retained, and starring Nelson Eddy and Risë Stevens); *A* *hattyú* (The Swan; 1920; filmed in 1956 with Grace Kelly and Alec Guinness); *Játék a kastélyban* (A Play at the Castle; adapted in 1926 by prolific Anglo-American comic novelist, short story writer, librettist, and playwright P. G. Wodehouse as *The Play's the Thing*, and in 1984 by Tom Stoppard as *Rough Crossing*.

Sean O'Casey [John Casey] (1880–1964; Irish) Poet, essayist, playwright known for his left-wing politics; twenty-two plays, mostly comedies and tragicomedies, among them *Juno and the Paycock* (1924); *The Plough and the Stars* (1926); *Purple Dust* (1944); *Cock-a-Doodle-Dandy* (1949); *The Bishop's Bonfire* (1955).

Joe Orton (1933–1967; English) Writer, playwright; three novels, one screenplay, nine black comedies, giving rise to the adjective "Ortonesque," meaning outrageously bizarre, macabre, and odd; *Entertaining Mister Sloane* (1964); *Loot* (1965); *The Erpingham Camp* (1967); *What the Butler Saw* (1969). In 1987, Stephen Frears' biographical film, *Prick Up Your Ears*—the title is an Ortonesque pun—screenplay by Alan Bennett and John Lahr (b. 1941), and starring Gary Oldman as Joe Orton and Alfred Molina as his lover and murderer, Kenneth Halliwell.

Marcel Pagnol (1895–1974; French) Playwright, memoirist, novelist, film producer, screenwriter; thirteen plays and thirty-five films, for which he wrote the scripts and many of which he also directed; best known for his sentimental, nostalgic romantic trilogy of comedies set in Marseille, *Marius* (1929; film 1931), *Fanny* (1931; film 1932), *César* (film, 1936; play adapted from film, 1946); *Jazz* (1926); *Topaze* (1928; films 1933, 1936); *La femme du boulanger* (The Baker's Wife; 1938), adapted from the short story by noted Provençal writer Jean Giono (1895–1970); *La fille du puisatier* (The Well-Digger's Daughter; 1940).

Harold Pinter (1930–2008; English) Actor, theater director, screenwriter, playwright; left-wing political activist; received twenty honorary degrees and many awards, including Nobel Prize in Literature, 2005;

twenty-seven screenplays, fifteen sketches, and twenty-nine stage plays, including the "comedies of menace," *The Room* (1957); *The Birthday Party* (1957); *The Hothouse* (1958; revised 1980); *The Caretaker* (1959); *The Dumb Waiter* (1959); *The Homecoming* (1964). The adjective "Pinteresque" describes an atmosphere of nameless dread and menace, but one with absurdist, ironic, comic overtones: "Pinteresque pauses."

Luigi Pirandello (1867–1936; Italian) Short-story writer, novelist, major playwright; influenced by naturalism, surrealism, and fantasies of illusion and reality; forty-four works for the theater in many genres, including twenty-one comedies, among them *Cecè* (Chee-Chee; written 1913; produced 1920); *Pensaci, Giacomino!* (Let's Think about It, Giacomino!; 1916); *Liolà* (1916), written in Sicilian, translated into Italian by Pirandello; *Il berretto e sonagli* (Cap and Bells; 1917); *Ma non è una cosa seria* (But It's Not a Serious Thing; 1918); *Il giuoco delle parti* (The Rules of the Game; 1918); *Sei personaggi in cerca d'autore* (Six Characters in Search of an Author; 1921), his most well known comedy; *Ciascuno a suo modo* (Each In His Own Way; 1924).

Terence Rattigan [Sir Terence Mervyn Rattigan] (1911–1977; English) Playwright, screenwriter; collaborated on twelve screenplays; six television plays; twenty-six superbly crafted, well-made stage plays, both comedy and drama, many of them later filmed; dramas include *The Winslow Boy* (1946; films, 1948; 1999); *The Browning Version* (1948; films, 1951; 1994); *The Deep Blue Sea* (1952; film, 1955); *Separate Tables* (1954; film, 1958); comedies include *French Without Tears* (1936; film 1940); *While the Sun Shines* (1943; film, 1947); *Love in Idleness* (1944); *The Sleeping Prince* (1953; filmed as *The Prince and the Showgirl*, 1957).

Jules Romain [penname of Louis Henri Jean Farigoule] (1885–1972; French) Novelist, known for his major series, *Les hommes de bonne volonté* (The Men of Good Will); member of the Académie Française; playwright; thirteen satirical fables and comedies, including *L'Armée dans la ville* (The Army in Town; 1911); the one-act *Amédée ou les messieurs en rang* (Amédée, or The Gentleman Lined Up; 1923); *Monsieur Trouhadec* *saisi par la débauche* (Monsieur Trouhadec Gripped by Debauchery; 1923); *Knock ou le triomphe de la médicine* (Knock, or The Triumph of Medicine; 1924; film, 1933, both starring Louis Jouvet), considered his masterpiece; *Le mariage de monsieur Trouhadec* (Monsieur Trouhadec's Marriage; 1925); *Donogoo* (1930).

Murray Schisgal (b. 1926; American) See also under Larry Gelbart, above; screenwriter, playwright; nine comedies as of this writing, including *Luv* (1964); *All Over Town* (1974); *Twice around the Park* (1982).

George Bernard Shaw (1856–1950; Irish) Lived and worked mostly in England; music and theater critic, novelist, essayist, playwright; Fabian Socialist activist; known for his wit and his "comedies of ideas," which he called "problem plays"; sixty-three plays, including *Arms and the Man* (1894; operetta adaptation by Oscar Straus as *Der Praliné-Soldat* [The Chocolate Soldier], 1908); *Candida* (1897); *The Devil's Disciple* (1897); *Caesar and Cleopatra* (1898; produced 1906; film 1945); *You Never Can Tell* (1899); *Pygmalion* (1913; film, 1938; Broadway musical adaptation by Lerner and Loewe as *My Fair Lady*, 1956); *Major Barbara* (1905; film 1941); *Man and Superman* (1905); *Androcles and the Lion* (1913; film 1952); *Heartbreak House* (written 1916–1917; produced 1920); *The Apple Cart* (1929); *The Millionairess* (1936; film, 1960); *"In Good King Charles's Golden Days"* (1939).

Neil Simon [Marvin Neil Simon] (b. 1927; American) Prolific television, film, and stage writer; thirty-seven screenplays and thirty-four plays as of this writing, among them *Come Blow Your Horn* (1961; film 1963); *Barefoot in the Park* (1963; film, 1967); *The Odd Couple* (1965; film 1968; television series, 1970–1975; Simon wrote six episodes for the 1970 season; the rest were written by many others); *Plaza Suite* (1968; film 1987); *The Prisoner of Second Avenue* (1971; film 1975); *The Sunshine Boys* (1972; film 1975); *The Good Doctor* (1973; television film, 1978); *Brighton Beach Memoirs* (1983; film 1986); *Biloxi Blues* (1985; film 1988); *Broadway Bound* (1986; film 1992); *Lost in Yonkers* (1991; film 1993); *The Goodbye Girl* (1993; film 1977); *Laughter on the 23rd Floor* (1993; television film 2001). Simon wrote the screenplays for the film and television adaptations.

Carl Sternheim (1878–1942; German) Critic, novelist, playwright, known for his satires of the German bourgeoisie and its values; thirty-one plays, including *Die Hose* (The Underpants; 1911), his most famous comedy in the Anglophone world; *Die Kassette* (The Strongbox; 1911); *Bürger Schippel* (Citizen Schippel; 1913); *Der Snob* (The Snob; 1914).

Tom Stoppard (b. 1937; Czech-born English) Radio, television, film, and theater writer of original plays and adaptations; ten original radio plays; seventeen film and television screenplays, including both original work and adaptations; thirty-three stage plays as of this writing, including *Rosencrantz and Guildenstern Are Dead* (1966); *The Real Inspector Hound* (1968); *Jumpers* (1972); *Travesties* (1974); *Dirty Linen and New-Found Land* (1976); *Rough Crossing* (1984), based on Ferenc Molnar's *A Play at the Castle* (1926); *Arcadia* (1993); *The Coast of Utopia* (2002), a trilogy: *Voyage*, *Shipwreck*, and *Salvage*.

Ben Travers (1886–1980; English) Novelist, playwright; twenty-one plays; known for his nine popular "Aldwych farces," produced at London's Aldwych Theatre from 1925 to 1933; the most famous is *Rookery Nook* (1926), adapted from his 1923 novel; *Plunder* (1928); *Turkey Time* (1931).

Pierre Véber (1869–1942; French) Journalist, operetta librettist, playwright, often with collaborators; novelist and short story writer, with thirty-three books to his credit; seventy full-length plays, forty-six one-act plays, most boulevard comedies; plays include *Dix ans après* (Ten Years Later; 1897), written in collaboration with Lucien Muhlfeld (1870–1902); *Loute* (translated as *The Lady from Rector's*; 1902); *Frère Jacques* (Brother Jacques; 1904); *Chambre à part* (A Separate Room; 1905); *Les grands* (The Adults; 1909), written in collaboration with Serge Basset (1865–1917); *La présidente* (Madame President; 1912), written with his frequent collaborator, Maurice Hennequin (1863–1926).

Louis Verneuil [Louis Jacques Marie Collin du Bocage] (1893–1952; French) Actor, stage director, playwright; author of sixty witty, insouciant boulevard comedies, including one written in English for Broadway, *Affairs of State* (1950; 610 performances); sixty-four original screenplays and screen adaptations of his works; many comedies written for the Romanian-born stage and screen actress, a ravishing beauty, Elvire Popescu (1894–1993), among them *Ma cousine de Varsovie* (My Cousin from Warsaw; 1923; television film, 1990); *Pile ou face* (Heads or Tails; 1924); *L'Amant de Madame Vidal* (Madame Vidal's Lover; 1928); *Une femme ravie* (A Delighted Woman; 1932).

Wendy Wasserstein (1950–2006; American) Award-winning playwright; screenwriter; author of five books; eleven plays, among them her first, *Any Woman Can't* (1973); *Uncommon Women and Others* (1977); *The Heidi Chronicles* (Pulitzer Prize and Tony Award; 1989); *The Sisters Rosensweig* (1992).

Lanford Wilson [Lanford Eugene Wilson] (1937–2011; American) Playwright; one of the founders of the Off-Broadway theater movement; twenty-one dramas and comedies, including the one-acter *The Madness of Lady Bright* (1964); the full-length plays, *Lemon Sky* (1970); *The Hot L Baltimore* (1973); *The Talley Trilogy: Talley's Folly* (1979), *Fifth of July* (1978), *Talley and Son* (1981).

P. G. Wodehouse [Pelham Grenville Wodehouse] (1881–1975; Anglo-American) Prolific comic novelist and short story writer, known for the Blandings Castle series, the Jeeves and Wooster series, the Mr. Mulliner stories, the Drones Club stories, and much more, many adapted for stage and screen; screenwriter, playwright, librettist; became an American citizen in 1955; twelve screenplays, thirty-six plays, including adaptations of his literary works, and musical comedy books, among the latter *Leave It to Jane* (1917); *Oh, Lady, Lady!* (1918), *Sally* (1920), *Anything Goes* (1934), all written with his frequent collaborator and fellow Anglo-American, Guy Bolton (1884–1979), and with music by Jerome Kern; *Oh, Kay!* (1926), with Guy Bolton, lyrics by Ira Gershwin, music by George Gershwin; plays include *The Play's the Thing* (1926; see above under Ferenc Molnar); *Her Cardboard Lover* (1927); *Good Morning, Bill* (1928).

Appendix Two

Major Comedy Screenwriters and Film Directors

Woody Allen [Allen Konigsberg] (b. 1935; American) Actor, screenwriter, playwright, satirist, director, film producer, composer, author; wrote or collaborated on seventy-three screenplays as of this writing; directed fifty films; actor in forty-five films; usually acts in the films he has written and directed, among them, *Bananas* (1971); *Sleepers* (1973); *Annie Hall* (1977); *Manhattan* (1979); *Zelig* (1983); *Broadway Danny Rose* (1984); *Hannah and Her Sisters* (1986); *Shadows and Fog* (1991); *Manhattan Murder Mystery* (1993); *Small Time Crooks* (2000); *The Case of the Jade Scorpion* (2001); also wrote and directed *The Purple Rose of Cairo* (1985); *Bullets Over Broadway* (1994), co-screenwriter Douglas McGrath (b. 1958); *Match Point* (2005), a sardonic comedy-drama; the romantic comedy *Vicky Cristina Barcelona* (2008); and the delightful *Midnight in Paris* (2011), starring the beautiful, charming Rachel McAdams, the brilliant comic actor Owen Wilson, and the superb Kathy Bates; *To Rome with Love* (2012); *Blue Jasmine* (2013), a comedy-drama that pays tribute to Tennessee Williams's *A Streetcar Named Desire*; *Magic in the Moonlight* (2014).

Andrew Bergman (b. 1945; American) Writer, director, producer; has written fourteen comedy projects as of this writing, including co-writing Mel Brooks's *Blazing Saddles* (1974) with Brooks, comedian Richard Pryor (1940–2005), Alan Uger, and Norman Steinberg (b. 1939); *Oh, God, You Devil* (1984); *The Freshman* (1990); *Soapdish* (1991), a screamingly funny satire of television soap operas, written with Robert

Harling (b. 1951), author of *Steel Magnolias* (film 1989); *The In-Laws* (2003), co-screenwriters Nat Mauldin, Ed Solomon (b. 1960).

Bertrand Blier (b. 1939; French) Screenwriter, director; author of twenty-two screenplays; director of twenty dramas and comedies as of this writing, among them *Sortez vos mouchoirs* (Get Out Your Handkerchiefs; 1978); *Buffet froid* (Cold Buffet; 1979); *La femme de mon pote* (My Best Friend's Girl; 1983).

Albert Brooks [Albert Lawrence Einstein] (b.1947; American) Actor, director, screenwriter, satirist; has written ten films and directed nine as of this writing; has appeared in several of his own films, which he wrote in collaboration with others, and/or directed, including *The Scout* (1994), co-screenwriter Andrew Bergman, directed by Michael Ritchie (1938–2001); *Mother* (1996); *The Muse* (1999).

Mel Brooks [Melvin "Mel" Kaminsky] (b. 1926; American) Actor, comedian, writer, satirist, composer, lyricist, director, producer; began writing career in television comedy shows; five comedy albums in the *2000 Year Old Man* series (1961–1998), created and written in collaboration with Carl Reiner (see below). As of this writing, he has acted in forty-four projects and directed twelve titles, including *The Producers* (1968; Broadway musical, 2001), for which he wrote the screenplay; *Young Frankenstein* (1974; music and lyrics for Broadway musical, 2007, book co-written with Thomas Meehan [b. 1934]), co-screenwriter and star Gene Wilder (b. 1933). Brooks frequently appears in his own film vehicles, which he also writes, sometimes with collaborators, and directs. They include *Blazing Saddles* (1974); *High Anxiety* (1977); *History of the World: Part I* (1981; "It's good to be the king!"); *Life Stinks* (1991); *To Be or Not To Be* (1983), a revised version of the 1942 Ernst Lubitsch (see below) and Edwin Justus Meyer (1896–1960) script; *Robin Hood: Men in Tights* (1993); *Dracula: Dead and Loving It* (1995).

Frank Capra [Francesco Rosario Capra; aka Frank R. Capra] (1897–1991; Italian-born American) Director, screenwriter, producer, editor;

wrote forty-two screenplays; directed fifty-five films, including famed World War Two propaganda films. His genial, beautifully crafted, sentimental, ironical comedies include *It Happened One Night* (1934); the fantasy *Lost Horizon* (1937), based on the novel by James Hilton (1900–1954); *You Can't Take It With You* (1938), based on the play by Kaufman and Hart; *Mr. Smith Goes to Washington* (1939); *Arsenic and Old Lace* (1944), based on the stage play by Joseph Kesselring (1902–1967); *It's A Wonderful Life* (1946), co-screenwriter writer with Frances Goodrich (1890–1984) and Charles Hackett (1900–1995) of this great Christmas classic; *State of the Union* (1948); *Pocketful of Miracles* (1961).

Charlie Chaplin [Sir Charles Spencer Chaplin] (1889–1977; English) Actor, writer, satirist, producer, director, composer; officer of the French Legion of Honor; created an iconic character, the "Little Tramp," complete with toothbrush mustache, derby, and cane; involved in eighty-seven film projects, including many shorts; directed seventy-six films, which he also wrote and acted in, among them *The Tramp* (1915); *The Kid* (1921); *The Gold Rush* (1925); *The Circus* (1928); *City Lights* (1931); *Modern Times* (1936); *The Great Dictator* (1940); *Monsieur Verdoux* (1947); *Limelight* (1952); *A King in New York* (1957).

Coen Brothers: Joel David Coen (b. 1954) and **Ethan Jesse Coen** (b. 1957) American award-winning producers, directors, screenwriters of fifteen sardonic dark comedies as of this writing, including *Fargo* (1996); *No Country for Old Men* (2007); *Burn After Reading* (2008).

Sacha Baron Cohen [Sacha Noam Baron Cohen] (b. 1971; English) Actor, writer, producer; television and film projects; known for his outrageous, satirical, iconoclastic, sometimes tasteless sense of humor; as of this writing has acted in thirty-five projects and written thirteen, including the films *Borat: Cultural Learnings of America for Make Benefit Glorious Nation of Kazakhstan* (2006), in which he played Borat, and which he co-wrote with Anthony Hines and three others; *Brüno* (2009), in which he played the title role, and which he co-wrote with Hines and five others.

George Cukor [George Dewey Cukor] (1899–1983; American) Director of sixty-seven films, including *A Bill of Divorcement* (1932); *Dinner at Eight* (1933); *Camille* (1936), a melodrama; *Holiday* (1938); *The Philadelphia Story* (1940); *Gaslight* (1944), a melodrama; *Born Yesterday* (1950); *Les Girls* (1957); *My Fair Lady* (1964, based on the Broadway musical adapted from George Bernard Shaw's *Pygmalion* by librettist Alan Jay Lerner [1918–1986] and composer Frederick Loewe [1901–1988]); *Travels with My Aunt* (1972), based on the novel by English author Graham Greene (1904–1991).

Blake Edwards [William Blake Crump] (1922–2010; American) Director, screenwriter, producer; married to Julie Andrews (b. 1935); wrote sixty-two film and television projects; directed forty-six films, including *Victor Victoria* (1982; Broadway musical, 1995), also wrote screenplay; *Pink Panther* series of nine films, which he also co-wrote, including: *The Pink Panther* (1963), with Maurice Richlin (1920–1990); *A Shot in the Dark* (1964), with William Peter Blatty (b. 1928); *The Return of the Pink Panther* (1975), with Frank Waldman (1919–1990); *Revenge of the Pink Panther* (1978), with Waldman and Ron Clark; and the last, *Son of the Pink Panther* (1993), with Richlin; *Operation Petticoat* (1959); *Breakfast at Tiffany's* (1961); *Darling Lili* (1970).

Nora Ephron (1941–2012; American) Writer, screenwriter, film director, actor; scripted fifteen films as of this writing; directed eight films, including the romantic comedies *When Harry Met Sally…* (1989); *Sleepless in Seattle* (1993); *You've Got Mail* (1998; an updated version of Ernst Lubitsch's *The Shop Around the Corner* [see below]), co-screen-writer Delia Ephron (b. 1944); *Julie and Julia* (2009), based on the book by co-screenwriter Julie Powell (b. 1974).

Federico Fellini (1920–1993; Italian) Director, screenwriter; made fifty-two films, many sardonic comedies with a touch of surreal-ism, including the following, which he directed and for which he co-wrote the screenplays with Ennio Flaiano (1910–1972) and Tullio Pinelli (1908–2009): *La strada* (The Road; 1954); *Le notti di*

Cabiria (Nights of Cabiria; 1957); *La dolce vita* (1961); *8½* (1963). Other films include *Fellini Satyricon* (1959), based on the book by Petronius (27–66), co-screenwriter Bernardino Zapponi (1927–2000); *Fellini's Roma* (1972), co-screenwriter Zapponi; *Amarcord* (I Remember; 1973), co-screenwriter Tonino Guerra (b. 1920); *Fellini's Casanova* (1976), co-screenwriter Zapponi; *Ginger and Fred* (1986), co-screenwriters Pinelli and Guerra.

W. C. Fields [William Claude Dukenfield] (1880–1946; American) Actor, screenwriter; acted in thirty-seven films, among them many shorts; wrote or co-wrote twenty-one screenplays; used funny penna-mes, such as the ones in parentheses after films he wrote as vehicles for himself, among them *It's a Gift* (Charles Bogle; 1934), co-written with nine contributors to the screenplay; *Man on the Flying Trapeze* (Charles Bogle; 1935), co-written with seven contributors to the screenplay; *You Can't Cheat an Honest Man* (Charles Bogle; 1939), co-written with six other screenwriters; *The Bank Dick* (Mahatma Kane Jeeves; the name was taken from a line in a vaudeville sketch: "My hat and cane, Jeeves"; 1940); *My Little Chickadee* (1940), co-screenwriter and co-star Mae West (1893–1980); *Never Give a Sucker an Even Break* (Otis Criblecoblis; 1941), co-screenwriters Prescott Chaplin (1896–1968) and John T. Neville (1886–1970).

Christopher Guest (b. 1948; American) Actor, screenwriter, direc-tor, composer, musician; known for his mockumentaries; actor in ninety-four projects, as of this writing; screenwriter for twenty-four projects; directed fifteen projects. The first mockumentary he wrote and starred in, *This Is Spinal Tap* (1984), was co-written with the film's director Rob Reiner (b. 1947), and actors Michael McKean (b. 1947) and Harry Shearer (b. 1943), who also appear in the film. Guest frequently collaborates on screenplays for mockumentaries with Canadian actor and screenwriter Eugene Levy (b. 1946), among them *Waiting for Guffman* (1996); *Best in Show* (2000); *A Mighty Wind* (2003); *For Your Consideration* (2006), all directed by Guest, with both himself and Levy in the cast.

Ben Hecht (1894–1964; American) Playwright, screenwriter, director, producer, novelist; wrote thirty-five books; scripted seventy films, many in collaboration with playwright and screenwriter Charles Macarthur (1895–1956); wrote or collaborated on one hundred fifty-seven screenplays and television plays, including many dramas and adaptations of literary works; films include *The Goldwyn Follies* (1938), co-screenwriter Sid Kuller (!910–1993); *Some Like It Hot* (1939) a Bob Hope (1903–2003) vehicle, not to be confused with Billy Wilder's film (see below), co-screenwriter Gene Fowler (1890–1960); *The Front Page* (1931; and versions for television), co-screenwriter Charles Macarthur, based on their Broadway play, and adapted as *His Girl Friday* (1940) by Charles Lederer (1910–1976), co-screenwriters Hecht and Macarthur.

Isobel Lennart (1915–1971; American) Wrote twenty-eight screenplays, mostly light comedies and musicals, among them *Holiday Affair* (1949); *A Life of Her Own* (1950), directed by George Cukor (see above); *My Wife's Best Friend* (1952); *Merry Andrew* (1958), starring Danny Kaye, co-screenwriter I. A. L. Diamant (1920–1988); *Please Don't Eat the Daisies* (1960), based on the book and stage play by co-screenwriter, Jean Kerr (1922–2003).

Shawn Levy [Shawn Adam Levy] (b. 1968; Canadian-American) Director, producer, actor in twenty-four projects; has directed thirty-three titles as of this writing, including *Big Fat Liar* (2002); *Just Married* (2003); *Cheaper by the Dozen* (2003); *The Pink Panther* (2006), a remake of the Blake Edwards film (see above); the fantasy comedies *Night at the Museum* (2006), *Night at the Museum: Battle of the Smithsonian* (2009), and *Night at the Museum: Secret of the Tomb* (2014), all starring Ben Stiller (see below), with Ricky Gervais and Robin Williams.

Jerry Lewis [Joseph Levitch] (b. 1926; American) Actor, comedian, television personality, screenwriter, film and television director; had long-term comedy partnership with actor and singer, Dean Martin [Dino Paul Crocetti] (1917–1995), the straight man of the act; has acted in seventy projects as of this writing; wrote or co-wrote twenty titles; directed twenty-two films including *The Bell Boy* (1960), which he wrote and starred in; *The Nutty Professor* (1963) and *Cracking Up* (1983), both of which he co-wrote with Bill Richmond and starred in; *Hardly Working* (1980), which co-wrote with Michael Janover (b. 1946) and starred in.

See also Frank Tashlin, below.

Anita Loos (1888–1981; American) Playwright, nonfiction author, novelist, screenwriter; one hundred thirty-two films, as story writer, scenarist, or screenwriter in both the silent and sound eras, many written in collaboration, most of them comedies, including *Gentlemen Prefer Blondes* (1953), based on her hit 1949 Broadway musical comedy, based on her best-selling novel *Gentlemen Prefer Blondes: The Intimate Diary of a Professional Lady* (1926).

Ernst Lubitsch (1892–1947; German-born American) Director, actor, screenwriter; known for his genial comedies and screen musicals; acted in thirty-eight films; wrote or co-wrote thirty-eight films; directed seventy-six films, including *Lady Windermere's Fan* (1925); *Paramount on Parade* (1930); *Trouble in Paradise* (1932); *The Merry Widow* (1934); *Ninotchka* (1939); *The Shop Around the Corner* (1940), co-screenwriters, the prolific Samson Raphaelson (1896–1983) and Ben Hecht (uncredited; see above), based on the stage play *Parfumerie* by Hungarian playwright Miklós László (1903–1973); *To Be or Not To Be* (1942).

S. J. Perelman [Simeon James Perelman; aka Sidney, or Sid] (1904–1979; American) Humorist, author, playwright, screenwriter; sixteen screenplays written in collaboration, including the Marx Brothers films *Monkey Business* (1931), co-screenwriter Will B. Johnstone (?–1947), *Horse Feathers* (1932), co-screenwriters Bert Kalmar (1884–1947) and Harry Ruby (1895–1974).

Carl Reiner (b. 1922; American) Actor, director, writer, producer; has acted in eighty-eight film and television projects as of this writing, including Sid Caesar's *Your Show of Shows* (1952–1954) and *The Dick*

Van Dyke Show (1961–1966), of which he was the creator; writer or co-writer on twenty-two projects; has directed twenty film and television comedies as of this writing, including Neil Simon's *Enter Laughing* (1967); *Oh God* (1977); *The Jerk* (1979); *The Man with Two Brains* (1983).

Morrie Ryskind (1895–1985; American) Playwright, comedy sketch writer, screenwriter; twenty-three screenplays, including the following three Marx Brothers films written in collaboration with George S. Kaufman: *The Cocoanuts* (1929), adaptation of Broadway hit; *Animal Crackers* (1931); *A Night at the Opera* (1935); also wrote the classic screwball comedy *My Man Godfrey* (1936), based on the novel by Eric Hatch (1901–1973), co-screenwriter.

George Seaton (1911–1979; American) Director, producer, screenwriter; wrote or co-wrote forty films; directed twenty-two films in various genres; best known for *Miracle on Thirty-Fourth Street* (1947), which he wrote and directed; also wrote *Charley's Aunt* (1941), based on the play by Brandon Thomas; co-wrote (uncredited) *A Night at the Opera* with Morrie Ryskind and *A Day at the Races* with Robert Pirosh (1910–1989) and George Oppenheimer (1900–1977); co-wrote *The Doctor Takes a Wife* (1940) with Ken Englund (1914–1993); directed light comedy *Junior Miss* (1945).

Mack Sennett (1880–1960; Canadian-American) Producer, actor, screenwriter, director; acted in three hundred fifty-seven projects; played Sherlock Holmes in eleven parodies; known for his slapstick, custard-pie throwing, crazy car chase Keystone Cops movies; produced one thousand one hundred nineteen projects, many of them short subjects; directed three hundred nineteen films, many of them shorts; wrote ninety-one scenarios, stories, and screenplays; worked with all the great comedians, including Charlie Chaplin (see above) and W. C. Fields (see above). Among the films he directed are several Chaplin vehicles, including *Tillie's Punctured Romance* (1914); *The Fatal Mallet* (1914); *Tango Tangles* (1914); *Mabel at the Wheel* (1914).

Ben Stiller [Benjamin Edward Stiller] (b. 1965; American) Actor, writer, film director, producer; son of famed comedy team, actors Jerry Stiller (b. 1927) and Anne Meara (b. 1929); has acted in one hundred eighteen films as of this writing; has directed fourteen films; has written or co-written ten projects, including *Reality Bites* (1994); *The Cable Guy* (1996); *Zoolander* (2001), a satire of the fashion industry, which he directed; *Tropic Thunder* (2008), a satire of war movies, which he directed, acted in, and co-wrote with Justin Theroux (b. 1971) and Etan Cohen; and has played male nurse Gaylord "Greg" Focker in the series of films co-starring the inimitable Robert De Niro (b. 1943) as his father-in-law Jack Byrnes, including *Meet the Parents* (2000), *Meet the Fockers* (2004), and *Little Fockers* (2010).

See also Shawn Levy, above.

Preston Sturges (1898–1959; American) Director, writer; wrote or co-wrote forty-five film comedies; directed thirteen films, all comedies; known for his screwball comedies, among them his first, *The Great McGinty* (1940); *The Lady Eve* (1941); *Sullivan's Travels* (1941), all three of which he both wrote and directed.

Quentin Tarentino (b. 1963; American) Actor, writer, producer, director, cinematographer; known for his sardonic, mordant comedies; has acted in thirty films, written or co-written twenty-three, and directed twenty films as of this writing, including *Reservoir Dogs* (1992); *Pulp Fiction* (1994); *Kill Bill: Vol 1* (2003); *Kill Bill: Vol 2* (2004); *Inglourious Basterds* (2009), all of which he wrote.

Frank Tashlin (1913–1972; American) Director, prolific writer of screen comedies; began career doing animated features and shorts; directed seventy-five films; wrote fifty-one titles, including *The Fuller Brush Man* (1948), starring Red Skelton (1913–1997); *Love Happy* (1949); *Kill the Umpire* (1950); *The Paleface* (1948), co-screenwriter Edmund L. Hartmann (1911–2003), and *Son of Paleface* (1952), which he also directed, co-screenwriter Robert L. Welch (1910–1964), both starring Bob Hope; *Artists and Models* (1955), which he also directed, starring Dean Martin and Jerry Lewis (see above); directed *Hollywood or Bust* (1956), starring Martin and Lewis; *The Girl Can't Help It* (1957), which he also directed, co-screenwriter Herbert Baker (1920–1983); *The Geisha Boy* (1958) and *Cinderfella* (1960), which he also directed, both starring Jerry Lewis.

Jacques Tati [Jacques Tatischeff] (1907–1982; French) Actor, writer, director, editor, producer; known for his satiric comedies about modern life; directed, co-wrote, and acted the character of Monsieur Hulot, which he created, in *Les vacances de Monsieur Hulot* (Mr. Hulot's Holiday; 1953); *Mon oncle* (My Uncle; 1958); *Play Time* (1967); *Trafic* (1971).

Peter Ustinov [Sir Peter Alexander Ustinov; born Peter Alexander, Baron von Ustinov; English; of German, Russian, and Ethiopian aristocratic descent] (1921–2004; English) Actor, playwright, screenwriter, stage designer, author, humorist, newspaper and magazine columnist, radio broadcaster, television presenter, wit and raconteur, diplomat, teacher; recipient of numerous awards; acted in ninety-four films; wrote twenty-eight television films and theatrical films, among them *Hot Millions* (1968), in which Ustinov co-starred with Maggie Smith (b. 1934), co-screenwriter Ira Wallach (1912–1995); among the nine films he directed are the satire of the Cold War, *Romanoff and Juliet* (1961), for which he wrote the screenplay, based on his 1956 stage play, in both of which he also acted.

Francis Veber (b. 1937; French) Director, screenwriter, producer, actor; as of this writing, has written forty titles and directed twelve films, among them *La chèvre* (The Goat; 1981); *Les compères* (ComDads; 1983); *Le dîner de cons* (The Dinner Game; Dinner for Schmucks; 1998); *Le placard* (The Closet; 2001), for all of which he wrote the screenplays. His screenplays include *Le grand blond avec une chaussure noire* (The Tall Blond Man with One Black Shoe), co-written with the film's director Yves Robert (1920–2002); *La cage aux folles* (1978), co-written with the author of the play on which the film is based, Jean Poiret (1926–1992), Edouard Molinaro (b. 1928), and Marcello Danon (?–1997).

Billy Wilder [Samuel Wilder] (1906–2002; Austro-Hungarian-born American) Director, screenwriter, producer, artist, journalist; involved in various capacities in more than sixty films, including the classic comedies he co-wrote and directed, *Sabrina* (1954), based on the stage play *Sabrina Fair* by Samuel A, Taylor (1912–2000), co-screenwriter with Wilder and Ernest Lehman (1915–2005); *The Seven Year Itch* (1955), based on the stage play by George Axelrod (1922–2003), co-screenwriter; *Some Like It Hot* (1959), co-screenwriter I. A. L. Diamond (1920–1988); *The Apartment* (1960), co-screenwriter Diamond.

Appendix Three

An Annotated Glossary of Comedy Terms

Notes: For ancient Greek and Roman comedy terms, see chapter seven. For a list of the standard character types in commedia dell'arte, see chapter four. A word in **boldface** within an entry is a cross-reference to another entry.

absurd. Meaningless; without intrinsic purpose or sense; in humor, something that is ridiculous or incongruous—for instance, juxtaposing two things that do not ordinarily go together. The **Theater of the Absurd** was an influential, innovative artistic movement in playwriting—but it might actually be absurd to call it a movement, since it was adhered to by only a few practitioners, who invented it in the late 1940s and early '50s.

act 1. To do something purposefully; for instance, what the performer does in furtherance of achieving a goal or objective when playing a character in a stage or media performance. **2.** To pretend to be a fictitious character in a stage play or in the media, playing the character, behaving like the character, and doing what the character would do. **3.** A comic routine; a comedian's stand-up series of jokes: *Her act was hilarious.* The act may be a solo or partnership performance.

action 1. Something an actor/character does or says purposefully at a specific **moment** in furtherance of an objective, goal, or task. In a comedy, a comic **bit** may be an action, and a **joke** line may be a verbal action, i.e., one that uses words as opposed to physical doing. **2.** The main throughline of a scene or story; its spine.

ad lib; adlib. [From Latin, *ad libitum*: at will] **1.** A spontaneously improvised line or lines, or bit of stage business, added during a performance; often done by comics or comic actors as part of a **routine** or as a **heckler squelcher**; or as a naturally occurring joke during a play. **2.** To make an off-the-cuff remark or add business during a show.

anticlimax. The intentional deflationary rhetorical device of proceeding from high to low, when proceeding even higher is expected by the audience; also called *bathos*.

aphorism. A laconic, pithy, memorable statement, maxim, or adage, often reducing a situation to a comment on it, or stating a principle or opinion, usually with a moral aspect to it, e.g., Oscar Wilde's dictum, "What is a cynic? A man who knows the price of everything and the value of nothing." (*Lady Windermere's Fan*, act 3)

assumption(s). What the audience to a joke thinks is the story or probable outcome of the joke, as it is set up by the comedian. The joke teller deliberately misleads the audience into assuming certain erroneous things, but things that it would be natural to assume. The audience's expectations will be dispelled by the **punch line**. The "target assumption" is the assumption the comedian wishes the audience to see as the correct one. See also **first story; reinterpretation; second story.**

attitude. Psychological disposition toward or relation to something, e.g., a character's feeling about his or her situation, or about another character; synonymous with **point of view (POV).**

bad laugh. An unexpected, undesired, undesirable audience reaction of hilarity to something that is supposed to be taken seriously; or because of an accident at a particularly unpropitious moment.

baggy-pants comic. A **low comedian**, particularly in **vaudeville** and **burlesque**. A clownish character, he wore ill-fitting trousers that looked as if they might fall down any minute, hence the name.

banana. A comedian, particularly in vaudeville or burlesque. The second banana is the top banana's sidekick. The third banana is the put-upon stooge or chump, the fall guy who takes the blame for the actions of the others.

bathos. See **anticlimax**.

bedroom farce. A sex comedy involving outrageous, but plausible situations, fast-paced action, and lubricious characters.

behavioral joke. A gag that depends not on a verbal line, but rather on some physical action, the physical but nonverbal expression of emotion, using body language, position, and even sound effects.

billy act. In vaudeville, a sketch or turn involving a caricatural American Southern hick mountain character, or hillbilly, complete with tattered straw hat, patched clothing, and corncob pipe.

bit 1. A piece of stage business. **2.** A comic piece of business.

black comedy. A play full of grim, mordant, sarcastic humor about the human condition, but without a tragic hero or a tragic ending. Subjects that are usually the occasion of sadness, tragedy, or misery, such as death, disease, drug abuse, war, domestic and other forms of violence, terrorism, insanity, murder, and the like, are treated satirically, ironically, or humorously. They are often done in a **deadpan** style, so that the audience is sometimes not sure if what they are seeing is even supposed to be funny.

bladder. An air-filled sac, sometimes mounted on a stick handle, used by a medieval jester or merry-andrew to hit the objects of their mockery.

blue joke(s). Comic material of a sexual nature, involving sexual situations; ribald, lewd, bawdy, sometimes obscene jests; synonymous with off-color joke; risqué joke.

boilermaker's convention. In vaudeville especially, performer's sarcastic slang for the audience.

bomb 1. A joke that falls flat, i.e., fails to elicit laughter. **2.** To fail to elicit laughter or other forms of appreciation from the audience; to fall flat.

Borscht Belt. Borscht is an Eastern European beet soup, popular in the Jewish community; hence the term, referring to the Catskill mountain Jewish resort hotels where mainly Jewish comedians used to do their acts from the 1920s through the 1960s, until most of the hotels went out of business; also called Borscht Circuit. Many of the comedians were vaudeville performers and went on to do radio, television, and film work.

Boston version. A burlesque act from which any obscenity or ribald reference has been excised, in deference to presumed New England puritanical, censorial attitudes.

boulevard comedy; boulevard farce. Comic plays and farces, or an individual comic play or farce, presented in Paris from ca. 1800 to the present day. The plays are usually realistic, elegant, and often light entertainment, frequently with satirical overtones. They are performed in theaters all over Paris, which has no central theater district. The term comes from theaters, now gone, where such plays were first performed, located on the boulevards in what is now Paris's fourth arrondissement (district).

break in. To refine a new act or routine in a variety, vaudeville or music hall show by first performing it a number of times to see what really works for an audience and what doesn't. The time involved in doing this is called a "break-in": *We're finished with the break-in, and now we're ready to cook.*

break up. Synonymous with **crack up**.

bring down the house. To elicit such merriment, laughter or applause by something an actor does on stage that a show must temporarily stop.

Britcom. British situation comedy, very popular in the United States, where public television stations and BBC-America show them regularly.

broad. Unsubtle, unrestrained; sometimes, vulgar; also, risqué, as in low comedy, sex farces, and the style of playing of low comedians: *broad comedy.*

burlesque 1. A satirical piece or play that parodies or mocks an existing play or persons. On television, Rowan Atkinson's hilarious *Blackadder* series is, along with its social satire, a burlesque of historical dramas and films. **2.** A form of theater that combines vaudeville comedy sketches, musical numbers, and ladies who strip for the audience, especially in a "burlesque house." **3.** To parody or lampoon an existing play or persons.

button 1. The final, climactic **moment** of a scene, joke, or beat, to be emphasized with finality and closure. **2.** The punch line of a joke, delivered in such a way as to cap the joke and make the audience laugh. **3.** In musical comedy, the end of a number, pointed up so as to elicit applause: *to put a button on it.*

callback 1. Any audition after an initial audition. **2.** A joke in a comedy that reminds the audience of a joke they had heard earlier in the show.

camp. Kitschy humor, full of facetious, fatuous remarks pointed up as if they were more important or witty than they are. "High camp" consists of repartee, delivered in an arch, flip manner, and as if it is clever, when it is merely clichéd; and the mockery or spoof of social norms and mores. "Low camp" elevates pop culture to a status it does not intrinsically deserve, and has a vulgar aspect, such as that of over-done drag queens, who wear feather boas as if they were expensive minks, and treat paste costume jewelry like diamonds. Camp humor is often associated with the homosexual world.

capa y espada [Spanish: cape and sword]. See **comedia de capa y espada**.

capper. The last joke in a series of recurring jokes or running gag, expected to get the biggest pay-off laugh.

cardboard character. A one-dimensional, flat character, without much psychological depth.

caricature 1. An exaggerated, often grotesque character, in which particular salient characterological features are isolated and thus held up to view for examination. The caricature creates an odd, comical effect, frequently for satirical purposes, as with some of the doctors in Molière's plays, or characters in ancient Greek comedies. A caricature may be more physical than psychological, with makeup emphasizing certain features outlandishly, and padded or otherwise distorted costumes, an awkward gait, and a funny voice. **2.** An exaggerated **imitation** of someone well known, emphasizing one or more aspects of the personality and/or physical appearance.

catchphrase. An ordinary sentence that, repeated over and over and delivered in the same way, becomes the trademark of a particular comedian or character; also called a tag line or catchword.

character joke. A routine, anecdote, one-liner or other kind of joke that depends for its humor on the audience's perception of a particular individual, as it has been set up, for instance, in a **situation comedy**;

e.g., Jack Benny's miserliness and poor violin playing, periodically made fun of or otherwise evoked in the course of his sitcoms.

character POV (point of view). The attitude of the person delivering the joke.

cheap laugh. A joke that relies for its humor on an obvious line, which may elicit as much groaning as laughter from the audience.

city comedy. An English genre of Jacobean and Caroline tragicomedy, known for its urbane, sophisticated wit. Ben Jonson was one of the writers associated with it.

closing line. The final punch line of the final joke in a stand-up comedy routine, expected to elicit the biggest laugh, and to provoke applause for the act as a whole.

clown 1. A circus performer whose job is to provoke laughter through outrageous physical slapstick comedy that is usually done without words, as a form of mime. Clowns have their individual, distinctive makeups, costumes and character specialties; and the art of clowning has a long history. **2.** A comic, especially a slapstick or knockabout comedian. **3.** To joke, act foolishly, or perform in a slapstick manner, whether as part of a circus act or other entertainment: *to clown around.*

comedia de capa y espada [Spanish: cape and sword comedy]. Spanish Renaissance comedies, or a single example of the genre, such as those by Lope de Vega Carpio, dealing with melodramatic intrigues often involving cloak and dagger plots, duels, and romantic entanglements. Called *capa y espada*, for short.

comedia de carácter [Spanish: comedy of character]. A genre of comedies, or an individual comedy, dealing with psychology and portraying rounded characters, such as *El burlador de Sevilla* (The Trickster of Seville) by Tirso de Molina, whose works exemplify the genre.

comedia histórica [Spanish: historical play/comedy]. A genre of comedy, or an individual comedy, with a historical setting and well known figures from the past.

comedian 1. An actor who performs in comedy. **2.** A funny, droll, amusing actor. **3.** A performer who does a comic act in various venues, including comedy clubs, television, nightclubs and cabarets: *a stand-up comedian*.

comédie de moeurs [French]. Comedy of manners.

comédie larmoyante [French: lachrymose, tearful, or sentimental comedy]. An eighteenth-century genre of romantic, sentimentalized, tearjerking comedies.

comédie rosse [French: The word *rosse* means "mare," and is also used as an epithet, just as we use the English noun "bitch"]. A subgenre and individual examples of it: bitter **social comedy**; e.g., *Les corbeaux* (The Crows; also known as The Vultures) by Henri Becque.

comedienne 1. An actress who performs in comedies. **2.** A female stand-up comic.

comedy 1. A genre of play or film, or an individual example of it, that has a happy ending and deals in a light-hearted, witty way with the situations it portrays; it is meant to provide amusement and to provoke laughter. **2.** Humor, funny stuff, jokes.

comedy of character. A play, film, or television show that depends for its humor on the specific persons involved in the situations, as opposed to one that relies more on plot, e.g. such television sitcoms as *The Honeymooners*, *I Love Lucy*, *The George Burns and Gracie Allen Show*, *The Golden Girls*, and *Will and Grace*. The situations are still important, of course, but we watch these shows more for the characters and how they go through the sometimes outlandish scrapes they get themselves into.

comedy of humors. An English Jacobean subgenre, popularized by Ben Jonson. It dealt with what we would now call psychological humor, i.e., the humor that arises from people's personalities, foibles, etc. It was based on the concept of the four humors in medieval medicine and physiology: a humor is a biophysical element that made the body function as it does: blood, phlegm, black bile, yellow bile. These humors were thought to determine a person's temperament, which could be phlegmatic, sanguine, choleric, or melancholic, respectively, depending on which element was dominant.

comedy of ideas. A play that revolves around a debate concerning ideas of politics, philosophy or religion, and the like, but in a humorous way. Characters often represent different points of view in the debate, as they do in the plays of George Bernard Shaw.

comedy of intrigue. A play in which the plot is all-important, and the characters—memorable though they may be—less so than the situations in which they are involved, as in some of the nineteenth-century farces of Georges Feydeau.

comedy of manners. A play that deals with upper-middle-class or upper-class mores, usually in a sophisticated, witty, sometimes even arch style. The setting is always in a society stratified by class, and class differences and behavior are readily apparent. Many Restoration plays are examples, as are some plays by Molière, the late nineteenth-century comedies of Oscar Wilde, and some of the twentieth-century plays of Noël Coward, such as *Private Lives*.

comedy of morals. Comic plays that deal with ethical issues in an amusing way, e.g., Molière's *Tartuffe*, and many of his other plays, or Oscar Wilde's *An Ideal Husband*.

comedy quartette. A team of four vaudeville comics: the comedian; the straight man; a tramp, who was usually drunk; and a schoolboy dressed in a beribboned, broad-brimmed straw hat, and wide lace collar.

comedy team. Especially in vaudeville, a pair of comedians who do an act together: one is the straight man, the other the comic.

comic 1. Another word for comedian, especially one who does a stand-up or vaudeville act. **2.** Droll; funny; amusing; provoking laughter and mirth.

comic opera. A comedic work for the musical stage that includes spectacle, dancing, songs, concerted numbers for chorus and soloists, and, often but not always, spoken dialogue, as in those by Jacques Offenbach and Gilbert and Sullivan. But many comic operas, especially Italian examples of the genre, such as *L'elisir d'amore* (The Elixir of Love) and *Don Pasquale* by Gaetano Donizetti, contain sung recitative instead of spoken dialogue. These works may be full-length or one-act pieces for two or more characters; in the latter case, chorus and spectacle elements may be but are not always eliminated. Gilbert and Sullivan's *Trial by Jury* and Offenbach's *La chanson de Fortunio* (Fortunio's Song) and *Le financier et le savetier* (The Financier and the Shoemaker) are for full casts, while Offenbach's *Pomme d'api* (Lady Apple) and *Le violoneux* (The Violinist) are each for three characters only. The stories of these operas are light-hearted, and often romantic and/or satiric, but never heavy or tragic. The eighteenth-century English ballad opera, the German Singspiel, and the Viennese operetta are forms of comic opera, and the American musical comedy is a close cousin, using different kinds of popular musical idioms.

comic relief. An amusing or droll interlude or several interludes in a serious drama or tragedy; meant to relieve tension by making the audience laugh, or at least smile. Comic relief is often in the form of a subplot in which the secondary characters are supposed to be funny; the comic subplot may mirror or contrast with the main dramatic story. Comic elements were not permitted in ancient Greek tragedy, but comic relief is a common device in Shakespearean tragedy.

commedia dell'arte [Italian: comedy of art]. An Italian form of popular improvisational comedy, and scripted comic plays based on standard, formulaic scenarios and using stock characters, such as Harlequin, Columbine, Pantaloon or Pantalone, Punchinello, and Scaramouche; it began in the sixteenth century.

commedia dell'improviso [Italian: comedy of improvisation]. An Italian form of popular improvisational comedy. It preceded the scripted commedia dell'arte, which became the general term for both improvised and scripted comedy.

commedia erudite [Italian: erudite comedy]. The humanist, witty comedies written for Renaissance Italian courts; the upper-class counterpart of commedia dell'arte.

comment. To show the audience by your attitude, by a raised eyebrow, or by an intonation or by other means what you as an actor, or what the character thinks of a remark, a situation, or, sometimes, the play as a whole or one's fellow actors. Commenting as an actor on the proceedings is generally to be avoided. When the character comments, this is part of the action you play as an actor.

connecter. A line or lines that permit of at least two interpretations: an erroneous one, and the one that is the point of the joke, as heard in the punch line, causing a laugh. The connector may be in the form of a **double entendre**. See also **assumption; reinterpretation.**

court comedy. English comic plays written for performance primarily at the courts of Queen Elizabeth I and King James I. Examples include plays by John Lyly (1553/1554?–1606) and Shakespeare's *Love's Labor's Lost.*

crack. Synonymous with **wisecrack**.

crack up. To laugh or otherwise break character in the midst of performing, so amusing does the comedian or comic actor find what is going on: *He cracked himself up.* Also called **break up**.

crank. A clever remark, such as a verbal conceit or witty joke: "I've gibe and joke / And quip and crank." (W. S. Gilbert, *The Yeomen of the Guard*)

custard-pie. Pertains to the kind of slapstick comedy routine seen in vaudeville and silent films, in which a custard pie is thrown by one actor at another, the other actor throws a pie back, and so forth.

deadpan. The kind of comedy, and of comic playing or performing, in which a comedian—called a deadpan, or a deadpan comedian—uses a neutral expression when uttering a joke or doing funny bits of business. The term comes from "pan," once a slang word for face.

decoy; decoy assumption. The idea planted in the audience's mind by the comedian, misleading them so as to set up the surprise conclusion to the joke. See **assumption**.

delivery. The way in which a speech or part of a speech is uttered; the general manner in which an actor recites his or her lines, or in which a comic tells a joke: *Her delivery of the joke was masterful.*

dialect act; dialect comedy. Vaudeville routines presenting stereotyped ethnic characters, usually played as idiotic, gullible, and naïve. The acts were comic turns or routines in which the performers used accents that were considered funny, and played on the undesirable stereotypical characteristics of the ethnic group.

dirty joke. A humorous sexual anecdote; synonymous with off-color joke; **blue joke**.

double entendre [French: double meaning]. A word or line susceptible of a dual, equally valid interpretation, often one that is straightforward in meaning, and a second one involving a risqué meaning (see **blue joke**) or several meanings, as in the phrase used by the psychopathic cannibal, Hannibal Lecter, in his concluding phone conversation in the film *Silence of the Lambs*, "I'm having an old friend for dinner."

doubletalk. A form of comic speech, or a comic routine, in which the comedian combines real words with nonsense syllables and words, forming a kind of gibberish. Imitating foreign language by using nonsense words but accurate sounds is another kind of doubletalk.

drag. [Etymology: presumably from the nineteenth-century long women's skirts that dragged on the ground.] Female dress worn by a male, or male dress worn by a female (despite the etymology). Of ancient tradition, since all actors were male, the assumption of the dress of a gender other than one's own is a frequent device in comedy for disguising a character, and the frequent occasion for humor, mockery, and laughter. A "drag queen" is a man who habitually dresses like and assumes the persona of a woman.

drawing-room comedy. A play featuring witty banter and airy persiflage, as well as a complicated plot, that takes place in a middle or upper-class milieu; sometimes referred to as high comedy; often synonymous with comedy of manners (a wider term). There are always formal scenes in a drawing room or salon, at a reception or other high society event, as in Oscar Wilde's *An Ideal Husband* and *The Importance of Being Earnest*.

elegiac comedy. A genre of comedies and dramas written in Latin in medieval France, in rhymed couplets. The subject is often sexual conquest.

embarrassed laugh. In stand-up comedy, the result of a joke that relies for its humor on an obvious insult to an audience member.

epigram. Originally, a short witty or amusing poem or couplet, like Benjamin Franklin's well known rhyme from *Poor Richard's Almanac*: "Early to bed, early to rise, makes a man healthy, wealthy, and wise." But in contemporary terms, an epigram is a concise witty phrase that has a twist to it; that is, an unexpected, but satisfying ending.

ethnic humor 1. Inauthentic outsider jokes that mock the groups and cultures to which people belong, and that deal in offensive, falsifying, and false stereotypes. See also **dialect act. 2.** Authentic humor that emanates from groups or cultures, and gently mocks traits perceived by the group to be common characteristics of itself, whether this perception is accurate or not.

extravaganza. In nineteenth-century England, an elaborate, spectacular show with a large cast. Beginning in the early 1830s, these eclectic pieces were a form of light comic burlesque with music.

farce. A fast-paced comedy that involves unlikely, far-fetched, absurd, and extreme situations, which are nevertheless plausible. Sexual innuendo, broad physical humor, word play, chase scenes, slapstick bits, mistaken identity, frustration, and misinterpretations of people and events by characters are some of the elements associated with farce.

farceur. A comic actor who plays in farce, and specializes in the slapstick humor and fast-paced playing necessary for the genre; cf. **light comedian**.

feed. To deliver the straight, or feed line(s) setting up a comedian's punch line.

female impersonator. A male performer who assumes and plays the persona of a woman and performs in **drag**; similar to but not to be confused with a drag queen.

first story. The audience's assumptions about the plot or point of a joke as it is set up by the comedian; these assumptions will be dispelled by the surprise of the punch line. See also **assumption(s)**; **second story**.

fright wig. A hairpiece with unruly shocks of hair sticking wildly up and out in every direction—looking as if its wearer were terrified—worn by circus clowns and low comedians.

high comedy. Witty, jocular plays dealing with the upper strata of society and their romantic problems, e.g., **comedy of manners**; **drawing-room comedy**.

gag 1. Another word for joke. **2.** A bit of comic business.

genteel comedy. Synonymous with **comedy of manners**, this term was coined by essayists Joseph Addison (1672–1719) and Sir Richard Steele (1672–1729) to characterize the Restoration comedies of such writers as Colley Cibber and John Vanbrugh, and the Augustan comedies of the early eighteenth century.

get the bird. To receive disapproving catcalls and have rotten eggs and vegetables thrown during a performance, especially in vaudeville and British music hall.

get the hook! An expression of disapproval, called out from the audience, particularly in the days of vaudeville and burlesque, meaning that the stage manager should use the large crook on the end of a long staff designed for the purpose of pulling a performer off the stage.

gibe 1. A sarcastic, ill-natured joke, jeering wisecrack, or taunt at someone else's expense. **2.** To make a taunting or heckling remark.

heckler. An obstreperous audience member who heckles the performer(s), that is, who challenges, annoys, attempts to humiliate, or otherwise interrupts a performer. The heckler is sometimes a **plant**, deliberately placed in the audience as part of an act.

heckler squelcher. A joke, usually an ad lib, meant to ridicule a heckler and stop him or her from continuing to annoy the comedian or the audience; also called **saver**; **stop joke.**

high comedy. Often synonymous with **comedy of manners.**

humor 1. A general term for the existential phenomenon of that which is considered comic, funny, and droll. What people find humorous depends on their individual temperaments. **2.** The ability to express and the manner of expressing comically something deemed absurd, incongruous, and ridiculous, provoking laughter: *Molière's humor still amuses after all these centuries.* **3.** A temporary mood: *He's in a foul humor.*

imitation. Aping or mimicking someone or something, often for comic effect; sometimes as a **caricature.**

immediacy. The present urgency of the **moment**, and of the immediate objective, which is very important in performing comedy, as well as in dram.

impersonation. A portrayal of another person, usually a celebrity, done by an actor who *impersonates* that individual. Impersonations are complete characterizations, e.g., the depictions of Truman Capote by Robert Morse in Jay Presson Allen's stage play *Tru*; Philip Seymour Hoffman in the title role of the film *Capote* (2005); and Toby Jones as Capote in *Infamous* (2006); Helen Mirren's Queen Elizabeth II in *The Queen* (2006); or Meryl Streep's Margaret Thatcher in *The Iron Lady* (2011).

impression. An imitation of someone using salient features of that person's physicality, i.e., gestures, movement, facial expressions, and vocal mannerisms. The impression may be a **caricature**, and is often a comic one, as in *Saturday Night Live* sketches.

in the aisles. In a state of near collapse from laughing so hard: *rolling in the aisles.*

in joke. A humorous anecdote that depends on the audience having knowledge of the subject of the joke; e.g., Milton Berle's joke to the audience about itself in *Great Comedians Talk About Comedy*: "I've seen better crowds at group therapy." If you don't know what group therapy is, the joke isn't funny.

inside joke. A humorous anecdote or droll remark that depends for its humor on the knowledge about its premise, shared by a limited group of listeners, who are involved in the situation or know the individual people that are the subject of the joke.

instant switch. A comic technique involving an instantaneous change from one emotion to another; e.g., from a smile to a scream, or from anger to calmness, or vice versa.

insult humor 1. In stand-up comedy, comic routines, jokes, or interactions with the audience that depend for laughs on ad hominem, personal remarks about or to someone. **2.** Put-downs and sarcastic remarks directed by one character to another; ubiquitous in television sitcoms and drawing-room comedy.

irony 1. Humor and humorous words that acknowledge and consist of a perception of the difference between what was intended and the actual result of a situation; this humor is sometimes rueful or wry. One form of irony is "poetic justice," a literary device—not always ironic: there is a happy ending where the good is rewarded and the bad punished, which may occur in literature, but not always in real life). An example: the plotline of a comedy built on the idea of "the biter, bit," where the person's harmful intention backfires, and the opposite of what was intended occurs, so that the "biter" gets his or her comeuppance. **2.** A literary device for pointing up contrasts, such as that between what is expected, desired, or intended, and what is.

jest 1. A frivolous, joking, witty remark or action. **2.** A playful mood: *She spoke in jest*. **3.** To make funny remarks or jokes, both physical and verbal.

jester. A medieval court fool who dressed in cap and bells and motley and, carried a zany and/or a bladder; a merry-andrew.

joke 1. A witty, funny, amusing brief anecdote or story, the last line of which is meant to provoke laughter. **2.** An utterance or a behavioral manifestation meant to be humorous and to arouse mirth and laughter. **3.** A witticism; a droll or comic remark. **4.** A trick played on someone, presumably for comic effect, in order to provoke laughter at that person's expense: *a practical joke.* **5.** To tell an amusing, funny story or anecdote. **6.** To kid around.

joke writer. A person who thinks up gags for a stand-up comic or television show, and writes witty, funny, amusing brief anecdotes, witticisms, droll one-liners, wisecracks, or skits. Also called a *gag writer.*

juggler. In medieval days, a jester, whose routines included sleight of hand tricks.

jumble. A quirky form of English eighteenth- and early nineteenth-century comic musical theater devised by the manager of the Haymarket Theatre in London, dramatist and memoirist George Colman "the Younger." It combined opera, farce, and tragedy, and was a hodge-podge of entertaining and ludicrous juxtapositions.

kicker. A surprise twist ending to a story, whether dramatized or written, or to a joke, in which case the word is synonymous with **punch line**.

kill 1. To ruin; to kill a joke is to ruin it totally. **2.** To give a wonderful performance that the audience loved: *We killed them!*

laugh 1. The mirthful, physical reaction to a joke. Hence, too, the noun *laughter:* the general reaction: *The result of his remark was laughter.* **2.** A synonym for **joke** in such terms as **cheap laugh** or **shock laugh**. **3.** To react with amusement, enjoyment and mirth to a joke or to a funny line in the play. The physical reaction involves the whole body, with the belly moving, the mouth open, and sounds, loud or softer, issuing from the larynx. Laughs can be chuckles, belly laughs, and everything in between.

laughing comedy. Oliver Goldsmith's term, coined in 1772, for comedies portraying and satirizing human foibles and follies, as opposed to romantic or **sentimental comedy**. He included his play *She Stoops to Conquer* in the genre.

laugh line 1. The final words of a joke or of an exchange of dialogue, on which an audience's laugh is hoped for. Synonymous with **punch line. 2.** Words in a play, whether a drama or comedy, meant to provoke the audience's reaction of audible, vocal mirth.

lay an egg. To fall flat, as when a joke does not get a laugh; to fail miserably.

lazzo. [Italian; plural, lazzi] In commedia dell'arte, a standardized physical or acrobatic trick, comic routine, or standard verbal quip or dialogue exchange.

leading comedian. The actor who plays the most important comic role or line of roles, especially in a comic opera or operetta, e.g., the line of patter-song roles in Gilbert and Sullivan, including Sir Joseph in *H.M.S. Pinafore* and Ko-Ko in *The Mikado*.

light comedian. A comic actor who plays in drawing-room comedy and light comedy, and whose specialty is charming, witty repartee, rather than physical humor.

light comedy. An amusing, delightful play or film that depends on witty dialogue rather than physical business, and does not have much depth or point, but abounds in laughs, e.g., Neil Simon's *Barefoot in the Park*; Noël Coward's *Hay Fever*.

low comedian. A comic actor whose brand of humor and performance style is crude, unsubtle, tasteless, and vulgar.

low comedy 1. Crude, coarse, tasteless humor. **2.** A vulgar farcical play that includes elements of slapstick, bad jokes, garish costumes and makeup, and a lack of subtlety or sophistication. **3.** An actor's unsubtle performance: *a low comedy performance.*

malapropism. The unconscious, unintentional use of a wrong word in place of the right one that was intended; from Mrs. Malaprop, the character in Sheridan's *The Rivals* who is always using the wrong word, which is similar in sound.

male impersonator. A woman dressed in male attire who plays a man in vaudeville and club **drag** acts; see also **trousers role.**

Middle Comedy. The ancient Greek school of comedy that followed the **Old Comedy** of Aristophanes, and attempted to change the rules. We have no complete plays from this school.

milk 1. To play a scene or a moment for all it is worth, so as to get the most out of it. **2.** To do all one can do and then do some more, whether appropriate or not, in order to get the maximum response from the audience.

moment 1. In acting terms, the brief duration of time during which something happens: living in the moment, i.e., being present and concentrated on what is happening. **2.** A particular noticeable occurrence that draws attention to itself and lasts for an instant; e.g., a **button**: an acting moment; a comic moment.

mug 1. Face: *Get a load of the mug on that guy!* **2.** A man: *See that mug over there?* **3.** To make faces on stage or for the camera, especially using outlandish, exaggerated expressions meant to provoke laughter.

musical comedy. See **comic opera**.

music hall. See **vaudeville**.

New Comedy. The kind of comic play written by the ancient Greek, Menander, and adapted by the Romans for their own theater.

nose joke. A surefire humorous anecdote, the punch line of which is so obvious that it practically punches the audience in the nose; synonymous with **platter joke**.

observational comic. A comedian whose act is based on various points of view about life, and on his or her perceptions and observations.

off-color joke. See **blue joke**.

Old Comedy. The plays of Aristophanes, and the school of satirical comedy preceding the **Middle Comedy** and the **New Comedy**.

one-liner. A quick, pointed joke, complete in itself, that requires no extra feed line, since it usually contains both its own feed and punch lines; e.g., Groucho Marx's joke: "I never forget a face, but in your case I'll make an exception."

operetta. See **comic opera**.

pantomime 1. Silent acting, using gesture and movement. Called *mime*, for short. **2.** A theater piece that is performed silently. **3.** A popular British light entertainment incorporating music, dialogue, spectacle, and such diverse elements as comic turns, acrobatics, and special magical effects; usually seasonal, e.g., the Christmas pantomime. Called a *panto*, for short.

paradox. A contradictory statement or situation that seems ridiculous or absurd, but that may actually be true. "How quaint the ways of paradox, / At common sense she gaily mocks," wrote W. S. Gilbert in *The Pirates of Penzance*, the plot of which hinges on a paradox.

parody 1. A piece that satirizes, mocks, spoofs and/or imitates another piece, as in mock opera or ballet performances. **2.** To perform such a piece, or to imitate or satirize someone or some style of behavior or performance.

pastiche. An imitation of a style, well-known piece, or genre; often with satirical intent.

patter. Words meant to be spoken or sung quickly, with excellent diction, as in the patter songs in Gilbert and Sullivan. Part of the effect of the complicated lyrics, with their intricate rhymes and alliterative consonants, depends on their rapid-fire delivery. But more important than speed is keeping the rhythm steady.

pay-off. The desired audience reaction that results from the actors having built a joke or scene or whole play up to a climax. In comedy, the pay-off for a joke is a huge laugh from the audience.

pear-shaped tones. Particularly elegant diction and elocution, with sounds that are resonant and beautiful to listen to; also used sarcastically to refer to an actor whose speech is too refined, overarticulated, and overdone. In fact, pear-shaped tones may be used to great comic effect, as they were in the episode called "Sense and Senility" in *Blackadder III*, with two hammy actors hired to teach elocution to Hugh Laurie as the dimwitted prince.

physical comic. A comedian whose act depends not on verbal quips and punch lines, but on behavioral manifestations, tricks and/or various physical mannerisms and positions.

pick up. To speed things up, as in the directions "Pick up the pace/ tempo!" or "Pick it up!" "Pick the scene up!" is the direction to play the scene with more energy, picking up the pace. The oft-heard directorial phrase "Pick up your cues!" means to speak immediately upon the termination of a speech, without pausing before speaking. Picking up cues is of paramount importance in creating the impression of real, ongoing conversation and in keeping up the pace, tempo and rhythm of a scene. Otherwise, the play can be deadly, and, in a comedy, very unfunny. **Timing** depends in part on picking up cues.

plant 1. A performer who is seated in the audience as part of the show; for example in a stand-up comedy act. **2.** Something mentioned, alluded to, or shown in a play or film that will prove in retrospect to have been important to the plot; e.g., the scene in the Southern diner in the classic comedy film, *My Cousin Vinny* (1992), where Vinny (played by Joe Pesci), a lawyer from New York, learns what grits are and how they are made: this will later prove important in the trial scene, where Vinny destroys the testimony of a witness, who was cooking grits for his breakfast. **3.** To set up a joke by imparting certain (usually erroneous) ideas to the audience, thus "planting" them in the audience's mind, and leading them to assume certain things. **4.** To put a performer in the audience as part of the show; e.g., a **heckler**.

platter joke. A surefire humorous anecdote that is so obvious it practically serves up the punch line to the audience on a platter; synonymous with **nose joke**.

play for a laugh. To point up a line vocally, perhaps using gestures or mugging as well, in order to elicit laughter from the audience.

point of view (POV). In comedy, the attitude of the actor toward the material being presented; this attitude is meant to arouse a similar attitude of approval, disapproval, etc. in the audience, who are expected to be on the side of, i.e., to sympathize with the attitude of the comedian.

practical joke. A physical jest at someone else's expense, such as offering to hold a chair for someone who is about to sit, then pulling the chair out from under that person, who then falls flat on the floor. Practical jokes are often used in **farce**.

pratfall. A fall onto an actor's rear end, or *prat*, in nineteenth-century slang (although the word *prat* dates from at least Elizabethan times); often one done with exaggeration.

premise 1. The principal concept or story that sets up a joke; the basis on which the story of the joke rests, often based on audience knowledge and consequent assumptions. **2.** The basic or concept idea underlying a story, and setting up the conflict.

prop comic. A comedian whose act depends upon the imaginative use of stage properties.

pun. A joking play on words that deliberately exploits their similarity. Shakespeare's *Richard III* begins with a pun: "Now is the winter of our discontent made glorious summer by this sun [son] of York."

punch 1. To point up the meaning of a line by emphasizing or stressing certain words. **2.** To make a moment or a line stand out, either by vocally stressing it or by doing a bit of business that points the moment up.

punch line. The last words of a joke; the **laugh line**; also called a gag line. A comedian may "punch" the line, i.e., point it up by using a specific vocal pattern of intonation and emphasis in order to get the laugh.

quip. A witty, usually off-the-cuff remark, which may be a sarcastic **gibe**, and is occasioned by a particular event or circumstance.

quipster. A person who is known for his or her quips, or who may be given to making quips on any occasion.

rant. A rambling comic routine that ranges widely over various subjects, and depends for its humor on the point of view of the comedian, to which the audience is expected to be sympathetic.

reinterpretation. The audience's instant switch in its understanding of the joke, after the original assumption about it (deliberately and misleadingly set up by the comedian) has been changed, often to its opposite, thus causing laughter. See also **assumption; connecter.**

repartee. A conversational exchange of witty ripostes, pointed quips, jests, and sallies in which, often, one interlocutor tries to outdo the other in terms of cleverness. Comedies of manners depend on such dialogue.

Restoration comedy. English comic plays written after the restoration in 1660 of King Charles II to the throne, and until ca. 1715.

reveal 1. In comedy, to expose the true meaning of a joke or moment suddenly in the **punch line**, allowing the audience to understand its true import, causing laughter. **2.** [Used as a noun] The word, phrase, or action that allows the audience's reinterpretation, leading them to understand the second story of the joke. See also **assumption(s); first story; second story.**

rhythm joke. A humorous anecdote or piece that depends for its effect on the regular tempo of its words, as in the comic verse of Lewis Carroll or W. S. Gilbert; such jokes may also depend on alliteration, assonance, or rhyme.

riff 1. In comedy, bantering remarks exchanged with the audience. **2.** An extended improvisational routine taking off from a particular theme or remark that sets off a train of thought. **3.** The action of bantering and/or of performing such an improvisational routine: *The comedian was riffing with the audience in the middle of the routine.*

rip; rip into. To attack in some way, usually verbally, the heckler who has been abusing the comedian; that is, in turn to insult, abuse, or otherwise annoy the annoying heckler.

risqué joke. See **blue joke**.

roast 1. To hold a person up to ridicule by poking fun and making jokes at that person's expense. **2.** A banquet for the purpose of honoring a guest through good-natured, friendly ridicule and jokes that poke fun at the guest of honor.

roll 1. A series of jokes. **2.** A series of successes in telling the jokes in a stand-up routine: *The comedian was on a roll.*

romantic comedy. A play or film dealing in a light-hearted, humorous, amusing way with love and its complications. Most comedies, not only the romantic kind, revolve around the idea that "the course of true love never did run smooth" (William Shakespeare, *A Midsummer Night's Dream*, act 1, scene 1).

routine. An act, especially in a variety show: *a comic routine.*

rule of three. The idea that when a running gag is repeated, it is on the third repeat that the gag gets the biggest laugh.

running gag. A joke or bit of comic business that recurs periodically in the course of a play or film; also called a running joke. The joke is designed to get the biggest laugh the last time it is played.

sarcasm. A kind of nasty humor in which insults, wisecracks, and put-downs abound. Sarcastic humor can be cruel, directed at its target with great contempt.

satire. A comedy, prose piece, essay, or poem that mocks or makes fun of social customs, mores, habits and ways of behaving. It is a general rule that you can only mock those more powerful than you, so the upper socioeconomic classes, for instance, come in for their share, particularly those who take themselves overly seriously. But satires of the poor, the mentally disadvantaged, the ethnically different, minorities, or the physically challenged fall flat, and are just not funny, in part because both the jokers and their audiences are simply catering to their own inferiority complexes and to their xenophobic and other phobias.

satyr plays. Lewd ancient Greek comedies and farces that were originally part of the religious rites involved in the worship of the god Dionysius.

saver 1. A strong joke that is meant to overcome a weak joke that did not get a laugh. It saves the comedian's act from being a flop. **2.** Synonymous with **heckler squelcher.**

school act. A vaudeville routine that takes place in a classroom, with a ludicrous teacher, adult actors playing students, and inane one-liners in answer to silly questions.

screwball comedy. An outrageously farcical piece with eccentric characters and situations; e.g., the film *My Man Godfrey* (1936). The 1930s was the heyday of the genre in Hollywood.

second story. The actual plot and point of a joke, as opposed to the first story, set up by the comedian to mislead the audience. See also **assumption(s)**; **first story.**

segue 1. In comedy, to make remarks that connect to and lead directly into the next joke or part of the routine: *The comic segued easily from one joke to another.* **2.** The remarks made for this purpose: *The comic's segues were almost as funny as the jokes.*

sentimental comedy. An eighteenth-century English genre of romantic comic play, or an individual example of the genre. Also called "weepy comedy." See also **laughing comedy.**

set. An extended comedy or musical routine.

set up 1. To establish the premise or basis of a joke in the audience's mind: *a set-up premise.* **2.** In an act with two comedians, for the straight man to feed the comic lines that lead to the punch line.

setup. The lines leading to the punch line, establishing certain misleading premises in the mind of the audience.

sex comedy. A comic play that revolves around sexual encounters and complicated love affairs, graphic in its physical and verbal humor; a bedroom farce.

shatter. To destroy the audience's assumptions about the outcome of a joke, those assumptions being based on the set-up premise; this shattering causes the audience to laugh when they hear the punch line.

shock laugh. A joke that ends with an obscene word, producing sometimes embarrassed laughter.

shoe horn 1. To insert incongruous, contrived material into the middle of a joke to which it is extraneous, and, although it may appear at first to have some connection to the joke, is meaningless in the context. **2.** The material so inserted, which is a joke in itself: *So you are an opera singer? Well, I drove past Lincoln Center the other day…*

shtick. [Yiddish: piece; bit] **1.** A bit of comic business; a comic routine. **2.** A particular intonation pattern, gesture, catchphrase, or distinctive movement that an actor or comic has made his personality trademark.

sight gag. A visual joke or bit of funny business that requires no words. In a famous seventeenth-century sight gag, Colley Cibber as Lord Foppington in Sir John Vanbrugh's *The Relapse* had his huge, extravagant powdered wig—which was almost as big as he was—carried on stage every night in a sedan chair, and donned it with elaborate ceremony, while the audience was laughing its heads off.

situation comedy; sitcom. A comedy—usually one that is part of a weekly television series; the term refers as well as the series as a whole—that depends for its humor on the circumstances that unfold and that the characters find themselves involved in, willy-nilly; rather than a comedy that depends more on the characters than the circumstances for its humor, although the term refers to comedies in which the same characters appear every week, so that much of the humor depends on the audience's knowledge of them.

sketch; skit. A short act of spoken dialogue in a television comedy show, such as *Saturday Night Live*; or in a vaudeville evening or revue; usually comic in nature, involving a simple story and funny comedy routines and characters; may be satirical.

slapstick. Broad clowning in comedy, involving physical bits of business such as falling, slipping on a banana peel and the like.

slow burn. An actor's technique for the lengthy buildup of anger that is held back until it can be held no longer, and finally explodes. Usually, the actor must avoid giving a joke or other moment away before the audience is supposed to know it, but in the case of a slow burn, the audience is supposed to realize what is happening before the other characters do, e.g., as in Jackie Gleason's reactions in his television series *The Honeymooners.*

social comedy. An early to mid-nineteenth century American subgenre of the comedy of manners, exemplified by Mrs. Moffatt's 1845 hit *Fashion; or, Life in New York.*

sotie. [French: a stupidity] A French subgenre of comedy in the late medieval and early Renaissance periods, and also the particular piece belonging to the subgenre: a licentious, satirical **farce** with elements of the medieval morality play, often satirizing the Church. It included the **satire** of well known political and other public figures, often portrayed in **caricature**.

spell it out. To make a point clearly and succinctly by emphasizing important words and speaking fairly slowly, making sure it sinks in. Comedians occasionally set up a joke in this manner. And sometimes, it is necessary for an actor to do this, particularly in verse plays involving complicated language; but sometimes it is merely patronizing and condescending to the audience.

spoof. A parody or lampoon of a person, film, opera, or other entertainment, etc. in which the object of the mockery is imitated, along with an exaggeration of typical characteristics, e.g., the fake TV news program on *Saturday Night Live*.

stand. A stop on a tour; and the amount of time the road company stays in a particular place; for example, a one-night stand.

stand-up comedy. Humorous routines and solo acts performed by an individual comic who tells a series of jokes or does a turn in various venues, e.g., nightclubs, cabarets, comedy clubs, television, or, sometimes, in a Broadway theater, e.g., Jackie Mason's or Dame Edna's Broadway shows. Although usually consisting of solo acts, stand-up comedy can involve teams, such as Abbott and Costello in their famous "Who's on First?" routine. In clubs where they perform, the comics stand and deliver their jokes, often using a hand mike, sometimes employing props. Called *stand-up*, for short. See also **Borscht Belt**.

step on a laugh. To kill a laugh, i.e., not to allow the audience to laugh; inadvertently and ineptly coming in too soon with the next line or bit of business, before the audience has finished laughing, or, sometimes, even started.

stichomythia. (STIH kuh MIH thee uh) Rapid-fire exchanges of sharp, pointed dialogue, as in some of Noël Coward's plays, e.g., *Private Lives*; or Tom Stoppard's *Rosencrantz and Guildenstern Are Dead*.

stooge 1. The straight man in a vaudeville comedy team. **2.** A put-upon chump, the comic victim of manipulation.

stop joke. A **one-liner** that is usually off the subject of the comic routine, and is often an ad lib, as in the case of a **heckler squelcher**.

story joke. An anecdote that has a beginning, middle, and end, and a punch line that concludes the story with a surprise.

straight man. The person in a comedy or comedy act who feeds, or sets up the comedian's jokes; the stooge.

tag line 1. Another word for **punch line**. **2.** A comedian's **catch-phrase**, often one heard at the end of an act or routine. The audience that is familiar with the tag line usually laughs as the comedian is exiting. **3.** A catchword associated with a product in a commercial, usually heard at the end of the spot.

take 1. A reaction in the form of a pointed look or stare, usually a comic one involving recognition of someone, some thing, or some circumstance; the verbal phrase is "to do a take." There are double and triple takes, which must be practiced to perfection, in order to have their full effect. **2.** A pointed look by an actor at another actor or object. **3.** In film and television, each continuous filming, taping, or digital video of a scene or part of a scene, from the moment the camera begins photographing it to the moment it stops.
Note: For a list of the different kinds of comedic takes, see chapter one.

target assumption. Also called a *target*, for short. See **assumption; decoy**.

telegraph 1. To convey information (often nonverbally) before it should be conveyed. **2.** To anticipate a reaction so that the audience understands what is about to happen before it should, e.g., when an actor flinches before the other actor is even ready to strike a blow. The word is often used in connection with giving away a joke before the audience should be aware of it. Sometimes telegraphing is called for, particularly in the case of the **slow burn**.

throw away. The technique of treating something, especially a line, as unimportant, casual or not worthy of notice or emphasis; used for comic or dramatic effect.

throwaway. A line or joke that is delivered in a casual offhand way.

time a laugh. To hold, i.e., to remain silent and stationary, temporarily suspending the action of the play, while the audience laughs, until the laughter is subsiding, and the right moment for delivering the next line arrives.

timing. The technique of making something happen at the exact carefully rehearsed moment when it is supposed to happen. Timing is essential in making an entrance or an exit, and is an elementary comedy technique, as well as being an essential of stage combat. Correct timing depends on setting up the right tempo, rhythm and pace.

top banana. The leading comedian in an act, especially in burlesque and vaudeville, but also sometimes in a play or musical.

topic. In comedy, the principal unifying subject of a routine.

topical comedian. A comic whose material is ephemeral because it is based on subjects that are contemporary and fleeting.

topical joke. A humorous anecdote, or a droll reference to a subject or person currently in public consciousness. Topical jokes are usually ephemeral and often depend for their humor on the audience's knowledge of some political or other subject in the news of the day.

topper 1. A joke that gets the climactic laugh in a **running gag**. **2.** A joke that elicits a greater response than the previous one.

tragicomedy. A hybrid genre of drama that began in the Elizabethan theater, and that crosses comedy and tragedy, and emphasizes the ironic and the humorous in human destiny; sometimes called a *heroic comedy*. Such plays often have a rueful ending: not tragic, but not happy either.

travesty 1. A parody, spoof, satire, or imitation of a well known work, style, or genre; e.g., Offenbach's travesties of Rossini and Meyerbeer; W. S. Gilbert's spoofs of Shakespeare; Sullivan's spoofs of Verdi in *The Pirates of Penzance*. **2. Drag**, i.e., cross-dressing, seen as a travesty of the dress of the gender that is not the actor's own. The French word for cross-dressing is *travesti*. **3.** A ludicrous semblance of the real thing: *The verdict was a travesty of justice*.

trousers role. A male character played by a woman in male attire in an opera or comic opera; for example, Cherubino in Mozart's *Le Nozze di Figaro* or Fragoletto in Offenbach's *Les Brigands*.

variety Entertainment at a music hall or other venue that includes musical numbers, comic acts, and specialty acts, such as those involving animals or acrobatics.

vaudeville 1. Originally, an eighteenth-century satirical song. Such numbers were often incorporated into comic operas. **2.** A one-act farce or sketch, especially in the nineteenth century. The term was used by Chekhov to characterize his one-act farces. **3.** A popular American and British form of variety entertainment, beginning in the 1890s and lasting through the 1930s. Comic acts were always an important part of the show, and many great comedians started their careers in vaudeville as "headliners" (featured performers), going from theater to theater on a "circuit" of theaters owned by particular producers, and went on to radio, television, and film. The British music hall, referring to both the venue and the kind of variety entertainment offered there, is similar.

wait for a laugh. To pause after a line that the actor expects will get a laugh from the audience. This is to be avoided: If the audience laughs, allow them to do so, do not **step on a laugh**, and **time a laugh**, but you as both actor and character cannot anticipate that a laugh will be there, so don't stop and wait for one.

warm up. To tell jokes to the audience before the taping of a television **situation comedy**, and so put them in the mood to laugh when the sitcom is performed; the job is given to a stand-up comedian.

warm-up. The routine a comedian does before the taping of a sitcom.

wisecrack. A sarcastic joke, usually a put-down or insult; also shortened to crack.

wit 1. Intelligence; particularly keen, quick perception: *She has a quick wit.* **2.** A feeling for what is ingeniously and cleverly humorous; a sharp, discerning sense of humor. **3.** A cleverly humorous, intelligent person who is particularly deft and quick at **repartee**, and clever in expressing perceptions comically. **Irony** and **sarcasm** are the stock in trade of the wit: *He has a sarcastic wit.* **4.** Clever, quick, perceptive humor.

witty. Pertaining to the quality of having a lively intelligence and a clever sense of humor; quick with a **quip**.

Selected Bibliography

Abrams, M. H. *A Glossary of Literary Terms*. 7th ed. New York: Heinle & Heinle, 1999.

Adler, Stella. *On the Technique of Acing*. Foreword by Marlon Brando. New York: Bantam Books, 1988.

Aitkin, Maria. *Style: Acting in High Comedy*. New York: Applause Theatre Book Publishers, 1996.

Aristotle. *Poetics; Longinus: On the Sublime; Demetrius: On Style (Loeb Classical Library No. 199)*. Revised edition. Cambridge, MA: Harvard University Press, 1995.

Astington, John H. *Actors and Acting in Shakespeare's Time: The Art of Stage Playing*. New York: Cambridge University Press, 2010.

Baker, Henry Barton. *English Actors from Shakespeare to Macready*. 2 vols. New York: Henry Holt and Company, 1879.

Barba, Eugenio and Nicola Savarese. *A Dictionary of Theatre Anthropology: The Secret Art of the Performer*. Translated by Richard Fowler. 2nd ed. New York: Routledge, 2006.

Barnes, Eric Wollencott. *The Lady of Fashion: The Life and the Theatre of Anna Cora Mowatt*. New York: Charles Scribner's Sons, 1954.

Benedetti, Jean. *Stanislavski: A Biography*. New York: Routledge, 1988.

Bergson, Henri. *Laughter*. Translation of *Le rire* by Wylie Sypher in *Comedy*. Baltimore: The Johns Hopkins University Press, 1956.

Bermel, Albert. *Farce: A History from Aristophanes to Woody Allen*. Carbondale, IL: Southern Illinois University Press, 1990.

Berry, Cicely. *The Actor and the Text*. New York: Applause, 1992.

Bloom, Harold. *Shakespeare: The Invention of the Human.* New York: Riverhead Books, 1998.

Blumenfeld, Robert. *Accents: A Manual for Actors.* Revised and expanded edition. New York: Limelight Editions, 2002.

—*Acting with the Voice: The Art of Recording Books.* New York: Limelight Editions, 2004.

—*Stagecraft: Stanislavsky and External Acting Techniques: A Companion to Using the Stanislavsky System.* New York: Limelight Editions, 2011.

—*Teach Yourself Accents: The British Isles: A Handbook for Young Actors and Speakers.* New York: Limelight Editions, 2013.

—*Teach Yourself Accents: Europe: A Handbook for Young Actors and Writers.* New York: Limelight Editions, 2014.

—*Teach Yourself Accents: North America: A Handbook for Young Actors and Writers.* New York: Limelight Editions, 2013.

—*Tools and Techniques for Character Interpretation: A Handbook of Psychology for Actors, Writers, and Directors.* New York: Limelight Editions, 2006.

—*Using the Stanislavsky System: A Practical Guide to Character Creation and Period Styles.* New York: Limelight Editions, 2008.

Boleslavsky, Richard. *Acting: The First Six Lessons.* Twenty-ninth printing. New York: Routledge, 1987.

Boucher, François. *20,000 Years of Fashion: The History of Costume and Personal Adornment.* Expanded edition. New York: Harry N. Abrams, Inc., 1983.

Bradley, Ian, ed. *The Complete Annotated Gilbert and Sullivan.* Introduced and Edited by Ian Bradley. New York: Oxford University Press, 1996.

Callow, Simon. *Acting in Restoration Comedy.* New York: Applause, 1991.

Campbell, Oscar James Jr. *The Comedies of Holberg.* Cambridge, MA: Harvard University Press, 1914.

Chekhov, Michael. *Lessons for the Professional Actor.* From a collection of notes transcribed and arranged by Deirdre Hurst du Pray. Introduction by Mel Gordon. New York: Performing Arts Journal Publications, 1985.

—*The Path of the Actor.* New York: Routledge, 2005.

—*To the Actor on the Technique of Acting.* Revised and expanded edition. Foreword by Simon Callow. Preface by Yul Brynner. New York: Routledge, 2002.

Dale, Alan. *Comedy is a Man in Trouble: Slapstick in American Movies.* Minneapolis, MN: University of Minnesota Press, 2000.

Esslin, Martin. *The Theatre of the Absurd.* New York: Doubleday, 1961.

Forman, Edward. *Historical Dictionary of French Theater.* Lanham, MD: The Scarecrow Press, Inc., 2010.

Freud, Sigmund. *The Basic Writings of Sigmund Freud.* Translated and Edited by Dr. A. A. Brill. *Psychopathology of Everyday Life; The Interpretation of Dreams; Three Contributions to the Theory of Sex; Wit and Its Relations to the Unconscious; Totem and Taboo; The History of the Psychoanalytic Movement.* New York: The Modern Library, 1995.

Frye, Northrop. *Anatomy of Criticism.* New York: Penguin, 1990.

Garcia, Manuel. *Hints on Singing.* New & revised edition. London: Ascherberg, Hopwood, and Crew, Limited,1894.

Giannetti, Laura and Guido Ruggiero, trans. and eds. *Five Comedies from the Italian Renaissance.* Baltimore, MD: The Johns Hopkins University Press, 2003.

Gidel, Henry. *Feydeau.* Paris: Flammarion, 1991.

Gordon, Mel. *Lazzi: The Comic Routines of the Commedia dell'Arte.* New York: PAJ Publications: 2001.

Gordon, Sarah. *Culinary Comedy in Medieval French Literature.* Purdue Studies in Romance Literatures, vol. 37. West Lafayette, IN: Purdue University Press, 2006.

Gozzi, Count Carlo. *The Memoirs of Count Carlo Gozzi.* 2 vol. Trans. John Addington Symonds. New York: Scribner and Welford, 1890.

Grantham, Barry. *Playing Commedia: A Training Guide to Commedia Techniques.* London: Nick Hearn Books, 2000.

Hagen, Uta. *A Challenge for the Actor.* New York: Charles Scribner's Sons, 1991.

Hagen, Uta, with Haskell Frankel. *Respect for Acting.* New York: Macmillan, 1973.

Hall, Peter. *Shakespeare's Advice to the Players*. New York: Theatre Communications Group, 2003.

Hathorn, Richmond Y. *Crowell's Handbook of Classical Drama*. New York: Thomas Y. Crowell Company, 1967.

Hayes, Kevin J., ed. *Charlie Chaplin Interviews*. Jackson, MS: University Press of Mississippi, 2005.

Hindman, James, Larry Kirkman, and Elizabeth Monk. *TV Acting: A Manual for Camera Performance*. New York: Hastings House Publishers, 1979.

Jouvet, Louis. *Le comédien désincarné* (The Disembodied Actor). Paris: Collection Champs Arts, Flammarion, 1954; 2009.

—*Témoignages sur le théâtre* (Essays on the Theater). Paris: Collection Champs Arts, Flammarion,1952; 2009.

Julleville, Louis Petit de. *Répertoire du Théâtre Comique en France au Moyen-Age* (Repertoire of Comic Theater in Medieval France). Ed. of 1886. Paris: Hachette, 2012.

Kaplan, Steve. *The Hidden Tools of Comedy: The Serious Business of Being Funny*. Studio City, CA: Michael Wiese Productions, 2013.

Keaton, Buster, with Charles Samuels. *My Wonderful World of Slapstick*. Garden City, NY: Doubleday, 1960.

King, Geoff. *Film Comedy*. London: Wallflower Press, 2002.

Lee, Josephine. *The Japan of Pure Invention: Gilbert and Sullivan's The Mikado*. Minneapolis, MN: University of Minnesota Press, 2010.

Lehmann, Lotte. *More Than Singing: The Interpretation of Songs*. London: Boosey and Hawkes, 1945.

Lever, Maurice. *Sade: A Biography*. New York: Mariner Books, 1994.

Linklater, Kristin. *Freeing Shakespeare's Voice: The Actor's Guide to Talking the Text*. New York: Theatre Communications Group, 1992.

Loy, Myrna and James Kotsilibas-Davis. *Myrna Loy: Being and Becoming*. New York: Alfred A. Knopf, Inc., 1987.

Luckhurst, Mary and Chloe Veltman, eds. *On Acting: Interviews with Actors*. New York: Faber and Faber, 2001.

Lumet, Sidney. *Making Movies*. New York: Alfred A. Knopf, 1995.

Malaev-Babel, Andrei. *The Vakhtangov Sourcebook*. New York: Routledge, 2011.

Meisner, Sanford, and Dennis Longwell. *On Acting.* New York: Random House Vintage Books, 1987.

Meredith, George. *An Essay on Comedy.* In *Comedy,* ed. Wylie Sypher. Baltimore: Johns Hopkins University Press, 1956.

Merlin, Bella. *The Complete Stanislavsky Toolkit.* Hollywood, CA: Drama Publishers, 2007.

—*Konstantin Stanislavsky.* New York: Routledge, 2003.

Mikhail, E. H., ed. *Oscar Wilde: Interviews and Recollections.* 2 vols. London: The Macmillan Press, Ltd., 1979.

Mongrédien, Georges. *Daily Life in the French Theatre at the Time of Molière.* Translated by Claire Eliane Engel. London: George Allen and Unwin Ltd, 1969.

Moore, Sonia. *The Stanislavsky Method: The Professional Training of an Actor.* Preface by Sir John Gielgud. Foreword by Joshua Logan. New York: The Viking Press, 1960.

Partridge, Eric. *Shakespeare's Bawdy: A Literary and Psychological Essay and a Comprehensive Glossary.* New York: E. P. Dutton & Co., 1947; Routledge reprint, 1991.

Proust, Marcel. *In Search of Lost Time.* Translation of *A la recherche du temps perdu* by C. K. Scott Moncrieff and Terence Kilmartin, revised by D. J. Enright. 6 vols. New York: The Modern Library, 1992.

Provenza, Paul and Dan Dion. *¡Satiristas!: Comedians, Contrarians, Raconteurs & Vulgarians.* New York: HarperCollins Publishers, 2010.

Robinson, Davis Rider. *The Physical Comedy Handbook.* Portsmouth, NH: Heinemann, 1999.

Rudlin, John. *Commedia dell'Arte: An Actor's Handbook.* New York: Routledge, 1994.

Sacks, Mike. *Poking a Dead Frog: Conversations with Today's Top Comedy Writers.* New York: Penguin Books, 2014.

Saint-Denis, Michel. *Theatre: The Rediscovery of Style.* Introduction by Sir Laurence Olivier. New York: Theatre Arts Books, 1960.

Sedita, Scott. *The Eight Characters of Comedy: A Guide to Sitcom Writing and Acting.* Los Angeles: Atides Publishing, 2006.

Senelick, Laurence. *The Changing Room: Sex, Drag and Theatre.* New York: Routledge, 2000.

Shurtleff, Michael. *Audition: Everything an Actor Needs to Know to Get the Part.* Introduction by Bob Fosse. New York: Bantam Books, 1978.

Skinner, Edith. *Speak with Distinction.* Revised with new material added by Timothy Monich and Lilene Mansell. Edited by Lilene Mansell. New York: Applause Theatre Book Publishers, 1990.

Spivak, Alice, written in collaboration with Robert Blumenfeld. *How to Rehearse When There Is No Rehearsal: Acting and the Media.* New York: Limelight, 2007.

Stanislavsky, Constantin. *An Actor Prepares.* Translated by Elizabeth Reynolds Hapgood. New York: Theatre Arts Books (1936; 23rd printing), 1969.

—*An Actor's Work: A Student's Diary.* A contemporary translation of *An Actor Prepares* and *Building a Character* by Jean Benedetti, trans. and ed. New York: Routledge, 2008.

—*Building a Character.* Translated by Elizabeth Reynolds Hapgood. New York: Theatre Arts Books (14th printing), 1949.

—*Creating a Role.* Translated by Elizabeth Reynolds Hapgood. New York: Theatre Arts Books, 1961; 6th printing, 1976.

—*My Life in Art.* Translated by G. Ivanov-Mumjiev. Moscow: Foreign Languages Publishing House, n.d.

—*My Life in Art.* Translated by J. J. Robbins. Orig. pub. Little, Brown and Company, 1924. New York: The World Publishing Co. Meridian Books, 1966.

—*On the Art of the Stage.* Introduced and Translated by David Magarshack. New York: Hill and Wang, 1961.

Strasberg, Lee. *A Dream of Passion.* New York: Penguin Plume Books, 1987.

—*The Lee Strasberg Notes.* Edited by Lola Cohen. New York: Routledge, 2010.

—*Strasberg at the Actors Studio: Tape-Recorded Sessions.* Edited by Robert H. Hethmon. 5th printing. New York: Theatre Communications Group, 2000.

Styan, J. L. *Restoration Comedy in Performance.* New York: Cambridge University Press, 1986.

Suzman, Janet. *Acting with Shakespeare: Three Comedies.* New York: Applause, 1996.

Sypher, Wylie. *Comedy: An Essay on "Comedy" by George Meredith; "Laughter" by Henri Bergson.* Edited, with an Introduction and Appendix. Baltimore: Johns Hopkins University Press, 1956.

Taylor, Millie. *British Pantomime Performance.* Chicago: Intellect, 2007.

Teague, Frances. *Acting Funny: Comic Theory and Practice in Shakespeare's Plays.* Madison, NJ: Fairleigh Dickinson University Press, 1994.

Terry, Ellen. *Ellen Terry's Memoirs.* With preface, notes, and additional biographical chapters by Edith Craig and Christopher St. John. London: Victor Gollancz Ltd., 1933.

Toporkov, Vasili. *Stanislavski in Rehearsal.* Translated and with an Introduction by Jean Benedetti. New York: Routledge, 2004.

Tucker, Patrick. *Secrets of Acting Shakespeare: The Original Approach.* New York: Routledge, 2002.

Webb, Clifton, with David L. Smith. *Sitting Pretty: The Life and Times of Clifton Webb (Hollywood Legends).* Foreword by Robert Wagner. Jackson, MS: University Press of Mississippi, 2011.

Wilde, Larry. *Great Comedians Talk about Comedy.* Mechanicsburg, PA: Executive Books, 2000.

About the Author

Robert Blumenfeld is the author of *Accents: A Manual for Actors* (1998; Revised and Expanded Edition, 2002); *Acting with the Voice: The Art of Recording Books* (2004); *Tools and Techniques for Character Interpretation: A Handbook of Psychology for Actors, Writers, and Directors* (2006); *Using the Stanislavsky System: A Practical Guide to Character Creation and Period Styles* (2008); *Blumenfeld's Dictionary of Acting and Show Business* (2009); *Blumenfeld's Dictionary of Musical Theater: Opera, Operetta, Musical Comedy* (2010); *Stagecraft: Stanislavsky and External Acting Technique—A Companion to Using the Stanislavsky System* (2011); *Teach Yourself Accents: The British Isles* (2013); *Teach Yourself Accents: North America* (2013); *Teach Yourself Accents: Europe* (2014); and the collaborator with noted teacher, acting coach, and actress Alice Spivak on the writing of her book *How to Rehearse When There Is No Rehearsal: Acting and the Media* (2007)—all published by Limelight. He lives and works as an actor, dialect coach, and writer in New York City, and is a longtime member of Equity, and SAG-AFTRA. He has worked in numerous regional and New York theaters, as well as in television and independent films. For ACT Seattle he played the title role in Ronald Harwood's *The Dresser*, and he has performed many roles in plays by Shakespeare and Chekhov, as well as doing an Off-Broadway season of six Gilbert and Sullivan comic operas for Dorothy Raedler's American Savoyards (under the name Robert Fields), for which he played the Lord Chancellor in *Iolanthe* and other patter-song roles. In 1979 he played the Pope and Coach Griffin in Christopher Durang's *The Nature and Purpose of the Universe*. In 1994, he performed in Michael John LaChiusa's musical *The Petrified Prince*, directed by Harold Prince at the New York Shakespeare Festival's Public Theater. He created the roles of the Marquis of Queensberry and two prosecuting attorneys in Moisés Kaufman's Off-Broadway hit play *Gross Indecency: The Three Trials of Oscar Wilde*, and was also the production's dialect coach, a job that he did as well for the Broadway musicals, *Saturday Night Fever* and *The Scarlet Pimpernel* (third version and national tour), and for the New York workshop of David Henry Hwang's rewritten version of Rodgers and Hammerstein's *Flower Drum Song*. At the Manhattan School of Music, he was dialect coach for Dona D. Vaughn's production of Strauss's *Die Fledermaus* (2009); and for Jay Lesenger's production of Weill's *Street Scene* (2008), which he also coached for Mr. Lesenger at the Chautauqua Opera. Mr. Blumenfeld has recorded close to 400 audiobooks. He currently records books for Audible, among them *Pale Fire* (joint recording with Mark Vietor) and *Bend Sinister* by Vladimir Nabokov, for both of which he was chosen by the Nabokov estate; *A Modest Proposal* by Jonathan Swift; and *Jurgen* by James Branch Cabell. Before working for Audible, he recorded more than 320 Talking Books for the American Foundation for the Blind, including the complete Sherlock Holmes canon, Victor Hugo's *The Hunchback of Notre-Dame*, Alexandre Dumas's *The Count of Monte Cristo*, a bilingual edition of Rainer Maria Rilke's previously unpublished poetry, and a bilingual edition of Samuel Beckett's *Waiting for Godot*, in Beckett's original French and the playwright's own English translation. He received the 1997 Canadian National Institute for the Blind's Torgi Award for the Talking Book of the Year in the fiction category, for his recording of Pat Conroy's *Beach Music*; and the 1999 Alexander Scourby Talking Book Narrator of the Year Award in the fiction category. He holds a BA in French from Rutgers University and an MA from Columbia University in French language and literature. Mr. Blumenfeld speaks French, German, and Italian fluently, and has smatterings of Russian, Spanish, and Yiddish.

CANDICE OLSON
EVERYDAY ELEGANCE

PHOTOGRAPHS BY BRANDON BARRÉ

Houghton Mifflin Harcourt
Boston • New York

Published by:
Houghton Mifflin Harcourt
Boston • New York
www.hmhbooks.com

For information about permission to reproduce selections from this book, write to Permissions, Houghton Mifflin Harcourt Publishing Company, 215 Park Avenue South, New York, New York 10003.

www.hmhbooks.com

The publisher and the author make no representations or warranties with respect to the accuracy or completeness of the contents of this work and specifically disclaim all warranties, including without limitation warranties of fitness for a particular purpose. No warranty may be created or extended by sales or promotional materials. The advice and strategies contained herein may not be suitable for every situation. This work is sold with the understanding that the publisher is not engaged in rendering legal, accounting, or other professional services. If professional assistance is required, the services of a competent professional person should be sought. Neither the publisher nor the author shall be liable for damages arising here from. The fact that an organization or Website is referred to in this work as a citation and/or a potential source of further information does not mean that the author or the publisher endorses the information the organization or Website may provide or recommendations it may make. Further, readers should be aware that Websites listed in this work may have changed or disappeared between when this work was written and when it is read.

Trademarks: All trademarks are the property of their respective owners. Houghton Mifflin Harcourt is not associated with any product or vendor mentioned in this book.

ISBN: 978-1-118-47747-2 (pbk)
ISBN: 978-0-544-17868-7 (ebk)

Printed in the United States of America

DOR   10   9   8   7   6   5   4   3   2

4500444956

Book and cover design by Tai Blanche

Note to the Readers:
Due to differing conditions, tools and the individual skills, Houghton Mifflin Harcourt assumes no responsibility for any damages, injuries suffered, or losses incurred as a result of following the information published in this book. Before beginning any project, review the instructions carefully, and if any doubts or questions remain, consult local experts or authorities. Because codes and regulations vary greatly, you always should check with authorities to ensure that your project complies with all applicable local codes and regulations. Always read and observe all of the safety precautions provided by manufacturers of any tools, equipment, or supplies, and follow all accepted safety procedures.